Ancestor Worship and the Elite in Iron Age Scandinavia

Ancestor worship is often assumed by contemporary European audiences to be an outdated and primitive tradition with little relevance to our societies, past and present. This book questions that assumption and seeks to determine whether ancestor ideology was an integral part of religion in Viking Age and early medieval Scandinavia. The concept is examined from a broad socio-anthropological perspective, which is used to structure a set of case studies which analyse the cults of specific individuals in Old Norse literature. The situation of gods in Old Norse religion has been almost exclusively addressed in isolation from these socio-anthropological perspectives. The public gravemound cults of deceased rulers are discussed conventionally as cases of sacral kingship, and, more recently, religious ruler ideology; both are seen as having divine associations in Old Norse scholarship. Building on the anthropological framework, this study introduces the concept of 'superior ancestors', employed in social anthropology to denote a form of political ancestor worship used to regulate social structure deliberately. It suggests that Old Norse ruler ideology was based on conventional and widely recognised religious practices revolving around kinship and ancestors and that the gods were perceived as human ancestors belonging to elite families.

Triin Laidoner received an MA in Old Nordic Religion from the University of Iceland and a PhD in History from the University of Aberdeen, UK. Prior to that, she studied Icelandic and Swedish philology, and literary translation. Her work focuses on pre-Christian religious beliefs and practices in northern Europe, Old Norse–Icelandic literature, mythology and folklore, social anthropology, kinship and social structures, and ancestor beliefs and rituals. She has published on connections between Sámi and Old Norse beliefs.

Studies in Medieval History and Culture
Recent titles include

The Charisma of Distant Places
Travel and Religion in the Early Middle Ages
Courtney Luckhardt

The Death Penalty in Late Medieval Catalonia
Evidence and Signification
Flocel Sabaté

Church, Society and University
The Paris Condemnation of 1241/4
Deborah Grice

The Sense of Smell in the Middle Ages
A Source of Certainty
Katelynn Robinson

Travel, Pilgrimage and Social Interaction from Antiquity to the Middle Ages
Edited by Jenni Kuuliala and Jussi Rantala

Ancestor Worship and the Elite in Late Iron Age Scandinavia
A Grave Matter

Triin Laidoner

Routledge
Taylor & Francis Group
LONDON AND NEW YORK

First published 2020 by Routledge

2 Park Square, Milton Park, Abingdon, Oxon OX14 4RN
605 Third Avenue, New York, NY 10017

Routledge is an imprint of the Taylor & Francis Group, an informa business

First issued in paperback 2021

Copyright © 2020 Triin Laidoner

The right of Triin Laidoner to be identified as author of this work has been asserted by her in accordance with sections 77 and 78 of the Copyright, Designs and Patents Act 1988.

All rights reserved. No part of this book may be reprinted or reproduced or utilised in any form or by any electronic, mechanical, or other means, now known or hereafter invented, including photocopying and recording, or in any information storage or retrieval system, without permission in writing from the publishers.

Notice:
Product or corporate names may be trademarks or registered trademarks, and are used only for identification and explanation without intent to infringe.

Publisher's Note

The publisher has gone to great lengths to ensure the quality of this reprint but points out that some imperfections in the original copies may be apparent.

British Library Cataloguing-in-Publication Data
A catalogue record for this book is available from the British Library

Library of Congress Cataloging-in-Publication Data
A catalog record for this title has been requested

ISBN: 978-0-367-00063-9 (hbk)
ISBN: 978-1-03-217506-5 (pbk)
DOI: 10.4324/9780429444746

Typeset in Times
By Deanta Global Publishing Services, Chennai, India

Contents

Acknowledgements vii
Abbreviations viii

Introduction 1

PART 1
Theoretical considerations 5

1 Old Norse religion: Approach, sources and method 7
   1.1 *Old Norse religion* 7
      1.1.1 *What is 'religion'?* 7
      1.1.2 *What is 'Old Norse'?* 9
      1.1.3 *The non-static and heterogenous nature of Old Norse religion* 10
      1.1.4 *Heterogenous conceptions of the afterlife in Old Norse religion* 11
      1.1.5 *Gravemounds and ancestors in Old Norse religion* 13
      1.1.6 *Folk vs. world religion* 15
      1.1.7 *Paganism and Christianity* 17
   1.2 *Primary sources* 18
   1.3 *Method* 23

2 Research on ancestor worship 31
   2.1 *The development of 'ancestor worship' as an academic term* 31
   2.2 *Ancestor worship in Old Norse research* 37

3 Ancestors in social anthropology: Definition and social use 47
   3.1 *'Ancestor worship' – the problem with terminology* 47
   3.2 *The role of ancestors in folk religions* 50

Contents

    3.3 Family, kinship and 'superior ancestors' 53
    3.4 'Superior ancestor worship' 57

4 Kings and gods in Old Norse religion   70
    4.1 The myth of 'sacral kingship' 70
    4.2 Euhemerism – medieval propaganda or just history? 74

PART 2
Case studies   83

5 Introduction to the case studies   85

6 Erik of Birka   89

7 The Ynglingar   102
    7.1 Background on the Ynglingar 102
        7.1.1 Sources 102
        7.1.2 The Ynglingar and sacral kingship 104
        7.1.3 Ynglingatal: authorial purpose 106
    7.2 Freyr 111
        7.2.1 Adam's Templum 113
        7.2.2 Adam's account of human sacrifice 113
        7.2.3 Icons and processions 115
    7.3 Hálfdanr svarti 118
    7.4 Óláfr Geirstaðaálfr 121

8 The Háleygjar   135
    8.1 The Háleygjar and sacral kingship 135
    8.2 Þorgerðr hǫlgabrúðr 140

9 The Settlers of Breiðafjǫrðr   155
    9.1 Þórólfr Mostrarskegg 156
    9.2 Auðr djúp(a)úðga 162

10 General conclusion   171

    Primary sources   175
    Index   178

Acknowledgements

Special thanks go to Stefan Brink, Terry Gunnell and Neil Price for all their help and support.

Abbreviations

Afv	*Austrfararvísur* (Skald 1)
Akv	*Atlakviða* (Ekv)
AUk	*Af Upplendinga konungum* (FSNL 2)
BrN	*Brennu-Njáls saga* (ÍF 12)
BsH	*Bósa saga ok Herrauðs* (FSNL 3)
BsS	*Bárðar saga Snæfellsáss* (ÍF 13)
CDE	*Chambers Dictionary of Etymology*
Chr	*Chronicon*
DN	*Diplomatarium Norvegicum*
DV	*Diarium Vazstenense*
Eir	*Eiríks saga rauða* (ÍF 4)
Ekv	*Eddukvæði*
Em	*Eiríksmál* (Skald 1)
QOs	*Qrvar-Odds saga* (FSNL 2)
Eyr	*Eyrbyggja saga* (IF 4)
Fær	*Færeyinga saga* (Flat 1)
Flat	*Flateyjarbók*
Fs	*Fljótsdæla saga* (ÍF 11)
Fsk	*Fagrskinna* (ÍF 29)
FSNL	*Fornaldarsǫgur norðurlanda*
GD	*Gesta Danorum*
Germ	*Germania*
Get	*Getica*
GH	*Gesta Hammaburgensis*
Gís	*Gísla saga Súrssonar* (ÍF 6)
GL	*Guta lag*
Grm	*Grímnismál* (Ekv)
Grs	*Grettis saga Ásmundarsonar* (ÍF 7)
Gylf	*Gylfaginning* (SnE)
GÞL	*Den ældre Gulathings-Lov* (NGL 1)
Háv	*Hávamál* (Ekv)
HB	*Helreið Brynhildar* (Ekv)

Herv	*Hervarar saga ok Heiðreks konungs* (*Hauksbók* 2)
Hhj	*Helgakviða Hjǫrvarðssonar* (Ekv)
Hkr	*Heimskringla* (ÍF 26–28)
HN	*Historia Norwegie*
HNb	*Hversu Noregr byggðist* (FSNL 2)
Hs	*Harðar saga* (ÍF 13)
HsF	*Hrafnkels saga Freysgoða* (ÍF 11)
Hsg	*Hákonar saga góða* (Hkr 1)
HsHá	*Haralds saga hins hárfagra* (Hkr 1)
Hss	*Hálfdanar saga svarta* (Hkr 1)
HþÞ	*Helga þáttr Þórissonar* (FSNL 4)
ÍF	*Íslenzk fornrit*
Ísb	*Íslendingabók* (ÍF 1)
IsG	*Illuga saga Gríðarfóstra* (FSNL 3)
Krm	*Kormáks saga* (ÍF 8)
Laxd	*Laxdæla saga* (ÍF 5)
Lnd	*Landnámabók* (ÍF 1)
Ls	*Lokasenna* (Ekv)
NC	*Kong Magnus Haakonsön's Nyere Christenret* (NGL 2)
NGL	*Norges gamle love indtil 1387*
NGþ	*Norna-Gests þáttr* (FSNL 1)
Ód	*Óláfsdrápa* (Skald 1)
Ósh	*Óláfs saga helga* (Hkr 2)
ÓshF	*Óláfs saga helga* (*Fornmanna sögur*)
ÓsT	*Óláfs saga Tryggvasonar* (Hkr 1)
ÓsTF	*Óláfs saga Tryggvasonar* (Flat 1)
prol	*Prologus* (Hkr 1)
Rett	*Kong Haakon Magnussöns Retterbod om Odelslösning* (NGL 3)
Saf	*Sǫgubrot af fornkonungum* (FSNL 1)
SC	*Kong Sverrers Christenret* (NGL 1)
Skald	*Skaldic Poetry of the Scandinavian Middle Ages*
Skáld	*Skáldskaparmál* (SnE)
Skm	*Skírnismál* (Ekv)
SL	*Skånske lov*
Sml	*Smålands lagen* (*Corpus iuris Sueo-Gotorum antiqui* 6)
SnE	*Snorra Edda*
SÓkhh	*Saga Óláfs konungs hins helga*
Sþ	*Sǫrla þáttr* (Flat 1)
VA	*Vita Ansgarii*
Vatn	*Vatnsdæla saga* (ÍF 8)
Vgl	*Västgötalagen* (*Corpus iuris Sueo-Gotorum antiqui* 1)
Vsp	*Vǫluspá* (Ekv)
Vþm	*Vafþrúðnismál* (Ekv)
Yng	*Ynglinga saga* (ÍF 26)

Abbreviations

Yngt	*Ynglingatal* (Skald 1)
Þd	*Þórsdrápa* (Skald 3)
Þkv	*Þrymskviða* (Ekv)
Þþ	*Þiðranda þáttr ok Þorhalls* (Flat 1)
Þþb	*Þorsteins þáttr bæjarmagns* (FSNL 4)
Þþj	*Þorleifs þáttr jarlaskálds* (Flat 1)

Introduction

This book argues that ancestor worship was an important element of Old Norse religion. It argues that a unified explanation can be found for phenomena as diverse as the worship of dead kings in Scandinavia and prominent Icelandic settlers, so-called 'sacral kingship' or 'religious ruler ideology', and the tendency of medieval scholars to 'euhemerise' gods; it could also be applied to account for the worship of collective ancestor beings in Old Norse literature (e.g. *dísir*) as well as for more recent folkloristic material (e.g. farm guardians), but this lies outside the scope of the present study. The unified explanation proposed here to account for these groups of phenomena is that they all ultimately have their roots in the worship of ancestors, and in particular in the political and public activities of the cult. This proposal is supported by Old Norse material using social anthropological research to provide parallels from other folk-religious societies around the world. Although Old Norse religion should not be viewed as a temporally or geographically stable and homogeneous belief system, it is better to account for what we know of it in terms of underlying tendencies that are as internally consistent as possible (and externally consistent with what is known of other cultures) than to view it as a hodgepodge of local beliefs that bear no relation to each other. This study argues that social anthropology, with its cross-cultural emphasis, has great potential to help us understand sociological and religious patterns in typical kinship-based societies such as that of pre-Christian Scandinavia.

Treatment of ancestors by social anthropologists has been generally ignored by scholars of Old Norse religion since structural–functionalist methods became dominant in the first half of the 20th century; since then, the focus of most anthropological work has moved to field studies in contemporary societies. Consequently, Old Norse scholars are often unaware of more recent developments in social anthropology which could have implications for their field. For early anthropologists, who were explicitly interested in the origins and development of culture from a Darwinian perspective, 'ancestor worship' was the core of religion. With the emergence of structural–functionalism, these earlier approaches started to wane, and focus was instead placed on the study of kinship and social structures in order to understand how these were related to the development of 'ancestor worship' in different societies. This shift led to a greater understanding of the extreme complexity of kinship systems in societies where ancestors

2 *Introduction*

are a conspicuous part of daily life, thus also leading to greater caution in the use of ancestor-related terminology, which has only recently started to diminish. This broad caution towards the use of the term was also assumed by Old Norse scholars who similarly started to avoid portraying any death-related practices as being linked to ancestor worship, both in terms of the daily religious practices of common people and of the public cults of rulers. The latter in particular became clearly separated from any discussion of ancestors and rather took its own course in the form of sacral kingship.

This study uses socio-anthropological treatment of ancestors to provide a unifying lens to view a set of case studies analysing the cults of specific elite individuals in the Old Norse literary tradition. One key concept discussed here is that of 'superior ancestors', a term employed by some social anthropologists to denote a form of political ancestor worship used deliberately to regulate social structures. This phenomenon usually occurs in typical kinship-based societies with social hierarchies where the power of the ancestors of the elite is presented as surpassing that of common ancestors on the small-scale domestic level, meaning that they must be worshipped by all. In Old Norse scholarship, instances of public worship have usually been placed within the 'sacral kingship' and more recently 'religious ruler ideology' paradigms. In these paradigms, the worshipped individuals are seen as having divine and mythical associations, and their suggested identity as real, distant ancestors of leading families in recorded genealogies and other written sources is explained as the euhemerism of medieval authors. This study argues that such an approach is intrinsically Christo-centric and that the analysis of such cases provides reasonably strong evidence to suggest that public offerings to prominent persons were too in effect ancestor cults, given the values and principles of typical kinship-based societies such as those of pagan Scandinavia. It argues that the phenomena observed in the corpus of material used – which have traditionally been accounted for by a number of disparate underlying processes, such as sacral kingship, cults of dead rulers, learned euhemerisation – can be reasonably explained in a unified and principled way by a single underlying belief in 'superior ancestors.'

When the idea for this study first took root, the intention was to write about ancestors in a more all-encompassing way and to include the cults of individuals that have survived in medieval descriptions, the cults of collective ancestor beings (e.g. *dísir*, *álfar*), and survivals in later folklore (e.g. farm guardians). The objective was to focus on the religious function of ancestors, with no particular intention of addressing political concepts. It soon became clear that this would not be easy, as ancestors are an integral part of not only religious life, but also of wider social, political, and legal spheres. In order to limit the scope of this work, it was decided to confine the analysis to the reported instances of cults of named individuals in Old Norse literature. It was to be expected that they would be found at the top of society, but this also means that their cults have frequently been interpreted through theories of sacral kingship in the past. Breaking from this tradition of analysis, Olof Sundqvist has critically examined the political aspects of rulership in a series of publications over the last two decades and his findings

Introduction 3

have led to a major shift in the way the religious role of rulers is understood today; Sundqvist's views are generally favoured in the present work. In spite of the ideas introduced by Sundqvist, however, the earlier theories of sacral kingship have led to the exclusion of characters depicted in literature from scholarly discussion of ancestor worship – a concept which itself has a long and complicated history – and this trend has largely remained. Consideration of ancestors in pagan Scandinavia is now made quite regularly from archaeological (and to a much lesser extent folkloristic) perspectives; however, this focuses mostly on the small-scale domestic forms of cults. The focus here is on characters in Old Norse literature that were reported to have been honoured on a public scale. Subsequently, discussions of 'sacral kingship' and 'religious ruler ideology' are essential companions to this study, although not its main focus.

This study consists of two parts: the first part focuses on the theoretical background, which forms a framework for the case studies examined in the second part. Issues relating to the background of the study of Old Norse religion and the main problems which arise when working with it will be discussed in Chapter 1. Chapter 2 continues with a discussion of 'ancestor worship' as discussed in research to date, from the development of the concept as a scholarly term in folklore studies in the early 19th century to evolutionary anthropology later in the century, and in Old Norse scholarship over this whole time-period. Chapter 3 follows with an examination of the views of some 20th-century anthropologists. Here problems with terminology will be discussed, with emphasis on the concept of 'god', which in folk religion is generally seen as conceptually close to family ancestors. This chapter also introduces the concept of 'superior ancestors', reflecting the views of some social anthropologists who have investigated ancestor cults in past and contemporary societies. Anthropologists' tying of superior ancestors to ancestor cults is fundamentally appealing and allows us to interpret the cults of elite individuals described in Old Norse literature as cults of 'superior ancestors' as well. Chapter 4 then follows with discussion of two related concepts: 'sacral kingship' and 'euhemerism' in Old Norse scholarship. The first is associated with the special religious role of rulers and their supposedly divine origin, which is sometimes used to explain the emergence of their cults. Building on the proposed 'superior ancestor' concept, this chapter argues that deceased rulers in Scandinavia and Iceland received public ritual attention as part of a general ancestor cult and that the remote ancestors of the elite were worshipped as 'gods.' Subsequently, it is also argued that the application of the popular 'euhemerism' theory in medieval literature – albeit influenced by classical histories – was a natural step for the medieval authors because the necessary ideas were already alive in native Nordic traditions.

While Part 1 of the thesis builds up a framework to understand the attested public cults of rulers in Old Norse literature as a form of ancestor cult, Part 2 examines the available sources on them and tests whether the concepts introduced in preceding chapters can be applied. Chapter 5 very briefly reviews the socio-political background in Scandinavia and Iceland in the pre- and early medieval period. This is followed by case studies that focus on elements in the written sources which are suggestive of ancestor beliefs and ideologies, and that consider the historical and authorial background of the sources. Chapter 6 discusses the reported deification of Erik of Birka, after which attention is given to the Ynglingar in Chapter 7. The Ynglingar have most frequently been discussed in the context of sacral kingship and ruler ideology, as have the Háleygjar, another influential group in Viking Age Norway. The discussion of the Háleygjar in Chapter 8 is concerned mainly with Þorgerðr hǫlgabrúðr, potentially the foremother of the last pagan king of Norway. Discussion of the worship of influential people in Scandinavia is then followed by two examples of Icelandic settlers – Auðr and Þórólfr in Chapter 9. These individuals have not conventionally been discussed within the 'sacral kingship' theory as they are not 'kings', although recent studies have also emphasised the importance of ruler ideology in these cases.

Part 1
Theoretical considerations

1 Old Norse religion
Approach, sources and method

1.1 Old Norse religion

1.1.1 What is 'religion'?

Much ink has been spilt by scholars from various disciplines in the debate over how to define religion, and thus the criteria proposed to help us determine what can be classified as 'religion' are often contradictory. The definitions can be broadly divided into substantive and functional scientific ideologies, and into disciplinary discourses (e.g. theological, psychological, philosophical, sociological) (Cox 2010: 1–23).[1] Substantive definitions explain religion in terms of its content: religion is present if there is belief in supernatural or transcendental power. Functional definitions, on the other hand, emphasise rather the effects of religion in people's lives: religion is not intended to explain existence, but to help people cope with it emotionally (Furseth & Repstad 2006: 16–23; Cox 2010: 8–9). In very simple terms, the substantive definitions are more restrictive and focus on the philosophical question of what religion is, whereas the functional definitions are very broad and focus on what religion does (Furseth & Repstad 2006: 16). Scholars from various disciplines often find themselves on either side of this broad scientific division. Psychological definitions, for example, are on the functional side and emphasise that religion is the bridge between an emotional or psychological state and an object which is seen as being greater than human. Theological definitions, on the other hand, support the substantive definition, insisting that religion refers to a belief in God (Cox 2010: 2–7). The theological definition is thus very restrictive because it explains religion as a doctrinal belief in one god, excluding other gods and forms of spiritual life. The substantive approach has also been followed by scholars of Old Norse religion, who have suggested that Scandinavian paganism should not be viewed as a 'religion' proper because it was not a 'formalised confessional religion with a corpus of holy texts' (Nordanskog 2006: 30–33) and because 'it had no holy scripture, but was basically a ritually and orally performed tradition' (Andrén 2011: 853).

Some scholars, particularly archaeologists who focus on the study of rituals and the examination of ceremonial sites rather than the literary sources, prefer to speak of ritualised traditions and use the term *forn siðr* in the Old Norse religious

8 Theoretical considerations

context rather than the term 'religion' (e.g. Jennbert 2011). The expression *forn siðr* ('old customs') comes from Old Norse sources where it is used to refer to the ways of life people followed before Christianity, and is sometimes used interchangeably with *heiðinn siðr* ('heathen customs'). This broad term encompasses ritual practices, faith, tradition, morality and customs and is therefore seen as more appropriate, because it was ritual that was central in Old Norse religious life, rather than belief in gods (Jennbert 2011: 164; Andrén 2011: 853). For example, the Swedish archaeologist Kristina Jennbert (2011: 220) writes that 'the concept of religion itself is [...] complicated to use, since it refers to belief and not to ritual, not to what people do'. Although rituals were certainly central to everyday life in pre-Christian Scandinavia and although there is no reason to object to using *forn siðr* as an alternative to 'religion', the latter term perhaps need not be taken in such a restrictive sense as this avoidance implies. The term 'religion' is indeed often confounded with Christianity in modern Western mindsets, but as noted above, there is no one explicit ostensive definition. Academics of most disciplines, including ethnological sciences such as anthropology, folkloristics and sociology, which rely upon direct observation of cultural phenomena, accept the term's meaning as always being context dependent. All religions involve rituals which are performed with the purpose of connecting the believers to specific objects or beings. The subdivisions of different branches of Christianity, too, have a great deal of internal and temporal variety, despite following certain established principles and involving the concept of one supreme God (Nordberg 2012: 121). Medieval Christians in Iceland, for instance, who recorded history in written form must have had different ideas about God and religion than those of modern theologians. This means that religious diversity applies generally to all religion. As Andreas Nordberg (2012: 120) explains – and I could not agree more – it is therefore rather unfortunate that the definition of 'religion' within Old Norse studies is so often based on Western theological convictions, rather than on anthropological, psychological or folkloristic perspectives, which generally take a far more wide-ranging and inclusive approach to the concept. To borrow again from Nordberg (2012: 119–122), I believe that the understanding of 'religion' referring only to an institutional religious structure where faith in a monotheistic God is central and is reinforced by holy scriptures is in its own right Christo-centric.

I should nevertheless stress that the aim here is not to criticise the use of expressions like *forn siðr*, 'ritual tradition', 'paganism' or any other alternative in the context of Old Norse religious life, but to simply justify the use of the term 'religion'. Although some theoretical foundations are necessary, getting overly involved in definitional critique means that we could endlessly come up with new expressions, which would all, in their own way, be problematic and open to challenge. The suggestion that, for example, *forn siðr* is a more valid expression to denote Old Norse religious practices than 'religion' because this was the term that was used by early Christian scribes and because it refers to religious activities in a broader sense might be disputed, in addition to what was said above, by the fact that Christianity is similarly called *kristinn siðr* ('Christian customs') or *nýi siðr* ('new customs') rather than 'religion' in Old Norse literature, and that the conversion is referred to as *siðaskipti* 'change of customs'. Clearly, people living in the Viking Age and early medieval era made no concrete distinction between ritual and religion in the terminology they used, and for the early Christians the old and new concepts existed in parallel. As long as it is accepted that the beliefs, traditions and practices involved in the spiritual and cultural life of the Norsemen did not involve a formal doctrinal religion, but a range of beliefs and ritual activities that were not subject to any strict rules, that evolved and changed over time and that had many regional variations, it is perfectly valid to call these 'religion'. It is in this sense that the term is used in this book.

1.1.2 What is 'Old Norse'?

Andreas Nordberg's (2012: 119–123) article, which offers perhaps the most thought-provoking approach to 'Old Norse religion' to date, calls attention also to the consideration of what 'Old Norse' means in the Nordic cultural context. The expression 'Old Norse' is essentially a philological term and designates a medieval manifestation of a west Nordic dialect that followed the scribal norms of Norway and Iceland and which was used in Icelandic literature, although it is often used to refer to both the west and east dialects and their sub-groups as a single unit.[2] Although first and foremost a linguistic term, it is commonly extended also to denote the people who spoke the Old Norse languages and dialects in the Viking Age, to the entire geographic area where the speakers of 'Old Norse' lived, and to their religious practices. Although this kind of unified language-based approach to the Germanic Scandinavian population as a whole is to some extent necessary and appropriate – a common language with only minor dialectal variations must have distinguished the Norsemen from other adjacent groups, like the speakers of Sámi and other Finno-Ugric languages (DuBois 1999: 12–20, 23–28) – it is important to acknowledge that most surviving texts that contain information about 'Old Norse religion' were written in west Nordic and thus represent primarily the west Nordic variant of the religion (Nordberg 2012: 123, 126). This means that the information found in medieval literature is not necessarily representative of the entire Germanic population in Scandinavia and must be interpreted with caution. Interdisciplinary co-operation has consequently become a necessity (e.g. Raudvere & Schjødt 2012).

We can of course within reason – and within a broader socio-cultural context – consider that the Norsemen shared a language and therefore a broadly similar lifestyle and worldview; however, influences from other cultures, too, must be taken into consideration in the study of Old Norse religion (DuBois 1999: 10–28). Disregarding the influence of the Sámi, in particular, whose populations reached as far south as the central regions of modern Scandinavia (Sandnes 1973; Price 2000, 2019; Zachrisson 2005) can give a distorted image of Scandinavia's pre-Christian past (e.g. DuBois 1999). Co-operation with neighbours must have been a key factor in successful cultural development, and the Norsemen's dense interaction with the *Fenni* (i.e. Sámi; see Valtonen 2007) is mentioned regularly in Old Norse sources and in the early histories by Roman and Greek historians.[3]

10 Theoretical considerations

The different languages may have restricted communication, perhaps creating a certain nervous wariness on either side, but the communities cannot have been immune to mutual influences and the Sámi, too (among many others), certainly contributed to the formation of what we today consider to be 'Old Norse religion'.

1.1.3 The non-static and heterogenous nature of Old Norse religion

The borders among ethnically and linguistically distinct communities in northern Europe, as well as among groups that did share a common language, are thus considered today to have been very blurred in the pre-Christian era. A number of academics over the last few decades have advanced the approach that the Scandinavian geographic area and its religious landscape must be interpreted openly regarding regionalism, diversity and temporal variation; they argue that the earlier tendency to lump the different and often conflicting elements found in literature together under a uniform, homogenous and static Old Norse religion distorts rather than clarifies our perception of life in pagan Scandinavia (e.g. DuBois 1999; Brink 2007; Price 2002; Gunnell 2007b; Shaw 2011; Nordberg 2012; Schjødt 2012). Following the ground-breaking Indo-European *Stammbaumtheorie* ('language-tree theory') developed by the German linguist August Schleicher (1861) and carried out in the spirit of 19th-century nationalism, scholars of philology and folklore became particularly keen in their attempts at reconstructing a common and systematic Indo-European ideology from which the Old Norse myths were believed to have descended and which could be fitted into a shared Germanic heritage (Arvidsson 2006: 22–32).[4] The ideas of a uniform Indo-European ideology and culture, propagated most famously by George Dumézil (1958) with his formulation of the tripartite paradigm of social structures, are today viewed with a critical eye (Schjødt 2012: 278–279). Such earlier views have, however, done a great deal to shape present-day approaches. Treatments of Old Norse religion are still often focused on the mythological tradition and centre around the idea of a shared religion, built around a hierarchical family of gods. This certainly holds true of popular culture; however, academics also – although usually paying at least lip service to the idea that no religious system is entirely static – still prefer to interpret the Old Norse gods as belonging to a fixed pantheon which was known across Scandinavia (e.g. Abram 2011: 91).

The idea of a fixed pantheon of Norse gods can be traced to the versions of Old Norse myths recorded by the Icelander Snorri Sturluson more than 200 years after his country's conversion to Christianity, which are the most frequently used sources for investigating Old Norse religion. Snorri's intention was probably to create a uniform northern mythology, analogous to the classical mythologies of the ancient Mediterranean cultures (Gunnell 2000: 118–121). He attempted to establish a hierarchical pantheon of gods who, led by the god of war, Óðinn, all had a subordinate characteristic role and were known and worshipped throughout Scandinavia and beyond: Freyr was the god of fertility, Þórr the god of thunder, and so on. In light of the consistency with which the 'pantheon' has been used as a foundation for studies of Old Norse religion, his attempt must indeed be considered fruitful. Recently, the more cautious and interdisciplinary approach is to acknowledge that the more-or-less reasonable and sequential narratives created by Snorri have many different origins and are often inconsistent with other evidence, both literary (e.g. poetry, laws) and non-literary (e.g. place names). A fresh evaluation, and possibly one of the most valuable and frequently quoted works within the last two decades, is the revision of theophoric place names in Scandinavia by Stefan Brink (2007), which reveals a much more inconsistent division of the gods than Snorri suggests. According to Brink's study, Óðinn was by far not the most popular deity in Scandinavia. His name can be associated with roughly 70 place names which are distributed more or less evenly in all the central sites in Scandinavia, suggesting that he was at least known in these places, but the names that figure most abundantly in Norway, Sweden and Denmark are Þórr, Ullr and Týr, respectively. This observation is striking considering that Týr (whose name appears most frequently in Danish place names but hardly at all in those of Sweden or Norway) and Ullr (rare in Danish place names but found commonly in Swedish and Norwegian ones) both play a trivial role in Snorri's mythology and that practically nothing is known about them. The uneven distribution of theophoric place names thus suggests that a pantheon such as Snorri depicted cannot be considered entirely viable. The 'anti-pantheon' work has been developed most actively by Terry Gunnell (e.g. 2000, 2007a, 2007b, 2015, 2017), who has convincingly demonstrated that the specific roles assigned to different gods, too, are problematic. A closer look at the different evidence about Þórr and Freyr, for example, who are conventionally classified as a thunder-god and a fertility-god, suggests that both these characters served a much more complex and ambivalent role than is usually recognised and were essentially independent 'all-purpose' gods, possibly linked to regional cults of ancestors (Gunnell 2015: 64–68).

1.1.4 Heterogenous conceptions of the afterlife in Old Norse religion

Considering that Óðinn is not mentioned in *Landnámabók* and that the only region in Scandinavia where his name is not found in place names is western Norway (Brink 2007: 111), where the majority of Icelandic settlers, including Snorri's ancestors (Jakob Benediktsson 1986: cxxx), are believed to have come from, his firm favouring of Óðinn as the ruler of all other gods seems to be linked to his personal social background and interests: for a man of an elite family of poets in 13th-century Iceland, the image of a masculine and aggressive godhead of war and poetry must have been most appealing (Gunnell 2000: 120). Opting for such an arrangement, Snorri also gives prominence to Valhǫll, the almost exclusively male otherworld run by Óðinn and restricted to the warrior elite, which is mentioned sporadically also in 10th-century poetry (e.g. Grm; Em). Regrettably, Snorri's zealous promotion of Valhǫll has contributed to its modern public image as *the* otherworld of the Norsemen and much less emphasis is placed on the numerous other lands of death mentioned in different texts, including those by Snorri himself. Hel rules over nine underworlds in Niflheimr and receives those who die of sickness or old age (Grm; Gylf ch. 34), Freyja receives dead warriors in Fólkvangr (Gylf ch. 24), some of the dead go to Niðavellir or to Brimir's beer hall (Vsp st. 36; Gylf ch. 52), to Gimlé (Vsp 62; Gylf ch. 52), to Hvergelmir (Gylf ch. 52) or to Nástrandir (Vsp sts 37–38; Gylf ch. 52), where murderers, liars, oath-breakers, seducers and slayers of kinsmen – the worst crime in many kinship-based societies (e.g. Goody 1962: 383; Newell 1976a: 19) – dwell. Some dead go to the land of the immortals (e.g. Herv ch. 1) or enter mountains (e.g. Eyr chs 4–11; Lnd pp. 98–99, 233), others seem to sail to unspecified otherworlds by boat (e.g. Vatn ch. 23; Laxd ch. 7) or simply continue living inside gravemounds (e.g. BrN ch. 78). In Iceland the dead become restless and must be forced through violence or legal prosecution to remain in their graves (e.g. Grs ch. 35; Eyr chs 50–53), while others stay put inside gravemounds fiercely guarding their treasures (e.g. Hs ch. 15). Otherworld concepts and perceptions of the dead are abundant, and we can assume that only a small fraction of them were recorded. Death and death-related phenomena, in fact, run like a common thread through Old Norse literature; no being, place or motif is ever entirely disassociated with it. This abundance itself must be taken as an indicator of the crucial part of ancestors in religious thinking. The vast variety of death-beliefs, customs and rituals is not confined to written evidence. As the archaeologist Neil Price (2012a: 20) points out, the diversity found in Viking Age funerary practices is so extreme that it is only graves which they share among them.

The age and origin of the different otherworlds remain uncertain, but a partial explanation for the conflicting concepts lies in the background of the social settings where they developed, some being broadly attached to the different races depicted in mythology. Loose analogies have been drawn between these afterlife concepts and mythological races on one hand and real-life social groups on the other. The belief of the dead entering mountains, for example, might have a link to the Sámi (Bäckman 1975; 1983; DuBois 1999: 75–77), the 'original' people in Scandinavia, who are paralleled with the *jǫtnar* – the primeval inhabitants of the world in mythology (Lindow 1995; Mundal 2000).[5] The Valhǫll concept, which in Snorri's systematic mythology is closely linked to Óðinn (who he considers the leader of the principal race of *æsir* and, unlike earlier rulers, was cremated), might have been adopted from a male-centred warrior cult that reached Scandinavia some time during the early Iron Age (Nordland 1966: 67–68; Motz 1996: 103–124; Gunnell 2007b: 353–361). Continued life in gravemounds, which is similar also to the cult of Freyr who was buried inside a large gravemound, can be associated with the ancient *vanir* system that has strong associations with fertility, kinship and family ideology, and which possibly represents an older Bronze Age cult; the war between the *æsir* and *vanir* in mythology (Vsp sts 21–24; Gylf ch. 22; Yng ch. 4) thus could reflect a supposedly hard transition from the Bronze Age to the Iron Age. The gravemound also seems to be an important aspect of the *álfar* – another social tribe presented in the mythological tradition – who might represent the ancient inhabitants of south-west Sweden and south-east Norway (Gunnell 2007a). Entrances into (unspecified) otherworlds are also often located on gravemounds (e.g. Þkv st. 6; Vsp st. 41; Skm sts 11–12) and, as one might logically expect, the 'gravemound' itself in all probability represents the oldest otherworld concept, although more complex and abstract afterlife ideas developed alongside it.

1.1.5 Gravemounds and ancestors in Old Norse religion

The pivotal importance of gravemounds in pagan (and early Christian) Scandinavia is made most evident in early medieval law texts, which repeatedly prohibit offerings and sacrifices to graves, indicating a regular, long-term and deeply ingrained practice. For example, Magnús Hákonsson's 13th-century law code which had authority over the larger part of Norway bans sacrifices to beings that dwell in gravemounds (NC pp. 307–308), a Gotlandic law prohibits prayers to gravemounds and other ancient holy places (GL ch. 4, p. 9), another Norwegian decree bans beliefs in gravemounds and *horgar* (GÞL p. 18) and king Sverrir's Christian law (SC p. 430) lists gravemounds and *horgar* as places where it was illegal to worship. Gravemounds certainly seem to have held a special religious meaning for people, in all probability because they were directly and intimately connected with family ancestors (e.g. Brink 2001: 88; Gunnell 2014). The religious importance assigned to gravemounds is, however, only one side of the story. Medieval laws (e.g. DN pp. 117–118; Rett pp. 120–121) note the requirement to name one's last five ancestors in the male line in order to legally inherit ancestral land – *telja langfeðr frá haugi* ('enumerate ancestors from gravemounds') or *til haugs ok heiðni* ('to gravemounds and heathen time') – and we may assume that the gravemounds, as tangible, physical evidence that contained the dead ancestors and which were in all probability located on the hereditary land, also played some role in the legal process. The five-generation principle for claiming the *óðal* is also suggested in Swedish runic inscriptions and in genealogical poetry (Gurevich 1977; Zachrisson 1994, 2017; Sundqvist 2002: 151–156; Brink 2012a: 103–106); even as late as the 14th century, an unbaptised child was still counted as a *høghæ man* ('barrow-man') according to an early Danish law (SL pp. 3–4).[6] The legal texts indicate that the presence of ancestors, exhibited by gravemounds, had a strong impact on both religious and secular routines.

The fact that 13th- and 14th-century laws often mention the sacrifices and offerings to gravemounds and that ancestors were clearly the backbone of social order and economic and legal norms shows that the traditions related to ancestors were so deeply established in early Scandinavia that they survived long after the conversion to Christianity, and even into the modern era. As Gunnell (2007b) points out, these beliefs and customs were more difficult to root out than the belief in gods who were relatively easily integrated into Christian culture, being cast as either the pagan counterparts of saints or as demonic characters resembling the Devil (e.g. Loki; Laidoner 2012). Beings whose origins are believed to be rooted in earlier ancestor beliefs, on the other hand, survived well into the modern era: the different farm guardians in Scandinavian folk belief often held to live inside gravemounds and identified as the original inhabitants of farms, received offerings of food even into the 18th and 19th centuries.[7] According to one report (Blom 1896: 137–138), cockerels were sacrificed to the beings inhabiting a *risahaug*

14 *Theoretical considerations*

in Setersdal in Norway in the 18th century. The word *risa* is connected to the Old Norse *risi*, which is usually interpreted according to its contemporary meaning 'giant', although it is believed to derive from *rísa* ('to rise') which also has the related meaning of 'a piece of rising ground' (CDE), pointing to a possible interpretation as 'raised gravemound' and subsequently explaining *risi* as a person underneath the raised ground (Perkins 1999: 199, note 4); the most common occurrence of *risi* in extant literature is that of *bergrisi*, whose initial element derives via PG **bergaz* ('mountain, hill') from PIE **bhergh* ('high, elevated'), also the origin of the word 'barrow'. The term *bergrisi* occurs mostly in the Icelandic context where mountains symbolically took over the function of gravemounds.[8]

Although the domestic practices related to different ancestor-figures in later folk belief were a relevant topic to folklorists and archaeologists in the late 19th and early 20th century, overall, Snorri's portrayal of the mythological framework has dominated research into Old Norse religion. The fragments of myths recorded, joined and modified by Snorri must of course have their roots in pagan Scandinavia; however, it is most doubtful whether these orally transmitted and highly varied fantasy stories had any real impact on believers' emotional attitudes and ritual behaviours. Mythological scenes are sometimes envisaged on rock carvings and picture stones (e.g. Nylén & Lamm 1988: 68–73; Ellmers 1995), allegedly supporting such contention. However, these interpretations are based on existing literature, which naturally focuses on the extraordinary rather than the ordinary. The images typically depict common activities: people on boats or horseback, people fishing or hugging. There is no reason why they could not depict simple everyday situations. Even if sometimes the different scenes could be stitched together to look like sequences from myths, this interpretation must nonetheless be viewed with caution; a horse with eight legs is not necessarily Sleipnir, but potentially a horse who runs fast, the same way a man on horseback is not necessarily a warrior headed for Valhǫll, but simply a man on horseback. The gods known from the mythological tradition were probably of much less significance compared to personal ancestors, and may have been called upon only in times of community-wide crisis, very likely as the ancestors of prominent kin groups, if we follow the typical worldview in 'folk religious' societies generally (see Chapter 1, Section 1.6).

Compared to earlier research, recent studies have generally placed more emphasis on the socio-political background of pre-Christian societies and it is now recognised that the communities of early Scandinavia are above all characterised by strong kinship ties across many generations (Vogt 2010; Vestergaard 2012). Consequently, ancestors have come to be seen as intimately linked with the social issues of the living, ranging from morality to group membership, and identity to politics. The legal requirements declared in law texts already mentioned for claiming the ancestral *óðal* and the motivation behind genealogical poetry imply the central importance of intergenerational relationships. Archaeologists also emphasise that the long-held tradition of burial grounds expresses strong generational connections and the need to communicate with one's ancestors (e.g. Baudou 1989; Zachrisson 1994, 2004; Gräslund 2001; Artelius 2004; Parker Pearson 2003;

Gardela 2016; Hem Eriksen 2019; Price 2019) and scholars who have used folkloristic material underline that a continuity of this kind can be seen in the legends associated with specific gravemounds in public memory (Zachrisson 1996; Gunnell 2014). The fact that people still knew through folk tales that some small knolls in the landscape were actually ancient graves suggests that these stories functioned almost as a form of protection, prohibiting human interference with the places where they were located (Zachrisson 1996: 102).[9] The spatial structure of *þing* mounds and their surroundings also suggests strong ancestral interference (Brink 2004). Overall, research has started to undergo a major shift with respect to the importance of kinship and the status of ancestors in early Scandinavian societies. However, the concept of 'god' is usually associated with the supernatural, and the Old Norse gods, too, are more often than not viewed as having had mythic and divine dimensions in the Norsemen's religious cognition, despite early Scandinavia's regional kinship-based social structures. It is habitually overlooked that the concept of 'divine' is in essence alien to typical folk religions such as those in pagan Scandinavia, the 'gods' of whom were usually found in the history, experiences and customs of humans, not in transcendent, remote or mythical divinities.

1.1.6 Folk vs. world religion

The term 'folk religion', like many other theoretical terms, must be used rather loosely here.[10] Linked to ideas about 'high' and 'low' mythology – terminology that was advanced by German scholars like Mannhardt and Schwartz in the late 19th century – 'folk religion' (*Volksreligion*) was traditionally used in the sense of a less sophisticated form of belief, as the opposite of 'high religion' (*Hochreligion*), which involves belief in the 'high gods', also sometimes labelled 'world', 'institutional', 'official' or 'universal' religion today. The narrow and polarised terminology can be problematic and misleading, as it suggests that, on the one hand, the 'high religion' is a religious domain without disparity, and on the other, that the 'lower' belief systems reveal less rich and complex traditions than the religions of 'advanced' societies. This dichotomy is untrue – it is often in small-scale cultures that we see religion manifest itself most elaborately (DuBois 1999: 27–28). The negative connotations of the word 'folk' have also consequently resulted in substitute terms being used (e.g. 'ethnic', 'indigenous', 'popular', 'lived' religion); out of these, 'vernacular religion' – advocated by the American folklorist and religious studies specialist Leonard Primiano (1995) – has been deployed perhaps most actively in recent years (e.g. Kuutma 2005; Bowman 2014; Bowman & Valk 2014; Alybina 2014). This term, Primiano (2014) explains, must not be viewed simply as a substitute expression for the old concept. It is rather a separate one that focuses less on 'religion' as an abstract phenomenon, instead allowing scholars to place more focus on people's personal beliefs and affairs and to understand how religion – in whatever mixed form – 'is lived: as human beings encounter, understand, interpret, and practice it' (Primiano 1995: 44). The claim is thus that all religion is 'vernacular' religion and that it is the perception of the 'individual' that is of interest because every person experiences religion differently – whether institutional or domestic or both – and mixes the traditions and teachings with their own private thoughts and understandings. Whether or not we accept this contention in entirety, it is clear that religious syncretism occurs extensively around the world and that aspects of an individual's religious life should not be distorted in order to conform to historically loaded and polarising terminology. The Chinese, for example, have amalgamated elements of four philosophies: Confucianism, Buddhism, Taoism and traditional folk religion, which usually overlap and blend with each other (Chamberlain 2009); this means that the borders between 'world' and 'folk' are far from neatly aligned and that they can be practised simultaneously, which is inconsistent with the earlier academic approach that sought an ostensibly more clear-cut scenario. However, as another author points out, importance should also be given to *how* the term 'folk religion' is used and whether or not sufficient acknowledgement is given to its ideological and semantic limitations (Kapaló 2013). Adopting a different, historically less burdening term has its benefits, but it can in turn blur the distinction between folk and world religion more than is necessary. There are a few key aspects which are particularly characteristic of each and we need not necessarily withdraw from relying on those aspects associated with what was formerly labelled 'folk religion'. Ancestors, too, are at the very core of 'folk religion'.

Broadly speaking, 'official' institutionalised belief systems that require worldwide membership – and that subsequently tend to be classified as world religions – are typically oriented towards the individual, while small-scale belief systems in kinship-based regional enclaves – or folk religions – are more collectively inclined. The main characteristic that separates world religion from folk religion is that the former has scriptures, holy books or other sacred teachings about faith, morality and ways of living that accumulate over centuries and are followed by all practitioners with fairly minimal differences. Folk religion, in contrast, does not follow any extensive or coherent body of theological knowledge; instead, beliefs and practices are learned piecemeal through personal, oral communication, passed down generation to generation and via a domestic environment. Even though these beliefs, too, are based on tradition, the focus is more on how these traditions fit into the local geography and contemporary social circumstances. Since they do not follow any strict written rules, but rather loose guidelines that can be adapted to fit particular conditions, they are constantly subject to change. This flexibility applies also to the genealogies that are at the heart of such kinship-based societies, making it much harder to study and to understand them, especially from the modern Western perspective accustomed to associate religion with Christian dogma.[11]

Regardless of the overall fluidity of folk religions, there are elements which are typically characteristic of them, and which have been excellently encapsulated by the human geographer Yi-Fu Tuan (2001: 152–154), whose work has been instrumental to understanding how people attach meaning to places and how this is influenced by sense of time. The foremost of these lies in the importance of continuity and family cohesion, including with dead family members, who are believed to remain firmly attached to the home and to continue to intervene in daily life. Unlike in most world religions such as Christianity, which is based on blind faith and trust in a monotheistic supreme God, and which is of concern in the early medieval Nordic context, security in folk religions is gained through a sense of continuity and links to the human past, and this is why ancestors in such cultures take on unique importance. Since folk religions lay great emphasis on kinship, the 'gods' who appear in rituals are closely linked to specific families and to the geographical territories where they physically reside. Since they are firmly attached to particular places, their ability to look after people – unlike that of the Christian God – does not usually extend beyond that particular region. This binds the members of folk religions to specific geographic areas and explains also why exile – also the highest criminal sentence in pagan Scandinavia and Iceland (Riisøy 2009) – is considered a particularly serious punishment in these societies; it deprives the outlaw not only of the physical amenities of life, but also from the protection granted by the local 'gods', who are the person's ancestors and guardians. These localised 'gods', as Tuan points out, are thus not perceived as anything like God in Christian theology, but belong to a hierarchy of beings that are intimately linked with family ancestors. Since each community is protected by its own ancestors, folk religions readily accept the existence of other 'gods' outside one's own regional borders. This kind of tolerance can be seen also by the uneven geographical distribution of theophoric place names in Scandinavia as previously noted. Even if the members of folk religions sometimes accommodate the idea of a universal transcendent power, the belief is usually remote and hazy compared to the belief in the local gods who influence human affairs more directly (Tuan 2001: 152–154; Goody 2010: 92). Generally, deities associated with the land are believed to be much more ancient than those associated with the sky or the upper air.

1.1.7 Paganism and Christianity

Consistent with the 'folk' versus 'world' dichotomy in religious terms, the meeting of paganism and Christianity in Scandinavia is sometimes mistakenly viewed as a swift clash of two opposite and extreme forms of spirituality. From a religious historical perspective, it is important to understand that the transition to Christianity did not happen overnight or bring about any radical changes during its earliest stages. As a complex and time-consuming process, the conversion took place at different times in different places and varied from region to region and individual to individual. The acceptance of Christianity by law – the event that is commonly considered to mark the end of the pagan period – was promoted by the rising elite and did not mean that the daily beliefs and practices of common people went through any sudden fundamental changes.[12] During the earlier stages of the conversion process, it must have been crucial for the missionaries to make Christianity fathomable to the people by attaching pagan elements to this new type of belief (Gunnell 2007b: 370–371). Placing Christian festivals on pagan feast days, for example, was an established practice and serves as a good example of this kind of transition (Kvideland & Sehmsdorf 1999: 11–12; Gunnell 2000). Transforming pagan cult houses into Christian churches instead of destroying

18 *Theoretical considerations*

them was another useful strategy for merging the new beliefs with the old; Bede's 7th-century *Historia Ecclesiastica Gentis Anglorum* (pp. 44–45) contains a copy of a letter from Pope Gregory to a missionary in England with the instruction to preserve the pagan temples and to transform them into Christian centres, as this would speed up conversion. Similarly, places where pagan cults had been celebrated in Scandinavia continued to function as religious centres after conversion (e.g. Jeppesen & Madsen 1990; Ljungkvist & Frölund 2015), and written sources bear witness to the fact that the formal acceptance of new and stricter ideological principles did not affect former beliefs, which were modified rather than exterminated, as is seen, for example, in the makeover of the *dísir* in *Þiðranda þáttr* (Flat 1, pp. 419–421; Kaplan 2000), or in Helgi magri's simultaneously friendly relation with Christ and Þórr (Lnd p. 250). The meeting of Old Norse religion and Christianity was certainly not accompanied by any sudden change of mentality, but rather generated a hybrid religious environment where boundaries and identities remained fluid for a long time.

Though it is impossible to separate Old Norse paganism from Christianity in absolute terms, from a typological point of view, it is of course possible and even necessary to draw an artificial line between the two, as there are some fundamental differences that led to wider social changes. The introduction of a new transcendent god whose power suddenly extended over the laws and elements of nature and over the entire world, freed people geographically; however, it also changed the *status quo* and challenged the social-moral sensibilities of early medieval Norse societies. Kinship that had been the decisive element in survival, success and strategic behaviour started to lose its importance and new foundations had to be found for social organisation. More importantly, as a consequence of the acceptance and promotion of Christianity – a religion of the book – literacy started to develop among the elite in the northern regions of Europe. Of the Old Norse speaking countries, Iceland became the cradle of vernacular writing; apart from the use of runes, pagan Scandinavian societies had essentially been oral, and it is from the Icelandic medieval manuscripts that we draw our greatest portion of knowledge about their past.

1.2 Primary sources

Broadly speaking, we can divide surviving primary literary sources into texts penned by foreign learned historians, and texts written by the Norsemen themselves in Latin or Old Norse. Archaeological finds, runes, place names, law texts and later folklore count as primary sources for Old Norse religion, but these must be interpreted, to a great extent, within the oldest literary tradition. Histories and chronicles written in Latin by various Roman, German and Scandinavian historians – ranging from the 1st century AD to the Middle Ages – offer some useful glimpses into the religious life of people in northern Europe. The ethnographic account of the Roman historian Tacitus, *Germania*, from 98 AD is the earliest report concerned with the religious customs among the tribes of the *Germani* whose religious ideology might bear some resemblance to that of the Norsemen in the Late Iron Age. However, the descriptions are written by a Roman politician for whom 'Germania' referred geographically to the area between the rivers Rhine, Danube, Vistula and the Baltic Sea – a region which was outside the control of the Roman Empire and thus attractive but also daunting for early chroniclers (Birley 1999).

Later Latin sources are also often valuable as comparative data for Old Norse descriptions, but most of these are written as missionary documents, shaped by the new religious order approaching from the south: Christianity. One of the earliest missionary efforts in Scandinavia was made by Ansgarius, later the archbishop of Hamburg–Bremen, who went first to Jutland and then to Birka where he established a minor Christian community, and whose life story was written by his successor Rimbert in the *Vita Ansgarii* (875 AD) (Palmer 2004). Another useful account written by an outsider in Latin is *Gesta Hammaburgensis* (1075) by the German chronicler Adam of Bremen. His text concentrates on the history of the bishopric of Hamburg–Bremen that had been entrusted with the Roman Catholic Church's missions to Scandinavia. It therefore includes descriptions of the pagan communities in Scandinavia, among others the famous description of the pagan cult house in Gamla Uppsala. It is one of the richest descriptions of a pagan cult; however, its reliability is diminished by the fact that it is based on second-hand missionary reports. He might have been inspired by stories or by other contemporary chronicles such as, for instance, the early 11th-century *Chronicon* by Thietmar of Merseburg, whose description of a communal sacrifice at the ancient Danish centre at Lejre – also based on hearsay – is similar to Adam's account. These Latin descriptions by churchmen were intended primarily as propaganda to draw attention to the pressing need for conversion in these areas (Tschan 2002).

Even though Thietmar, Adam and other authors mentioned above describe religious worldviews which they did not empathise with or even understand, the texts are useful, not least because they are often concerned more with real-life social situations than with the mythology which abounds in some later texts in Old Norse (e.g. *Snorra Edda*) or written by Scandinavians in Latin. Saxo Grammaticus' patriotic account *Gesta Danorum*, for example, which was completed at the beginning of the 13th century, recounts the pagan and early Christian history of the Danes and Scandinavians, but is to a large extent fantastic in character and probably largely based on orally preserved *fornaldarsaga*-like stories which he took from Icelanders. Saxo is the earliest native Christian author writing in Latin prose who produced versions of Old Norse myths and gods. As a learned author familiar with Latin teachings, his interpretation is strongly euhemeristic – pagan gods were originally rulers who became worshipped for their success by the ignorant masses – and he credits them with supernatural virtues to explain such an achievement, partially based on mythological tradition (Ellis Davidson 1998).

Of other Scandinavian authors, the Icelander Ari fróði Þorgilsson, living in the late 11th and early 12th centuries, should be mentioned. He is the earliest-known composer of a historical record of Iceland in the vernacular and is believed to be behind the composition of *Íslendingabók* and *Landnámabók*, which deal with events in Iceland from its settlement until Ari's own time (Jakob Benediktsson 1986; Grønlie 2006). *Landnámabók* contains the ancestral lines of the families that claimed land in Iceland, and since it essentially describes the creation of a new nation, it is unlikely that the information could have been based on earlier texts. *Íslendingabók* puts more emphasis on ecclesiastical matters and in the extant version the author refers to an earlier lost version, which evidently contained a chronology of Norwegian kings; fragments of this chronology have survived elsewhere (e.g. the *langfeðgatal* ('enumeration of ancestors') which ends with Ari himself). By the author's own time, Iceland had been settled for over 200 years, but its political history was very much linked with the rule of the group related to Haraldr hárfagri, whose policies might have led to emigration to Iceland; an account of the kings of Norway would have been a natural way of contextualising the early history of Iceland. Both accounts contain fictionalised scenes and their reliability as accurate historiography is questionable; however, they are essentially historical accounts and function as valuable references for the later and anonymous *Íslendingasǫgur*, where same events and characters can be found.[13]

The *Íslendingasǫgur* depict the interactions of prominent Icelandic families between settlement and the beginning of the Icelandic Commonwealth (Vésteinn Ólason 1998; Clover 2005; Clunies Ross 2010). Genealogies, feuds and other important aspects of daily life are recurring themes in these narratives, but they appear side by side with pagan rituals and the supernatural world. The events described may not always be historically correct, but their setting and context are on the whole historical and realistic. Although the sagas' dating has been a matter of considerable dispute, the majority of them are believed to have been written around the 13th century. The debate over their origin started in the 19th century and divided scholars into two opposing sides: advocates of Freeprose and Bookprose. According to the Freeprose theory, the sagas originate from the Viking period and are based on oral tradition, which kept events alive in the form of folklore until they were recorded in written form. The Bookprose theory, initiated and developed a short while after, primarily by Icelandic scholars, posited that the sagas are literary compositions in their own right, composed by the authors of the Middle Ages. In the spirit of the academic vision promoted today, which questions rather than supports any clear-cut boundaries, recent studies have taken a looser approach with regard to these matters. The consideration of Gísli Sigurðsson (2004) of the importance of oral tradition in the creation of the Icelandic sagas has been especially valuable, and it is now generally accepted that a portion of the sagas' content must have been transmitted orally for a long time prior to their recording. Although Gísli argues for the importance of verbal transmission, he does not support the existence of purely oral sagas, as some Freeprose supporters did; it is most likely that inter-authorial and inter-literary influences were at work. Regardless of the precise origin of the sagas, they expose the mindsets of early Icelanders and provide kernels of insight into pagan Scandinavian traditions.

Prior to the *Íslendingasǫgur* but following the tradition of Ari and other early Norwegian–Icelandic antiquarians, the sagas of individual kings were written. These accounts revolve to a great extent around Óláfr helgi and Óláfr Tryggvason, who were the descendants of Haraldr hárfagri and thus members of the 'Ynglingar'. Like Latin sources, the kings' sagas focus more on religion than mythology and are concerned chiefly with the genealogical traditions of the ruling families (Andersson 2009). The most extensive and well-known collection is the 13th-century *Heimskringla* by Snorri Sturluson, which provides a kind of 'learned prehistory' for Scandinavia (Whaley 1991; Finlay & Faulkes 2011). It begins with a prologue which explains geographical matters and where Snorri acknowledges his debt in composing the collection to Ari and to Þjóðólfr úr Hvíni, a skald at Haraldr's court who composed *Ynglingatal* in the 9th century. However, Snorri must have borrowed from oral reports as well as other written traditions, some of which have been lost or are preserved only via Snorri, meaning that their accuracy cannot be verified by comparing multiple versions. The collection begins with *Ynglinga saga*, which is based on *Ynglingatal*, and continues with individual sagas of 15 Norwegian kings of the hárfagri family. In the prologue Snorri ascribes their ancestry to Yngvifreyr, while *Ynglinga saga* starts with Óðinn's emigration from Troy to Scandinavia, which is consistent with the prologue to the 13th-century *Edda*, which portrays Old Norse mythology. As noted earlier, the main purpose behind the regularly inconsistent genealogies of kings, which abound in early medieval literature, is believed to have been the need to aid certain individuals' rightful claims to power (e.g. Gurevich 1977; Zachrisson 1994). They are thus valuable sources in terms of the importance of ancestry and kinship in Scandinavia until and during the conversion to Christianity. With *Heimskringla*, Snorri broke new ground in documenting royal historiography. As Diana Whaley (1991: 46–47) has pointed out, the later collections of kings' sagas – although interspersed with material that Snorri did not use – are all basically compendious adaptations of his work. A considerable collection of this kind is the 14th-century *Flateyjarbók* – the largest Icelandic manuscript, written by the Icelandic priests Jón Hákonarson and Magnús Þórhallson – whose dominant subject is the life of Óláfr Tryggvason and the conversion of Norway. The sagas, as told in *Flateyjarbók*, have many additions of a supernatural kind, drawn from earlier sources and oral traditions (Ashman Rowe 2005).

The Icelandic sources, and particularly Snorri's texts, often cite skaldic verse dating from the 9th to 13th centuries (Gade 2000; Frank 2005; Whaley 2005; Clunies Ross 2011). The subject matter in these poems is mostly commemorative and historical: the authors usually celebrate a specific event and are concerned with the genealogical background of real Norwegian kings at whose demand the poems were composed, making it easier to date them, although mythological content is present, too. The poems thus belong to the world of the elite and are generally subject to strict rules with respect to both metre and structure, and contain elaborate types of strophes and a great deal of *kenningar* ('juxtapositions'), *heiti* ('synonyms') and *fornǫfn* ('nicknames'), making it hard to understand the poems without additional context or explanation (such as that given by Snorri, who quoted the poems). For Snorri – a man born into a powerful family in the Icelandic

Commonwealth, educated in both literature and law and who himself became a retainer in the service of Norwegian kings – it was thus natural to ground his royal histories by using skaldic verses as evidence.[14] Overall, the creation of skaldic poetry is acknowledged as having been an individual and conscious artistic effort, unlike that of Eddic poetry, which is believed to be a reworking of old lore known to many people, and which Snorri utilised elsewhere.

The fact that Snorri's interests extended beyond political topics is seen in his perhaps most popular work – the 13th-century *Edda* – which is designed as a handbook for poets, and consists of four sections, which to varying degrees all centre on mythological themes and rely heavily on Eddic poetry. Unlike skaldic poetry, the Eddic poems are structurally simple and are quoted by Snorri without giving the name of any particular author or scribe (Gunnell 2005; Clunies Ross 2011). This does not necessarily indicate the absence of authorial purpose in the composition of a traditional narrative; however, the fact that the poems are narratively and metrically flexible, of anonymous authorship, and deal with the mythological past suggests that they were part of common cultural heritage. The dating of these poems is therefore difficult, although some elements found in them are believed to be of great antiquity and to originate from different parts of northern Europe. Their thematic tendency is to describe the ancient Norse gods and heroes and their exploits: the mythological poems employ themes related to cosmogony and the supernatural and seem to be Scandinavian tradition, and the heroic lays celebrate the deeds of aristocratic warriors from the Migration Period in Europe. Snorri's interest in collecting and preserving pre-Christian folklore – or whatever of it had remained in 13th-century Iceland – was unusual in his time. It is important to notice though that the names 'skaldic' and 'Eddic' are ultimately constructed by scholars and do not indicate any exclusive type of poetic model, and that the qualities used to differentiate them often blend. Essentially, the Eddic poems' categorisation as a unit derives from the fact that they are anonymous and preserved in a continuous and more or less complete form, mainly in a single manuscript, *Codex Regius*. This means that the rest of Old Norse vernacular poetry, which is usually preserved in single stanzas and scattered over a number of prose texts from many medieval Icelandic manuscripts, has become traditionally labelled 'skaldic'.

The themes and elements contained in the main literary sources, which will be addressed throughout the book, must have their roots in Scandinavian and Icelandic paganism; however, our ability to interpret them is limited by their varied background and preservation. We only know that the extant manuscripts were produced in Iceland from the 13th century onwards and that they contain the understanding of paganism of medieval Icelandic Christians. It is consequently impossible to tie any of these texts definitively to actual religious practices and experiences in pagan Scandinavia, let alone view them as reflections of a belief 'system' followed by the entire population of Scandinavia. The Latin histories are early and concerned more with religion than myth, but are written by foreigners who were Christian. Synoptic histories, kings' sagas and royal biographies are written by native authors and draw material from earlier local traditions, but focus on kings and are influenced by Latin cultural traditions. *Landnámabók* and *Íslendingabók* might be broadly classified as historical, but are concerned mainly with prominent Icelandic families, as are the later mostly anonymous *Íslendingasǫgur*, which combine the Icelandic settings with the supernatural. Old Norse poetry is older than the sagas and closer to the pagan Scandinavian world, although it was recorded contemporaneously with the later material by the same medieval Icelandic scribes. Eddic poems present the ancient lore of common people and are recorded in a more or less continuous line, but are anonymous and therefore difficult to date. Skaldic poems deal with the authors' contemporaries, but they are usually fragmentary and focus on the elite. Medieval authors wrote texts of many different types and conflicts of this kind – pagan/Christian, Icelandic/Scandinavian, historical/fantastical, elite/common – that are inevitably present in surviving works. All extant literature, whichever genre it is identified with in the academic world, is helpful and problematic at the same time. The major challenge for scholars who are working with Old Norse religion is to attempt to work out which elements are likely pre-Christian, whether or not they display certain common patterns and how far it is possible to reconstruct the bigger picture from them. A degree of scepticism and caution when working with the texts is critical for the conduct of such research, as are insights drawn from other disciplines.

1.3 Method

This study is above all a literary–historical investigation of the role of the ancestors of the elite in Old Norse religion, which is construed here as a typical orally transmitted folk religion where temporal, geographical and local variations were always present. The study combines textual evidence from native and foreign authors with modern anthropological studies in order to understand and identify the meaning of practices related to ancestor cults in the context of the socio-cultural patterns and values of typical folk religions in general. It is my belief that the results of previous and current anthropological research, which focus on the study of human societies, cultures and religions of past and present societies around the world, provide a useful context for understanding underlying patterns in typical kinship-based communities, including in pre-Christian Scandinavia. They offer a valuable setting for understanding the concept of 'god' in folk religions and cultures, which is often confused and obscured in discussions of Old Norse religion by the Christian theological tradition. The theoretical framework drawn from social anthropological assessments is used as a lens for the subsequently examined case studies, which focus on the content of texts that provide descriptions of *post mortem* cults of specific individuals in Scandinavia and Iceland. In addition, authorial agendas and the political and social background will be considered in connection with each case study. References are regularly made to folklore, philology, toponymy, archaeology and the history of religion, although these remain secondary to the textual sources and to the socio-anthropological analogues of ancestor cults in other cultures.

Notes

1 See Furseth & Repstad (2006); Cox (2010).
2 See Barnes (2005); Nordberg (2012: 122–124, 125–126).
3 The *Fenni* and their distinct lifestyle is mentioned by many early historians like Tacitus (Ger chs 1, 46, ed. pp. 3, 47–48, tr. pp. 101, 140–141), Ptolemaeus (*Geographia* 2, ch. 10, ed. pp. 110–113, tr. p. 65), Jordanes (Get ch. 3, ed. p. 59, tr. p. 56), Paulus Diaconus (*Historia Langobardorum* 1, ch. 5, ed. pp. 54–55, tr. pp. 7–8), Adam of Bremen (GH IV, chs 24–25, ed. pp. 172–173, tr. pp. 205–206), Saxo Grammaticus (GD V, IX, ed. pp. 133, 138, 258, tr. pp. 148, 153, 28), the geographer of Ravenna (*Ravennatis anonymi Cosmographia et Gvidonsis Geographica*, I, IV, V, chs 11–13, 28, 46, ed. pp. 28, 201, 324, 417) and many others.
4 Concerning the history of comparative philology in Old Norse studies, see Jackson (2012), in folklore, see Kvideland & Sehmsdorf (1999: 3–37).
5 The suggestion that the Sámi are connected with the mythical *jǫtnar* was first made by Þormóður Torfason, who in his *Historia Rerum Norvegicarum* (pp. 241–252) from 1711 discussed the geographical location of *Jǫtunheimar* and suggested that since this region was located towards the north or east by Norse authors, it points to the Sámi districts in today's Kola Peninsula and its neighbourhood.
6 In later manuscripts the *høghæ* has been replaced by *hedhen* ('heathen') (SL p. 4, note a).
7 For further information and discussion concerning these characters, see Schetelig (1911); Feilberg (1918); Lid (1933); Birkeli (1938: 85–203); Lindow (1978: 136–144); Kvideland & Sehmsdorf (1999: 238–248); Gunnell (2014).
8 In the Eddic poem *Grottasǫngr*, two women who grind riches with a magic millstone descend from a *bergrisi* (sts 9–10, 24). The poem reveals that they had been nourished under the earth and that they had moved a *setberg* ('flat-topped mountain') from its place and a boulder from the *risi*'s residence (sts 10–12). It seems that the supernatural object is obtained from an otherworld of some sort; after having spent time under the earth (in a grave?) and removing a flat-topped mountain (a mound?) and a rock (a memorial stone) from a *risi*'s dwelling, they deliver a magic millstone to the king. In *Gylfaginning* (ch. 47) *setberg* is in the residence of Útgarða-Loki of the 'outer realm', the name of which broadly corresponds to Ugarthilocus in *Gesta Danorum* (VIII, ed. pp. 244–246, tr. 267–270), who resides in a burial mound-like cavern filled with treasures, a rotten smell and decay (Ellis 1968: 186, 191–194). The place name Setberg is common in western Iceland, where it usually designates a flat-topped mountain (Cleasby & Vigfússon 1874: 524).
9 Continuity of belief of this kind is visible in Iceland, where a motorway project was halted less than a decade ago because elves were believed to live in the rocks located where the road was meant to pass through (Kirby 2014).
10 Useful discussion about 'folk religion' is found in Mensching (1964); Schneider (1964); Yoder (1974), Tuan (2001: 149–160). Of recent studies, the collection of articles edited by Bowman and Valk (2014) offers especially valuable insights, as well as the articles by Primiano (1995) and Bowman (2014).
11 By Western Christian perspectives, I do not mean that the ideas should derive from personal religious convictions, but rather from the tendencies in the general worldview that most Western societies share.
12 Concerning the Christianisation of the Nordic countries, see e.g. Finnestad (1990); Orri Vésteinsson (2003); Carver (2005); Berend (2007); Brink (2012b).
13 Further on Norse historiography, see Würth (2005).
14 Concerning Snorri's life, see Faulkes (2012).

Secondary sources

Abram, Chris, 2011, *Myths of the pagan north: the gods of the Norsemen*, Continuum International Publishing Group, London and New York.

Alybina, Tatiana, 2014, 'Vernacular beliefs and official traditional religion. The position and meaning of the Mari worldview in the current context', *Approaching Religion*, vol. 4, no. 1, pp. 89–100.

Andersson, Theodore, 2009, 'The formation of kings' sagas', *Scripta Islandica*, vol. 60, pp. 77–88.

Andrén, Anders, 2011, 'Old Norse and Germanic religion', in T. Insoll (ed.), *The archaeology of ritual and religion*, University Press, Oxford. pp. 846–862.

Artelius, Tore, 2004, 'Minnesmakarnas verkstad. Om vikingatida bruk av äldre gravar och begravningsplatser', in Å. Berggren et al. (eds.), *Minne och myt. Konsten att skapa det förflutna*. Vägar till Midgård 5. Nordic Academic Press, Lund. pp. 99–120.

Arvidsson, Stefan, 2006, *Aryan idols: Indo-European mythology as ideology and science*, University of Chicago Press, Chicago and London.

Ashman Rowe, Elizabeth, 2005, *The development of Flateyjarbók. Iceland and the Norwegian dynastic crisis of 1389*, University Press of Southern Denmark, Odense.

Bäckman, Louise, 1975, *Sájva: Föreställningar om hjälp- och skyddsväsen i heliga fjäll bland samerna*, Almqvist & Wiksell International, Stockholm.

Bäckman, Louise, 1983, 'Förfäderskult? En studie i samernas förhållande till sina avlidna', *SáDS áigecála*, vol. 1, pp. 11–48.

Barnes, Michael, 2005, 'Language', in R. McTurk (ed.), *A companion to Old Norse-Icelandic literature and culture*, Blackwell, Malden, Oxford and Victoria. pp. 173–189.

Baudou, Evert, 1989, 'Hög – gård – helgedom i Mellannorrland under den äldre järnåldern', *Arkeologi i norr*, vol. 2, pp. 9–43.

Benediktsson, Jakob, 1986, 'Formáli', in Jakob Benediktsson (ed.), *Íslendingabók. Landnámabók*, Hið Íslenzka fornritafélag, Reykjavík.

Berend, Nora (ed.) 2007, *Christianization and the rise of Christian monarchy: Scandinavia, Central Europe and Rus' c. 900–1200*, Cambridge University Press, Cambridge.

Birkeli, Emil, 1938, *Fedrekult i Norge. Et forsøk på en systematisk-deskriptiv fremstillning*. Skrifter utgitt av Det Norske Videnskaps-Akademi i Oslo II. Hist.-Filos. Klasse, no. 5. I kommisjon hos Jacob Dybwad, Oslo.

Birley, Anthony, 1999, 'Introduction', in A. Birley (ed.), *Tacitus. Agricola and Germany*. Oxford University Press, Oxford. pp. xi–xxxix.

Blom, Peter, 1896, *Beskrivelse over Valle prestegjeld i Sætersdalen: med dets prestehistorie og sagn*, Oplændingens tr, Gjøvik.

Bowman, Marion, 2014, 'Vernacular religion, contemporary spirituality and emergent identities. Lessons from Lauri Honko', *Approaching Religion*, vol. 4, no. 1, pp. 101–113.

Bowman, Marion, and Ülo Valk (eds.) 2014 [2012], *Vernacular religion in everyday life: expressions of belief*, Routledge, London and New York.

Brink, Stefan, 2001, 'Mythologizing landscape. Place and space of cult and myth', in M. Stausberg (ed.), *Kontinuitäten und Brüche in der Religionsgeschichtem*, de Gruyter, Berlin and New York. pp. 76–112.

Brink, Stefan, 2004, 'Mytologiska rum och eskatologiska föreställningar i det vikingatida Norden', in A. Andrén et al. (eds.), *Ordning mot kaos. Studier av nordisk förkristen kosmologi*. Vägar till Midgård 4. Nordic Academic Press, Lund. pp. 291–316.

26 Theoretical considerations

Brink, Stefan, 2007, 'How uniform was the Old Norse religion?' in J. Quinn et al. (eds.), *Learning and understanding in the Old Norse world: essays in honour of Margaret Clunies Ross*. Medieval texts and cultures in northern Europe 18. Brepols, Turnhout, pp. 105–135.

Brink, Stefan, 2012a [2002], 'Law and legal customs in Viking Age Scandinavia', in J. Jesch (ed.), *The Scandinavians from the Vendel Period to the tenth century: an ethnographic perspective*, Boydell Press, Woodbridge, pp. 87–117.

Brink, Stefan, 2012b [2008], 'Christianisation and the emergence of the early church in Scandinavia', in S. Brink and N. Price (eds.), *The Viking world*, Routledge, London and New York, pp. 621–628.

Carver, Martin (ed.) 2005 [2003], *The cross goes north: processes of conversion in Northern Europe, AD 300–1300*, The Boydell Press, Woodbridge.

Chamberlain, Jonathan, 2009, *Chinese gods. An introduction to Chinese folk religion*, Blacksmith Books, Hong Kong and London.

Cleasby, Richard, and Guðbrandur Vigfússon (eds.) 1874, *Icelandic-English dictionary*, Clarendon Press, Oxford.

Clover, Carol, 2005 [1985], 'Icelandic family sagas (Íslendingasögur)', in C. Clover and J. Lindow (eds.), *Old Norse-Icelandic literature: a critical guide*, University of Toronto Press, Toronto, pp. 239–315.

Clunies Ross, Margaret, 2010, *The Cambridge introduction to the Old Norse-Icelandic saga*, Cambridge University Press, Cambridge and New York.

Clunies Ross, Margaret, 2011 [2005], *A history of Old Norse poetry and poetics*, DS Brewer, Cambridge.

Cox, James, 2010, *An introduction to the phenomenology of religion*, Continuum International Publishing Group, London and New York.

DuBois, Thomas, 1999, *Nordic religions in the Viking Age*, University of Pennsylvania Press, Philadelphia.

Dumézil, George, 1958, *L'idéologie Tripartiz des Indo-Européens*, Collection Latomus, Brussels.

Ellis, Hilda, 1968, *The road to Hel: a study of the conception of the dead in Old Norse literature*, Greenwood Press, New York.

Ellis Davidson, Hilda, 1998, 'Introduction', in P. Fisher and H. Ellis Davidson (eds.), *Saxo Grammaticus. The history of the Danes. Books 1–9*, D. S Brewer, Cambridge, pp. 1–16.

Ellmers, Detlev, 1995, 'Valhalla and the Gotland stones', in O. Crumlin-Pedersen and B. Munch (eds.), *The ship as symbol in prehistoric and medieval Scandinavia*, Nationalmuseet, Copenhagen, pp. 165–171.

Faulkes, Anthony, 2012 [2008], 'Snorri Sturluson: his life and work', in S. Brink and N. Price (eds.), *The Viking world*, Routledge, London and New York, pp. 311–314.

Feilberg, Henning, 1918, *Nissens historie*. Danmarks folkeminder, 18. Schønberg, Copenhagen.

Finlay, Alison, and Anthony Faulkes, 2011, 'Introduction', in A. Finlay and A. Faulkes (eds.), *Snorri Sturluson. Heimskringla, vol. 1. The beginnings to Óláfr Tryggvason*. Viking Society for Northern Research. University College London, London, pp. vii–xv.

Finnestad, Ragnhild, 1990, 'The study of the Christianization of the Nordic countries. Some reflections', in T. Ahlbäck (ed.), *Old Norse and Finnish religions and cultic place-names*, Donner Institute for Research in Religious and Cultural History, Åbo, pp. 256–272.

Frank, Roberta, 2005 [1985], 'Skaldic poetry', in C. Clover and J. Lindow (eds.), *Old Norse-Icelandic literature: a critical guide*, University of Toronto Press, Toronto, pp. 157–196.

Furseth, Inger, and Pål Repstad, 2006, *An introduction to the sociology of religion: classical and contemporary perspectives*, Ashgate Publishing Limited, Aldershot.

Gade, Kari Ellen, 2000, 'Poetry and its changing importance in medieval Icelandic culture', in M. Clunies Ross (ed.), *Old Icelandic literature and society*, Cambridge Studies in Medieval Literature, 42. Cambridge University Press, Cambridge, pp. 61–95.

Gardela, Leszek, 2016, 'Worshipping the dead: Viking Age cemeteries as cult sites?' in M. Egeler (ed.), *Germanische Kultorte. Vergleichende, historische und rezeptionsgeschichtliche Zugange*, Herbert Utz Verlag, München, pp. 169–205.

Gísli, Sigurðsson, 2004, *The Medieval Icelandic saga and oral tradition: a discourse on method*, Harvard University Press, Cambridge.

Goody, Jack, 1962, *Death, property and the ancestors: a study of the mortuary customs of the Lodagaa of West Africa*, Stanford University Press, Stanford.

Goody, Jack, 2010, *Myth, ritual and the oral*, Cambridge University Press, Cambridge.

Gräslund, Anne-Sofie, 2001, 'Living with the dead', in M. Stausberg (ed.), *Kontinuitäten und Brüche in der Religionsgeschichte: Festschrift für Anders Hultgård zu seinem 65. Geburtstag am 23.12. 2001*. Reallexikon der germanischen Altertumskunde, 31. de Gruyter, Berlin and New York, pp. 222–235.

Grønlie, Siân, 2006, 'Introduction', in A. Faulkes and A. Finlay (eds.), trans. S. Grønlie *Íslendingabók. Kristni saga. The book of the Icelanders. The story of the conversion*. Viking Society for Northern Research, XVIII. University College London, London, pp. vii–xlvii.

Gunnell, Terry, 2000, 'The season of the *Dísir*: the winter nights and the *Dísablót* in early Scandinavian belief', *Cosmos*, vol. 16, pp. 117–149.

Gunnell, Terry, 2005, 'Eddic poetry', in R. McTurk (ed.), *A companion to Old Norse-Icelandic literature and culture*, Blackwell, Malden, Oxford and Victoria, pp. 82–100.

Gunnell, Terry, 2007a, 'How Elvish were the Álfar?' in A. Wawn et al. (eds.), *Constructing nations, reconstructing myth: essays in honour of T. A. Shippey*, Brepols, Turnhout, pp. 111–130.

Gunnell, Terry, 2007b, 'Viking religion: Old Norse mythology', in R. North and J. Allard (eds.), *Beowulf & other stories: a new introduction to Old-English, Old Icelandic & Anglo-Norman literatures*, Pearson, New York, pp. 351–375.

Gunnell, Terry, 2014, 'Nordic folk legends, folk traditions and grave mounds. The value of folkloristics for the study of old Nordic religions', *FF Communications*, vol. 307, pp. 17–41.

Gunnell, Terry, 2015, 'Pantheon? What Pantheon? Concepts of a family of gods in pre-Christian Scandinavian religions', *Scripta Islandica*, vol. 66, p. 55–76.

Gunnell, Terry, 2017, 'How high was the highest one?' *Acta Scandinavica*, vol. 7, pp. 105–129.

Gurevich, Aron, 1977, 'Representations of property during the high Middle Ages', *Economy and Society*, vol. 6, no. 1, pp. 1–30.

Hem Eriksen, Marianne, 2019, *Architecture, society, and ritual in Viking Age Scandinavia: doors, dwellings, and domestic space*, Cambridge, Cambridge University Press.

Jackson, Peter, 2012, 'The merits and limits of comparative philology. Old Norse religious vocabulary in a long-term perspective', in C. Raudvere and J. P. Schjødt (eds.), *More than mythology: narratives, ritual practices and regional distribution in pre-Christian Scandinavian religions*, Nordic Academic Press, Lund, pp. 47–64.

Jennbert, Kristina, 2011, *Animals and humans: recurrent symbiosis in archaeology and Old Norse religion*, Nordic Academic Press, Lund.

28 Theoretical considerations

Jeppesen, Jens, and Hans Madsen, 1990, 'Stormansgård og kirke i Lisbjerg', *Kuml* (1988–1989), pp. 289–310.

Kapaló, James, 2013, 'Folk religion in discourse and practice', *Journal of Ethnology and Folkloristics*, vol. 7, no. 1, pp. 3–18.

Kaplan, Merrill, 2000, 'Prefiguration and the writing of history in 'Þáttr Þiðranda ok Þórhalls', *The Journal of English and Germanic Philology*, vol. 99, no. 3, pp. 379–394.

Kirby, Emma, 2014, 'Why Icelanders are wary of elves living beneath the rocks', *BBC News*, 20 June. viewed 24 October 2018, <https://www.bbc.co.uk/news/magazine-27907358>.

Kuutma, Kristin, 2005, 'Vernacular religions and the invention of identities behind the Finno-Ugric wall', *Temenos*, vol. 41, no. 1, pp. 51–76.

Kvideland, Reimund, and Henning Sehmsdorf, 1999 [1988], *Scandinavian folk belief and legend*, University of Minnesota Press, Minneapolis.

Laidoner, Triin, 2012, 'The flying Noaidi of the north: Sámi tradition reflected in the figure Loki Laufeyjarson in Old Norse mythology', *Scripta Islandica*, vol. 63, pp. 59–91.

Lid, Nils, 1933, *Jolesveinar og grøderikdomsgudar*. Skrifter utgitt av Det Norske Videnskaps-Akademi i Oslo II. Hist.-Filos. Klasse, 1932. No. 5. I kommisjon hos Jacob Dybwad, Oslo.

Lindow, John, 1978, *Swedish legends and folktales*, University of California Press, Berkeley, Los Angeles and London.

Lindow, John, 1995, 'Supernatural others and ethnic others: a millennium of world view', *Scandinavian Studies*, vol. 67, no. 1, pp. 8–31.

Ljungkvist, John, and Per Frölund 2015, 'Gamla Uppsala: the emergence of a centre and a magnate complex', in F. Herschend, P. Sinclair and N. Price (eds.), *Journal of Archaeology and Ancient History*, 16. Uppsala University, Uppsala.

Mensching, Gustav, 1964, 'Folk and universal religion', in L. Schneider (ed.), *Religion, culture and society: a reader in the sociology of religion*, John Wiley & Sons, New York, London and Sydney.

Motz, Lotte, 1996, *The king, the champion and the sorcerer: a study in Germanic myth*, Fassbaender, Wien.

Mundal, Else, 2000, 'Coexistence of Saami and Norse culture: reflected in and interpreted by Old Norse myths', in G. Barnes and M. Clunies Ross (eds.), *Old Norse myths, literature and society: proceedings of the 11th International Saga Conference 2–7 July 2000*, University of Sydney, Sydney, pp. 346–355.

Newell, William, 1976a, 'Good and bad ancestors', in W. Newell (ed.), *Ancestors*, Mouton, Hague and Paris, pp. 17–29.

Nordanskog, Gunnar, 2006, *Föreställd hedendom: Tidigmedeltida skandinaviska kyrkportar i forskning och historia*. Vägar till Midgård, 9. Nordic Academic Press, Lund.

Nordberg, Andreas, 2012, 'Continuity, change and regional variation in Old Norse religion', in C. Raudvere and J. P. Schjødt (eds.), *More than mythology: narratives, ritual practices and regional distribution in pre-Christian Scandinavian religions*, Nordic Academic Press, Lund, pp. 119–151.

Nordland, Odd, 1966, 'Valhall and Helgafell: syncretistic traits of the Old Norse religion', in S. Hartman (ed.), *Syncretism: based on papers read at the Symposium on Cultural Contact, Meeting of Religions, Syncretism held at Åbo on the 8th–10th of September, 1966*. Almqvist & Wiksell, Stockholm, pp. 66–99.

Nylén, Erik, and Jan Peder Lamm, 1988, *Stones, ships and symbols: the picture stones of Gotland from the Viking Age and Before*, Gidlund, Stockholm.

Palmer, James, 2004, 'Rimbert's Vita Anskarii and Scandinavian mission in the ninth century', *Journal of Ecclesiastical History*, vol. 55, no. 2, pp. 235–256.

Parker Pearson, Michael, 2003 [1999], *The archaeology of death and burial*, Sutton Publishing, Stroud.

Perkins, Richard, 1999, 'The gateway to Trondheim: two Icelanders at Agdenes', *Saga-Book*, vol. 25, pp. 179–213.

Price, Neil, 2000, 'Drum-time and Viking Age: Sámi-Norse identities in early medieval Scandinavia. Identities and cultural contacts in the Arctic', in M. Appelt et al. (eds.), *Proceedings from a conference at the Danish National Museum*, The Danish National Museum & Danish Polar Center, Copenhagen, pp. 12–27.

Price, Neil, 2002, *The Viking way: religion and war in late Iron Age Scandinavia*, Uppsala University Department of Archaeology and Ancient History, Uppsala.

Price, Neil, 2012a, 'Mythic acts: material narratives of the dead in Viking Age Scandinavia', in C. Raudvere and J. P. Schjødt (eds.), *More than mythology: narratives, ritual practices and regional distribution in pre-Christian Scandinavian religions*, Nordic Academic Press, Lund, pp. 13–46.

Price, Neil, 2019, *The Viking way: magic and mind in late Iron Age Scandinavia*, 2nd edition, Oxford, Oxbow Books.

Primiano, Leonard, 1995, 'Vernacular religion and the search for method in religious folklife', *Western Folklore*, vol. 54, no. 1, pp. 37–56.

Primiano, Leonard, 2014 [2012], 'Afterword. Manifestations of the religious vernacular: ambiguity, power, and creativity', in M. Bowman and Ü. Valk (eds.), *Vernacular religion in everyday life: expressions of belief*, Routledge, London and New York, pp. 382–394.

Raudvere, Catharina, and Jens Peter Schjødt (eds.) 2012, *More than mythology: narratives, ritual practices and regional distribution in pre-Christian Scandinavian religions*, Nordic Academic Press, Lund.

Riisøy, Anne, 2009, *Sexuality, law and legal practice and the reformation in Norway*, Brill, Leiden.

Sandnes, Jørn, 1973, 'Om samenes utbredelse mot sør i eldre tid', *Historisk tidsskrift*, vol. 52, pp. 111–137.

Schetelig, Haakon, 1911, 'Folketro om gravhauger', *Maal og Minne*. Festskrift til H. F. Heiberg, pp. 206–212.

Schjødt, Jens Peter, 2012, 'Reflections on aims and methods in the study of Old Norse religion', in C. Raudvere and J. P. Schjødt (eds.), *More than mythology: narratives, ritual practices and regional distribution in pre-Christian Scandinavian religions*, Nordic Academic Press, Lund, pp. 263–287.

Schleicher, August, 1861, *Compendium der vergleichenden Grammatik der indogermanischen Sprachen*, Hermann Böhlau, Weimar.

Schneider, Louis (ed.) 1964, *Religion and culture in society: a reader in the sociology of religion*, Wiley, New York.

Shaw, Philip, 2011. *Pagan goddesses in the early Germanic world: Eostre, Hreda and the cult of Matrons*. London: Bristol Classical Press.

Sundqvist, Olof, 2002, *Freyr's offspring. Rulers and religion in ancient Svea society*, Uppsala Universitet, Uppsala.

Tschan, Francis, 2002, 'Introduction', in F. Tschan (ed.), *History of the archbishops of Hamburg-Bremen*, Columbia University Press, New York, pp. xxv–xlvi.

30 Theoretical considerations

Tuan, Yi-Fu, 2001 [1977], *Space and place: the perspective of experience*, University of Minnesota Press, Minneapolis and London.

Valtonen, Irmeli, 2007, 'Who were the Finnas?' in J. Bately and A. Englert (eds.), *Ohthere's voyages. A late 9th-century account of voyages along the coasts of Norway and Denmark and its cultural context*. Maritime culture of the North, 1. The Viking Ship Museum, Roskilde, pp. 106–107.

Vésteinn Ólason, 1998, *Dialogues with the Viking Age. Narration and representation in the sagas of the Icelanders*, trans. A. Wawn. Mál og Menning, Reykjavík.

Vésteinsson, Orri, 2003 [2000], *The Christianization of Iceland. Priests, power and social change 1000–1300*, Oxford University Press, Oxford.

Vestergaard, Elizabeth, 2012 [2002], 'Kinship and marriage: the family, its relationships and renewal', in J. Jesch (ed.), *The Scandinavians from the Vendel Period to the tenth century: an ethnographic perspective*, Boydell Press, Woodbridge, pp. 59–86.

Vogt, Helle, 2010, *The function of kinship in medieval Nordic legislation*, Brill, Leiden and Boston.

Whaley, Diana, 1991, *Heimskringla. An introduction*. Viking Society for Northern Research, University College London, London.

Whaley, Diana, 2005, 'Skaldic poetry', in R. McTurk (ed.), *A companion to Old Norse-Icelandic literature and culture*, Blackwell, Malden, Oxford and Victoria, pp. 479–502.

Würth, Stefanie, 2005, 'Historiography and pseudo-history', in R. McTurk (ed.), *A companion to Old Norse-Icelandic literature and culture*, Blackwell, Malden, Oxford and Victoria, pp. 155–172.

Yoder, Don, 1974, 'Toward a definition of folk religion', *Western Folklore*, vol. 33, no. 1, pp. 2–15.

Zachrisson, Inger, 2005, 'Ethnicity: conflicts on land use. Sámi and Norse in Central Scandinavia in the Iron Age and the Middle Ages', in I. Holm et al. (eds.), *'Utmark': the outfield as industry and ideology in the Iron Age and the Middle Ages*, Universitetet i Bergen, Bergen, pp. 193–201.

Zachrisson, Torun, 1994, 'The Odal and its manifestation in the landscape', *Current Swedish Archaeology*, vol. 2, pp. 219–238.

Zachrisson, Torun, 1996, 'Folkliga föreställningar', in M. Buström et al. (ed.), *Fornlämningar och folkminnen*, Riksantikvaieämbetet, Stockholm, pp. 87–103.

Zachrisson, Torun, 2004, 'The holiness of Helgö', in H. Clark and K. Lamm (eds.), *Excavations at Helgö*, XVI. Kungl Vitterhetsakademien, Stockholm, pp. 143–175.

Zachrisson, Torun, 2017, 'The background of the odal rights: an archaeological discussion', *Danish Journal of Archaeology*, vol. 6, no. 2, pp. 118–132.

2 Research on ancestor worship

2.1 The development of 'ancestor worship' as an academic term

The greatest question in the study of religion is that of origin. Different ideas, ranging from sociological and political to personal and faith-based theories have been proposed by so many scholars from so many various disciplines over the years that it would be impossible to cover them in any single study. One discipline that has paid significant attention to studying and attempting to understand religion is anthropology, whose various sub-disciplines examine the physical, cultural, social and linguistic development of humans from pre-historic times to the present. While some consider social anthropology to have acquired academic status in the early to middle 20th century when scholars like Bronislaw Malinowski and Alfred Radcliffe-Brown published their first major field studies, others see it as an outgrowth of the Age of Enlightenment of the 17th and 18th centuries, when European intellectuals began systematically examining human behaviour and social institutions.[1] The great majority of anthropologists agree, however, that social anthropology emerged during the second half of the 19th century when evolutionist ideas became dominant. No matter when one dates the beginning of anthropology as a scholarly discipline, the foundations for the study of religion and culture of which anthropology, in the modern sense, was a fundamental part, existed long before the 20th century (see Barnard 2004: 15–26).

The development of evolutionary anthropology is closely linked to theories of folklore which emerged from national–romantic ideas and which evolved over the course of the 18th and 19th centuries. The gathering of oral tradition, inspired by the works of philosophers of the Romantic School who helped form the ideological background for the collection and publication of folktales, had already begun in the late 18th century (Harvilahti 1997: 737), but reached its peak in the following century when Jacob and Wilhelm Grimm published their comprehensive collections of folklore.[2] The humiliation of occupation by Napoleon's army in the early 19th century stimulated nationalist sentiments in Germany and provoked interest in its past; however, since materials about its ancient religion were scarce, attempts at recreating a unified, uniquely Germanic culture were made by using the relatively rich corpus of Old Norse literature (Arvidsson 2006: 124, 131–132). That Old Norse myths and sagas could be used as potential sources of information for Germany's history had been noted in the 18th century, but it was the Grimm brothers who gave the study of folklore greater recognition. Although sharing earlier collectors' passion for Old Norse mythology, they brought a novel perspective by also incorporating folktales from the contemporary German peasantry. Their aim was to combine the motifs found in folktales with mythology and linguistics in order to determine which elements were local and which had been borrowed from other cultures (Grimm 1835: 7–8; see Arvidsson 2006: 131–132).

The work of the Grimm brothers was a watershed, representing one of the most intriguing and valuable discussions of the time. It resulted in the publication of *Kinder-und Hausmärchen* in 1812–1815 and *Deutsche Sagen* in 1816 and 1818. These collections were followed by the monumental *Deutsche Mythologie*, which was published in 1835 and which was mainly concerned with Old Norse mythology. Their radical approach to using folklore was generally well received and their conceptual understanding – though still quite vague – started to influence folklore research throughout the continent. Inspired by their sense of nationalism, almost every nation made an attempt to create their own mythology from unreliable and conflicting sources, thereby creating many new, uniform and previously non-existent mythologies (Harvilahti 1997: 737–738). These collections have done a great deal to shape the views of following generations – most interpretations of Old Norse paganism through the mid-20th century were rooted in the Grimms' pioneering work and, as discussed previously, many still imagine pre-Christian beliefs as having been static religious systems following contemporary geographical borders.

The Grimms' observations and ideas gave rise to the so-called nature-myth school, with German scholars Adalbert Kuhn and Max Müller its main representatives, and soon after the discipline of evolutionary anthropology, which was initiated by the English scholars Edward Tylor and Herbert Spencer. Both disciplines were strongly influenced by folklore (see de Vries 1984; Csapo 2005: 19–30), but while evolutionary anthropologists placed great emphasis on indigenous cultures and saw folk traditions as survivals of the most primitive forms of religion, Müller and his followers developed a theory that identified the origins of myths and gods with natural phenomena. The theory of 'solar mythology', which sought to interpret Indo-European myths as metaphors for the worshipped sun, became highly influential; folklore was seen as a dim reflection of the 'original' Aryan solar myth (see Arvidsson 2006: 126–131). With this limited and speculative approach, the nature-mythologists made themselves easy targets for criticism. Although both schools influenced research into the second half of the 19th century, Müller's theories soon fell out of fashion and their romantic ideas about the high cultural heritage of the Aryans were deflated by evolutionary anthropology (Arvidsson 2006: 125–131; Goody 1962: 13–30). His work was even parodied: first published anonymously in 1870, a satire of Müller's methods written by theological writer Richard Littledale (1973) went so far as 'proving' that both 'Max' and 'Müller' did not really exist and were in fact actually himself a solar myth.

Evolutionary anthropologists, on the other hand, made considerable use of folklore, which they saw as a survival of primitive beliefs shared by all peoples during the earlier stages of evolution. While scholars who studied human culture and religion prior to the second half of the 19th century based their theories primarily on the theological views of pre-historic religions and compared contemporary modern Western societies with those of Greek and Roman antiquity (Ackermann 2002: 2–4), evolutionary anthropologists gradually started to base their theories on observations of contemporary indigenous cultures, which they believed had preserved these 'primitive' beliefs and traditions. This was the time when European imperialism reached its peak, and even though field research in anthropology did not really begin until the very end of the 19th century (see Urry 1972), Western scholars came into increased contact with contemporary non-Western cultures at that time. First-hand observation of these cultures, even if initially only made by missionaries and merchants, opened a whole new avenue into the understanding of religious history: the core of religious life in these cultures was not gods, but ancestors. The beliefs and rituals in these 'folk' religions were often perceived as social activities rather than proper spiritual practices, but Western scholars were very interested in their origins, hoping that they would also provide useful information about the history of religion in their own countries (see Urry 1993; Bowie 2006).

Folklore studies and the core ideas of evolutionism had thus been popular for some time, but the study of the earliest religious beliefs reached its height in the second half of the 19th century after Charles Darwin published his epoch-defining *On the Origin of Species by Means of Natural Selection, or the Preservation of Favoured Races in the Struggle for Life* (1859) and established the doctrine of evolution. Darwin's controversial theory about the development of species via their struggle for survival suggested that human beings are the result of evolution from lower life forms, spurring investigation into 'primitive' religions and eventually leading to the rise of evolutionary anthropology.[3] Evolutionary anthropology's heyday, considered to have begun in the 1860s with the theories of 'armchair' anthropologists such as Edward Tylor and Herbert Spencer, lasted until the 1890s, although such ideas held sway into the 20th century. Led by the Grimms' folklore and Darwin's theory of evolution, evolutionary anthropologists came to use the idea of social evolution as their primary explanatory framework. They suggested that the primitive religious practices which had survived among so many native communities and allegedly also left remnants in contemporary European folklore formed the primeval religion of all mankind – modern Western societies had simply evolved to higher forms of religion due to civilisation and inherently superior traits. Discussion was centred mostly around mortuary practices, cults of the dead, vegetation rituals, the growth of funeral rites into worship and above all, ancestor worship, which was seen by some as the archetypal form of all religion.[4]

The first serious cross-cultural comparative study of indigenous cultures to argue that ancestor worship was a fundamental part of early religion was by Tylor (1871, 2: 103, 169), who developed the argument that animism – belief in the soul – was one of the most primitive forms of religion and that it frequently took the form of ancestor worship. His main question regarding ancestor worship was whether it should be considered a primitive form of religious belief from

34 *Theoretical considerations*

which the 'high' hierarchical religions had emerged or if it is an inevitable part of human nature and thus, a natural part of all religion. The same question was also addressed by Spencer in his *The Principles of Sociology* (1897: 286–287, 294, 403, 422, 429), originally published in 1874–1875, which proposed a historical sequence of how different beliefs had developed: first, there was belief in the survival of the soul, followed by funeral rites, which allowed the propitiation of the soul, then persistent ancestor worship, after which the souls of the most distinguished ancestors subordinated those of ordinary ancestors and transfigured into gods. The native words for different god figures – which often meant 'ancestor' in local languages – were used to support this theory (Spencer 1897: 303). Spencer's proposed distinction between common and distinguished ancestors was thus neo-euhemeristic (see Chapter 4, Section 4.2) in its own way: gods are simply dead men. His conviction that every religion originates in 'ancestor worship' – a term which he defined broadly as applying to all forms of religion not only to the worship of direct relatives – made him a target for criticism (e.g. Hartland 1894: 203), mostly because many of his contemporaries held fast to the idea that ancestor worship was the cult of the 'family' (e.g. Jevons 1896: 189–205), which was inconsistent with the fact that some gods were worshipped by entire communities (see Goody 1962: 15–16, 18–19). As a social unit, family was considered to have been absent in the early stages of human evolution, which for these scholars meant that ancestor worship could not have been the most ancient and elementary form of religion. These objections were significantly weakened by Edward Westermarck (1891), who came up with the hypothesis that humans, even in their most primitive stages, were designed by nature to avoid incest and become attracted only to unfamiliar persons outside their own kin group. This meant that the institution of marriage and the concept of family must have formed the oldest social units in human history, consequently allowing the development of ancestor worship to be pushed much further back in time. Family systems, and the dynamics of human religious behaviour within the family, became a particularly fascinating subject for early psychologists, who argued that ancestral–familial relationships are present in most aspects of religion, including gods who are projections of parental power and comfort (e.g. Freud 1918: 152–265; Flügel 1921: 124, 133–155; Jung 1981: 62), although many of these scientists discredited Westermarck's theory.[5]

Émile Durkheim (1895, 1915: 48–70), for example, attacked the hypothesis of family as an ancient social unit by arguing that Westermarck's definitions of 'family' and 'marriage' were too generic and that ancestor worship cannot have been the most basic form of religion because, unlike totemism (the worship of totems, which are spirit-filled animals, plants and objects and which Durkheim himself favoured as the most original form of religion), it is found only in more advanced societies; if revered entities had emerged from deceased ancestors, then this should be seen among the lowest strata of society, which according to Durkheim was not the case. The question whether or not totemism, too, should be considered as a distinct form of ancestor worship has since been a matter of dispute: some scholars have supported Durkheim's claim and classified those groups that do not worship their human ancestors but revere totemic plants and animals as non-ancestor worshipping (e.g. Lehmann & Myers 1985: 285), while others find this division limiting and argue that even though totems are not identified as human ancestors, they identify a person with a line of ancestors and are thus comparable to ancestors (e.g. Goody 1962: 16–18; 410–411; Lévi-Strauss 1964: 73–74, 77; Steadman & Palmer 2008: 55–82). The main novelty in Durkheim's work, however, was that he did not identify early religious beliefs as attached to any particular kind of being, group or behaviour, but insisted that various social systems, such as family, religion and economy, function together for the benefit of the society as a whole and that the similar patterns that they display – i.e. the 'idea' behind these typical principles – must form the foundation of religion (Durkheim 1915: 34–42). Even though formulated through evolutionist reasoning and partly still concerned with the question of the age and primacy of ancestor worship, Durkheim's explanations started taking on a functionalist flavour by examining the role of religion in relation to its functions in society.

Following Tylor and Spencer's treatments of the subject, ancestor worship quickly gained ground in scholarly research. Even though it caused much disagreement among scholars with regard to the particulars of the practice, it came to be considered as a central aspect of early religion. The ensuing debate revolved mainly around two issues: the antiquity of ancestor worship and the nature of ancestors (Goody 1962: 15). The first, instigated by evolutionist thinking and the search for origins, was concerned with the direction in which religion developed. Three main strands emerged: ancestor worship, totemism and belief in 'high gods'; scholars espoused different views on the linear ordering of these phenomena in the development of religion. One scholar who spoke against Spencer's theory of ancestor worship as the archetype of all religion was Andrew Lang, who re-opened the discussion of the 'high gods', which due to the folkloristic spirit of the time had been previously left without much attention. Despite attributing some gods with a possible previous existence as humans, and agreeing that euhemerism must have occurred in societies that were still familiar with ancestor worship, Lang (1898: 275, 1913: 308–313) objected to the view that gods were the culmination of religious history and that they had emerged from ancestors. He emphasised that the spiritualism attached to the 'high gods' is different from that attached to the dead; to him this meant that god worship may have preceded all other forms of worship (Lang 1913: 310–311). Overall, his argument did not attract much support: the majority of scholars of the time singled out totemism as the earliest form of religion (e.g. Lubbock 1870: 126–127, 232; Freud 1918: 182; Durkheim 1915: 48–70). Ancestors were commonly placed on a middle ground between totems and gods, but their overall importance in religion was not seriously examined for approximately half a century.

Another issue that aroused considerable debate and controversy was the question of the attitude of the deceased towards the living.[6] Were ancestors considered to be allies or enemies? Some scholars were of the opinion that the relations between the dead and their living descendants were of a positive nature (e.g. Robertson Smith 1901: 54–55; Jevons 1896: 47–58); others maintained that the spirits of the dead were probably perceived as hostile towards humans, deriving from the fear of the physical body of the deceased (e.g. Frazer 1913–1924, 1966; Malinowski 1925: 48–49). Freud (1918: 87–107) rejected this suggestion and instead linked the emotion of fear to the idea of unconscious guilt. He posited a novel association among funerary rites, mourning behaviour and fear of revenge by ancestors. He believed that family relations were always characterised by affection as well as unconscious hatred, which, after a death, generated anxiety and guilt in the survivors. Feelings of hostility, including even wishing death upon one's closest relatives whilst alive, were thus projected onto the dead. In order to reduce one's guilt, it was necessary to convince oneself that the dead person was hostile and potentially harmful and to propitiate them with offerings.

In the same way that folklore and social Darwinism influenced evolutionary anthropologists, their ideas also had an impact on folklore studies. Sparked by the German folklorist Wilhelm Mannhardt's publication of *Die Korndämonen* in 1867 and the two-volume *Wald- und Feldkulte* (1875–1877), in which he attempted to separate mythology from folklore and to focus on beliefs in spirit-like beings rather than gods, a new phase emerged in folklore studies. Mannhardt maintained that these traditions and beliefs had been the original religion of the Indo-Germans and that interpreting these in their own right – instead of as a corrupted form of a lost 'high mythology' – would provide a more authentic image of Germanic prehistory (see de Vries 1984: 31–36; Arvidsson 2006: 135–141). The 'folkloristic' mythology model and the combined interest in folklore and evolutionary anthropology led to investigations of death practices, the worship of vegetation spirits and ancestors and everything else that had left remnants in popular culture and that had so far been considered to be part of the 'low' strata of religion. For example, it was suggested that the protective farm spirits that had survived in folk beliefs were connected with the first ancestors of the household and the cult of the hearth-fire (Schrader 1910: 24). These ideas were enthusiastically taken up by scholars interested in Old Norse religion (e.g. Feilberg 1918; Lid 1928, 1933; Birkeli 1938, 1944). As a consequence, less attention was paid to the study of gods, who were assumed by most evolutionary anthropologists to have evolved much later. According to the German scholar Wilhelm Schwartz (1885: xiii), for example, there were no gods during Indo-Germanic times, only 'nature beings'. Schwartz was the first scholar to call the nature, death, vegetation and spirit beliefs 'lower mythology', a term which later had negative connotations, even though he did not see folk belief in a negative light as a mere fragment of an ancient 'high' religion: for him, folk belief was the basis from which a 'high god' mythology had developed.

Later in the 20th century, social Darwinism and the early 'evolutionary' approaches became generally regarded as inadequate and racist by contemporary anthropologists; earlier theories were discarded, although ancestor worship – now seen in a less evolutionary sense – remained a key aspect of religion also for the following generations of scholars. The study of folklore, too, generally fell out of fashion in Europe after World War II. As a counter-reaction to the earlier overenthusiasm regarding the central role of ancestor worship in early religion, anthropologists took to questioning the supposed all-pervasiveness and universality of the practice. For 20th-century anthropologists, who had gradually adopted the developing ideas of functionalism and structural–functionalism (shaped most resolutely by Bronislaw Malinowski and Alfred Radcliffe-Brown), the direction their research took was to not discuss the antiquity of ancestor worship, but to study kinship systems in order to understand the principles crucial for the occurrence of ancestor cults. Although early functionalists did not deny the evolution of religion, their focus shifted towards experimentation, the technique called systematic introspection, and comparison of contemporary societies. Most subsequent research concerning ancestor worship was undertaken on lineage-based (usually patrilineal) modern societies (see Barnard & Spencer 2002: 469–480). Different definitions of 'kinship', disputes over the questions of which types of kin-structures are most common in ancestor-worshipping communities and whether biological descent is more important than non-biological alliance dominated anthropological research throughout the 20th century. Even though investigations of religion and field research in ancestor traditions continued, scholars became very careful with attempting to define what exactly could be classified as 'ancestor worship'. With the shift in focus, anthropologists paid relatively little attention to the relationship of religion to human behaviour. By the 1960s the study of religion within anthropology had essentially reached a 'state of a general stagnation' (Geertz 1993: 88).

2.2 Ancestor worship in Old Norse research

In accordance with the generally folkloristic character of research and the ideas initiated by European intellectuals in the late 19th and early 20th centuries, scholars of Old Norse religion, too, placed considerable focus on subjects such as vegetation rituals, seasonal festivals, mortuary practices, otherworld concepts and ancestors.[7] The myriad death-related concepts and characters depicted in Old Norse literature provided common ground among scholars of various backgrounds, most of whom supported the idea that ancestor worship had been a natural part of Old Norse religion. The worship of both collective supernatural beings (e.g. dísir, álfar) and outstanding individuals (e.g. Freyr, Þorgerðr holgabrúðr, Óláfr Geirstaðaálfr) were generally accepted as having been closely connected with the cult of ancestors (e.g. Vigfússon & Powell 1883: 413–417; Storm 1893; Chadwick 1907; Phillpotts 1913). These early scholars generally supported the idea that the public cults of distinguished persons, who may have assumed the role of gods after death, existed alongside the private worship of family ancestors, and were essentially extended versions of the domestic cults (e.g. Chadwick 1907: 339–340, 1908: 467). This approach to the cults of kings and gods waned around the middle of the 20th century after the new focus on fieldwork in anthropology led to a more cautious delineation of what counted as 'ancestor worship', after interest in folk belief had subsided and after 'sacral kingship' had become strongly established in the early Scandinavian context (see Chapters 3 and 4).

Even though folklore had been important in the study of Old Norse religion from very early on, interest in the domestic and private side of religious belief and practice was particularly strong during the first half of the 20th century.

38 *Theoretical considerations*

The Mannhardtian folkloristic approach was adopted by many scholars who had become interested in ancient beliefs and practices, believing that they had survived in contemporary folk belief. A particularly popular subject addressed in many extensive monographs and collections was the traditions concerned with farm guardians (e.g. *gardvord, tomte, nisse, haugebonde, haugkall*), who received regular offerings from people – especially during important seasonal celebrations like Yule – in return for maintaining the safety and prosperity of the farm, and who were often associated with gravemounds. The finds from archaeological excavations of Viking Age graves in Norway were often in accordance with legends still known and remembered in the rural areas; for example, according to one local legend a specific ancient mound contained a ring and a cup, which proved to be correct when the grave was opened (Schetelig 1911: 207). The legends, it was argued, thus acted as agents of cultural continuity, contributing to respect for old gravemounds; even if the people who told the stories could no longer recognise the grave as a grave, they remembered these locations and passed on stories about them (Schetelig 1911: 211–212). The archaeologist who worked on this project – the Norwegian Haakon Schetelig – concluded that the farm guardians that had survived in contemporary folk stories had their origin in the graves located near farms and were manifestations of the ancestors who had once lived there (Schetelig 1911: 211). The idea that the memories of ancient gravemounds survived in folktales and legends long after they were in use has been more recently picked up by Torun Zachrisson (1996).

The largest portion of research on the topic of farm guardians being remembered and kept alive in folktales and legends was, of course, carried out by folklorists. Henning Feilberg (1904, 1918), who pursued Mannhardt's and Spencer's ideas and who saw ancestor cults as the basis of religious activity, argued in a series of studies that contemporary traditions had their roots in ancestor worship, which originated in the belief that the soul continued living inside the gravemound. He believed that the most significant winter festivals like Yule, which became central in the ensuing discussion, were originally the commemoration of ancestors who came to visit during the darkest time of the year (Feilberg 1904, 2: 299–314). Yule time seems to have held particular importance as the period when the dead were expected to visit their families: food and drink were prepared for them, the sauna was heated where the visitors could wash themselves, and beds were made up so that they could spend the night. These visits were reported to have sometimes left traces: earth was found in beds and the drinks that had been left out for the dead overnight were filled with supernatural energies (e.g. Olrik & Ellekilde 1926–1951, 2: 1053–1058). To borrow a thought from Terry Gunnell (2000: 127–128), as it is the cold and dark time of the year when nature shows signs of death and decay and has become unsafe, the subsequent moving of all life indoors meant that this was the most natural time for the dead to become active.

Among the most comprehensive and valuable collections of ancestor beliefs in Scandinavian folklore from that period, one should note the work of Axel Olrik, published posthumously by his associate Hans Ellekilde (1926–1951), and that of Ingjald Reichborn-Kjennerud (1928–1947), who wrote about ancient medicinal remedies and who linked the farm guardians with the traditions of *álfar* who could inflict illness on people through *álfskot* ('elf-shot'). Other important works concerning ancestors were published by Emil Birkeli (1932, 1938, 1943, 1944), who combined folklore with the history of religion, archaeology and social anthropology, and Nils Lid (e.g. 1928, 1933, 1942), who combined folklore and history of religion with a new emphasis on etymological studies and ethnology. As a theologian, Birkeli went on a missionary trip to Madagascar, which aroused his interest in ancestor traditions and inspired him to use comparative material from other distant cultures that still practised ancestor worship, in order to draw analogies to the Norwegian *fedrekult* ('forefather cult'), which he, too, connected to the gravemound and the farmhouse. Lid was particularly interested in vegetation rituals and deities, as well as Yule traditions, most notably the *oskoreia* tradition – the ride of the visiting dead on Yule night.[8] These investigations are still the most frequently quoted works on ancestor worship in Scandinavia, although the subject has more recently been reopened by Terry Gunnell, who has addressed ancestor-related issues in a number of papers, for example, in connection with the 'winter-nights' (2000), Christmas celebrations (2004), *álfar*-lore (2007a), the Scottish *broonie* (2011) and the gravemound cult (2014). The cults of dead individuals contained within Old Norse literature – which are almost exclusively concerned with distinguished persons – were also used in the earlier folkloristic treatments, but usually as illustrative cases of worship of some sort rather than as ancestor cults in their own right. As noted by Lid (1942: 99), for example, the cults of kings were built around the idea that they were one with the gods; he had thus already started to lean towards the idea of sacral kingship, separating folklore and the practices revolving around ancestors from those of dead rulers found in Old Norse literature.

Whereas the scholars of the late 19th and early 20th centuries were rather bold in their treatments of beliefs and practices as examples of 'ancestor worship', with the changing direction of interest in social anthropology came a changing of attitude in Old Norse research as well: Old Norse scholars' interest in social anthropology became heavily reduced. Judgements on Old Norse religion must be based on scattered and uncertain written evidence from almost a millennium ago, offering only limited resources for the study of kinship and its relationship to ancestor traditions, which often involve abstract death concepts and unclear relationships between the worshippers and cult objects, for example, when dead rulers receive ritual attention from an entire society, not just their own relatives. Therefore, social anthropology had little to contribute to ongoing Old Norse research, which seems to have taken two virtually separate paths: the study of abundant death-related concepts and customs, usually discussed in the context of folklore and archaeology, and the question of the communal worship of gods and rulers, who were enthusiastically attached to sacral kingship by scholars. Methodological discussions from anthropological perspectives were not common; however, influenced by the general tenor of European intellectual life, researchers became increasingly wary of the use of the term 'ancestor worship' towards the middle of the 20th century and often replaced it with alternative words and terminologies.

Louise Hagberg's (1937) vast study of death beliefs and customs in contemporary Sweden not once mentions the word 'ancestor', let alone 'ancestor worship' or 'ancestor cult', but simply addresses the 'dead'. A similar tendency is visible in the work of Reidar Christiansen (1946), according to whom it would be dangerous to speak of 'ancestor worship' in its own right in the Old Norse context, despite admitting that the traces left in folklore are suggestive of a once-existing ancestor cult. Nora Chadwick (1946) chose an alternative term in her hypothesis of pagan kings deliberately entering ancestral barrows in the hope of rebirth: she referred to these beliefs and related rituals as the cult of the *draugr* ('ghost') or *haugbúi* ('mound-dweller'). The novelty in Chadwick's work lies primarily in the fact that she addressed the issue of ancestors in connection with the cults of rulers, an aspect which had received little attention at the time and whose link to ancestor worship was generally either left open (e.g. Radin 1930: 54) or ruled out (Ström 1954).

The argument of Folke Ström (1954: 34) that the scope and importance of ancestor worship had been greatly exaggerated in the past and that the worship of kings reflects sacral kingship rather than ancestor worship marked the beginning of a new phase in the debate. Even though these ideas had been addressed previously, his study of the cult of the *dísir* became the spawning ground for subsequent debate. Ström did not entirely reject the existence of ancestor cults in pagan Scandinavia – he wrote that the *förfäderskult* can be linked to later seasonal ceremonies, funerary customs and various supernatural beings in modern folklore (1960). However, he suggested that the *dísir* cult had been primarily a cult of vegetation and that its relationship to foremothers was of a secondary nature (Ström 1954: 96, 102). Furthermore, the cult that had been originally associated with the *dísir* shifted its focus over time and became associated with dead kings. The reason for the public celebrations revolving around the kings, however, was not that they were dead, but because they were seen as promoters of fertility and growth – the *ár ok friðr* ('good harvests and peace') – and had a relationship of some sort with female fertility deities (Ström 1954: 34). Ström (1954: 54) distinctly supported and promoted the sacral kingship ideology in pre-Christian Scandinavia.

The adoption of the sacral kingship paradigm as a means of interpreting the cults of dead rulers gradually formed a new academic wave, and the general caution around the term 'ancestor worship' contributed further to the lack of discussion about ancestors of any kind in Old Norse religion. Even though most scholars at that time still acknowledged that ancestors had played some role in religion, the scope became much narrower than before. The claims of earlier authors like Feilberg and Birkeli, who had traced the various farm and household guardians back to the worship of ancestors, became criticised through the existence of different guardian-like characters (e.g. *landdísir*) that were also found in unsettled lands like Iceland where no ancestors existed (de Vries 1970, 1: 256–260, 445–483); the ensuing argument was that the farm spirits in Scandinavia could not have developed merely from the concept of ancestors, but must rather be looked upon as beings of nature. Other scholars preferred to speak of the 'veneration of the dead' or the 'cult of the dead' in connection with the guardian-type figures.

Gabriel Turville-Petre discussed the *álfar* and *dísir*, whom he saw as representing the dead (Turville-Petre 1963), but avoided any direct claims that these traditions represented ancestor worship (Turville-Petre 1964: 225–231). Instances concerning the worship of kings and gods were seen by him as unrelated to this overall ancestor veneration. Like Lid and Ström, Turville-Petre discussed these cases within the context of 'divine kingship' (Turville-Petre 1964: 190–195, 274). Hilda Ellis Davidson also took a more cautious approach towards ancestor worship, although a few times she used the phrase synonymously with the 'cult of the dead' (e.g. Ellis 1968: 99). She spoke of elves, land spirits and kings, but referred to the beliefs as 'cult of the dead' or 'veneration of the dead' (Ellis 1968: 99–120, Ellis Davidson 2001: 122–123, 142). She acknowledged that there were elements of ancestor worship in the tale of Óláfr Geirstaðaálfr and in the cult of Freyr, but treated these as something different from ordinary ancestor beliefs. In her opinion, kings had not been worshipped as ancestors, but because they were seen as intermediaries between people and gods (Ellis Davidson 2001: 100, 136, 142). She was thus biased towards the theory of sacral kingship, taking it for granted that pagan gods were actually 'gods', and were simply viewed as the ancestors of kings by medieval authors. Following the initial enthusiasm about ancestors, which led to difficulties over definitions and perhaps over-caution in addressing any character as an 'ancestor', the entire subject tapered off for a time.

The wariness of speaking about 'ancestor worship' has subsided over the last few decades, owing first and foremost to archaeological excavations, which have revealed long-term continuity of ritual activities on burial grounds, such as the enduring practice of consuming food and drink on gravesites, as well as the practice of re-building new cemeteries on top of old ones, expressing the need of communication (e.g. Baudou 1989; Arrhenius 1990; Zachrisson 1994, 1998, 2004; Artelius 2000, 2004; Gräslund 2001; Insoll 2011; Gardela 2016). The importance of intergenerational bonds has also been noted in the literature, for example in the profusion of genealogical records, as well as in the prohibition of gravemound offerings in law texts. Folkloristic exploration of ancestor beliefs, as noted earlier, has also been re-invigorated; although it would be unwarranted to talk about unbroken traditions in such a context, a combined study of narrative folklore of the modern period and Old Norse literature, which is itself also to a great extent folklore, certainly deserves further exploration by using more up-to-date folkloristic methods and perspectives.[9] Discussion of the link between the worship of rulers and general ancestor cults is not absent in scholarship, but it is certainly less pronounced. Social anthropological approaches, however, have been more or less ignored since the mid-20th century since functionalist theories became dominant. Overlooking a vast field of cultural–religious study such as social anthropology limits our ability to address issues that demand refinement. If we want to understand 'ancestor worship', how religious experience emerges from it and how it is tied to broader societal concerns (for example in relation to rulership and religion), it is important to consider the perspective of the one field of research specifically aimed at studying human behaviour, social relationships and religion from a cross-cultural, comparative and historical perspective.

Notes

1 About the development of British social anthropology, see Urry (1993); Goody 1995; Kuklick (2008); Barnard (2004: 1–26).
2 Concerning the life and work of the Grimm brothers, see Zipes (2002) and Shippey (2005).
3 For further information, see Goody (1962: 13–30); de Vries (1984); Ackermann (2002: 29–45); Barnard (2004: 27–46); Arvidsson (2006: 124–131).
4 A very useful overview of the history of research of ancestor worship from which I have borrowed here is by Jack Goody (1962: 13–30).
5 Jung coined the term 'collective unconscious' – the inherited part of the brain – which he understood as the common and universal element of the psyche. As he explained: 'possession is caused by something that could perhaps most fitly be described as an "ancestral soul", by which I mean the soul of some definite forebear. [...] such cases may be regarded as striking instances of identification with deceased persons. [...] Not only are ancestral spirits supposed to be reincarnated in children, but an attempt is made to implant them into the child by naming him after an ancestor. So, too, primitives try to change themselves back into their ancestors by means of certain rites' (Jung 1981: 123–124).
6 For an overview and discussion, see Goody (1962: 20–23); Newell (1976a).
7 A useful review of research history of ancestor worship in the context of Old Norse religion is found in Nordberg (2013).
8 See Eike (1980).
9 For a discussion and re-evaluation of the methods and problems of using folklore in the Old Norse context, see Bek-Pedersen & Sävborg (2014); Heide & Bek-Pedersen (2014); Valk & Sävborg (2018).

Secondary sources

Ackermann, Robert, 2002, *The myth and ritual school: J. G. Frazer and the Cambridge Ritualists*, Routledge, London and New York.
Arrhenius, Birgit, 1990, 'Utgrävningen av den östligaste storhögen på gravfältet Ormknös, Raä 111, Björkö, Adelsön, Uppland', *Laborativ Arkeologi*, vol. 4, pp. 65–80.
Artelius, Tore, 2000, 'Bortglömda föreställningar. Begravningsritual och begravningsplats i halländsk yngre järnålder', *RAÄ Arkeologiska undersökningar*. Skrifter 36/Gotarc B: 15.
Artelius, Tore, 2004, 'Minnesmakarnas verkstad. Om vikingatida bruk av äldre gravar och begravningsplatser', in Å. Berggren et al. (eds.), *Minne och myt. Konsten att skapa det förflutna*. Vägar till Midgård 5. Nordic Academic Press, Lund, pp. 99–120.
Arvidsson, Stefan, 2006, *Aryan idols: Indo-European mythology as ideology and science*, University of Chicago Press, Chicago and London.
Barnard, Alan, 2004 [2000], *History and theory in anthropology*, Cambridge University Press, Cambridge.
Barnard, Alan, and Jonathan Spencer (eds.) 2002 [1996], *Encyclopaedia of social and cultural anthropology*, Routledge, London and New York.
Baudou, Evert, 1989, 'Hög – gård – helgedom i Mellannorrland under den äldre järnåldern', *Arkeologi i norr*, vol. 2, pp. 9–43.
Bek-Pedersen, Karen, and Daniel Sävborg (eds.) 2014, *Folklore in Old Norse – Old Norse in folklore*. Nordistica Tartuensia, 20. Tartu University Press, Tartu.
Birkeli, Emil, 1932, *Høgsetet: Det gamle ondvege i religionshistorisk belysning*, Dreyers Grafiske Anstalt, Stavanger.

Birkeli, Emil, 1938, *Fedrekult i Norge. Et forsøk på en systematisk-deskriptiv fremstillning.* Skrifter utgitt av Det Norske Videnskaps-Akademi i Oslo 2. Hist.-Filos. Klasse, no. 5. I kommisjon hos Jacob Dybwad, Oslo.

Birkeli, Emil, 1943, *Fedrekult fra norsk folkeliv i hedensk og kristen tid*, Dreyer, Oslo.

Birkeli, Emil, 1944, *Huskult og hinsidighetstro. Nye studier over fedrekult i Norge.* Skrifter utgitt av Det Norske Videnskaps-Akademi i Oslo 2. Hist.-Filos. Klasse, no. 1. I kommisjon hos Jacob Dybwad, Oslo.

Bowie, Fiona, 2006, 'Anthropology of religion', in R. Segal (ed.), *The Blackwell companion to the study of religion*, Wiley-Blackwell, Malden, Oxford and Victoria, pp. 3–24.

Chadwick, Hector, 1907, *The origin of the English nation*, University Press, Cambridge.

Chadwick, Hector, 1908, 'Ancestor worship and cult of the dead (Teutonic)', in J. Hastings (ed.), *Encyclopædia of religion and ethics*, 1. Charles Scribner's Sons and T. & T. Clark, New York and Edinburgh, pp. 466–467.

Chadwick, Nora, 1946, 'Norse ghosts: a study in the *Draugr* and the *Haugbúi*, 1–2', *Folklore*, vol. 57, 2 and 3, pp. 50–65, 106–127.

Christiansen, Reidar, 1946, 'The dead and the living,' *Studia Norvegica*, vol. 2, pp. 3–96.

Csapo, Eric, 2005, *Theories of mythology*, Blackwell, Oxford.

Darwin, Charles, 1859, *On the origin of species by means of natural selection, or the preservation favoured races in the struggle for life*, John Murray, London.

de Vries, Jan, 1970 [1956–1957], *Altgermanische Religionsgeschichte*, 1–2. Grundriss der germanischen philologie. Walter de Gruyter & Co, Berlin.

de Vries, Jan, 1984, 'Theories concerning "nature myths"', in A. Dundes (ed.), *Sacred narrative. Readings in the theory of myth*, University of California Press, Berkeley, Los Angeles and London, pp. 30–40.

Durkheim, Émile, 1895, 'Origine du marriage dans l'espèce humaine d'après Westermarck', *Révue Philosophique*, vol. 40, pp. 606–623.

Durkheim, Émile, 1915 [1912], *The elementary forms of religious life*, trans. J. Swain. George Allen & Unwin Ltd, London.

Eike, Christine, 1980, 'Oskoreia og ekstaseriter', *Norveg*, vol. 23, pp. 227–309.

Ellis, Hilda, 1968, *The road to Hel: a study of the conception of the dead in Old Norse literature*, Greenwood Press, New York.

Ellis Davidson, Hilda, 2001 [1993], *The lost beliefs of Northern Europe*, Routledge, London and New York.

Feilberg, Henning, 1904, Jul, *Allesjælestiden, hedensk, kristen julefest; Julemørkets löndom, juletro, juleskik*, 2 vols, Det Schubotheske forlag, Copenhagen.

Feilberg, Henning, 1918, *Nissens historie*. Danmarks folkeminder, 18, Schønberg, Copenhagen.

Flügel, John, 1921, *The psycho-analytic study of the family*, The International Psycho-Analytical Press, London, Vienna and New York.

Frazer, James, 1913–1924, *The belief in immortality and the worship of the dead*, 1–3, McMillan and Co, London.

Frazer, James, 1966 [1933–1936], *The fear of the dead in primitive religion*, Biblio & Tannen Booksellers & Publishers, Inc, New York.

Freud, Sigmund, 1918 [1913], *Totem and taboo. Resemblances between the psychic lives of savages and neurotics*, Moffat, Yard & Company, New York.

Gardela, Leszek, 2016, 'Worshipping the dead: Viking Age cemeteries as cult sites?' in M. Egeler (ed.), *Germanische Kultorte. Vergleichende, historische und rezeptionsgeschichtliche Zugange*, Herbert Utz Verlag, München, pp. 169–205.

44 Theoretical considerations

Geertz, Clifford, 1993, 'Religion as a cultural system', in C. Geertz (ed.), *The interpretation of cultures: selected essays*, Fontana Press, London, pp. 87–125.

Goody, Jack, 1962, *Death, property and the ancestors: a study of the mortuary customs of the Lodagaa of West Africa*, Stanford University Press, Stanford.

Goody, Jack, 1995, *The expansive moment: the rise of social anthropology in Britian and Africa 1918–1970*, Cambridge University Press, Cambridge.

Gräslund, Anne-Sofie, 2001, 'Living with the dead', in M. Stausberg (ed.), *Kontinuitäten und Brüche in der Religionsgeschichte: Festschrift für Anders Hultgård zu seinem 65. Geburtstag am 23.12. 2001*. Reallexikon der germanischen Altertumskunde, 31. de Gruyter, Berlin and New York, pp. 222–235.

Grimm, Jacob, 1835, *Deutsche mythologie*, Dieterichsche Buchhandlung, Göttingen.

Grimm, Jacob, and Wilhelm Grimm, 1812–1815, *Kinder- und Hausmärchen*, Realschulbuchhandlung, Berlin.

Grimm, Jacob, and Wilhelm Grimm, 1816–1818, *Deutsche sagen*, Nicolaischen Buchhandlung, Berlin.

Gunnell, Terry, 2000, 'The season of the *Dísir*: the winter nights and the *Dísablót* in early Scandinavian belief', *Cosmos*, vol. 16, pp. 117–149.

Gunnell, Terry, 2004, 'The coming of the Christmas visitors: folk legends concerning the attacks on Icelandic farmhouses made by spirits at Christmas', *Northern Studies*, vol. 38, pp. 51–75.

Gunnell, Terry, 2007a, 'How Elvish were the Álfar?' in A. Wawn et al. (eds.), *Constructing nations, reconstructing myth: essays in honour of T. A. Shippey*, Brepols, Turnhout, pp. 111–130.

Gunnell, Terry, 2011 (26 May), *The nordic roots of the Broonie and other mound dwellers*. Seminar Series. Centre for Nordic Studies, University of the Highlands and Islands, Scotland.

Gunnell, Terry, 2014, 'Nordic folk legends, folk traditions and grave mounds. The value of Folkloristics for the study of Old Nordic religions', *FF Communications*, vol. 307, pp. 17–41.

Hagberg, Louise, 1937, *När döden gästar: svenska folkseder och svensk folktro i samband med död och begravning*, Wahlström & Widstrand, Stockholm.

Hartland, Edwin, 1894, *Legend of Perseus: a study of tradition in story custom and belief*, David Nutt, London.

Harvilahti, Lauri, 1997, 'Romantic nationalism', in T. Green (ed.), *Folklore: an encyclopaedia of beliefs, customs, tales, music, and art*, 2, ABC-CLIO, Santa Barbara, pp. 737–741.

Heide, Eldar, and Karen Bek-Pedersen (eds.) 2014, *New focus on retrospective methods: resuming methodological discussions: case studies from Northern Europe*, Academia Scientiarum Fennica, Helsinki.

Insoll, Timothy, 2011, 'Ancestor cults', in T. Insoll (ed.), *The Oxford handbook of the archaeology of ritual and religion*, University Press, Oxford, pp. 1043–1058.

Jevons, Frank, 1896, *An introduction to the history of religion*, Methuen & Co, London.

Jung, Carl Gustav 1981 [1934–1954], *The archetypes and the collective unconscious. The collected works of C. G. Jung*, 9, 1, trans. R. Hull. Princeton University Press, Princeton.

Kuklick, Henrika (ed.) 2008, *A new history of anthropology*, Blackwell, Malden, Oxford and Victoria.

Lang, Andrew, 1898, *The making of religion*, Longmans, Green & Co, London, New York and Bombay.

Lang, Andrew, 1913 [1887], *Myth, ritual and religion*, 1. Longmans, Green & Co, London, New York, Bombay and Calcutta.
Lehmann, Arthur, and James Myers, 1985, 'Ghosts, souls, and ancestors: power of the dead', in A. Lehmann and J. Myers (eds.), *Magic, witchcraft, and religion*, Mayfield Publishing Company, Palo Alto and London, pp. 284–287.
Lévi-Strauss, Claude, 1964, *Totemism*, trans. R. Needham, Merlin Press, London.
Lid, Nils, 1928, *Joleband og Vegetasjonsguddom*. Skrifter Utgitt av det Norske Videnskaps-Akademi i Olso, 2. Hist.-Filos. Klasse. 1928. No. 4. I kommisjon hos Jacob Dybwad, Oslo.
Lid, Nils, 1933, *Jolesveinar og grøderikdomsgudar*. Skrifter utgitt av Det Norske Videnskaps-Akademi i Oslo 2. Hist.-Filos. Klasse, 1932. No. 5. I kommisjon hos Jacob Dybwad, Oslo.
Lid, Nils, 1942, 'Gudar og Gudedyrkning', in N. Lid (ed.), *Religionshistorie*. Nordisk Kultur, 26. Albert Bonniers Förlag, H. Aschehoug & Co.s Forlag and J. H. Schultz Forlag, Stockholm, Oslo and Copenhagen, pp. 80–153.
Littledale, Richard, 1973, 'The Oxford solar myth. A contribution to comparative mythology', *Folklore Forum*, vol. 6, pp. 68–74.
Lubbock, John, 1870, *The origin of civilisation and the primitive condition of man; mental and social condition of savages*, Longman, Green & Co, London.
Malinowski, Bronislaw, 1925, '*Magic, science and religions*', in J. Needham (ed.), *Science, religion and reality*, The MacMillan Company, New York, pp. 19–84.
Mannhardt, Wilhelm, 1867, *Die Korndämonen: Beitrag zur germanischen Sittenkunde*, Ferd. Dümmler's Verlagsbuchhandlung, Berlin.
Mannhardt, Wilhelm, 1875–1877, *Wald- und Feldkulte*, 2 vols (*Der Baumkultus der Germanen und ihrer Nachbarstämme; Antike Wald- und Feldkulte aus Nordeuropäischer Überlieferung*), Gebrüder Borntraeger, Berlin.
Newell, William, 1976a, 'Good and bad ancestors', in W. Newell (ed.), *Ancestors*, Mouton, Hague and Paris, pp. 17–29.
Nordberg, Andreas, 2013, *Fornnordisk religionsforskning mellan teori och empiri. Kulten av anfäder. Solen och vegetationsandar i idéhistorisk belysning*, Kungl. Gustav Adolfs Akademien för svensk folkkultur, Uppsala.
Olrik, Axel, and Hans Ellekilde, 1926–1951, *Nordens gudeverden; vol 1: vætter og helligdomme; vol. 2: årets ring*, G. E. C. Gads Forlag, Copenhagen.
Phillpotts, Bertha, 1913, *Kindred and clan in the middle ages and after: a study in the sociology of the Teutonic races*, at the University Press, Cambridge.
Radin, Paul, 1930, 'Ancestor worship', in E. Seligman and A. Johnson (eds.), *Encyclopaedia of the social sciences*, 2. The Macmillan Company, New York, pp. 53–55.
Reichborn-Kjennerud, Ingjald, 1928–1947, *Vår gamle trolldomsmedisin*, 5 vols. Jacob Dybwad, Oslo.
Robertson Smith, William, 1901 [1889], *Lectures on the religion of the Semites. First series. The fundamental institutions*, Adam and Charles Black, London.
Schetelig, Haakon, 1911, 'Folketro om gravhauger', *Maal og Minne. Festskrift til H. F. Heiberg*, pp. 206–212.
Schrader, Otto, 1910, 'Aryan religion', in J. Hastings (ed.), *Encyclopædia of religion and ethics*, 2. Charles Scribner's Sons and T. & T. Clark, New York and Edinburgh, pp. 11–57.
Schwartz, Wilhelm, 1885, *Indogermanischer Volksglaube: Ein Beitrag zur Religionsgeschichte der Urzeit*, Verlag von Oswald Seehagen, Berlin.

46 Theoretical considerations

Shippey, Tom (ed.) 2005, *The shadow-walkers. Jacob Grimm's mythology of the monstrous*, Arizona Center for Medieval and Renaissance Studies, in collaboration with Brepols, Tempe.

Spencer, Herbert, 1897 [1874–1875], *The principles of sociology*, 1. D. Appleton & Company, New York.

Steadman, Lyle, and Craig Palmer, 2008, *The supernatural and natural selection. The evolution of religion*, Paradigm Publishers, Boulder and London.

Storm, Gustav, 1893, Vore Forfædres tro paa sjælevandring og deres opkaldelsesystem. *Arkiv for nordisk filologi*, vol. 9, pp. 199–222.

Ström, Folke, 1954, *Diser, norner, valkyrjor. Fruktberhetskult och sakralt kungadöme i norden*, Almqvist & Wiksell, Stockholm.

Ström, Folke, 1960, 'Förfäderskult', *Kulturhistorisk leksikon for nordisk middelalder fra vikingetid til reformationstid*, vol. 5, Rosenkilde og Bagger, København, pp. 120–121.

Turville-Petre, Gabriel, 1963, 'A note on the landdisir', in A. Brown and P. Foote (eds.), *Early English and Old Norse studies: presented to Hugh Smith in honour of his sixtieth birthday*, Methuen, London.

Turville-Petre, Gabriel, 1964, *Myth and religion of the north: the religion of Ancient Scandinavia*, Greenwood Press, Connecticut.

Tylor, Edward, 1871, *Primitive culture: researches into the development of mythology, philosophy, religion, language, art, and custom*, 2 vols, John Murray, London.

Urry, James, 1972, 'Notes and queries on anthropology and the development of field notes in British anthropology, 1870–1920', *Proceedings of the royal anthropological institute of great Britian and Ireland*, pp. 45–57.

Urry, James, 1993, *Before social anthropology: essays on the history of British anthropology*, Harwood Academic Publishers, Chur.

Valk, Ülo, and Daniel Sävborg (eds.) 2018, *Storied and supernatural places: studies in spatial and social dimensions of folklore and sagas*. Studia Fennica Folkloristica, 23. Finnish Literature Society, Helsinki.

Vigfússon, Guðbrandur, and York Powell, 1883, *Corpvs Poeticvm Boreale: the poetry of the old Northern tongue from the earliest times to the thirteenth century*: *Eddic poetry*, 1. The Clarendon Press, Oxford.

Westermarck, Edward, 1891, *The history of human marriage*, Macmillan & Co, London and New York.

Zachrisson, Torun, 1994, 'The Odal and its manifestation in the landscape', *Current Swedish Archaeology*, vol. 2, pp. 219–238.

Zachrisson, Torun, 1996, 'Folkliga föreställningar', in M. Buström et al. (ed.), *Fornlämningar och folkminnen*, Riksantikvaieämbetet, Stockholm, pp. 87–103.

Zachrisson, Torun, 1998, *Gård, gräns, gravfält. Sammanhang kring ädelmetalldepåer och runstenar från vikingatid och tidigmedeltid i Uppland och Gästrikland*. Stockholm Studies in Archaeology, 15. Stockholms universitet, Stockholm.

Zachrisson, Torun, 2004, 'The holiness of Helgö', in H. Clark and K. Lamm (eds.), *Excavations at Helgö*, XVI. Kungl. Vitterhetsakademien, Stockholm, pp. 143–175.

Zipes, Jack, 2002, *The brothers Grimm: from enchanted forests to the modern world*, Palgrave Macmillan, New York and Hampshire.

3 Ancestors in social anthropology
Definition and social use

3.1 'Ancestor worship' – the problem with terminology

The first thing one realises when embarking on the study of ancestor practices is how expansive the subject is. Attitudes towards the dead in different parts of the world vary greatly and so do the ways in which ancestors interact with the living. Ancestors can be regarded as benevolent, caring and kind, but also sad, lonely or vindictive, often capricious and even cruel; often these contrasting characteristics interact in complex ways (Newell 1976b). Ancestors may be named or anonymous, related to specific individuals or entire communities, approached collectively or individually. Consistent with the exceedingly varied characteristics associated with ancestors, attitudes and practices relating to them also vary. Some groups bury the dead within their residences and make offerings to them before every meal (Firth 1936: 75–81, 112–113), while others do not see their ancestors as bound to the soil and therefore do not give much attention to where they are buried (Evans-Pritchard 1940: 209–210). The primary focus of ancestor practices can be to console or comfort ancestors, to secure the protection they provide (Fortes 1976: 9–13) or to keep them content because they pose a threat to the living (Lee 1984). Sometimes the nature and influence of ancestors change over time: those who are still personally remembered are good ancestors, but as time passes and they are forgotten, they become potentially malicious nameless spirits (Mbiti 1970). The requirements that determine a person's eligibility to become an ancestor vary too, and this may be restricted to those who come from specific social groups or meet certain conditions (e.g. chieftains, elders, distinguished individuals, or those who died healthy or violently) (Czaplicka 1914: 159; Hunter 1961: 231, 228; Goody 1962: 383; Fortes 1976: 8; Newell 1976a: 18–19; Blackburn 1985).

The variety of beliefs and practices associated with ancestors across the globe means that scholarly definitions of the concept are either very simple and deficient or very expansive and diffuse. With the development of evolutionary anthropology, ancestor worship came to be investigated more commonly across disciplines. The baggage the term carries in connection with evolutionary approaches to religion, however, has led to much criticism and almost excessive caution among contemporary anthropologists. There is seemingly endless disagreement in

48 Theoretical considerations

scholarship as to what an 'ancestor' is, what 'worship' means, how, why, when and where ancestors are worshipped and so forth. The term 'ancestor worship' itself is now often seen as overly restrictive, antiquated and misleading (e.g. McAnany 1995: 1–16; Park 2010: 1–8; Kubuya 2018: 28–30), and its pervasive use in archaeological contexts to explain almost any pre-historic burial practice as such has been criticised (Whitley 2002). I will, however, avoid getting ensnared in overly intricate and specialised definitions here; for the purpose at hand, it is sufficient to outline the core complexities and problems with the term and to explain what is meant by it in the present work.

In most general encyclopaedias the word 'ancestor' is defined as referring to a deceased progenitor who receives ritual attention from the living members of one's family (entries in Fowler & Fowler 1986; Doniger 1999). Subsequently, 'ancestor worship' is defined as the beliefs and ritual practices concerned with deceased predecessors (entries in Doniger 1999; Hardacre 2005). The view that many scholars have shared since the decline of evolutionary anthropology, however – that the term 'ancestor worship' as a general reference to ancestor beliefs is too restrictive – derives from a Western perspective and is connected to a specific period in research history. Copious alternative terms incorporating one or more phrases such as 'communication', 'remembering', 'rite', 'service', 'ritual', 'reverence', 'devotion', 'veneration', 'religion', 'cult', 'living with the ancestors' and 'family-worship', to name a few, have been proposed as more appropriate in the context of ancestors (e.g. Abraham 1966: 63; Mbiti 1970: 9, 131; Feeley-Harnik 1991; McAnany 1995; Park 2010; Insoll 2011; Lo 2012: 134; Johnston 2015: 54; Kubuya 2018).

Indeed, the English term 'ancestor worship' might be considered as too generic or even inappropriate considering the markedly diverse nature of practices linked to the dead, as well as the fact that societies which European scholars often classified as having ancestor worship do not usually have only one corresponding word or phrase in their language for all the different types of ritual practice (Berentsen 1985: 26–28). However, the alternative terms proposed – sometimes used to simply replace 'ancestor worship' without much critical reconsideration of the terms' ideological content – are equally dangerous as they can also obscure meaning. If we were to settle for, let us say, 'ancestor cult', 'ancestor veneration' or 'ancestor rituals' (which are among the more widely accepted terms today because they avoid the sticky 'worship' element that has often become restricted to Christian Church practice), we still need to consider the meaning of 'ancestor.'[1] John Mbiti (2015: 69), a renowned theologian whose work has been focal in the debates on African religions where ancestors are a conspicuous feature, has criticised the use of this word in religious contexts, suggesting that we ought to speak about the 'living dead', considering their active engagement in daily life. Furthermore, as will be discussed later in this chapter, ancestors may be individuals biologically unrelated to the worshippers, for example, where the cults of rulers have expanded to include entire communities (Sheils 1980). In such cases the 'ancestors' are strictly speaking not the progenitors of the believers, thus falling outside the conventional definition of the word.[2]

However, the negative associations of the term 'ancestor worship' seem to derive primarily from the word 'worship', another term which has no single agreed definition without cultural contextualisation. In European terminology 'worship' is usually limited to Christian theological beliefs and activities, and this has caused a disparity between scholars with different personal religious convictions. As a Christian philosopher, Mbiti (1970: 9), for example, has strongly criticised the use of the word 'worship' in the African context because the offerings given to the dead there are according to him primarily symbols of family continuity, contact and respect, not 'worship'. The activities performed in European graveyards, such as lighting candles, or placing flowers or pictures of the dead on graves, are often more firmly established than anywhere in Africa; the Africans performing these acts do not see themselves as 'worshipping' the dead, but rather 'remembering' them (Mbiti 1970: 9). The strong tone of annoyance in Mbiti's work concerning Western scholars' 'harping about "ancestor worship" in connection with African traditions seems to spring largely from the author's personal worldview. For a Christian scholar, the 'worship' of ancestors – no matter how culturally and politically important they may be – cannot co-exist with the Christian belief where 'worship' is directed to God.

Scholars whose work bears slighter trace of personal Christian belief have less restrictive criteria for the use of the term 'worship', even though they too use specific parameters to limit the term to use in certain circumstances. Meyer Fortes (1976: 5), a leading figure in British social anthropology in the middle of the 20th century, whose greatest contribution lies in the analysis of kinship systems and their political implications, acknowledges that the interaction between the people and their ancestors is effectively a 'channel of communication' and yet, in almost all his studies we find the phrase 'ancestor worship' (e.g. Fortes 1970, 1976, 1987). For Fortes (1987: 67) the main prerequisite for a practice to be 'strictly defined' as 'ancestor worship' was commemoration of ancestors by name. Other anthropologists (e.g. Goody 1962: 379–382) have suggested that the 'worship' of ancestors must be motivated by the belief that the soul – as a separate substance – survives death and continues to participate in the everyday affairs of the living; evidence of this belief might be found in more overt ritual activities such as the daily ritual feeding of specific ancestors, blood offerings, etc. The European custom of placing flowers on graves falls rather in the category of commemorative rites, as it does not usually involve the concept of survival (Goody 1962: 379). However, the question of determining one's personal motivations remains. Most people in all parts of the world are not analytical of their own beliefs and motivations; specific ritual acts (wherever they take place) may simply be performed because they have always been done this way, thus deriving essentially from habit or societal norms and expectations. The border between belief and tradition seems vague, at best.

Even though earlier use of 'ancestor worship' in indigenous contexts, as an overarching framework for all beliefs and practices concerned with ancestors, might have been too broad and all-encompassing in scholarly debates at the time, the tendency to define the concept in an overly narrow sense creates problems too. Groups that do not fall within any given closed definition have been categorised as having no 'ancestor worship' in the past and subsequently (and misleadingly), as having no interest in ancestors (this will be discussed in the next chapter). The presence of other spiritual beings in religion (e.g. Supreme Being, Mother Goddess, nature spirits), for example, is often understood by European scholars as more important than that of ancestors, leading to such exclusion. Too often scholars overlook the fact that most ethnic cultures, as has been discussed previously, attach the greatest importance to ancestors even where they are believed to co-exist with transcendental beings (Tuan 2001: 149–160; Goody 2010: 92). Thus, the same way 'worship' could be an overstatement of the practices associated with ancestors, 'veneration' could conversely be a substantial understatement, let alone 'communication' or 'remembrance' (Berentsen 1985: 26–28).

'Ancestor worship' is not an easy concept to define, and considering how much baggage the term carries in research history it is important to be aware of the countless issues involved in assessing the role of ancestors in people's religious experience. Even though the conventional definition of the term is now strongly disputed, there are those who have adopted a less stringent view concerning 'ancestor worship' and its semantic scope. Despite criticism, 'ancestor worship' is still frequently listed as a current term in encyclopaedias (e.g. Doniger 1999: 54; Bloch 2002; Hardacre 2005) and in academic books and articles, though these at least usually pay lip service to its complexity (e.g. Lindsay 1996; Steadman et al. 1996; Steadman & Palmer 2008; Liu 2000; Lakos 2010; Ephirim-Donkor 2012; Sayers 2013; Harrington 2013; Keightley 2014; Hüwelmeier 2016; Anning & Tian 2018). It is also used by scholars of Old Norse religion (e.g. Baudou 1989; DuBois 1999; Sundqvist 2002; Steinsland 2005: 344–346; Gunnell 2007: 23–25; Brink 2013: 39; Murphy 2017, 2018). 'Ancestor worship' as an umbrella term for a vast variety of beliefs and ritual acts might be misleading; however, simply acknowledging the complexity of the term might altogether be less misleading than substituting it for another. Definitional obstacles, as shown by the myriad variations used in an attempt to replace the term, could continue indefinitely, making any single explanation somewhat deficient.

The present study is concerned with the content of texts which shed light on the importance of ancestors and ancestry in Old Norse religion and an exhaustive anthropological exploration is not within its scope. It is sufficient to recognise the problems of terminology associated with ancestors, which have perhaps been dealt with too aggressively in the recent past. This study discusses the religious encounters depicted in Old Norse literature, where the relationship between the living and the dead sometimes takes the form of public cult; on occasion I will refer to these beliefs and practices as 'ancestor worship'.

3.2 The role of ancestors in folk religions

One of the most characteristic features of ancestors in religion is that they are never the exclusive power within any system, but co-exist with other beings of a supernatural nature and often also in combination with universalistic faiths (e.g. Klass 1996; Nakamaki 2012). What sometimes escapes scholars' attention is that the presence of these other beings does not necessarily mean that they are seen by practitioners as superior to ancestors. For example, the !Kung living in the Kalahari Desert are reported to have a high god and a lesser god whose roles are confused, as well as many minor spirits. However, the most immediate role in their religious life is held by the 'recently deceased !Kung'; the high god is not actually revered, but viewed as being responsible for people's misfortunes (Lee 1984: 103–118). The shamanistic Tungus people in north-eastern Siberia revere an all-powerful celestial creator, but their religious leaders communicate primarily with the 'clan's own ancestral spirits' (Lewis 2003: 45, 134–159). The Lugbara (located in the present-day West Nile district of Uganda) believe that a god created the world but that ancestors formed society, which is why they establish 'the rules of social behaviour' (Middleton 1960: 27). The presence of celestial and creator beings thus does not necessarily indicate that ancestors are unimportant, and in fact they may even be the predominant actors of religious life. Their power to influence human affairs is usually considered to be more direct than that of distant and abstract creator beings whose roles – unlike that of the Christian God – are obscure (Tuan 2001: 152).

The fact that the boundaries between gods and ancestors are subtle and unclear was noticed by early anthropologists, who theorised that the idea of god stemmed from societies' arrangements in kinship groups where people saw their most remote ancestors as gods (e.g. Spencer 1897; Robertson Smith 1894: 54–55). A more scientific and reliable approach to the subject was brought to anthropology via actual research in indigenous communities, which finally provided some first-hand evidence. One of the earliest field studies, that of the British psychiatrist and anthropologist William Rivers (1906: 442–460), who surveyed a hill tribe – the Toda – in southern India, showed that the people gave offerings to spirits and to the dead generally, as well as to an infinite number of gods and goddesses and to personalised ancestors who, according to the people, were the same: 'when Teitnir gave a buffalo after the death of his wife, some said it was given to the gods, while others said it was given to Teitnir's grandfathers, and when I tried to inquire more definitely into this point the two things were said to be the same'. Rivers (1906: 446) writes further that many of the infinite number of gods and goddesses are believed to be once-living known persons and that they reside inside hills which are revered. In her pioneering study of the Samoyed of eastern Siberia, Maria Czaplicka (1908: 174–175) attempts to stratify their belief system into nature spirits, a Mother God, a sky deity, a vast range of national and domestic gods and goddesses, high clan-gods and domestic god-spirits. These characters are divided into generic groups (e.g. tribe, clan, family); however, people's perception of them is, according to the author, again based on ancestors, some more directly and intimately than others. These and other first-hand accounts of societies where ancestors are a prominent part of religion suggest that they can co-exist with other gods, and that they can be transformed into gods over time; often the believers themselves are not sure or interested in where the difference lies (e.g. Blackburn 1985).

Notwithstanding the earlier statement that the Toda give regular offerings to personalised ancestors and to gods who are seen as historical persons, Rivers

52 Theoretical considerations

(1906: 293, 297, 446–447) nonetheless arrived at the conclusion that on the whole there is little evidence to indicate that 'ancestor worship' played any significant part in the Toda religion. This unexpected reaction derives essentially from the ever-increasing wariness of the term itself which, following its earlier use in the second half of the 19th century, started to be considered too strong, gradually leading to highly specific definitions and a near-requirement that most practices be classified as *not* representing ancestor worship. The Samoyed, too, have been noted as having no (i.e. absent) belief in ancestors (Swanson 1964: 18), and the Tungus mentioned earlier have been classified as having a 'non-ancestral' religion because it includes 'more autonomous deities which are not simply sacralised versions of the living' (Lewis 2003: 29, 41, 134–159), and despite the fact that their religious leaders are said to control the clan's ancestor spirits and that their own souls apparently go to live with their dead relatives. The syncretic presence of ancestors and god- or spirit-like characters appears to have caused a conflict in the modern Western mindset which is geared towards not only wanting to separate the two, but also to rank the hotchpotch of different god figures higher than mere humans that have died. As was mentioned previously, some anthropologists have challenged the downplaying of the importance of ancestors in their research, demonstrating that ancestors are central to most indigenous groups around the world, irrespective of religious syncretism (Steadman et al. 1996; Steadman & Palmer 1994, 2008).

Another reason why anthropologists have questioned the centrality of ancestors is that they are sometimes not remembered by name – as was noted earlier, Meyer Fortes (1987: 67) was one of several scholars who saw remembering ancestors by name as a key requirement for classifying a practice as 'ancestor worship' – or that the agents that evoke ritual commitment are not specifically called 'ancestors'. The Mardu tribe of western Australia, for example, is reported to have not memorised the names of specific ancestors, and thus is consequently found not to practise ancestor worship (Tonkinson 1978: 52, cited in Steadman et al. 1996: 64). The religion of the Yanomamö people of the Amazon rainforests is often categorised as 'shamanic' and subsequently concerned more with spirits – the *hekura* – than ancestors (see Steadman et al. 1996: 64). Again, in both cases, Steadman et al. (1996: 63) have shown ancestors to be duly important. The Mardu beliefs and rituals revolve around beings they consider to be inherently 'ancestral' (Steadman et al. 1996: 63), and the main actors in the spiritual life of the Yanomamö, the *hekura*, literally represent the 'original people' in their language (Chagnon 1983: 92, cited in Steadman et al. 1996: 64), a term which points to their identity as the most distant ancestors of the Yanomamö (Steadman & Palmer 2008: 56–57, 111). Misconceptions have thus often occurred in the mistranslation of indigenous terms, forcing entire concepts to fit one unifying word palatable to Western scholars – most often this word is 'god', but 'spirit', 'deity', etc. are also often used. These concepts do not necessarily have one clear equivalent nor unambiguous meanings even in local languages. The word *hekura*, for example, is sometimes translated as 'gods' (e.g. Mitchell 2004: 45), and even though this word can be used in different contexts in English as well, in Christian theology it has been insistently associated with God or at least with someone more supernatural or autonomous than simply dead humans. Thus, the presence of beings who are described as 'gods' in early field reports – which as a rule were communicated through translators – has incorrectly led to the by no means justified understanding that ancestors have an inferior role in religious life or are absent. Rivers, for example, collected his information about Toda beliefs through interpreters (Sanjek 1990: 203–207), and there is no record of what the 'gods and goddesses' mentioned in his report were called by the Toda at the time. His comment that they were apprehended by the people as 'once-living people' seems straightforward and fairly uncontroversial. One way or another, the god concept in most folk religions appears intimately connected to people's memory of their ancestors (Goody 1962: 18–19; Littlewood 2001: 57–71; Tuan 2001: 149–160). Where ancestors are traced back by their names in recorded dynastic annals which go back to great antiquity (e.g. in China), their prominent position, despite the concurrent existence with various deities and spirits, is generally not questioned and is more often than not referred to as 'ancestor worship' (Lakos 2010; Keightley 2014; cf. Kubuya 2018).

Scholarly disagreement over the particulars of beliefs and practices concerned with ancestors is nearly endless and any sweeping generalisation based on a selection of only a few examples is not conclusive or beyond reproach. I should therefore stress that my intention is not to oversimplify religious and spiritual matters, the rich diversity of which cannot be adequately summarised in any one study. However, the aim of the present work is not to provide a conclusive or comprehensive anthropological interpretation of ancestor traditions, but to use existing anthropological insights to examine specific religious processes in pagan Scandinavia. Thus, the specifics and intricacies do not affect the analysis presented here, which looks for universal patterns and general principles rather than absolute truths about specific cultural manifestations, variations and inflections. It is important to keep in mind that ancestors – although typically present in almost every culture – are never the exclusive power in traditional societies, nor are they seen as divine, despite possessing more power than the living. As a religious category they do not prohibit the votaries from relying upon the aid of other supernatural beings, such as gods or spirits, but nor are they clearly separable from them. These are useful starting points when investigating the cults of the dead in Old Norse religion.

3.3 Family, kinship and 'superior ancestors'

As the above discussion indicates, the involvement of ancestors in the affairs of the living depends on culture and differs greatly from one society to another. It is therefore unsurprising that social anthropologists struggle with the question of how practices concerned with ancestors should be defined. One aspect that has often been understood as giving ancestor worship a specific character is its central location in the domestic sphere. The preservation and replication of one's genes is obviously a crucial feature of survival, and 'family' forms the natural basis for achieving this end. Early anthropologists (e.g. Jevons 1896: 189–205) saw ancestor worship – one of the earliest and most primitive forms of religion in their mind – as primarily a family cult, and later scholars have also emphasised the importance of this parameter (e.g. Newell 1976a: 19–20; Fortes 1976: 3). Subsequently, the authority given to ancestors has been interpreted as an extension of the respect given to family elders, while the primary purpose of ancestor rituals is seen to be the creation of a sense of solidarity among the living members of a kin network and the encouragement of social cooperation (Driberg 1936; Kopytoff 1971). This approach was rejected by others on the grounds that becoming an ancestor lends a person a wholly different status and value; as Fortes (1976: 2) writes about the Tallensi, 'one can argue with living elders, but not with ancestors'. A comprehensive discussion of the multifaceted and vastly complex issue of kinship falls outside the scope, purpose and capacity of the present study, and there are many details which need not concern us here. One phenomenon is, however, of particular relevance in the present context. This is the phenomenon of ancestors of ruling groups who frequently receive religious attention not only from their own descendants and kinsmen, but from entire communities. For common people, these ancestors are personally distant, less accessible and therefore perhaps more 'god-like' according to our logic than ancestors in the traditional sense – their influence extends beyond their physical territory and family members. However, they are still perceived as once-living humans linked to specific living people. It is this aspect of ancestor worship that will be explored further in this chapter, and it will give us a way of interpreting depictions in Old Norse sources of individual ancestors of leading groups who are trusted by entire communities. Most of these individuals have conventionally been treated as 'gods' or 'sacral kings' in Old Norse scholarship. Before taking a closer look at this phenomenon we will, however, briefly consider the issue of kinship – probably the most challenging branch of social anthropology, and one which scholars have actively debated throughout the 20th century and beyond.

The initial focus on family and descent in connection with 'ancestor worship' held that discussion of it should be confined to occasions when a clear genealogical relationship – direct descent from the same lineage – exists between specifically named ancestors and the people who carry out the related rites (e.g. Radcliffe-Brown 1961: 163; Goody 1962: 381). This approach has been criticised as later investigations into kinship have shown that the relationship between family structures and ancestor cults is complex beyond measure and so diverse that it is virtually impossible to determine what specific aspects of kinship are crucial to the emergence of ancestor cults (Sheils 1975: 428–429).[3] This brings up a number of related questions: what constitutes a 'family' in kinship-based societies? Does a family consist of two parents and their children or involve other relatives, too? If so, how far do the horizontal lines in a genealogy go? Is family a household, a descent lineage, a clan or a whole tribe?[4] Do the descent groups need to be unilineal or bilateral? Are they traced through the male or the female line? And what about marriages, extensions through foster relationships and other artificial arrangements that can be reinforced by claims of kinship? Can membership be modelled on entirely fictive kinship? Anthropologists have surveyed the status of kinship in different societies since the late 19th century in order to answer these and other related questions and to get a better understanding of social ties (see Barnard & Good 1984; Peletz 1995; Good 2002). Even though it has generally been agreed upon that some connection exists between ancestor rituals and family ideology, it soon became clear to earlier anthropologists that kinship is never simply a matter of biology, but a complex social construct through which relations – no matter how distant and even unreal – are artificially arranged and categorised. Thus, despite the fundamentally domestic nature of ancestor beliefs and practices – in the sense that they can and do crop up in domestic small-scale contexts and are built around the idea of family or close kinship – it does not necessarily follow that concrete biological links exist between ancestors and the people who hold such beliefs and undertake such rites. As the anthropologist Ian Cunnison (1967: 75) explains, it is that 'people behave among themselves in a certain way and therefore they are related in a certain way: not that people are related in a certain way and therefore they behave in a certain way'.

As early as 1930, Malinowski noticed that people often do not follow the biological definition of kinship when seeking to create kinship ties, which are nothing but the social extensions of actual genetic bonds. These extended kinship networks – lineages and clans – are designed to help connect distant relatives and unrelated individuals (Malinowski 1930: 28). Although reinforced by the idea of family and common descent from the same ancestor, they function in different domains of social life: legal, economic and ceremonial (Malinowski 1930: 23, 28). Alluding to remote ancestors, or even characters known to people living across wide geographic areas and whom we might call 'gods', provides a way of adding more people to your collective 'kin', while a limited number of individuals can actually trace their common ancestry through the generations (Steadman et al. 1996: 73). A person's genealogical knowledge is usually restricted to approximately four to five generations back (and less when collateral lines are included), so this kind of manipulation is a useful and extensively used strategy in kinship-based societies. I shall return to this later in the chapter.

The complexity of kinship creates countless challenges; however, the nature of ancestor cults would remain unclear without any understanding of social organisation. Numerous attempts have therefore been made by anthropologists to identify how religious behaviour – and the belief in ancestors in particular – relates to kinship systems and social structure. I will only mention two important surveys here. The first was made by Guy Swanson (1964), whose well-known and still debated cross-cultural analysis of ancestor beliefs in 50 non-Western societies attempted to classify 'ancestor worship' in terms of the degree to which the ancestors interfere with lives of their descendants. Swanson (1964: 97–108, 210–211) divided beliefs in ancestors into four categories: 1. inactive ancestors that do not influence the living (absent); 2. ancestors who are believed to exist, but whose actions are unspecified (present); 3. active ancestors that aid or punish their living descendants (active); 4. ancestors that can be invoked by their descendants to assist in earthly affairs (invoked). Any clear-cut categorisation such as this is of course problematic because it does not take into account any diversity of belief. Swanson's analysis has been criticised for being overly statistical, restricted and even incompetent (Tatje & Hsu 1969; Hallpike 2003: 128), and some scholars (Steadman et al. 1996), as noted previously, have challenged his entire study by showing that for every single society which he coded as 'absent' or 'present' in relation to ancestor beliefs, evidence can be adduced for strong claims that ancestors do influence and are influenced by the living. From his data, Swanson (1964: 108) nevertheless drew the interesting and still accepted conclusion that the presence of any dominant kin group larger than the nuclear family (e.g. clan, lineage) significantly influences the belief that ancestors are active in human affairs. This observation is significant because as well as indicating that the nuclear family is not the only unit in ancestor cults, it suggests that broader kinship systems are actually a prerequisite for its development, at least in its most elaborate and advanced form.

The second study was made a few years after Swanson's report by the anthropologist Terrence Tatje together with Francis Hsu, a pioneer in the field of psychological anthropology. These scholars criticised Swanson's 'active' versus 'non-active' dichotomy as overly simplistic and as an alternative they suggested a more expansive system consisting of seven types of beliefs about ancestors (i.e. absent, neutral, undifferentiated, malicious-capricious, punishing, rewarding-punishing, benevolent-rewarding) (Tatje & Hsu 1969: 156). Societies which are considered by most anthropologists as definitely practising ancestor worship fall, according to them, into the last four types (Tatje & Hsu 1969: 156–157). Their analysis agreed, however, with Swanson's proposal in one respect: it is possible to detect specific patterns in attitudes towards ancestors with respect to differences in kinship systems. The strongest type of ancestor cult is according to them, too, found most frequently in societies organised on the basis of lineages and clans, and they added that type of organisation is particularly common in patrilineal systems (Tatje & Hsu 1969: 155, 167). They argued that societies dominated by patrilineal father–son kinship organisation frequently display characteristics such as 'continuity, inclusiveness, authority', and an attitude to life which is characterised by respect for elders and their intervention, close relations between the generations and the glorification and preservation of ties with the past and with ancestors; ritual attention given to ancestors is consequently an extension of male values and associated modes of behaviour in a society (Tatje & Hsu 1969: 163). The hypothesis may be weakened somewhat by the fact that unilineal and particularly patrilineal societies are the ones that have been studied most extensively (Goody 1962: 19); however, both above-mentioned analyses provide reason to suspect that strong ancestor cults tend to be observed in patrilineal societies which recognise large units of people as corporate groups. The fact that kinship systems in Scandinavia and Iceland were also dominated by patrilineal lines (Vogt 2010; Vestergaard 2012) thus offers some support for the idea that the Norsemen, too, likely practised similar wide-scale ancestor cults which served broader sociopolitical purposes.

Despite these and numerous other proposed classifications, anthropologists have still not fully agreed on how kinship structures relate to ancestor practices.

Mainly as a result of the ever-increasing understanding of the endless inconsistencies in kinship structures, the long-held interest in kinship diminished greatly towards the end of the 20th century, although recent years have seen a revival (Shenk & Mattison 2011; Godelier 2011; El Guindi & Read 2016). The fact that there is no explicit and commonly accepted definition of 'kinship' in anthropological research is actually liberating, as Anthony Good (2002: 469) has phrased it, because this allows scholars to understand kinship for what it is to any individual: a broad and open-ended system of opportunities and constraints rather than a strict social boundary. The only uncontroversial trait that has arisen from century-long study is that kinship systems are quite distinct from biological relationships despite the sense of familial affiliation attached to them. This quite basic point, however, raises the intriguing possibility of ancestors sometimes being venerated by people outside their own kin group.

3.4 'Superior ancestor worship'

The belief that ancestors other than a person's own can have vital influence over that person occurs across many societies and has been referred to by some anthropologists as 'superior ancestor worship' (e.g. Sheils 1980; Levinson 1996: 6), while others have discussed similar phenomena in different cultures under the title 'royal ancestor worship' (e.g. Tcherkézoff 1987; Suriano 2010; El Shazly 2015). This section will primarily rely on the analysis by the American anthropologist Dean Sheils (1975, 1980), who criticised most studies in this field at the time as being heavily predisposed to classifying different types of ancestor worship as one. He emphasised that societies exhibit two distinct types of venerated ancestors – those who are worshipped privately within each family and those who are worshipped communally and who have a political agenda attached to them. The distinction between private domestic cults and those that assume a public character, and what Maurice Freedman (1979: 274) has called 'extra-domestic' and '(quasi)public', had of course been noticed by anthropologists prior to Sheils' study (e.g. Radin 1930; Malinowski 1930; Cunnison 1967: 75). However, the focus in previous discussion was mostly on the plasticity of kinship, whereas the link to ancestor worship – partly due to the many sets of rules designed to have a defining and limiting effect on the elements classifiable as such – was generally left open.

In order to introduce the concept, we shall begin with a few examples of contemporary societies where the ancestors of the leading kin groups are believed to affect the lives of ordinary people. In Swaziland and among the Ashanti of Ghana for instance, where each kin group is attached to their own ancestors, the ancestors of the most dominant group are seen as having the ability to protect the nation as a whole (Kuper 1947: 192–195; Busia 1951: 202, cited in Sheils 1980: 248). The Bantu-speaking people of South Africa have distinct ancestral gods for each individual lineage, but those of their royal clans are worshipped by the entire kingdom (Murphy 1949: 151; Lehmann & Myers 1985: 285); among the Ba-Thonga of south-east Africa, ancestor worship is said to reflect the system of political stratification (Junod 1913: 373–428; see also Goody 1962: 380). The Dahomeans' respect for their living ruler is said to be based on the unique relationship between the king and the ancestors of his clan, who are viewed as having the ability to aid or punish any person in the community (Goode 1951: 148, cited in Sheils 1980: 248); the focus of the Sakalava monarchy in Madagascar is said to rest on the spiritual relationship between the royal ancestors and the people as a whole (Feeley-Harnik 1978: 404).

Considering how relevant ancestors are in African societies, it is perhaps expected that they would have acquired a role also in their politico-religious structures; the phenomenon is, however, not confined to Africa. Ancestors are arranged in similar hierarchies in many other places around the world, too. Nobility in Hawaii, for example, are traced back directly to the founding ancestors who had more power than others, whereas ordinary people have no personal genealogies but are linked to the aristocratic lineage on a more distant and therefore inherently subordinate level (Valeri 1990: 165, 181 note 25). The 'named' ruling houses among the Tanimbar islanders of Indonesia are also linked to ancient ancestors, whereas the 'unnamed' common houses relate only to their own immediate and effectively inferior ancestors (McKinnon 1991: 97–98, 104). The same idea is found also in pre-historic religions. The descent of chiefs in ancient Mayan society for example was also traced back to the founding ancestors who protected the entire society (Hill 1992: 92; McAnany 1995); the Roman emperor cult expanded the traditional and common worship of ancestors to include collective rituals dedicated to the *Lares Praestites* or the 'city ancestors of Rome' (Sommer 2007: 30–33; Susina 2011). The reverence of one's family ancestors in combination with imperial ancestors in Japan, again linking the practice to political power, is believed to go back to the Nara period (Klass 1996: 60); the ancestors of China's first historical dynasty – the Shang – were clustered into generic groups (e.g. greater, lesser, superior), with the most powerful group comprised of the pre-dynastic ancestors and the first five kings who received more cult than others (Keightley 2004: 17–18). The Shang are described as having profoundly worshipped their ancestors – rites and offerings (predominantly dedicated to ancestors) are estimated to have taken up nearly one-third of each year (Fu 2003: 638). Attributing the ancestors of elite groups with more power than those of ordinary people is thus a common, long-standing and worldwide tradition, and is also found in contemporary societies where beliefs in ancestors have a role in religious life.

Superior ancestors, like strong ancestor cults, occur according to Sheils (1980: 248) most commonly in patrilineal societies which have a tendency to organise the central states in kinship terms and to be dominated by a specific kin group that has the solitary right to rule – 'a royal clan, lineage or extended family'. The power division between the ordinary members of the community and leaders results in social, political and economic inequality, so it is clear that the 'common' groups must accept claims of superiority for this system to work successfully (see Rappaport 1979: 261–262). In a society built around kinship relations and where ancestors are seen as having the power to sanction the customs and behaviour of the living, the only way for a ruler to legitimately justify their claim to superiority and secure their superordinate position is via a link to ancestors (Sheils 1980: 248). This means that the ancestors of the ruling group must be viewed as being more powerful and having wider-scale influence than those of ordinary people, whose powers are usually confined to the lives of their own descendants. The superior status bestowed upon the rulers' ancestors by the community as a whole is expected to take effect and to ensure protection during extraordinary situations like epidemics, bad harvests or war that pose a threat to all members of a society (Sheils 1980: 249). While the incentive for the community in this kind of arrangement is that the superiors will ensure society-wide protection in situations which go beyond their own ancestors' power, the leading group benefits by gaining more power and control.

Since the idea of kinship forms the nucleus of ancestor cults, the right and ability to call upon superiors in times of trouble is acknowledged by the community as being confined to the current ruler and his family, who are their legal and authorised descendants (Sheils 1980: 249; see Helms 1998: 6, 120). This rule applies to several of the above-mentioned groups and various others, whose leaders are said to have legitimised their public authority through claims of descent from ancestors whom only they could invoke (e.g. Junod 1913: 386; Kuper 1947: 192–195; Busia 1951: 203, cited in Sheils 1980: 249; Goode 1951: 148, cited in Sheils 1980: 248; Bonte 1981: 53; Hill 1992: 92; Lippy & Williams 2010: 1391). The exclusive and publicly accepted privilege of the rulers reinforces their power to command and to be obeyed by other groups, but it also requires distinctive social behaviour (Sheils 1980: 249–250), such as not being allowed to die a natural death (Kopytoff 1987: 66, cited in Helms 1998: 116). It also sanctions their right to restrict succession to people in their own kin group, essentially turning the entire society into their 'property' (Sheils 1980: 248–249). Other groups – aware that they lack the genealogical relatedness necessary to invoke the superiors – come to see the ruling kin group, along with their superior ancestors, as crucial to their own well-being and are therefore bound to readily accept ruling kin group succession (Sheils 1980: 249; Helms 1998: 118). Any confrontation or conflict with the ruler could result in such favours being denied (Sheils 1980: 249). The representation of Scandinavian rulers, who are sometimes reported to have been sacrificed or died ridiculous deaths (a feature that has puzzled scholars who logically expect to find glorification of nobility in the genealogical lore or 'praise poems'), might perhaps also be partly rooted in former codes and expectations of rulers' social behaviour which were still present in people's memory when the genealogies were written. The exaggerated burlesque fashion used to describe the deaths was possibly with the implicit purpose of making them manifest and memorable.

Regardless of the far-reaching influence and supernatural power ascribed to the superior ancestors, perhaps the least recognised and most important point to remember in the present context is that they are not identifiable as 'gods'. The influence they are believed to provide is society-wide; while this can only be requested by their own offspring, reverence is demanded of all members of the community, making superior ancestors somewhat like 'gods' according to our logic, or at least less ancestor-like. This feature is again likely to have contributed to the earlier-discussed scholarly tendency to exclude groups from being classified as worshipping ancestors. As Sheils emphasises, it is important to recognise that these superior ancestors are not seen by the people as 'gods' – they are not divine, cosmic, all-powerful or abstract – nor as 'generalised ghosts', but as historical rulers identified by people with a particular kin group (Sheils 1980: 247–248). A similar point regarding the ideological proximity and spatial closeness of gods and ancestors in the Old Norse context has been brought up by Jens Peter Schjødt (2010), who emphasises that our understanding of the reported 'deifications' of individuals in pagan Scandinavia depends first and foremost on how the concept of 'god' is understood; it might refer to family ancestors, which means that each family had their own localised 'gods'. Schjødt adds though that the rulers were probably seen as having qualities which were more numinous and powerful than those of common people. The anthropologist Mary Helms (1998: 6, 9 115–120) has characterised the ruling sector quite similarly as 'superior living ancestors', owing to their own inherent 'ancestral' qualities which they acquire through mediation with the dead ancestors. According to Helms (1998: 119) the living rulers' nature is located somewhere between 'those who are physically alive but spiritually limited (members of ordinary houses) and those who are spiritually fulfilled but physically dead (true ancestor-beings)'. The numinous qualities of religious leaders, be they kings, chiefs, priests or shamans, are usually conveyed through their knowledge of myths, rituals and even secret languages known only to them, as well as 'remembering' the genealogies of the entire community (Steadman & Palmer 1994: 179–180; Eliade 2004: 13; Brink 2005: 64–66). As prime preservers of genealogies, religious leaders would have considerable freedom to modify them at will, a privilege that they have always undoubtedly enjoyed: 'historians who collect genealogies in oral societies will usually find that there are many more versions than they might have preferred' (Henige 1982: 98).

The collection of genealogies from non-European indigenous peoples forms a natural and substantial part of anthropological fieldwork in kinship studies. Ever since William Rivers and his American counterpart Lewis Henry Morgan, who is often credited as the pioneer of the study of kinship, created the first genealogical surveys, the systematised genealogical method became a standard procedure for social anthropologists undertaking first-hand field studies and remained so through to the 1960s (deRoche 2007: 21–24). The overall pattern that surfaced from the genealogical data strongly indicated that the purpose of genealogies in these predominantly oral societies was not to create 'faithful' reports, but to constantly adapt them to suit current political and social realities. The native genealogies of the Tiv of Nigeria, for example, which had first been communicated orally, but then recorded by British administrators for the purpose of settling disagreements between individuals in court, showed substantial differences only 40 years later (Goody & Watt 1963: 309–310). Much disagreement arose between the anthropologists who saw the genealogical records crafted by the earlier administrators as records of fact and the Tiv who claimed them to be inaccurate; this suggests that specific components in the oral genealogies had been instinctively and regularly dropped and added by the Tiv according to what was socially desirable at the time of remembering (Bohannan 1952: 314–315; Goody 1962: 382; Goody & Watt 1963: 309).

As a general rule, an individual's genealogical memory is said to encompass four or five generations above themselves at the most, which means that oral genealogies are easily manipulated. For example, it is not uncommon that ruling dynasties, whose remembered genealogies are usually longer than those of common people, claim more than one origin – a phenomenon termed 'genealogical schizophrenia' by David Thornton (1998: 87) – in order to support current political or social structures. Rulers can even present themselves as the offspring of pre-historic and widely known characters – if such are present – despite the lack of genuine kin ties. This evidently common practice of selective memory, which has been called 'structural amnesia' (Barnes 1947: 48–56) and the 'homeostatic process of forgetting' (Goody & Watt 1963: 344) in anthropology, may be obvious to a scholar investigating the genealogies and perhaps to the person recording them in writing, but not to the people or even to the ruler who may have actually believed in their superior descent from specific pre-historic persons (Bohannan 1952: 314; Thornton 1998: 87). Kinship exploitation is thus a natural part of social organisation in oral societies where genealogies are inherently fluid, but for modern scholars this is often difficult to grasp. As Thornton (1998: 87) rightly points out, as historians we are only aware of adaptations in genealogies if several conflicting accounts have survived and then the tendency is to try to seek out the 'correct' version. However, by no means are any of the differing versions false. They all served different functions and purposes that were valid and inherently true for someone, somewhere, at some point in history (Bohannan 1952: 314–315; Vansina 1985: 101, 182). Although orality and literacy often co-exist and are no longer seen as polar opposites in scholarship, recording genealogies in written form inevitably leads to reduced flexibility.[5] However, since the flexibility of kinship networks is essential in ancestor cults, the introduction of literacy weakens them (Tatje & Hsu 1969: 154–155). 'Genealogical schizophrenia' is also visible in the conflicting Old Norse king lists, which medieval scribes copied and transformed at the time when literacy had made progress in northern Europe through Christian missionary work.[6]

In summary, 'superior ancestor worship' functions to enhance the cohesion upheld by ordinary ancestor worship at the descent level of common kin groups (Sheils 1980: 249, 254). It is built around the idea of kinship ties and familial solidarity and the associated obligations and privileges, but functions primarily for the benefit of the ruling family. Both cult types are geared towards protecting a specific group of people, but whilst ordinary ancestors are limited in their influence to their closest lineal descendants and territorial borders, the superiors also have a society-wide impact which is politically oriented. In order to gain more authority and to reinforce power, kinship may be heavily manipulated and may even be pseudo-ancestral. It is crucial, however, that the rulers' authority is reinforced through the idea of descent from specific ancestors who are seen as once-living human rulers. The special abilities ascribed to the Nordic elite, such as securing good harvests via mediation with the gods, are conventionally explained by their divine origin from characters like Óðinn or Freyr and addressed within the sacral kingship framework. In the light of the social patterns outlined in this chapter, it is intuitively appealing to adopt the view that their 'unique abilities' were also believed to derive from precursors who were perceived by the people as real historical persons, representing the elementary privileges reserved for legal descendants in a typical kinship-based society.

* * * * *

The information provided here covers only a fraction of the beliefs and practices connected with ancestors and cannot serve as more than a general illustration. For present purposes, however, this is enough: simply accepting that there is no one type of ancestor religion in the world and no single coherent definition of the practice, but that ancestors play a crucial part in most small-scale religions, is a good starting point. The generally varied nature of beliefs and practices relating to ancestors across the world probably says more about their overall importance in religious cognition than any set of clear-cut principles restricted to a limited number of contexts. In my view, the sociological patterns outlined above prove extremely useful when approaching Old Norse religion. It is important to acknowledge the intrinsic way in which ancestors and gods are compatible in typical folk-religious societies – something which is commonly (and perhaps consciously) ignored in the pagan Scandinavian context – and how reliance on ancestors of lineages other than one's own can arise with the social distancing of the elite. This phenomenon has been labelled 'superior ancestor worship' and entails the idea that the ancestors of leading families have the power to influence an entire society and must therefore receive worship from everyone. Building upon the ideological proximity between ancestors and gods, I propose that gods in Old Norse tradition should also be approached as 'superior ancestors': the historical human predecessors of leading families.

Even though the importance of ancestry and kinship continued long into Christianity, especially as a component of inheritance laws, the introduction of one god started to gradually diminish the importance ascribed to ancestors as 'local gods', and the development of literary culture reduced the flexibility of genealogies, particularly aristocratic ones which were the first to be recorded. Based on what was said above, we may assume that neither Nordic oral genealogical traditions nor the early recorded 'pseudo-histories' were concerned with historically truthful descent at any time. This, however, does not mean that they were not 'real' for practitioners. There is no strong reason to attribute the descents from pre-historic kings and inconsistencies recorded in the genealogies by Scandinavian and Icelandic court poets and historians only to medieval authorial fantasy and religious agendas. They served the purpose of creating an ideological foundation for the power of the elite and were seen as a logical process in a society where ancestry and kinship were crucial elements. The extant recorded genealogies in Viking Age and early medieval Scandinavia belong to an early stage of the written culture confined to the few, when the lists were still very flexible; this can be seen in the way medieval scribes copied and transformed the texts. Nonetheless, this is also the period when stable social hierarchies and political systems in Scandinavia had started to gain ground. Orality and literacy cannot always be clearly separated; however, the coming of the written word must have gradually 'fixed' certain individuals' claims to rulership. From then on, elite kinship could only be exploited by attaching new rulers to names which had been recorded in writing. This might explain why the later Norwegian hárfagri clan appears to be referred to as Ynglingar.

These ideas link up with sacral kingship and euhemerism in Old Norse scholarship, where the former traces living rulers' descent from gods, and the latter 'lowers' gods into once-living kings. In social anthropology the underlying connection between ancestor cults and these concepts is largely acknowledged, while in Old Norse scholarship they are often treated as separate. The introduction of euhemerism is usually ascribed to conspiracy-driven medieval scribes who desired to detract from pagan gods by portraying them as real people. Discussions of sacral kingship are focused on divine links between kings and gods or mythical beings, and ancestor worship is commonly studied within the folkloristic framework of small-scale domestic beliefs and practices (Gunnell 2014; Murphy 2018). By introducing the concept of 'superior ancestor worship', this study does not dispute the existence of political ideologies, belief in the sacrosanct nature of rulers or the importance of elite propaganda, but rather brings these phenomena into the theory's scope. By simply accepting that it was the reverence for ancestors that provided the foundations for sacral kingship or religious ruler ideology and contributed to the theory of euhemerism, we can explain why dead rulers received public cult and why the relationship between rulers and gods was readily accepted by society as unique: it did not derive from beliefs in the ruler's divine, cosmic or other abstract supernatural origin or intervention, but from belief in their privileged descent from former human rulers – superior ancestors.

Notes

1 This view is also supported by some scholars of Old Norse religion (e.g. Nordberg 2013).
2 Attempts have also been made to distinguish between 'ancestor worship' and 'cult of the dead' (e.g. Fortes 1976: 2–4). This has caused debate and confusion among scholars, as their particular meanings – as of any man-made concept – are subject to interpretation. The anthropologist Annemarie de Waal Malefijt (1968: 156–158), for example, suggested that the distinction should be based on the two key beliefs concerning the dead: they either remain active or leave society. If the dead are socially separated from the living, then their return is feared and a cult of the dead arises; if they are seen as 'living' active members of the group, then their return is desired and ancestor worship develops. Although de Waal Malefijt is right in that the dead can be feared more or less in different societies, which shapes attitudes towards them, such dichotomised reasoning overlooks conflicting attitudes within one society. For example, the fear of the return of the unwanted dead also occurs in societies where the dead are generally esteemed. This fear is also directly connected to time-based changes

within the nature of the dead. In some African cultures, for example, the dead that are still remembered by name represent beneficent ancestors and receive worship, but those who died long ago and whose identities have been forgotten become malicious (Lehmann & Myers 1985: 285). Similar disagreements have also arisen in Old Norse scholarship (e.g. Phillpotts 1913; Sverdrup 1927: 20–27, 54, 64).
3 For specific approaches, see Malinowski (1930); Fortes (1976); Schusky (1965); Scheffler (1966); Lévi-Strauss (1969); Tatje and Hsu (1969); Goody (1969); Barnard and Good (1984).
4 Lineage is a unilineal descent group that traces common descent from a known ancestor. It consists of three or more generations, including both living and dead members. In developed kinship systems, related lineages are united into a clan.
5 Useful discussion concerning the orality–literacy debate can be found in Henige (1982: 81–87); Ong (1982); Vansina (1985: 120–123); Goody (1987); Finnegan (1988: 117–120, 175); Thornton (1998: 85–87).
6 Concerning the transition from an oral society to a literate one in Scandinavia, and for further references, see Jesch (2001); Brink (2005).

Secondary sources

Abraham, William, 1966, *The mind of Africa*, University of Chicago Press, Chicago.
Anning, Hu, and Felicia Tian, 2018, 'Still under the ancestors' shadow? Ancestor worship and family formation in contemporary China', *Demographic Research*, vol. 38, pp. 1–36.
Barnard, Alan, and Anthony Good, 1984, *Research practices in the study of kinship*, Academic Press, London.
Barnes, John, 1947, 'The collection of genealogies', *Rhodes-Livingstone Journal*, vol. 5, pp. 48–55.
Baudou, Evert, 1989, 'Hög – gård – helgedom i Mellannorrland under den äldre järnåldern', *Arkeologi i norr*, vol. 2, pp. 9–43.
Berentsen, Jan-Martin, 1985 [1932], *Grave and gospel*, Zeitschrift für Religions- und Geistesgeschichte, 30, E. J. Brill, Leiden.
Blackburn, Stuart, 1985, 'Death and deification: folk cults in Hinduism', *History of Religions*, vol. 24, no. 3, pp. 255–274.
Bloch, Maurice, 2002 [1996], 'Ancestors', in A. Barnard and J. Spencer (eds.), *Encyclopedia of social and cultural anthropology*, Routledge, London and New York, pp. 66–67.
Bohannan, Laura, 1952. 'A genealogical charter', *Africa: Journal of the International African Institute*, vol. 22, pp. 301–315.
Bonte, Pierre, 1981, 'Kinship and politics: the formation of the state among the pastoralists of the Sahara and the Sahel', in J. Claessen and P. Skalnik (eds.), *The study of the state*, Mouton, Hague, pp. 35–58.
Brink, Stefan, 2005, 'Verba volant, scripta manent? Aspects of the oral society in Scandinavia', in P. Hermann (ed.), *Literacy in medieval and early modern Scandinavian culture*, the Viking collection 16, University Press of Southern Denmark, Odense, pp. 59–117.
Brink, Stefan, 2013, 'Myth and ritual and pre-Christian Scandinavian landscape', in S. Nordeide and S. Brink (eds.), *Sacred sites and holy places. Exploring the sacralization of landscape through time and space*, Brepols, Turnhout, pp. 33–51.
Busia, Kofi, 1951, *The position of the chief in the modern political system of Ashanti*, Oxford University Press, London.

Cunnison, Ian, 1967, *The Luapula peoples of Northern Rhodesia: custom and history in tribal politics*, Manchester University Press, Manchester.

Czaplicka, Maria Antonina, 1908, 'Samoyed', in J. Hastings et al. (eds.), *Encyclopaedia of religion and ethics*, vol. 11, Charles Scribner's Sons, New York, pp. 172–177.

Czaplicka, Maria, 1914, *Aboriginal Siberia*, Clarendon Press, Oxford.

de Waal Malefijt, Annemarie, 1968, *Religion and culture. An introduction to the anthropology of religion*, Macmillan Company, New York.

deRoche, Constance, 2007, 'Exploring genealogy', in M. Angrosino (ed.), *Doing cultural anthropology*, Waveland Press, Inc, Long Grove, pp. 19–32.

Doniger, Wendy (ed.) 1999, *Merriam-Webster's encyclopedia of world religions*, published in cooperation with the *Encyclopedia Britannica*, Merriam Webster, Springfield.

Driberg, Jack, 1936, 'The secular aspect of ancestor worship in Africa', *Journal of the Royal African Society*, vol. 35, no. 138, pp. 1–21.

DuBois, Thomas, 1999, *Nordic religions in the Viking Age*, University of Pennsylvania Press, Philadelphia.

El Guindi, Fadwa, and Dwight Read, 2016, 'Back to kinship II: a general introduction', *Structure and Dynamics, eJournal of Anthropological and Related Sciences*, vol. 9, no. 2, pp. 1–15.

El Shazly, Yasmin, 2015, *Royal ancestor worship in Deir el-Medina during the new kingdom*, Abercromby Press, Wallasey.

Eliade, Mircea, 2004 [1964], *Shamanism: archaic techniques of ecstasy*, Princeton University Press, Princeton.

Ephirim-Donkor, Anthony, 2012, *African religion defined: a systematic study of ancestor worship among the Akan*, University Press of America, Maryland.

Evans-Pritchard, Edward, 1940, *The Nuer: a description of the modes of livelihood and political institutions of a Nilotic people*, Clarendon Press, Oxford.

Feeley-Harnik, Gillian, 1978, 'Divine kingship and the meaning of history among the Sakalava of Madagascar', *Man*, vol. 13, no. 3, pp. 402–417.

Feeley-Harnik, Gillian, 1991, *A green estate: restoring independence in Madagascar*, Smithsonian Institute Press, Washington.

Firth, Raymond, 1936, *We, the Tikopia: a sociological study of kinship in primitive Polynesia*, George Allen & Unwin, London.

Fortes, Meyer, 1970 [1969], *Kinship and the social order: the legacy of Lewis Henry Morgan*, Routledge & Kegan Paul, London.

Fortes, Meyer, 1976, 'An introductory commentary', in W. Newell (ed.), *Ancestors*, Mouton, Hague and Paris, pp. 1–16.

Fortes, Meyer, 1987, *Religion, morality and the person: essays on Tallensi religion*, Cambridge University Press, Cambridge.

Fowler, Francis, and Henry Fowler, 1986, *The Oxford handy dictionary*, Chancellor Press, London.

Freedman, Maurice, 1979, *The study of Chinese society. Essays by Maurice Freedman*, W. Skinner (ed.), Stanford University Press, Stanford.

Fu, Pei-Jung, 2003, 'Religions', in A. Cua (ed.), *Encyclopedia of Chinese philosophy*, Routledge, New York.

Godelier, Maurice, 2011, *The metamorphoses of kinship*, trans. N. Scott, Verso, London and New York.

Good, Anthony, 2002 [1996], 'Kinship', in A. Barnard and J. Spencer (eds.), *Encyclopedia of social and cultural anthropology*, Routledge, London and New York, pp. 469–480.

Goody, Jack, 1962, *Death, property and the ancestors: a study of the mortuary customs of the Lodagaa of West Africa*, Stanford University Press, Stanford.
Goody, Jack, 1969, *Comparative studies in kinship*, Routledge & Kegan Paul, London.
Goody, Jack, 1987, *The interface between the written and the oral*, Cambridge University Press, Cambridge.
Goody, Jack, 2010, *Myth, ritual and the oral*, Cambridge University Press, Cambridge.
Goody, Jack, and Ian Watt, 1963, 'The consequences of literacy', *Comparative Studies in Society and History*, vol. 5, no. 3, pp. 304–345.
Gunnell, Terry, 2007, 'How Elvish were the Álfar?' in A. Wawn et al. (eds.), *Constructing nations, reconstructing myth: essays in honour of T. A. Shippey*, Brepols, Turnhout, pp. 111–130.
Gunnell, Terry, 2014, 'Nordic folk legends, folk traditions and gravemounds: the potential value of Folkloristics for the study of Old Norse religions', in E. Heide and K. Bek-Pedersen (eds.), *New focus on retrospective methods*. Folklore Fellows' Communications 307. Academia Scientarum Fennica, Helsinki, pp. 17–41.
Hallpike, Christopher, 2003 [1971], 'Some problems in cross-cultural comparison', in T. Beidelman (ed.), *The translation of culture: essays to E. E. Evans-Pritchard*, Routledge, London, pp. 123–140.
Hardacre, Helen, 2005, 'Ancestors', in L. Jones (ed.), *Encyclopedia of religion*, Thomson Gale, Detroit, pp. 320–325.
Harrington, Nicola, 2013, *Living with the dead: ancestor worship and mortuary ritual in ancient Egypt*, Oxbow Books, Oxford.
Helms, Mary, 1998, *Access to origins. Affines, ancestors and aristocrats*, University of Texas Press, Austin.
Henige, David, 1982, *Oral historiography*, Longman, London.
Hill, Robert, 1992, *Colonial cakchiquels. Highland maya adaptations to Spanish rule 1600–1700*, Harcourt, Brace, Jovanovich, Fort Worth.
Hunter, Monica, 1961 [1936], *Reaction to conquest: effects of contact with Europeans on the Pondo of South Africa*, Oxford University Press, London, New York and Toronto.
Hüwelmeier, Gertrud, 2016, 'Cell phones for the spirits: ancestor worship and ritual economies in Vietnam and its diasporas', *Material Religion*, vol. 12, no. 3, pp. 294–321.
Insoll, Timothy (ed.) 2011, *The Oxford handbook of the archaeology of ritual and religion*, University Press, Oxford.
Jesch, Judith, 2001, *Ships and men in the late Viking Age. The vocabulary of runic inscriptions and skaldic verse*, The Boydell Press, Woodbridge.
Jevons, Frank, 1896, *An introduction to the history of religion*, Methuen & Co, London.
Johnston, Reginald, 2015 [1934], *Confucianism and modern China*. The Lewis Fry Memorial Lectures, 1933–1934, delivered at Bristol University, Cambridge University Press, Cambridge.
Junod, Henri, 1913, *The life of a South African tribe*, II: *the psychic life*, Imprimerie Attinger Freres, Neuchatel.
Keightley, David, 2004, 'The making of the ancestors: late Shang religion and its legacy', in J. Lagerwey (ed.), *Religion and Chinese society*, 1. *Ancient and medieval China*, The Chinese University of Hong Kong, Hong Kong, pp. 3–64.
Klass, Dennis, 1996, 'Grief in an eastern culture: Japanese ancestor worship', in D. Klass et al. (eds.), *Continuing bonds. New understandings of grief*, Routledge, New York, pp. 59–70.
Kopytoff, Igor, 1971, 'Ancestors and elders in Africa', *Africa*, vol. 42, no. 2, pp. 129–142.

Kubuya, Paulin, 2018, *Means and controversy within Chinese ancestor religion*, Macmillan, Palgrave.

Kuper, Hilda, 1947, *An African society: rank among the Swazi*, Oxford University Press for the International African Institute, London.

Lakos, William, 2010, *Chinese ancestor worship: a practice and ritual oriented approach to understanding Chinese culture*, Cambridge Scholars Publishing, Newcastle upon Tyne.

Lee, Richard, 1984, *The Dobe !Kung*, Holt, Rinehart & Winston, New York.

Lehmann, Arthur, and James Myers, 1985, 'Ghosts, souls, and ancestors: power of the dead', in A. Lehmann and J. Myers (eds.), *Magic, witchcraft, and religion*, Mayfield Publishing Company, Palo Alto and London, pp. 284–287.

Lévi-Strauss, Claude, 1969 [1949], *The elementary structures of kinship*, trans. J. Harle Bell & J. R. von Sturmer, Eyre & Spottiswoode, London.

Levinson, David, 1996, *Religion: a cross-cultural encyclopedia*, ABC-CLIO, Santa Barbara.

Lewis, Ioan, 2003 [1971], *Ecstatic religion: a study of shamanism and spirit possession*, Routledge, London and New York.

Lindsay, Hugh, 1996, 'The Romans and ancestor worship', in M. Dillon (ed.), *Religion in the ancient world: new themes and approaches*, A. M. Hakkert, Amsterdam, pp. 271–285.

Lippy, Charles, and Peter Williams (eds), 2010, *Encyclopedia of religion in America*, 3, CQ Press, Washington.

Littlewood, Roland, 2001, *Religion, agency, restitution: the wilde lectures in natural religion, 1999*, Oxford University Press, Oxford.

Liu, Li, 2000, 'Ancestor worship: an archaeological investigation of ritual activities in Neolithic North China', *Journal of East Asian Archaeology*, vol. 2, no. 1–2, pp. 129–164.

Lo, Ping-Cheong, 2012, 'Confucian rites of passage: a comparative analysis of Zhu Xi's' family rituals', in D. Salomon et al. (eds.) *Ritual and the moral life: reclaiming the tradition*, Springer, Dordrecht, pp. 119–141.

Malinowski, Bronislav, 1930, 'Kinship', *Man*, vol. 30, no. 2, pp. 19–29.

Mbiti, John, 1970, *African religions and philosophies*, Doubleday, Garden City and New York.

Mbiti, John, 2015 [1975], *Introduction to African religion*, Waveland Press, Long Grove.

McAnany, Patricia, 1995, *Living with the ancestors. Kinship and kingship in ancient Maya society*, University of Texas Press, Austin.

McKinnon, Susan, 1991, *From a shattered sun. Hierarchy, gender and alliance in the Tanimbar Islands*, University of Wisconsin Press, Madison.

Middleton, John, 1960, *Lugbara religion: ritual and authority among an East African people*, Oxford University Press, London, New York and Toronto.

Mitchell, Tim, 2004, *Intoxicated identities. Alcohol's power in Mexican history and culture*, Routledge, New York.

Murphy, John, 1949, *The origins and history of religions*, Manchester University Press, Manchester.

Murphy, Luke, 2017, '*Familial religion in pre-Christian Scandinavia? Ancestor-worship, mother-priestesses and offerings for the Elves*', *family in the premodern world: a comparative approach workshop*, Princeton University, USA. http://www.academia.

68 Theoretical considerations

edu/33387975/Familial_Religion_in_Pre-Christian_Scandinavia_Ancestor-Worship_ Mother-Priestesses_and_Offerings_for_the_Elves (accessed 13 April 2018).

Murphy, Luke, 2018, 'Paganism at home: pre-Christian private praxis and household religion in the Iron-Age North', *Scripta Islandica*, vol. 69, pp. 49–97.

Nakamaki, Hirochika, 2012 [2003], *Japanese religions home and abroad: Anthropological perspectives*, Routledge, New York.

Newell, William, 1976a, 'Good and bad ancestors', in W. Newell (ed.), *Ancestors*, Mouton, Hague and Paris, pp. 17–29.

Newell, William (ed.) 1976b, *Ancestors*, Mouton, Hague and Paris.

Nordberg, Andreas, 2013, *Fornnordisk religionsforskning mellan teori och empiri. Kulten av anfäder. Solen och vegetationsandar i idéhistorisk belysning*, Kungl. Gustav Adolfs Akademien för svensk folkkultur, Uppsala.

Ong, Walter, 1982, *Orality and literacy: the technologizing of the word*, Methuen, London and New York.

Park, Chang-Won, 2010, *Cultural blending in Korean death rites: new interpretive approaches*, Continuum International Publishing Group, London and New York.

Peletz, Michael, 1995, 'Kinship studies in late twentieth-century anthropology', *Annual Review of Anthropology*, vol. 24, pp. 343–372.

Phillpotts, Bertha, 1913, *Kindred and clan in the middle ages and after: a study in the sociology of the Teutonic races*, Cambridge University Press, Cambridge.

Radcliffe-Brown, Alfred, 1961 [1952], *Structure and function in primitive society: essays and addresses*, Cohen & West Ltd, London.

Radin, Paul, 1930, 'Ancestor worship', in E. Seligman and A. Johnson (eds.), *Encyclopaedia of the social sciences*, 2, The Macmillan Company, New York, pp. 53–55.

Rappaport, 1979 [1971], 'Ritual, sanctity, and cybernetics', in W. Lessa and E. Vogt (eds.), *Reader in comparative religion: an anthropological approach*, HarperCollins, New York.

Rivers, William, 1906, *The Todas*, Macmillan, London.

Robertson Smith, William, 1894 [1889], *Lectures on the religion of the Semites*, Adam & Charles Black, London.

Sanjek, Roger (ed.) 1990, *Fieldnotes: the makings of anthropology*, Cornell University Press, New York.

Sayers, Matthew, 2013, *Feeding the dead: ancestor worship in ancient India*, University Press, Oxford.

Scheffler, Harold, 1966, 'Ancestor worship in anthropology: or observations on descent and descent groups', *Current Anthropology*, vol. 7, pp. 541–551.

Schjødt, Jens Peter, 2010, 'Ideology of the ruler in pre-Christian Scandinavia: mythic and ritual relations', *Viking and Medieval Scandinavia*, vol. 6, pp. 161–194.

Schusky, Ernest, 1965, *Manual for kinship analysis*, Holt, Rinehart & Winston, New York.

Sheils, Dean, 1975, 'Toward a unified theory of ancestor worship: a cross-cultural study', *Social Forces*, vol. 52, no. 2, pp. 427–440.

Sheils, Dean, 1980, 'The great ancestors are watching: a cross-cultural study of superior ancestral religion', *Sociological Analysis*, vol. 41, no. 3, pp. 247–257.

Shenk, Mary, and Siobhán Mattison, 2011, 'The rebirth of kinship', *Human Nature*, vol. 22, pp. 1–15.

Sommer, Carl, 2007, *We look for a kingdom: the everyday lives of the early Christians*, Ignatius Press, San Francisco.

Spencer, Herbert, 1897 [1874–1875], *The principles of sociology*, 1, D. Appleton & Company, New York.

Steadman, Lyle, and Craig Palmer, 1994, 'Visiting dead ancestors: shamans as interpreters of religious traditions', *Zygon*, vol. 29, no. 2, pp. 173–189.
Steadman, Lyle, and Craig Palmer, 2008, *The supernatural and natural selection. The evolution of religion*, Paradigm Publishers, Boulder and London.
Steadman, Lyle et al., 1996, 'The universality of ancestor worship', *Ethnology: An International Journal of Cultural and Social Anthropology*, vol. 35, no. 1, pp. 63–76.
Steinsland, Gro, 2005, *Norrøn religion. Myter, riter, samfunn*, Pax Forlag, Oslo.
Sundqvist, Olof, 2002, *Freyr's offspring. Rulers and religion in ancient Svea society*, Uppsala Universitet, Uppsala.
Suriano, Matthew, 2010, *The politics of dead kings: dynastic ancestors in the book of kings and ancient Israel*, Mohr Siebeck, Tübingen.
Susina, Emily, 2011, 'Don't fear the reaper: the purpose of religious festivals in ancient Rome', *Constructing the Past*, vol. 12, no. 1, p. 13.
Sverdrup, Georg, 1927, *Fra gravskikker til dødstro i nordisk stenalder*. Skrifter utgitt av Det Norske Videnskaps-Akademi i Oslo II. Hist.-Filos. Klasse, no. 8, i kommisjon hos Jacob Dybwad, Oslo.
Swanson, Guy, 1964 [1960], *The birth of the gods: the origin of primitive beliefs*, University of Michigan Press, Ann Arbor.
Tatje, Terrence, and Francis Hsu, 1969, 'Variations in ancestor worship beliefs and their relation to kinship', *Southwestern Journal of Anthropology*, vol. 25, no. 2, pp. 153–172.
Tcherkézoff, Serge, 1987, *Dual classification reconsidered: Nyamwezi sacred kingship and other examples*, Cambridge University Press, Cambridge.
Thornton, David, 1998, 'Orality, literacy and genealogy in early medieval Ireland and Wales', in H. Pryce (ed.), *Literacy in medieval Celtic societies*, Cambridge University Press, Cambridge, pp. 83–98.
Tuan, Yi-Fu, 2001 [1977], *Space and place: the perspective of experience*, University of Minnesota Press, Minneapolis and London.
Valeri, Valerio, 1990, 'Constitutive history: genealogy and narrative in the legitimation of Hawaiian kingship', in E. Ohnuki-Tierney (ed.), *Culture through time: anthropological approaches*, Stanford University Press, Stanford, pp. 154–192.
Vansina, Jan, 1985, *Oral tradition as history*, Madison, University of Wisconsin Press.
Vestergaard, Elizabeth, 2012 [2002], 'Kinship and marriage: the family, its relationships and renewal', in J. Jesch (ed.), *The Scandinavians from the Vendel Period to the tenth century: an ethnographic perspective*, Boydell Press, Woodbridge, pp. 59–86.
Vogt, Helle, 2010, *The function of kinship in medieval Nordic legislation*, Brill, Leiden and Boston.
Whitley, James, 2002, 'Too many ancestors?' *Antiquity*, vol. 76, no. 1, pp. 119–126.

4 Kings and gods in Old Norse religion

4.1 The myth of 'sacral kingship'

The idea that kings embody unique virtues and are seen as having divine authority has been associated with many pre-historic societies in scholarship (see de Maret 2011; Brisch 2012). The kings are believed to be juxtaposed with the gods: they are incarnations of the gods on earth or descend from them, and act as sacred mediums between gods and men, thus ensuring the welfare of the community. Towards the end of the 19th century, when the first forms of religion were an area of particular interest in academic writing across many disciplines, this phenomenon caught the eye of folklorists and social anthropologists (e.g. Mannhardt 1875–1877; Spencer 1851; Robertson Smith 1894), who combined the king-god idea with ideas of vegetation magic and ancestor worship. It came to be labelled 'sacral kingship', a term coined by James Frazer in his *The Golden Bough: A Study of Comparative Religion* in 1890.

Frazer was an evolutionistic thinker and concentrated on the early forms of this phenomenon in the large empires of the ancient Middle East. He developed the theory from a story told, among others, by the Latin poet Virgil (70–19 BC), who wrote that fugitive slaves could assume the role of a priest of the goddess Diana, whose shrine stood in a grove by the Lake of Nemi in Italy (*Aeneid* VII, lines 761–783, pp. 40–41). According to the story's interpretation by Frazer (1890: 1–6), the slave who acted as a priest of Diana could be challenged by any other male slave who broke a branch from the sacred tree in the grove – the golden bough; if victorious, the challenger became his replacement. Frazer's explanation of this story, which was central to the hypothesis of sacral kingship, was that the priest was a spirit of vegetation who came to be regarded as the husband of the goddess, and developed into a king or a god. Influenced by Mannhardt's ideas of vegetation magic, Frazer argued that the tale of the Nemi priesthood was an example of a worldwide myth of a sacral king who must die as part of a seasonal fertility rite. In Frazer's definition the sacral king was treated as a god (i.e. he received public sacrifices), he was responsible for the welfare of his people (i.e. secured good crops), he was married to the fertility goddess (i.e. by *hieros gamos*), his role was that of a religious priest (i.e. he mediated with gods) and he could be killed or sacrificed by a rival (i.e. as part of a fertility ritual).

Frazer's ideas regarding sacral kingship have since been subject to extensive criticism, but they were very influential in the development of the theory.[1] Building upon the idea that there was a uniform Middle Eastern culture, many British (e.g. Harrison 1912; Hooke 1933; i.e. the 'Myth and Ritual School') and Scandinavian (e.g. Widengren 1943; Engnell 1943; i.e. the 'Uppsala School') scholars of the early 20th century started to apply Frazer's theory and saw the king as a god incarnate. A few scholars (e.g. Frankfort 1948, 1951) questioned the validity of Frazer's 'patterns', arguing that the sacral king concept embodies myriad transitional varieties in different societies and time-periods, but for the majority the theory remained attractive (e.g. *La Regalità Sacra: The Sacral Kingship*, 1959). The elements that were discussed most frequently in the literature were those that Frazer had introduced: the king's ability to provide protection and fertile land in return for ritual sacrifices, his holy marriage to the earth goddess and his role as a sacrificial victim and as a religious mediator between the people and gods.

These theories were soon enthusiastically applied also to the study of ancient continental Germanic, Anglo-Saxon, Celtic and Scandinavian kingship. The source central to the discussion by Old Norse scholars at the time was the 9th-century poem *Ynglingatal* which lists the names and burial places of Swedish and Norwegian kings. The poem is contained in the 13th-century *Ynglinga saga* where it is interpreted and elaborated by Snorri, who places Freyr at the very top of the genealogy. Freyr has strong links to vegetation and fertility elsewhere in Old Norse literature; he is included as a *vanir* god in the mythological pantheon and, according to *Skírnismál*, entered a union of some sort with Gerðr, who, following the classical analysis of Magnus Olsen (1909), is often recognised as an earth goddess. And so the Ynglingar – seen as their descendants – came to be interpreted as sacral or divine kings mediating between the world of gods (i.e. Freyr) and the common people (e.g. Schück 1904; Wessén 1924; Schröder 1924; Grönbech 1931; von Friesen 1932–1934; Ström F. 1954, 1968, 1983; de Vries 1956; Ström 1959; Turville-Petre 1964: 190–195). Even though the kings' descent from a god is not a universal feature of sacral kingship and thus not always part of the general definition of the theory (Frazer's own *locus classicus*, the priest at Nemi, did not descend from a god but was a vegetation spirit who married an earth goddess), this became a central element in scholars' analyses of Old Norse religion. Elements that were interpreted within this sacral kingship framework included communal sacrifices to Freyr and his alleged descendants, the *hieros gamos* motif, the kings' inborn ability to secure the *ár ok friðr* ('prosperity and peace') by mediating with the gods, which went alongside the concept of 'royal luck' derived from divine descent, and perhaps the most controversial of all – the sacrificing of kings in order to restore harvests.[2] These different 'Frazerian' aspects dovetailed in the mid-20th century and 'sacral kingship' became strongly established in the Old Norse context. In the oft-quoted words of Åke Ström (1959: 702), 'that kingship in Old Scandinavia was entirely sacral, is nowadays considered as a mere matter of fact'.

This trend continued until 1964 when the enthusiastic adoption of the sacral kingship theory was challenged by the German scholar Walter Baetke, who, in his book *Yngvi und die Ynglinger*, started criticising earlier scholars for building

72 Theoretical considerations

their claims on unreliable evidence. One of his main objections was that the earlier arguments were based on medieval Christian reports that all stemmed from Icelandic historians' learned euhemerism (Baetke 1964: 97–99). Baetke made several interesting observations, such as that living pagan kings are never viewed in the sources as possessing divine qualities, receiving prayers or sacrifices, or operating as agents between people and gods; instead, public cults dedicated to kings always start at their gravemounds. To Baetke this meant that these cults should more likely be interpreted as a general *ahnenkult* ('ancestor cult') than the worship of kings because of their divine descent or godly nature and that the kings' religious role was consequently not sacral in character (Baetke 1964: 39–47, 98–99, 139–164). Furthermore, since features similar to those attributed to kings – such as sacrifices after their death – also occur in connection with Icelandic chieftains, they cannot be confined to kings in pagan Scandinavia (Baetke 1964: 45). Baetke concluded that the only cases that might serve as examples of sacral kingship concern Christian kings like Óláfr helgi.

Baetke's radical views were supported (e.g. Lönnroth 1986; Ejerfeldt 1971) and criticised (e.g. Hallberg 1966; Ström 1968), but on the whole most scholars were forced to at least take his ideas into consideration. I find that, while his arguments are not indisputable (e.g. Sundqvist 2002: 37–38), they did draw attention to the shortcomings of the previously fervent application of Frazer's theory and opened up new perspectives. Most studies after Baetke have treated sacral kingship with more caution and studied the religious aspects of rulership from a broader theoretical perspective, focusing a great deal on the restrictive dimensions of the term itself (Lönnroth 1986; McTurk 1974–1977, 1994; Faulkes 1978–1979; Sundqvist 2002, 2012, 2015; Schjødt 2010; Steinsland 2011). Some of these scholars have addressed the phenomenological side of the concept, something which received little or no attention before Baetke's time when discussion revolved around the question whether or not sacral kingship existed in pagan Scandinavia. Baetke's own work focused on source criticism and lacked analysis of sacral kingship as a religious phenomenon. For instance, his prerequisite that the king must be regarded by people as a 'god' or as 'divine' in order to meet the criteria of a 'sacral king' is problematic in its own way because it is not obvious what is meant by such terms. Rory McTurk (1974–1977: 156, 1994: 30–31), among others, proposed a more cautious definition of sacral kingship and suggested that the king should be associated with the 'supernatural' rather than the 'divine' because the latter is commonly understood as referring to someone divinely superhuman. In agreement with Baetke that the classic criteria of a 'sacral king' do not apply to the pagan Scandinavian kings, McTurk (1974–1977: 139, 149) thus opened up a new chapter in sacral kingship research, although his definition of the term has been considered too general (Steinsland 1991: 312).

Recent studies have drawn attention to further problems with terminology, for example, the use of the term 'kingship' in religious contexts and the meaning of 'gods'. Olof Sundqvist (2002, 2012, 2015) has in a series of studies criticised previous research for the tendency to assume that there was a static and centralised power structure in pre-Christian Scandinavia which revolved around a male ruler – a king.[3] As he demonstrates, this was not the case as it was only in the 12th or 13th century that, for instance, Svealand, also associated with some of the Ynglingar including Freyr, developed into a centralised state. Previously, the role of cultic leaders was taken by local chieftains, including women. The term 'sacral kingship', however, cannot be applied to individuals that are not kings. Sundqvist has therefore proposed a more open term, 'religious ruler ideology', which captures the broad nature of the phenomenon more appropriately and which has recently gained considerable popularity among scholars (e.g. Schjødt 2010; Steinsland 2011; Nygaard 2016). Regardless of the difficulties with terminology, Sundqvist makes a strong case for the existence of ruler ideology as far back as early paganism. While earlier investigations determined to find specific aspects of Frazer's paradigm in pagan Scandinavia cannot be fully accepted, Sundqvist believes that the heavy criticism that followed Baetke's investigation is overly sceptical. For example, Sundqvist (2002: 37–38) looks unfavourably on Baetke's source criticism: just because the evidence is medieval does not mean that it necessarily is permeated with Christian euhemerism and cannot contain genuine pagan traditions and ideologies. Gamla Uppsala was an important religious centre from at least the Migration Period to the Middle Ages and it is reasonable to assume that the leading families there were naturally engaged in cultural–political activities and had a key role in public rituals, such as securing the *ár ok friðr*, from early paganism and well into the Christian period (Sundqvist 2002: 63–140, 293–364).

A similar approach has been taken by Jens Peter Schjødt (2010), who reasons that it is possible to speak of ruler ideology in both pagan and Christian Scandinavia, but he stresses the importance of acknowledging the limitations of the god concept in such contexts. For example, Schjødt (2010: 164–168, 179) rejects Baetke's (1964: 39) claim that a ruler is sacral only if he possesses some divinity himself, arguing that the notion of 'divine' did not exist in paganism when gods were probably imagined rather in terms of human ancestors than seen as being transcendent or divine in the same way as the Christian God. This, however, does not mean that rulers were not credited with unique abilities, which were also related to their high-ranking status. As Schjødt (2010: 167, 172–176, 180–181, 188) emphasises, the rulers' role as mediators would not have been accepted by the community unless they were seen as having qualities which were more influential than those of common people. The human form of gods, however, created an efficient way for the leading families to present the living ruler as their descendant and thus legal representative and even as one of the gods when he (or she) died, something that is seen in sources like Rimbert's 9th-century *Vita Ansgarii* (ch. 26, ed. p. 56, tr. pp. 89–90), which depicts a Swedish king's transformation into one of the gods after his death.

The views taken by Schjødt are for the most part compatible with the proposed 'superior ancestor' theory. It is very likely that the local gods in pagan Scandinavia – including those that have left traces in the written sources, place names and iconography, and who are often accordingly dealt with as the Nordic pantheon – were perceived as the human ancestors of prominent families. This link to gods who had acquired more elaborate forms and greater geographical

74 *Theoretical considerations*

dispersion strengthened rulers' authority in religious, social and economic affairs. However, the unique ability of the ruler to mediate with the gods or 'superior ancestors' was not rooted in beliefs about divine descent – an essential component in the sacral kingship paradigm – but was accepted because the right to contact ancestors is, as a rule, confined to legal descendants. Ancestors innately held higher social status than living people, but those associated with the living ruler were also themselves seen as rulers and thus superior to others' ancestors. The socio-political agendas that seem to characterise early Norse societies make it possible to speak of religious ruler ideology, as the studies by Sundqvist and Schjødt, among others, amply demonstrate. However, I find that it was the society-wide reverence for ancestors that provided a foundation for this ideology. The fuzzy boundary suggested to have existed between pagan gods and human ancestors will inevitably take us to one more closely related academic theory – euhemerism.

4.2 Euhemerism – medieval propaganda or just history?

Euhemerism – where the origin of pagan gods is traced to the deification of historical human rulers – takes its name from the Greek writer Euhemerus of Messene, who lived in the late 4th century BC and took this approach to the classical Greek gods. Despite its origin in the distant pagan era, there is a long and complex history of euhemeristic interpretation which has many conflicting strands and which continues to the present day (see Seznec 1995: 11–13). A type of neo-euhemerism was introduced, for instance, in the late 19th century by Herbert Spencer, who argued that belief in gods is rooted in the worship of human kings. Spencer's euhemerism was criticised for its simplicity by some of his contemporaries, who saw ancestor cults as an exclusively domestic affair and who believed in the primacy of gods in ancient religions, although it was accepted that the theory of euhemerism itself arose as the natural reaction of people still familiar with ancestor worship (e.g. Hartland 1894: 203; Chisholm 1910: 207; Lang 1898: 275, 1913: 308–313). With the decline of evolutionary ideas, Spencer's euhemerism was generally forgotten, although later studies have emphasised the validity of this approach (e.g. Murphy 1949: 151; Littlewood 1998, 2001: 57–71; Goody 1962: 18–19; Littleton 2005: 302).

A period often mentioned in academic discussion of euhemerism is that of the conversion of Europe to Christianity, when the tendency to interpret pagan gods as men became particularly popular throughout the continent (Seznec 1995: 12–13). The humanisation of pagan gods made it possible to attack them as real historical individuals and in so doing to create a dichotomy between them and the Christian God. Medieval euhemerism has thus often come to be interpreted by scholars as an intellectual tool of early Christians who sought to explain pagan religion as a distorted historical phenomenon that contained no spiritual truth. Even though at first sight such an interpretation seems like a validation of paganism, almost a defence of the pagan gods and a condemnation of Christian authors for belittling them, the criticism is itself theocentric and conservative in character. What it suggests is that pagan gods – as metaphysical identities of some sort – did exist, but were humanised by propaganda-driven Christian authors. This means that the ideological dimensions of the god concept in pre-Christian religions are considered to be limited by scholars of Old Norse religion, and they are essentially imagined as similar to the Christian God. Similar attitudes prevail in the study of Old Norse religion, where euhemerised medieval genealogies are often explained as being rooted in conventional Christian ideas (e.g. Baetke 1964: 70–103; Krag 1991: 58–59).

The euhemeristic tradition is found in various Latin histories describing the early Germanic tribes as well as in medieval Icelandic accounts where the most widely known Nordic gods are presented as ancient human kings who had been turned into gods after death by their adherents.[4] Tacitus, for example, writes in his *Germania* (ch. 7, ed. p. 10, tr. p. 41) in the 1st century AD that the Germanic people chose their kings based on their noble birth, which is sometimes taken to indicate descent from a god, possibly Óðinn (e.g. Cusack 1998: 35–39), and the 6th-century historian Jordanes writes that the Goths – who in his understanding came from Scandinavia – traced their leaders back to Gapt who was revered as a god (Get chs 14–15, ed. p. 76, tr. p. 15) and who probably again refers to Óðinn (Birkhan 1965; Andersson 1996). Snorri uses this method in the prologue to *Snorra Edda* and in *Ynglinga saga* by presenting the *æsir* – led by Óðinn – as the (human) Trojan ancestors of several lineages of Scandinavian kings. Ari Þorgilsson's 12th-century *langfeðgatal* (Ísb pp. 27–28) also traces the author's own ancestry back to Yngvi, who is similarly presented as a human king of the Turks, and Snorri's prologue to *Heimskringla* traces the ancestry of the historical Norwegian Ynglingar family to Yngvifreyr. The typical recorded genealogy of the early medieval Nordic elite thus traces their ancestry to two main individuals: some sources go back to Yngvi, a character that occasionally merges with Freyr; in others, Óðinn assumes the role of initial ancestor. The scholarly tradition commonly associates Freyr with the Yngling family and Óðinn with the Háleygjar, although this division is often imprecise.

The tendency to euhemerise the pagan gods and to interweave them into human genealogies is often understood in scholarship as deriving either from the Icelandic authors' desire to imitate classical writings, from their conscious Christianity-driven attempt to explain and to disparage the pagan gods, or from the wish to promote their own social and economic interests by establishing a respectable family line. Although reasonable and justified – probably all contain some truth – none of these explanations considers the possibility that the gods could indeed have been imagined by the public – as well as the authors – as the real human ancestors of elite families at the time when the euhemerising works were written. This overprivileged view of the god concept is problematic in the light of typical folk religions where the distinction between gods and men is generally fluid. Even though we are dealing with inconsistent pseudo-histories in such cases, the genealogies reflect the current social values that supported the promotion and acceptance of the euhemerist theory. The Icelandic authors' familiarity with the erudite theories about prehistory – albeit demonstrating remarkable literary and cultural awareness – does not mean, as Schjødt (2010: 177–180) has pointed out, that the perception of pagan gods as men was not a natural part of paganism.

The foreign and native euhemerising accounts of Scandinavian rulers commonly refer to the gods as *deus* (pl. *dei*) or *goð* (pl. *goð*). Tacitus (Germ chs 2, 7 ed. pp. 4–5, 10, tr. pp. 38, 41) writes that Germanic peoples saw their tribal ancestors as *dei*, and according to Jordanes (Get chs 5–6, 14–15, ed. pp. 64, 67, 76, tr. pp. 9, 10, 15) the Goths worshipped some dead men as *semidei*. Rimbert (VA ch. 26, ed. p. 56, tr. pp. 89–90) depicts a dead Swedish king's transformation into one of the *dei* and Adam of Bremen notes in the 11th century (GH IV, ch. 26, ed. pp. 174–175, tr. p. 207) that blood sacrifices were given during a *blót* to the three *dei* Þórr, Óðinn and Freyr who were 'made of men' (*ex hominibus factos*). According to Snorri, Óðinn began being called a *goð* after he died (Yng ch. 7) and Njǫrðr and Freyr were turned into *blótgoða* ('sacrificial priests') (Yng ch. 4). Even though the deification of rulers could sometimes occur already in their lifetime according to the euhemerist theory (de Angelis and Garstad 2006: 219–221), the Old Norse gods seem to be identified mostly with dead humans in available descriptions.

Deification is of course a complex product of the human imagination and there is no manual that would help scholars determine the precise meaning that these characters, denoted by educated historians by the words *deus* or *goð*, had for the people who were engaged in religious activities. Prior to the association with the Christian God in Late Latin, the word *deus* was used as a generic term for 'deity' in the Greco-Roman polytheistic context – another highly ambiguous word whose possible references are never homogenous (Wood 1987: 264). The scholarly understanding of the beings whom the authors call *dei* as divine could thus derive chiefly from a later association of the word with Christian monotheism. Given the explanations that human aristocrats became worshipped 'as' gods, it is most likely that the authors themselves saw the gods as human (Lindow 2005: 36–37), and the consistent association of the *deus* and *goð* with earth, ancestors and gravemounds points in the same direction. According to Jordanes (Get ch. 6, ed. p. 67, tr. p. 10), for example, dead kings were sometimes worshipped as *numina* – someone with numinous powers – but the worship was conducted in ways which were equal to the commitment given to 'parents' (*parenti*). Thietmar of Merseburg (Chr I, ch. 17, ed. p. 11, tr. p. 80) writes that the people at Lejre gave the greatest sacrifices to the *dei* believing that these would 'do service for them with those who dwell beneath the earth' and according to *Vita Ansgarii* (ch. 26, ed. p. 56, tr. pp. 89–90) the *dei* whom a newly deceased king joined were the 'owners of the land' who quite literally inhabited the soil. Snorri (Hsg 14: 167–168), too, emphasises that the toasts made during a *blót* were reserved for Óðinn, Njǫrðr and Freyr, and for the *frændr framliðnir* ('passed kinsmen') in gravemounds. This practice was regularly prohibited by medieval Swedish and Norwegian laws (e.g. GL p. 9; GÞL p. 18; SC p. 430) and is mentioned in the kings' sagas (e.g. Yng ch. 40; Fsk 20: 124–125) and in poetry (e.g. Hhj prose following st. 30). Some sources, like *Guta saga* (pp. 4–5), which again states that people concurrently believed in gravemounds and gods, specify that ritual activities ranged from modest domestic offerings to communal sacrifices.

The indication here is probably that personal daily requests were addressed to one's own ancestors, while major requests, for things such as fertile lands or peace, were directed towards the ancestor gods of the ruling group – a feature not uncommon in societies where ancestors play an important role in religious life (Radin 1930: 54). The well-known 10th-century description of the human sacrifice among the Viking Rus by Ibn Fadlan (*Risala* pp. 17–18), too, suggests that the recipients of the slave in the otherworld were believed to be ancestors, not any god in particular (Ellis Davidson 1992: 338; cf. Price 2012a: 27). Even though some of the above-mentioned accounts, such as those by Adam and Rimbert, most likely used established euhemeristic patterns, the overall representation of the gods in the available descriptions suggests that people's perception of them was not far removed from that of dead ancestors.

* * * * *

As for the Old Norse equivalent, *goð* ('god'), it is believed to be the origin of the word *goði* (pl. *goðar*) 'chieftain or priest' (de Vries 2000: 181), and this connection has led many to believe that the *goðar* served a sacral function as cultic leaders before Christianity (e.g. Byock 1990: 59, 2002: 4; Sundqvist 2015: 56–57). The assumption thus again seems to be that *goð* refers to an ultimately different entity that existed prior to *goðar*, who, only due to their interaction with the *goð*, inherited a similar title. However, although an etymological connection exists between *goð* and *goði*, it is not obvious how and in which direction the meaning of these words developed. The *goðar* are mentioned primarily in the Icelandic context as governors of its administrative regions who sometimes undertook religious duties, suggesting this could be a later development. However, the word is found also in Scandinavian place names and runic inscriptions that go far back into the pre-Christian era, suggesting that this title and office are very old.[5] It is as likely that the regional chieftains were the *goð* to begin with, perhaps after they died, than that they inherited the title *goði* because they had a religious role as agents between the people and the *goð*. Njǫrðr and Freyr, often mentioned as *dei* together with Óðinn in the Latin sources and understood as Old Norse gods, were assigned the status of *blótgoða* (*Njǫrð ok Frey setti Óðinn blótgoða*; Yng ch. 4), an accusative plural form of *goði*. The meaning of and relationship between these words are unclear and open to interpretation.

With the above in mind, Icelandic authors were certainly influenced by the classical, learned prehistories in Europe and ecclesiastical as well as personal agendas were probably involved in the creation of their works. Snorri most likely had a political agenda of his own in *Heimskringla* (Bagge 1991; Sawyer 2008) and he was clearly familiar with the learned prehistories of the ancient Mediterranean world (e.g. descent from Troy). His texts, however, are recorded in Icelandic and concerned mainly with native traditions. It is possible that Snorri, like Ari fróði who is very likely to have followed the Venerable Bede in his vernacular historiography (Würth 2005), followed Latin models translated into the vernacular, since lost, or that his ideas were based on knowledge from vernacular preaching in churches (Faulkes 2012: 311). It is not known, however, that he used a specific Latin text for his euhemerism. In the light of other evidence such as early law texts which potentially provide the most realistic, albeit limited, vision of religious activities in Scandinavia and Iceland, it is possible that Snorri employed the learned euhemerism because the idea of gods as deceased human rulers was already present and deep-rooted in the consciousness of the Norsemen. If people were accustomed to constructing and expressing their identity through ancestry then euhemerism was a natural and straightforward way of depicting it. Driven by ulterior motives or not, the euhemerised genealogies would not have appeared so often unless the authors and their audiences accepted their legitimacy. It is doubtful that the euhemerism in the sources derives from medieval authors' inherent anti-paganism or that the gods at the top of family trees were perceived as anything but historical rulers, albeit with potentially overriding qualities and more far-reaching influence, given their identity as superior ancestors.

* * * * *

Sacral kingship or ruler ideology and euhemerism are like two sides of the same coin, and should not be approached as unrelated, as is sometimes done. Nordic rulers in the pre-Christian era might have been seen as possessing supernatural qualities of some sort; however, this is not necessarily attributable to belief in their divine or mythical origins. The unique abilities and privileges scholars associate with them, such as invoking the gods to ask for fertile land, peace or victory in war, can be attributed to their status as the legal descendants of superior ancestors – a phenomenon which intrinsically builds on the wider laws and regulations pertinent to other forms of ancestor ritual, with the exception of extension to the entire community. Anthropological studies show that genealogies in oral societies are inherently 'alive' and constantly adjusted according to present needs, serving particularly the purpose of promoting and securing the social status of present rulers. From this point of view, it might be said that every genealogy in the world is euhemerised; scholars simply do not always acknowledge the status of those farthest back in the lines as gods because they have not acquired high status and are thus unfamiliar with them. And yet this does not mean that the people and the rulers themselves did not come to believe in the veracity of the family trees. As an integral part of a general ancestor cult, the superior ancestor model also offers an explanation of why Old Norse rulers were venerated cheek by jowl with ancestors, and why their cults acquired a (quasi)public and community-wide status.

Icelandic historians may have utilised learned euhemerism in their writings in an attempt to imitate mainland European genealogical records. Unless these principles existed in their own society and were familiar to their audiences, however, this would have been an impossible task. The alleged 'euhemerism' in the sources probably abounds to a great extent with a genuine understanding of how gods were perceived by Scandinavians in the pre-Christian era. Seeing it as purely a political tool stems rather from modern-day audiences' habits and desires to maintain the ingrained romantic image of Vikings, Old Norse gods and myths portrayed in more recent times through literature – fictitious as well as academic – and visual media. In light of knowledge about the religious ideologies and practices of many folk religious societies, it is important to question the assumption that myths were turned into history and gods into men by learned authors; it might be just as reasonable to assume that humans and history existed prior to the creation of gods and myths. The understanding of gods in pre-Christian Scandinavia must be euhemeristic in its own right.

Social and religious contexts are never as simple and straightforward as the approach taken here perhaps suggests. With this reservation, it will be used as a theoretical framework for the case studies and the overall argument which follows. Combining the views of Sundqvist and Schjødt – who have taken a middle path between earlier polarised and often exaggerated theoretical positions – with the 'superior ancestor' hypothesis, I will discuss how ruler ideology was a natural part of pagan and early medieval Scandinavia, where it co-evolved and interacted with a pervasive ancestor cult. As the anthropologist Paul Radin (1930: 55) has put it, 'Where men can become gods so easily and mechanically, these same gods may likewise become men'.

Notes

1 A useful summary regarding the development of the theory and the different approaches can be found in Sundqvist (2002: 20–27).
2 The most discussed example of this kind is Dómaldi; see Ström (1968); Chaney (1970: 15, 20–21, 86); Lönnroth (1986); McTurk (1974–1977: 156–160); cf. Baetke (1964: 54–55); Abram (2011: 91–92).
3 Sundqvist's most recent and comprehensive publication dealing with ruler ideology is from 2015. However, as this book was not present during the earlier stages of the present work, references to his research are given on the basis of his earlier publications (e.g. 2002, 2012).
4 For discussion, see Faulkes (1978–1979); Beck (2000); Lindow (2005).
5 See references cited in Byock (1990: 59) and Sundqvist (2002: 77–79).

Secondary sources

Abram, Chris, 2011, *Myths of the pagan north: the gods of the Norsemen*, Continuum International Publishing Group, London and New York.
Andersson, Theodore, 1996, 'Götar, goter, gutar', *Namn och bygd*, vol. 84, pp. 5–21.
Baetke, Walter, 1964, *Yngvi und die Ynglinger. Eine quellenkritische Untersuchung über das nordische 'Sakral-köningtum'*. Sitzungsberichte der Sächsische Akademie der Wissenschaften zu Leipzig. Philologisch-historische Klasse: Sitzungsberichte, 109, 3. Akademie-Verlag, Berlin.
Bagge, Sverre, 1991. *Society and politics in Snorri Sturluson's Heimskringla*, University of California Press, Berkeley.
Beck, Heinrich, 2000, 'War Snorri Sturluson ein Euhemerist?' *Hesperides*, vol. 12, pp. 61–72.
Birkhan, Helmut, 1965, 'Gapt und Gaut', *Zeitschrift für deutsches Altertum*, vol. 94, pp. 1–17.
Brisch, Nicole (ed.) 2012 [2008], *Religion and power: divine kingship in the ancient world and beyond*. Oriental Institute Seminars, 4. The University of Chicago, Chicago.

80 Theoretical considerations

Byock, Jesse, 1990 [1988], *Medieval Iceland: society, sagas, and power*, University of California Press, Berkeley and Los Angeles.
Byock, Jesse, 2002, 'The Icelandic Althing: dawn of parliamentary democracy', in J. Fladmark (ed.), *Heritage and identity: shaping the nations of the north*, Donhead, Shaftesbury, pp. 1–18.
Chaney, William, 1970, *The cult of kingship in Anglo-Saxon England: the transition from paganism to Christianity*, University of California Press, Berkeley and Los Angeles.
Chisholm, Hugh (ed.) 1910, *Encyclopædia Britannica: a dictionary of arts, sciences, literature and general information*, II. 11th edition. Cambridge University Press, Cambridge.
Cusack, Carole, 1998, *Rise of Christianity in Northern Europe, 300–1000*, Cassell, London and New York.
de Angelis Franco, and Benjamin Garstad, 2006, 'Euhemerus in context', *Classical Antiquity*, vol. 25, no. 2, pp. 211–242.
de Maret, Pierre, 2011, 'Divine kings', in T. Insoll (ed.), *The Oxford handbook of the archaeology of ritual and religion*, University Press, Oxford, pp. 1059–1067.
de Vries, Jan, 1956, 'Das Königtum bei den Germanen', *Saeculum*, vol. 7, pp. 289–309.
de Vries, Jan, 2000 [1957–1960], *Altnordisches etymoligisches wörterbuch*, Brill, Leiden, Boston and Köln.
Ejerfeldt, Lennart, 1971, *Helighet, 'karisma' och kungadöme i forngermansk religion*. Skrifter utgivna av Religionshistoriska Institutionen, 7. Almqvist & Wiksells, Uppsala.
Ellis Davidson, Hilda, 1992, 'Human sacrifice in the late pagan period in North-Western Europe', in M. Carver (ed.), *The age of Sutton Hoo: the seventh century in North-Western Europe*, Boydell, Woodbridge, pp. 331–340.
Engnell, Ivan, 1943, *Studies in divine kingship in the ancient near east*, University of Uppsala, Uppsala.
Faulkes, Anthony, 1978–1979, 'Descent from the gods', *Medieval Scandinavia*, vol. 11, pp. 92–125.
Faulkes, Anthony, 2012 [2008], 'Snorri Sturluson: his life and work', in S. Brink and N. Price (eds.), *The Viking world*, Routledge, London and New York, pp. 311–314.
Frankfort, Henri, 1948, *A study of ancient near eastern religion as the integration of society & nature*, University of Chicago Press, Chicago.
Frankfort, Henri, 1951, *The problem of similarity in ancient near eastern religions*. The Frazer Lecture 1950. Clarendon Press, Oxford.
Frazer, James, 1890, *The golden bough: a study in magic and religion*, Macmillan & Co, New York and London.
Goody, Jack, 1962, *Death, property and the ancestors: a study of the mortuary customs of the Lodagaa of West Africa*, Stanford University Press, Stanford.
Grönbech, Wilhelm, 1931 [1909–1912], *The culture of the Teutons*, I, trans. W. Worster, Oxford University Press and Jespersen og pios forlag, London and Copenhagen.
Hallberg, Peter, 1966, 'Medeltidslatin och sagaprosa: Några kommentarer till Lars Lönnroths studier i den isländska sagalitteraturen', *Arkiv för nordisk filologi*, vol. 81, pp. 258–276.
Harrison, Jane, 1912, *Themis: a study of the social origins of Greek religion*, Cambridge University Press, Cambridge.
Hartland, Edwin, 1894, *Legend of Perseus: a study of tradition in story custom and belief*, David Nutt, London.
Hooke, Samuel, 1933, 'The myth and the ritual pattern of the ancient east', in S. Hooke (ed.), *Myth and ritual. Essays on the myth and ritual of the Hebrews in relation to the culture pattern of the ancient east*, Oxford University Press, London, pp. 1–14.

Krag, Claus, 1991, *Ynglingatal og Ynglingesaga: en Studie i historiske kilder*. Studia humaniora, 2. Rådet for humanistisk forskning, Oslo.

La Regalita Sacra: The Sacral Kingship. Contributions to the central theme of the VIIIth international congress for the history of religions. 1959. Studies in the History of Religions, 4. Brill, Leiden.

Lang, Andrew, 1898, *The making of religion*. Longmans, Green & Co., London, New York and Bombay.

Lang, Andrew, 1913 [1887], *Myth, ritual and religion*, I. Longmans, Green & Co, London, New York, Bombay and Calcutta.

Lindow, John, 2005 [1985], 'Mythology and mythography', in C. Clover and J. Lindow (eds.), *Old Norse-Icelandic literature: a critical guide*, University of Toronto Press, Toronto, pp. 21–67.

Littleton, Scott, 2005, *Gods, goddesses, and mythology*, 10. Marshall Cavendish, New York.

Littlewood, Roland, 1998, 'Living gods. In (Partial) defence of Euhemerus', *Anthropology Today*, vol. 14, no. 2, pp. 6–14.

Littlewood, Roland, 2001, *Religion, agency, restitution: the Wilde lectures in natural religion, 1999*, Oxford University Press, Oxford.

Lönnroth, Lars, 1986, 'Dómaldi's death and the myth of sacral kingship', in Lindow et al. (eds.), *Structure and meaning in Old Norse literature: new approaches to textual analysis and literary criticism*, Odense University Press, Odense.

Mannhardt, Wilhelm, 1875–1877, *Wald- und Feldkulte*, 2 vols, Gebrüder Borntraeger, Berlin.

McTurk, Rory, 1974–1977, 'Sacral kingship in ancient Scandinavia', *Saga-Book*, vol. 19, no. 2–3, pp. 139–169.

McTurk, Rory, 1994, 'Scandinavian sacral kingship revisited', *Saga-Book*, vol. 24, no. 1, pp. 19–32.

Murphy, John, 1949, *The origins and history of religions*, Manchester University Press, Manchester.

Nygaard, Simon, 2016, 'Sacral rulers in pre-Christian Scandinavia: the possibilities of typological comparisons within the paradigm of cultural evolution,' *Temenos*, vol. 52, no. 1, pp. 9–35.

Olsen, Magnus, 1909, 'Fra gammelnorsk myte og kultus', *Maal og Minne*, vol. 1, pp. 17–36.

Price, Neil, 2012, 'Mythic acts: material narratives of the dead in Viking Age Scandinavia', in C. Raudvere and J. P. Schjødt (eds.), *More than mythology: narratives, ritual practices and regional distribution in pre-Christian Scandinavian religions*, Nordic Academic Press, Lund, pp. 13–46.

Radin, Paul, 1930, 'Ancestor worship', in E. Seligman and A. Johnson (eds.), *Encyclopaedia of the social sciences*, II. The Macmillan Company, New York, pp. 53–55.

Robertson Smith, William, 1894 [1889], *Lectures on the religion of the Semites*, Adam & Charles Black, London.

Sawyer, Birgit, 2008, 'Snorri Sturluson's two horses', in Auður Magnúsdóttir et al. (eds.), *Vi ska alla vara välkomna!': nordiska studier tillägnade Kristinn Jóhannesson*, Meijbergs arkiv för svensk ordforskning, 35, Göteborg University, Göteborg, pp. 37–54.

Schjødt, Jens Peter, 2010, 'Ideology of the ruler in pre-Christian Scandinavia: mythic and ritual relations', *Viking and Medieval Scandinavia*, vol. 6, pp. 161–194.

Schröder, Franz, 1924, *Germanentum und Hellenismus. Untersuchungen zur germanischen Religionsgeschichte*, C. Winter, Heidelberg.

Schück, Henrik, 1904, *Studier i nordisk litteratur- och religionshistoria*, Gebers, Stockholm.

82 Theoretical considerations

Seznec, Jean, 1995 [1953], *The survival of the pagan gods: the mythological tradition and its place in renaissance humanism and art*. Originally published in French *La Survivance des dieux antiques*, 1940. Princeton University Press, Princeton.

Spencer, Herbert, 1851, *Social statics or, the conditions essential to human happiness specified, and the first of them developed*, John Chapman, London.

Steinsland, Gro, 1991, *Det hellige bryllup og norrøn kongeideologi: En analyse av hierogami-myten i Skírnismál, Ynglingatal, Háleygjatal og Hyndluljóð*, Solum, Oslo.

Steinsland, Gro, 2011, 'Origin myths and rulership. From the Viking Age ruler to the ruler of medieval historiography: continuity, transformations and innovations', in G. Steinsland et al. (eds.), *Ideology and power in the Viking and Middle Ages. Scandinavia, Iceland, Ireland, Orkney and the Faeroes*, Brill, Leiden and Boston, pp. 15–67.

Ström, Åke, 1959, 'The king god and his connection with sacrifice in Old Norse religion', in *The sacral kingship. Contributions to the central theme of the VIIIth international congress for the history of religions*. Studies in the History of Religions, 4. Brill, Leiden, pp. 702–715.

Ström, Folke, 1954, *Diser, norner, valkyrjor. Fruktberhetskult och sakralt kungadöme i norden*, Almqvist & Wiksell, Stockholm.

Ström, Folke, 1968, 'Kung Domalde i Svitjod och "kungalyckan"', *Saga och Sed*, vol. 34, pp. 52–66.

Ström, Folke, 1983, '*Hieros gamos*-motivet i Hallfreðr Óttarssons Hákonardrápa och den nordnorska jarlavärdigheten', *Arkiv för nordisk filologi*, vol. 98, pp. 67–79.

Sundqvist, Olof, 2002, *Freyr's offspring. Rulers and religion in ancient Svea society*, Uppsala Universitet, Uppsala.

Sundqvist, Olof, 2012, '"Religious ruler ideology" in pre-Christian Scandinavia. A contextual approach', in C. Raudvere and J. P. Schjødt (eds.), *More than mythology: narratives, ritual practices and regional distribution in pre-Christian Scandinavian religions*, Nordic Academic Press, Lund, pp. 225–261.

Sundqvist, Olof, 2015, *An arena for higher powers. Ceremonial buildings and religious strategies for Rulership in late Iron Age Scandinavia*, Brill, Leiden and Boston.

Turville-Petre, Gabriel, 1964, *Myth and religion of the north: the religion of ancient Scandinavia*, Greenwood Press, Connecticut.

von Friesen, Otto, 1932–1934, 'Har det nordiska kungadömet sakralt ursprung?' *Saga och Sed*, vol. 1, pp. 15–34.

Wessén, Elias, 1924, *Studier till Sveriges hedna mytologi och fornhistoria*. Uppsala Universitets Årsskrift. Almqvist & Wiksell, Uppsala.

Widengren, Geo, 1943, 'Det sakrala kungadömet bland öst- och västsemiter. Några synpunkter med anledning av ett nyutkommet arbete', *Religion och Bibel*, vol. 2, pp. 49–75.

Wood, Allen, 1987, 'Deity', in M. Eliade and C. Adams (eds.), *Encyclopedia of religion*, 4. Macmillan, New York.

Würth, Stefanie, 2005, 'Historiography and pseudo-history', in R. McTurk (ed.), *A companion to Old Norse-Icelandic literature and culture*, Blackwell, Malden, Oxford and Victoria, pp. 155–172.

Part 2
Case studies

5 Introduction to the case studies

The second part of this book consists of case studies that scrutinise the cults of named individuals in Scandinavia and Iceland as they are depicted in the literature. Reports documenting the cultic worship of specific people are limited, but they exist. As one might expect, the surviving literary examples of the worship of named individuals usually concern people who held influential positions in their lifetime, such as kings or local chieftains and the descriptions are always influenced by the attitudes, assumptions and goals of those who had them written. This investigation is primarily concerned with the content of texts that provide evidence of certain individuals being worshipped on a public scale as ancestors; the specific social and economic aspects of leadership in any specific context will not be analysed here. I treat all of the individuals in the following chapters as local elites: people seen as having more power and influence in society than others. A few words should therefore be said about the social and political contexts of pagan Scandinavia (especially Norway) and Iceland, the cultural settings of which help define most of the relevant content in available reports.

These societies differed from each other in terms of their organisation, and cultural and political structures.[1] The socio-political organisation of Iceland during the colonisation period (c. AD 871–930) was essentially tribal in character and scope. The settlers who came from various backgrounds – recent genetic studies show that the colonists had predominantly Norse origins although a considerable degree of the settlers' matrilineal ancestry is also Gaelic (Sunna Ebenesersdóttir et al. 2018) – were essentially self-sufficient and free to establish any law they saw fit to govern their newly established society. The rights of landowners in Norway and elsewhere in Scandinavia, on the other hand, who belonged to a historical and cultural continuum in which the expanding aristocracy played a crucial part, were more restricted (Byock 1990: 70–71). By AD 872, Haraldr hárfagri had formally subjugated most Norwegian petty kingdoms, and it is widely believed that some of the local chieftains who subsequently fell out of favour with Haraldr relocated to Iceland hoping to re-establish their independence and self-governance (Byock 1990: 54–55). Despite Haraldr hárfagri's position as king of a nation in the second half of the 9th century, the expansion of his authority in Norway was not a straightforward matter. Sources give inconsistent information concerning the chronology of his conquests, and it seems that his rule, especially in the northern parts of

Norway, was for a long period only formal while local chieftains continued to hold the real power. For example, Hákon Grjótgarðsson, the earl of Hlaðir in Trøndelag, whose family came from Hálogaland and whose grandson was Hákon Sigurðsson (later the archenemy of Haraldr's successor Óláfr Tryggvason), was probably in effect equally as powerful as Haraldr (Byock 1990: 53; Krag 2012: 647). It was not until the early 11th century that the unification of Norway – in parallel with the process of Christianisation advanced most actively by Haraldr's descendants Óláfr Tryggvason and Óláfr Haraldsson (alias Óláfr helgi) – took a single direction, and not until the 13th century that political stability was achieved (Krag 2012: 648). The same applies to Sweden, whose early society, despite some concentration of power around the 5th or 6th century, consisted of districts governed by independent petty kings; the description of the 9th-century king Erik in the Mälaren region which was dominated by Haraldr's rivals suggests that the king did not have absolute power, but was controlled by a public assembly (Sundqvist 2012: 246; Lindqvist 2012: 668–669). The development into a coherent political unit ruled by one king did not start there until the 12th century, again proceeding hand in hand with conversion and the rise of Christian monarchy (Line 2007; Lindqvist 2012: 668–669), and the same applies to Denmark (Gelting 2007). In this sense, the system of chieftaincies in Iceland during the settlement period was perhaps not so different from the situation in Scandinavia, at least with regard to farmers. It lacked, nonetheless, the same kind of historical and cultural depth, an executive legal system, the centralising tendencies of Haraldr and his followers and other military, political and religious pressures.

The fresh start and the apparent social equilibrium of Iceland's early society do not mean, of course, that social hierarchy was absent. A proportion of the settlers probably had poor economic status, and a considerable number, particularly those who came from Scotland and Ireland, are believed to have been brought along as slaves by the free farmers, many of whom were the descendants of wealthy and respected Norwegian chieftains (Sunna Ebenesersdóttir et al. 2018: 1030). It was not long until the local elite in Iceland started to reiterate and expand their authority and power. The need for a central decision-making unit led to the establishment of the Alþingi in 930 when the land, which was owned by independent farms scattered across the island, was divided into four administrative regions, each governed by nine effectively self-appointed *goðar* who settled regional disputes (Byock 1990: 58–76). The *goðar* usually belonged to groups of free-born men whose status was assured by respectable Norwegian ancestry and who were of similar political and social status. This administrative arrangement in Iceland lasted until the early 13th century when some dominant families fell into power struggles, which finally resulted in the acceptance of the supremacy of the Norwegian crown (Byock 1990: 70–76).

As was noted in Part 1, the role that ancestors and kinship played in pagan Scandinavian religions and inheritance laws was a critical one. The presence of pre-Christian burial mounds on family lands and knowledge about their inhabitants were solid proof that one's ancestors had owned particular parts of the land in the past. Even though Haraldr's taxation of the family lands held by petty kings, jarls and other independent landowners had already started to alter the long-standing *óðal* landholding system in the 9th century (Byock 1990: 53–54), there was no explicit rule on royal succession even in 11th- and 12th-century Norway (Krag 2012: 649) when it was still necessary to legitimise power according to pagan customs. This seems to be the purpose behind genealogical works such as *Ynglingatal*, *Ynglinga saga* and *Háleygjatal* among others, which will be discussed in the following chapters. Early Icelanders were naturally greatly influenced by their Norwegian roots when setting up their own government and legal system, and there is reason to believe that the time-honoured laws of inheritance were used as a basis for land ownership also in Iceland. However, for the settlers these ancestral markers were absent and alternative means had to be employed for securing claims over land possessions.

The cults of specific single individuals mentioned in the literature have been conventionally explained by scholars of Old Norse religion as offshoots of beliefs in the rulers' divine descent. They have often been fitted into the sacral kingship model discussed previously (see Chapter 4, Section 4.1), particularly the hárfagri dynasty and the jarls of Hlaðir. That sacral kingship itself is very likely to be an offshoot of general ancestor cults is often overlooked by scholars of Old Norse religion, whose interpretations were until recently more or less uniformly focused on Frazer's model. Emphasis has been mainly on myths and mythological elements (e.g. *hieros gamos*), consequently leading to the idea that the Nordic kings – several of whom initiated local cults – were believed to be of divine descent. The fact that the gods known from mythology (e.g. Freyr) are frequently presented as the human ancestors of later kings in the genealogical records and elsewhere in Old Norse literature is believed to derive from medieval authors' euhemerism and Christianity-driven agendas, not from social reality.

The following chapters consider the Old Norse evidence within the framework of the superior ancestor hypothesis outlined in Part 1. The available examples, however, are examined as case studies in their own right; each of these is designed to provide a synopsis of a range of elements suggestive of the idea that these individuals were seen and dealt with as once-living human ancestors rather than divinities, consequently supporting the overall argument that public offerings to prominent persons, too, were in effect ancestor cults, based on the values and principles of a typical kinship-based society. The discussion begins with the examination of cults in Sweden and Norway and then moves to Iceland. The present discussion is concerned with those cases which claim that specific individuals were worshipped publicly after death. I have excluded examination of other individuals who might also be important in the context of 'superior ancestors' (e.g. Freyja in connection with the *dísir* cult), but whose cults are not explicitly stated in the sources to have begun following their death.

Note

1 For further information about early society in Iceland, see Byock (1990, 2002); Leonard (2010); Jón Viðar Sigurðsson (2012). Concerning state formation in Scandinavia, see articles by Lindqvist, Krag and Roesdahl in Brink and Price (2012) and articles by Gelting, Bagge and Nordeide, and Blomkvist, Brink and Lindkvist in Berend (2007).

Secondary sources

Berend, Nora (ed.) 2007, *Christianization and the rise of Christian monarchy: Scandinavia, Central Europe and Rus' c. 900–1200*, Cambridge University Press, Cambridge.

Brink, Stefan, and Neil Price (eds.) 2012 [2008], *The Viking world*, Routledge, London and New York.

Byock, Jesse, 1990 [1988], *Medieval Iceland: society, sagas, and power*, University of California Press, Berkeley and Los Angeles.

Byock, Jesse, 2002, 'The Icelandic Althing: dawn of parliamentary democracy', in J. Fladmark (ed.), *Heritage and identity: shaping the nations of the north*, The Heyerdahl Institute and Robert Gordon University. Donhead, Shaftesbury, pp. 1–18.

Gelting, Michael, 2007, 'The kingdom of Denmark', in N. Berend (ed.), *Christianization and the rise of Christian monarchy: Scandinavia, central Europe and Rus' c. 900–1200*, Cambridge University Press, Cambridge, pp. 73–120.

Jón Viðar Sigurðsson, 2012 [2008], 'Iceland', in S. Brink and N. Price (eds.), *The Viking world*, Routledge, London and New York, pp. 571–578.

Krag, Klaus 2012 [2008], 'The creation of Norway', in S. Brink and N. Price (eds.), *The Viking world*, Routledge, London and New York, pp. 645–651.

Leonard, Stephen, 2010, 'Social structures and identity in early Iceland', *Viking and medieval Scandinavia*, vol. 6, pp. 147–159.

Lindqvist, Thomas, 2012 [2008], 'The emergence of Sweden', in S. Brink and N. Price (eds.), *The Viking world*, Routledge, London and New York, pp. 668–674.

Line, Philip, 2007, *Kingship and state formation in Sweden, 1130–1290*. The Northern World, 27. Brill, Leiden.

Sundqvist, Olof, 2012, 'Religious ruler ideology in pre-Christian Scandinavia. A contextual approach', in C. Raudvere and J. P. Schjødt (eds.), *More than mythology: narratives, ritual practices and regional distribution in pre-Christian Scandinavian religions*, Nordic Academic Press, Lund, pp. 225–261.

Sunna Ebenesersdóttir et al., 2018, 'Ancient genomes from Iceland reveal the making of a human population', *Science*, vol. 360, pp. 1028–1032.

6 Erik of Birka

The description of Erik on the island of Björkö (ON Birka) on Lake Mälaren is one of the earliest surviving descriptions of a public cult dedicated to a deceased king in Scandinavia. According to this Latin source, the king was accepted as one of their gods by the community and he received sacrifices in a temple that was built for him. The description is short and does not contain much detail with regard to how or how widely the rituals were carried out or what motivated them. However, there are aspects, alongside other evidence, which support the proposed theory of superior ancestors: sacrifices which only start after the death of the king, the king being incorporated into the ranks of the 'gods' who are the owners of the land, the cult-house-type construction that might relate directly to gravemounds, and the ceremonial journey taken by new rulers to legitimise their power, whose name *eriksgata* might derive from a that of a line of kings in that area. These facts lend support to the hypothesis of a superior ancestor cult in Late Iron Age and early medieval Scandinavia.

The earliest description of a cult dedicated to a historical king in Birka – an important trade centre that existed in Lake Mälaren in Sweden from c. 750 to 975 (Ambrosiani 2012) – is given in *Vita Ansgarii*, the hagiography of Saint Ansgarius written in the 9th century by his disciple and hagiographer Rimbert.[1] According to this text, a king named Erik was transformed into a *deus* ('god') after he died. The country had long enjoyed happiness and prosperity under Erik's rule and protection, and it was therefore considered necessary to honour the king with offerings in order to retain this good fortune after his death. According to Rimbert, a certain man who felt particularly unfavourable towards the approaching Christian religion insisted that he had been present at a meeting of the old gods (*dei*), and he announced it to be their wish that Erik be worshipped as one of them (VA ch. 26, ed. p. 56; tr. pp. 89–90).[2] It is said that by the time Ansgarius arrived in Birka, a temple had been built for Erik where sacrifices were offered to him. While lacking detail, this concise report lends considerable support to the general hypothesis of the existence of a superior ancestor cult in pre-Christian Scandinavia.

Discussion of the cults of dead rulers by scholars of Old Norse religion has commonly, as mentioned previously, revolved around the question of whether these rulers were regarded as divine or not by the people, whether they played a role in a fertility cult, and whether they should consequently be interpreted as sacral kings. Erik, whose reign according to Rimbert brought his people bountiful harvests and who therefore became a local cult figure, has also been associated with sacral kingship (e.g. de Vries 1956; Ström 1959; Turville-Petre 1964: 195; Ström & Biezais 1975). However, the account contains no allusions to phenomena regarded as most characteristic of sacral kingship in the earlier debates, such as the *hieros gamos* or the sacrifice of living rulers, nor is there a genealogical record tracing Erik's ancestry to any specific god known from the mythological tradition. It was therefore incorporated into the general theory to a much lesser extent than the accounts of the Ynglingar or the Háleygjar which will be discussed in subsequent chapters. However, scholars at this time were eager to seek out any features that would bolster the 'sacral kingship' hypothesis. For example, attempts were made to prove that Erik himself was an ancient Indo-European god by tracing the name *Erik* or *Erich* from Old Norse *Eiríkr* < *einrikr*, from Old Swedish *AinarikijaR ('alone powerful'); it was seen further as cognate with the Bavarian and Austrian word for Tuesday *ertag, eritag, erchtag* < Erichtag. Further links with the Alemannic *Zistac* < *Tiwaz-dag ('god-day') led to the hypothesis that *Einrikr* may have been a byname for *Tiwaz*, Proto Indo-European *deiuos ('deity', 'god') (Ström Å. & Biezais 1975: 161–163). It was not until after Baetke (1964) challenged the entire sacral kingship theory that the description of Erik came to be considered in any way other than as a divine king or a god.

As mentioned in Chapter 4, Baetke argued that the various sacral kingship hypotheses were based on sources heavily influenced by learned Christian euhemerism and therefore lacked foundation. Since Rimbert's report, too, is a clerical piece and represents the views of a Frankish-born archbishop, Baetke assumed that the part about Erik's deification was the result of the author's misunderstanding; the cult may have been created by pagan Swedes as a counterreaction to the Christian mission with the purpose of demonstrating to the missionaries that they already had gods that were equal to Christ (Baetke 1964: 47–51). The interpretation of the story as a 'mock' cult seems far-fetched and improbable; however, Baetke rightly highlights that Erik is depicted simply as a human by Rimbert. In the report he is indeed presented as a king to whom people started to give votive offerings and sacrifices 'as a god' (*tanquam deo*) only after his death (VA ch. 26, ed. p. 56; tr. p. 90), a comment which as Sundqvist (2002: 290) notes would have been unnecessary had Erik been perceived as such already in his lifetime. Considering that Ansgarius arrived in Birka after the king's death – following a short visit about 20 years earlier – he may have been unaware of the precise treatment received by Erik as a living king; however, based on other similar instances from early Scandinavia, as well as evidence from more contemporary ethnic groups, there is no valid reason to think that living kings were considered god-like. If aspects of the cult were exaggerated by Rimbert in the report, they sprung from his wish to reinforce the mission's importance by showing that the people in Birka were in dire need of religious assistance and thus encourage his fellow missionaries to travel to the potentially perilous north (Sundqvist 2002: 290; Palmer 2004: 239, 247).

Like Baetke, Sundqvist points out that Rimbert may have employed euhemerism in his description, especially since Adam of Bremen, who refers to Ansgarius' report in the *Gesta Hammaburgensis* (IV, ch. 26, ed. p. 175; tr. p. 207), also states that the Swedes worshipped gods made from people (*deos ex hominibus factos*) – a phrase used widely in works by medieval Christians as it provided a precedent for condemning pagan gods as false idols.[3] Rimbert was Ansgarius' disciple and successor as archbishop of the Hamburg–Bremen diocese, founded specifically to convert the northern world and to claim ecclesiastical authority there. His outlook in the *vita* is hagiographic; some theological–political as well as personal motivations have indeed been identified in his work (see Palmer 2004: 239–242; Mellor 2008). At the same time, the description of Erik's cult in the *Vita Ansgarii* (as opposed to in the work of Adam who merely quotes this work about 200 years later) is likely based on first-hand observation and not a retelling of Ansgarius' experience (Palmer 2004: 238). This does of course not prove that Rimbert did not use euhemerism; however, if he was personally familiar with the indigenous religious substratum in which ancestors clearly mattered, then the cults around rulers were by nature euhemeristic. The Christian agenda behind this historical account is not an indication that the cult of Erik was not real, like Baetke believed, but neither does this mean that the inhabitants of Birka perceived Erik as a god, like Ström and Biezais proposed. Rimbert himself does not use the conventional 'gods made from men' phrase and calls the *dei* the 'owners of this land' (*terram incolatus*) (VA ch. 26, ed. p. 56; tr. p. 89). Alongside the fact that the *dei* were seen by their audiences as disposed to accept humans among their company, this explanation suggests rather that the *dei* whom Erik joined were the former rulers of that area – Erik's predecessors – who had owned the land and who now quite literally inhabited the earth.

The proposed etymology connecting *Erik* with Proto Indo-European *deiuos is far-fetched and obscure; however, Ström and Biezais may have been on the right track when connecting it with *einrikr* ('alone powerful') and assuming that the name carried a special meaning for the people in Birka. For example, Sundqvist (2001: 633–637, 2002: 155–156, 311) has proposed that the name *Erik* or *Erich*, which was used as a personal name for kings since the 8th or 9th century and possibly even earlier, may have been a general epithet for rulers.[4] Giving a ruler a specific name steeped in tradition is not uncommon and it was probably also an important element in pre-Christian Germanic kingship (see Chaney 1970: 22; Uspenskij 2011). Modern naming customs, particularly those of royal families, may simply follow convention; in earlier times, however, passing down names from progenitors to descendants was intended to strengthen bonds between past ancestors and future generations, and encapsulated the idea of rebirth. Belief in rebirth is a global feature that exists in many religions and it is also strongly attested in Scandinavia's neighbouring Arctic and Finno–Ugric cultures (Bäckman 1975: 124).[5] Pre-Christian Norse name-giving traditions are not clearly attested, although *Gísla saga* (ch. 18) states that children's names were changed if they had been named after a relative whose characteristics did not match with those of the child (when they grew), and *Njáls saga* (ch. 42) contains a part of a proverb, which has survived to this day, according to which one-quarter of a person is the name, while the rest is parents and foster parents; the qualities associated with the name, then, likely also refer to more distant ancestral relationships.[6] There is thus reason to believe that ideas similar to those in neighbouring groups, and especially the Sámi, also existed in Scandinavia and that these naming conventions extended naturally also to rulership. This is suggested in some sources (e.g. Þþb ch. 5), with the most remarkable example found in the story of Ólafr Geirstaðaálfr of Norway, whose grandchild inherits his name and through this act also some of his qualities (Flat II, pp. 7–9; SÓkhh pp. 726, 735; see Heinrichs 1993). The shared name of successive rulers probably helped construct affinity between them and also transferred a degree of authority to the living ruler, perhaps even more so at the time when succession to power was not inherited through direct descent. Sundqvist's suggestion that the name *Erik* was a general appellation for rulers is intuitively appealing and, if this suggestion is accepted, such a title must have held special allure for Birka's inhabitants, although perhaps not in the same sense or to the same degree as Ström and Biezais's etymological arguments suggest. It is worth mentioning here that a particular 'Erik' has also survived in Scandinavian folklore – a devil-like character named Gammel-Erik ('Old Eric'), who is associated with the *oskoreia* motif widely known in Norway and in parts of Sweden during the Middle Ages and onwards (Birkeli 1944: 174). A direct association with Rimbert's Erik (e.g. Grimm 1882: 235; Palmer 1910: 546–547) is unlikely; however, considering that the *oskoreia* crowds – dead people that arise from gravemounds or appear from mountains at Yule time and overcome the farms – are believed to be a remnant of earlier customs revolving around ancestors, it is quite possible that they could be seen in some places as being commanded by caricatures of former pagan rulers who had received cultic honours in their gravemounds.

The idea that *Erik* may have been a general title for rulers is supported perhaps most clearly by the protracted inauguration ceremony known as *eriksgata* ('Erik's path'), which newly elected kings were required to undergo in Sweden according to some medieval laws (see Sundqvist 2001; Line 2007: 197–205). Tenuous associations have been made between this custom and Rimbert's Erik, on the grounds of his being one of the first known kings with this name (e.g. Grimm 1882, I: 360–361; Hultgård 1992: 73). With the idea of a symbolic title for rulers in mind, it would be rational to link the origins of this tradition with rulership more generally, rather than to one specific historical figure. The precise age of this legal process is unknown; however, it is probably a pre-Christian concept (Sundqvist 2001: 634–635) and is known to have lasted until at least the mid-16th century, when royal succession became hereditary and replaced the prior election of kings, consequently transforming the *eriksgata*'s former literal function into a symbolic one.[7] The word *gata* means 'path' and the election ceremony, which started on the Mora stone in Uppland near the south-east coast of Sweden, continued literally as a route through the surrounding districts where local *þing* assemblies could accept or reject the election.[8] The route usually passed by ancient runestones and gravemounds and culminated at the central provincial *þing* sites, which were used for public announcements. Stefan Brink (2004a: 309–312; 2004b) has drawn attention to the landscape features shared by these sites: waterways crossing old paths, rows of memorial stones leading to the site and an ancient large gravemound with a standing stone at the centre. As Brink (2004a: 308–313) argues, these places probably functioned as intersections between the people, gods and ancestors who sanctioned society's customs and whose approval was considered important for the legislation of power. The ancestors buried inside the graves thus quite literally escorted the new ruler along the path to the central gravemound which ostensibly contained the predecessors of the most prominent families – the superior ancestors according to this study's hypothesis.[9] Archaeological excavations have indicated uninterrupted long-term use of burial sites in Sweden (e.g. Baudou 1989; Arrhenius 1990; Zachrisson 1994; Artelius 2000, 2004), and this is also visible in Birka – one of the three great mounds in the Ormknös cemetery was in use from the early Roman Iron Age until the Viking Age, probably symbolising affinity with former ancestors (Arrhenius 1990: 74). Rimbert's *dei*, too, may well represent the ancestors of those who held power in that locality and whose physical gravemounds played a role in legitimising ownership of the land and securing continuity, as well as perhaps fertility in a wider sense.[10]

That gravemounds operated as genealogical markers in eastern Sweden is not as clearly attested in literature as it is in Norway, where genealogies, as mentioned earlier (see Section 1.1.5), were reckoned *til haugs ok heiðni*. Indications of such a custom, however, are found in runic inscriptions, skaldic poetry and archaeological evidence (Sundqvist 2002: 151–156). Medieval Swedish laws (e.g. Sml p. 110) also state that burials in old graves were confined to the members of the kin group, implying a strong sense of genealogical unity. More often than not, the surviving descriptions link public cults of individuals in Scandinavia to gravemounds. The offerings to Erik however were, according to Rimbert, brought to a *templum* ('temple') that was built explicitly for him after his death.[11] As a Christian missionary, Rimbert obviously employed a term familiar to him to describe the cult site. However, in the modern use of the term, 'temple' is again inextricably linked to the idea of a sanctuary for God, and this has probably again contributed to the often-prevalent understanding of the *dei* as something more than human ancestors. The pagan Scandinavian and Icelandic equivalent that abounds in the vernacular literature – *hof* – has various designations (see below), but as a rule, appears to be bound to gravemounds, thereby supporting the assumption that the cult of Erik reflects the superior aspects of a general ancestor cult. Due to the world-religious connotations of the word 'temple' in modern English, *hof* has usually been translated as 'cult house' or 'cult building' in recent scholarship (e.g. Sundqvist 2009a; Gräslund 2012: 249–253). I will briefly mention some additional facts about these *hof* structures, which have been subject to quite extensive debate in research and which shed some light on the building Rimbert describes.[12]

The Latin term *templum* corresponds broadly with the Old Norse word *hof*; for example, Adam of Bremen calls the religious centre of Gamla Uppsala a *templum* (GH IV, ch. 26, ed. pp. 174–175; tr. p. 207), while Snorri talks about this place as *hof* (Hsg ch. 14) (see Section 7.2.1). Following a comprehensive study by the

94 Case studies

Danish archaeologist Olaf Olsen (1966), which found that *hof* may refer simply to the dwellings of local chieftains in major farm houses that were used also for public religious ceremonies, the existence of separate purpose-built cult houses, such as the one Rimbert mentions, came to be questioned for some decades. Recent archaeological excavations, however, have brought to light fresh evidence and have shown that individual cult houses – sometimes enclosed and usually located near large halls – did already exist in late Iron Age Scandinavia (e.g. Vikstrand 2001: 256–258; Jørgensen 2002; Söderberg 2005). The precise meaning of *hof* is still considered uncertain by reason of its varied uses in the literature (Brink 1996; Vikstrand 2001; Gunnell 2001; Orri Vésteinsson 2007); as one study has shown, it can be used variously to refer to large or small halls, rooms, cultic objects, a type of architecture and structures where cult leaders were present (Sundqvist 2009a: 74–75).[13]

The word *hof* itself might have roots in a related word in west Norwegian dialects where it has the meaning of 'height' or 'small hill', and place names containing this element are found copiously in both Scandinavia and Iceland, suggesting that these localities were in regular and widespread use and probably had cultic significance (Brink 1990: 460–474, 1996: 260–261; Vikstrand 2001: 253).[14] It is thus possible – and even probable – that *hof* had a fundamental connection to gravemounds. That cult buildings may at some point have been erected on top of mounds, thus altering the meaning of the word *hof*, might be suggested by the 9th-century inscription of the Danish Snoldelev memorial runestone, which – albeit not mentioning *hof* – contains the word *salhauku(m)* ('on the hall of mounds') (see Brink 1996: 256–258; Sundqvist 2009b: 660), as well as by the word's recurring relationship with *hǫrgr* (e.g. Vþm 38, Vsp 7, Hhj 4; SC p. 430; GÞL p. 18), another exceedingly hazy term that has its own associations with gravemounds. Its designations, like those of *hof*, include a high wooden construction or cult building, an altar inside a *hof*, a stone heap, a mountain or other natural formations, and related words in other Germanic languages have various meanings such as 'height', 'rocky ground', 'cairn', 'mountain with steep sides and flat top', etc. (Heide 2014). Early medieval law texts frequently prohibit the worship at *hauga ok hǫrga* ('gravemounds and *hǫrgar*'), implying their connection to each other and demonstrating their prominence even as late as the 13th century.

Archaeologists have suggested that the small cult houses that have been recovered in the last few decades could be identified as *hǫrgar* (e.g. Jørgensen 2002; Söderberg 2005: 109, 195–196), but the idea has not found much support. Generally scholars agree with Olsen (1966: 105–106, 110, 281–282) that *hǫrgr* was at least originally a stone heap outdoors that functioned as a sacrificial altar (Hultgård 1996: 29–30; Sundqvist 2009a); this interpretation is based chiefly on *Hyndluljóð* (st. 10) according to which a *hǫrgr* was built to a dead woman and was made of piled-up stones that were reddened with blood. If this source is to be trusted, then *hǫrgr* seems to represent a more primitive outside structure than *hof* and it would be logical to assume that cultic rituals outdoors preceded activities inside actual cult houses. Other written sources, as was mentioned earlier, contradict this information and suggest that *hǫrgr* in Old Norse literature could be a gravesite, an altar, an altar inside a house or even a separate house (Røthe 2007: 49–51; Heide 2014).[15] The practice of entering a coffin into a wooden box with windows or building a small 'house' above the grave is widespread among Finno–Ugric groups (e.g. the Sámi, Holmberg 1964: 31–32) and is still alive in northern Russia's rural areas (Rybakov 1987: 108–109; Zelenin 1991: 348; Jordan 2003: 222). Such constructions are not a far cry from the one in the description of Freyr in Gamla Uppsala who around the 5th or 6th century received offerings in his *haugr* through windows and who was later worshipped inside a large *hof* (Yng 10: 23–25).

We could perhaps draw on the idea of sequential development here, made previously by Olsen (1966: 281–282), that over time the initial outdoor stone altars in Scandinavia developed into small wooden shelters without walls and then actually into small and sometimes large buildings. At the latest by the 13th century, when anyone who 'piles up a gravemound or builds a house and calls it *hǫrgr*' (*lœðr hauga eða gerer hús ok kallar hǫrg*) became legally bound to 'forfeit every coin of their property' (SC p. 430). Overall, however, we must settle for relative uncertainty regarding the precise meaning, function and scope of these structures at any specific time-period, if such clear-cut definitions ever existed. It is most likely that *hǫrgr* and *hof* coexisted for some time (Kaliff 2011: 56–57) and interacted with each other over time. The only aspect which seems certain at the present state of research is that both had cultic significance and that both were associated with gravemounds. We may not be able to reconstruct the exact appearance or function of the *templum* described in *Vita Ansgarii*, but we are justified in believing – on the basis of what is known about cult-house-type structures in early Scandinavia – that it was not merely the fruit of the author's fantasy or ecclesiastical propaganda. Man-made buildings of worship existed, and were in all probability dedicated to the foremost individuals or kin groups after their death. It is likely that they grew out of the general custom of raising altars or other less prominent structures on gravemounds as part of a general ancestor cult.

* * * * *

Vita Ansgarii is a hagiography. As such, its primary purpose was not to provide a detailed and truthful account of the life of Saint Angarius, nor to describe the Scandinavian religious landscape (beyond emphasising the need for conversion), but to provide a model for living the Christian life, to popularise the faith and to propagate the archbishop's rights and supremacy over the North. The source certainly contains polemic elements, but it is an important document composed by a man whose existence has been verified historically. Considering the purpose and background of the author, this source in some ways outweighs its vernacular counterparts in value. The agendas behind the Old Norse–Icelandic genealogical accounts which occasionally comment on public cults are believed to have often been preoccupied with the scribes' desire to trace their own ancestry from the kin groups they depict and to thereby boost their personal genealogical authority (e.g. the Ynglingar, see Chapter 7); this might have motivated them to exaggerate the degree to which these individuals were worshipped. Rimbert had no such purpose when depicting Erik; he may have had other great ambitions when accompanying Ansgar, as the missions eventually led to him being granted the archbishopric of Hamburg–Bremen; however, there is no evident reason why his descriptions of Birka, including that of Eric's cult, would have been unrealistically extravagant, let alone entirely invented.

The *vita* suggests that sacrifices to dead members of aristocratic lineages were not uncommon in 9th-century Sweden and that these cultic activities took place on a public scale. There is no mention of sacrifices or any special honours taking place in the king's lifetime; the initiative behind these activities seems to be connected solely to his death, that is to say, to his promotion to a different rank inherently connected to the realm of ancestors. The *templum* erected for the recently deceased king probably also represents an actual pagan cult building intimately linked to ritual activities performed at gravemounds. Considering that rulers at that time were elected (albeit from a select circle), rulership may have been reinforced by giving them a joint title *erik* 'alone powerful' saturated by tradition; this might also be manifested in the *eriksgata* procession. The spatial structure of the physical environment where the *eriksgata* route passed indicates again that ancestors of both the common and elite social classes were vital witnesses to such processions. We have previously discussed the innate ties of local gods to ancestors in traditional societies, as well as people's attachment to and rights over the physical locations where those ancestors are buried, both in Scandinavia and across the globe. Rimbert's understanding of the *dei*, whom he identifies as the owners of this part of the land and who readily accept a new human king as one of them in the eyes of the Birka inhabitants, does not point to sacral kingship. It is rather, as some authors (e.g. Sundqvist 2002: 153–155), and archaeologists in particular (e.g. Kaliff 1997: 72–73; Gräslund 2001: 225), have already noted, to be associated with the practice of ancestor worship. Representing the ancestors of Erik (and of other individuals bound artificially into the ruling kin group in that area), the *dei* were known and acknowledged by the entire community. It is, however, unlikely that they were perceived as 'gods' in the modern sense of the word; Rimbert's description of the cult fits well into the superior ancestor hypothesis and affirms the existence of this politico-religious form of ancestor worship in pre-medieval and early medieval Scandinavia.

Notes

1 A useful discussion of the background and purpose of this source can be found in Palmer (2004) and Mellor (2008).
2 The message of the gods declared the following: *Si itaque nos vobis propitious habere vultis, sacrificial omissa augete et vota maiora persolvite. Alterius quoque dei culturam, qui contrarian obis docet, ne apud vos recipiatis et eius servicio ne intendatis. Porro, si etiam plures deos habere desiderates, et nos vobis non sufficimus, Ericum quondam regem vestrum nos unanimes in collegiums nostrum asciscimus, ut sit unus de numero deorum* (If you desire to enjoy our goodwill, offer the sacrifices that have been omitted and pay greater vows. And do not receive the worship of any other god,

who teaches that which is opposed to our teaching, nor pay any attention to his service. Furthermore, if you desire to have more gods and we do not suffice, we will agree to summon your former King Eric to join us so that he may be one of the gods) (VA ch. 26, ed. p. 56; tr. pp. 89–90).

3 Adam of Bremen refers to *Vita Ansgarii* in his description of the Swedes: *Colunt et deos ex hominibus factos, quos pro ingentibus factis immortalitante donant, sicut in Vita sancti Anscarii leguntur Hericum regem fecisse* (The people also worship heroes made gods, whom they endow with immortality because of their remarkable exploits, as one reads in the *Vita* of Saint Ansgar they did in the case of king Eric) (GH IV, ch. 26, ed. p. 175; tr. p. 207).

4 Sundqvist (2002: 155–156) draws attention to the fact that three out of the four Birka rulers mentioned by Rimbert have alliterative names and that a similar structure is seen on the Sparlösa runestone (c. 800).

5 Children's characteristics and responses may be observed before naming to determine which of the ancestors has been reborn (Mancini Billson & Mancini 2007: 86), names can be changed if children fall ill (this being a sign that a wrong name had been chosen and that a specific ancestor wishes to be reborn) (Kildal, cited in Reuterskiöld 1910: 93–94; Bäckman & Hultkrantz 1978: 62, notes 55, 103), and children can be given names only after the mother dreams of a specific ancestor or if a religious leader carries out an act of prophecy that reveals which of the dead relatives wants to be reborn (Karjalainen 1918: 39, 45–46; DuBois 1999: 75).

6 *Njáls saga* states simply that one-fourth of a child's personage is made of the qualities and characteristics of foster parents. The modern Icelandic proverb adds that one-quarter of a person is the father, and another quarter the mother, one-quarter of a man are those who bring you up, and one-quarter is the name (Jónas Jónasson 1961: 264; Sölvi Sveinsson 1995).

7 The last recorded instance of the journey is from the 15th century: *Privilegia vero ecelesiarum cathedralium & statua provincialia generose confirmavit & sigillavit in equitatu, qui dicitur Eriksgata. [...] Rex Christoferus Sveciæ & Daciæ equitatum fecit, qui dicitur Eriksgata, fecundum lum leges patriæ [...]* (But the privileges of the Dome Church and the provincial laws he [Kristofer] confirmed and sealed willingly under the royal riding tour that is called *Eriksgata*. [...] Kristofer, the King of Sweden and Denmark made the royal ride called *Eriksgata*, according to the laws of the country.) (DV, p. 86).

8 The journey was potentially perilous – one early 12th-century ruler is reported to have been murdered during the tour for ignoring the custom of taking along hostages from prominent families in order to pledge their loyalty (Vgl, pp. 300–301). See Sundqvist (2001: 633–637).

9 Þing mounds may also have been purpose-built, as some of them contain no burial (e.g. Allerstav et al 1991: 38–42, 124).

10 Scholars in the late 19th century were keen on linking *eriksgata* with 'the great road of King Oree' known widely in Manx folklore (e.g. Grimm 1882: 234–235, 360–361; Moore 1891: 10–12, 190; Kermode 1904: 13; Palmer 1910: 546–548). The semi-mythical Oree or Orry was linked etymologically with Erik and in turn identified with Rígr – a byname for Heimdallr, who guards the path by which the gods descend to earth in Old Norse mythology. These folk-etymological constructions are far-fetched and contentious; however, it is noteworthy that Orry is commonly identified with Guðrøðr Crovan, an 11th-century Norse–Gaelic ruler who inherited this name after conquering the Isle of Man in 1079 and who is believed to have established the Manx legal system. Viking settlements are known to have existed on the island from the 9th century and Guðrøðr's descendants ruled there until the mid-13th century; the long-term Norwegian rule left behind a considerable legacy, including the island's most distinctive landmark – Tynwald Hill (from ON 'Þingvǫllr') – a *þing* mound which is traditionally believed to have been built with stones and soil from all the island's parishes,

surrounded by ancient graves (including a megalithic chambered mound known in legend as the grave of King Orry) and accompanied by a route known as the Royal Road (see Darvill 2004; McDonald 2007; McDonald 2012: 19–21, 166–170). Many of the elements are reminiscent of ruler-making traditions in the Scandinavian context.

11 *Nam et templum in honore supra dicti regis dudum defuncti statuerunt et ipsi tanquam deo vota et sacrificia offerre coeperunt* (for they had resolved to have a temple in honour of the late king, and had begun to render votive offerings and sacrifices to him as to a god) (VA ch. 26, ed. p. 56; tr. p. 90).

12 See also Brink (1996).

13 The existence of purpose-built cult houses does not mean, of course, that farmhouses may not have been used for religious activities like Olsen argued; the dual function of chieftains' dwellings has also been discussed more recently by Terry Gunnell (2001), who has convincingly argued that they functioned also as microcosms where enactments of scenes from Old Norse poetry helped promote the chieftain's religious authority in the eyes of local communities.

14 E.g. *Frøyshov* 'Freyr's *hof*' (c. 400–1100) (see Sundqvist 2009a: 68).

15 *Vǫluspá* (st. 7), for example, notes that both *hǫrgr* and *hof* were 'high and made of wood' (*hátimbruðu*); this harmonises with the high-timbered *hǫrgr* mentioned also in *Grímnismál* (st. 16), as well as the *hof* in *Eyrbyggja saga* (ch. 4), which was a 'great house', and in *Vatnsdœla saga* (ch. 4) where a *hof* is said to have been a hundred feet long. *Gylfaginning* (ch. 14), too, states that a *hof* was made for the *æsir* and a *hǫrgr* for the *ásynjur* and both were beautiful houses (*hús*).

Secondary sources

Allerstav, Agneta et al., 1991, *Fornsigtuna. En kungsgårds historia*, Stift Upplands-BroFornforskning, Upplands-Bro.

Ambrosiani, Björn, 2012 [2008], 'Birka', in S. Brink and N. Price (eds.), *The Viking world*, Routledge, London and New York, pp. 94–100.

Arrhenius, Birgit, 1990, 'Utgrävningen av den östligaste storhögen på gravfältet Ormknös, Raä 111, Björkö, Adelsön, Uppland', *Laborativ Arkeologi*, vol. 4, pp. 65–80.

Artelius, Tore, 2000, 'Bortglömda föreställningar. Begravningsritual och begravningsplats i halländsk yngre järnålder', *RAA Arkeologiska undersökningar*. Skrifter 36/Gotarc B: 15.

Artelius, Tore, 2004, 'Minnesmakarnas verkstad. Om vikingatida bruk av äldre gravar och begravningsplatser', in Å. Berggren et al. (eds.), *Minne och myt. Konsten att skapa det förflutna*. Vägar till Midgård 5. Nordic Academic Press, Lund, pp. 99–120.

Bäckman, Louise, 1975, *Sájva: Föreställningar om hjälp- och skyddsväsen i heliga fjäll bland samerna*, Almqvist & Wiksell International, Stockholm.

Bäckman, Louise, and Åke Hultkrantz, 1978, *Studies in Lapp shamanism*, Acta Universitatis Stockholmiensis, Stockholm.

Baetke, Walter, 1964, *Yngvi und die Ynglinger. Eine quellenkritische Untersuchung über das nordische 'Sakral-köningtum'*. Sitzungsberichte der Sächsische Akademie der Wissenschaften zu Leipzig. Philologisch-historische Klasse: Sitzungsberichte, 109, 3. Akademie-Verlag, Berlin.

Baudou, Evert, 1989, 'Hög – gård – helgedom i Mellannorrland under den äldre järnåldern', *Arkeologi i norr*, vol. 2, pp. 9–43.

Birkeli, Emil, 1944, *Huskult og hinsidighetstro. Nye studier over fedrekult i Norge*. Skrifter utgitt av Det Norske Videnskaps-Akademi i Oslo II. Hist.-Filos. Klasse, no. 1. i kommisjon hos Jacob Dybwad, Oslo.

Brink, Stefan, 1990, 'Cult sites in northern Sweden', in T. Ahlbäck (ed.), *Old Norse and Finnish religions and cultic place-names*, The Donner Institute for Research in Religious and Cultural History, Åbo, pp. 458–489.
Brink, Stefan, 1996, 'Political and social structures in early Scandinavia. A settlement-historical pre-study of the central place', *Tor*, vol. 28, pp. 235–281.
Brink, Stefan, 2004a, 'Mytologiska rum och eskatologiska föreställningar i det vikingatida Norden', in A. Andrén et al. (eds.), *Ordning mot kaos. Studier av nordisk förkristen kosmologi*. Vägar till Midgård 4. Nordic Academic Press, Lund, pp. 291–316.
Brink, Stefan, 2004b. 'Legal assembly sites in early Scandinavia', in A. Pantos and S. Semple (eds.), *Assembly places and practices in medieval Europe*, Four Courts Press, Dublin and Portland, pp. 205–216.
Chaney, William, 1970, *The cult of kingship in Anglo-Saxon England: the transition from paganism to Christianity*, University of California Press, Berkeley and Los Angeles.
Darvill, Timothy, 2004, 'Tynwald hill and the "things" of power', in A. Pantos and S. Semple (eds.), *Assembly places and practices in medieval Europe*, Four Courts Press, Dublin and Portland, pp. 217–232.
de Vries, Jan, 1956, 'Das Königtum bei den Germanen', *Saeculum*, vol. 7, pp. 289–309.
Du Bois, Thomas, 1999, *Nordic religions in the Viking Age*, University of Pennsylvania Press, Philadelphia.
Gräslund, Anne-Sofie, 2001, 'Living with the dead', in M. Stausberg (ed.), *Kontinuitäten und Brüche in der Religionsgeschichte: Festschrift für Anders Hultgård zu seinem 65. Geburtstag am 23.12. 2001*. Reallexikon der germanischen Altertumskunde, 31. de Gruyter, Berlin and New York, pp. 222–235.
Gräslund, Anne-Sofie, 2012 [2008], 'The material culture of Old Norse religion', in S. Brink and N. Price (eds.), *The Viking world*, Routledge, London and New York, pp. 249–256.
Grimm, Jacob, 1882, *Teutonic mythology*, I. 1st English edition by J. Stallybrass. George Bell & Sons, London.
Gunnell, Terry, 2001, 'Hof, Halls, Godar and Dwarves: an examination of the ritual space in the pagan Icelandic hall', *Cosmos*, vol. 17, pp. 3–36.
Heide, Eldar, 2014, '*Hǫrgr* in Norwegian names for mountains and other natural features', *Namn og Nemne*, vol. 31, pp. 7–51.
Heinrichs, Anne, 1993, 'The search for identity: a problem after the conversion', *Alvíssmál*, vol. 3, pp. 43–62.
Holmberg, Uno, 1964 [1927], 'Finno–Ugric, Siberian', in J. MacCulloch (ed.), *The mythology of all races*, IV. Cooper Square Publishers, New York.
Hultgård, Anders, 1992, 'Religiös förändring, kontinuitet och ackulturation/syncretism i vikingatidens och medeltidens skandinaviska religion', in B. Nilsson (ed.), *Kontinuitet i kult och tro från vikingatid till medeltid*, Projektet Sveriges kristnande, Uppsala, pp. 49–103.
Hultgård, Anders, 1996, 'Fornskandinavisk kult – finns der skriftliga källor?' in K. Engdahl and A. Kaliff (eds.), *Argeologi från stenålder till medeltid. Artiklar baserade på Religionsarkeologiska nätverksgruppens konferens på Lövstadbruk den 1–3 december 1995*. Riksantikvarieämbetet, Linköping, pp. 25–57.
Jónas Jónasson 1961 [1934], *Íslenzkir þjóðhættir*. Einar Ól. Sveinsson bjó undir prentun. Ísafold, Reykjavík.
Jordan, Peter, 2003, *Material culture and sacred landscape: the anthropology of the Siberian Khanty*, Rowman Altamira, Walnut Creek.

100 Case studies

Jørgensen, Lars, 2002, 'Kongsgård – kusted – marked. Overvejelser omkring Tissøkompleksets struktur og funktion', in K. Jennbert et al. (eds.), *Plats och praxis – studier av nordisk förkristen ritual*, Nordic Academic Press, Lund, pp. 215–247.

Kaliff, Anders, 1997, *Grav och kultplats. Eskatologiska föreställningar under yngre bronsålder och äldre järnålder i Östergötland*, vol. 24, Acta Universitatis Uppsaliensis, Uppsala.

Kaliff, Anders, 2011, 'Fire', in T. Insoll (ed.), *The Oxford handbook of the archaeology of ritual and religion*, University Press, Oxford, pp. 51–62.

Karjalainen, Kustaa, 1918, *Jugralaisten uskonto*. Suomensuvun uskonnot, 3, Söderström, Porvoo.

Kermode, Philip, 1904, *Traces of the Norse mythology in the Isle of Man*, Bremrose & Son Limited, London.

Line, Philip, 2007, *Kingship and state formation in Sweden, 1130–1290*. The Northern World, 27. Brill, Leiden.

Mancini Billson, Janet, and K. Mancini, 2007. *Inuit women: their powerful spirit in a century of change*, Rowman and Littlefield, Maryland and Plymouth.

McDonald, Andrew, 2007, *Manx kingship in its Irish Sea setting, 1187–1229. King Rǫgnvaldr and the Crovan dynasty*, Four Courts Press, Dublin and Portland.

McDonald, Neil, 2012, *Isle of Man a megalithic journey*, Megalithic Publishing, Lancashire.

Mellor, Scott, 2008, 'St. Ansgar: his Swedish mission and its larger context', in T. DuBois (ed.), *Sanctity in the North: saints, lives, and cults in medieval Scandinavia*, University of Toronto Press, Toronto, Buffalo and London, pp. 31–64.

Moore, Arthur, 1891, *The Folk-lore of the Isle of Man: being an account of its myths, legends, superstitions, customs, & proverbs*, Brown & Son and D. Nutt, Isle of Man and London.

Olsen, Olaf, 1966, *Hørg, hov og Kirke: historiske og arkæologiske vikingetidsstudier*, Gad, Copenhagen.

Orri Vésteinsson, 2007, 'Hann reisti hof mikið hundrað fóta langt... Um uppruna hof- örnefna og stjórnmál á Íslandi í lok 10 Aldar', Saga. Tímarit Sögufélags, vol. 45, pp. 53–91.

Palmer, James, 2004, 'Rimbert's Vita Anskarii and Scandinavian mission in the ninth century', *Journal of Ecclesiastical History*, vol. 55, no. 2, pp. 235–256.

Palmer, Smythe, 1910, 'Folk-lore in world-lore', *The Nineteenth Century and After*, vol. 68, pp. 545–557.

Reuterskiöld, Edgar, 1910, *Källskrifter till lapparnas mytologi*, Nordiska Museet, Stockholm.

Røthe, Gunnhild, 2007, 'Þorgerðr Hölgabrúðr. The *fylgja* of the Háleygjar family', *Scripta Islandica*, vol. 58, pp. 33–55.

Rybakov, Boris A., 1987, *Yazychestvo drevnei rusi*, Nauka, Moscow.

Söderberg, Bengt, 2005, *Aristokratiskt rum och gränsöverskridande. Järrestad och sydöstra Skåne mellan religion och rike 600–1100*. Riksantikvarieämbetet Arkeologiska undersökningar Skrifter, 62. Riksantikvarieämbetets förlag, Stockholm.

Sölvi Sveinsson, 1995, *Íslenskir málshættir með skýringum og dæmum*, Iðunn, Reykjavík.

Ström, Åke, 1959, 'The king god and his connection with sacrifice in Old Norse religion', in *The sacral kingship. Contributions to the central theme of the VIIIth international congress for the history of religions*. Studies in the History of Religions, 4. Brill, Leiden, pp. 702–715.

Ström, Åke and Biezais Haralds, 1975, *Germanishce und Baltische religion*, Verlag W. Kohlhammer, Stuttgart, Berlin, Köln and Mainz.

Sundqvist, Olof, 2001, 'Features of pre-Christian inauguration rituals in the medieval Swedish laws', in J. Hoops and H. Beck (eds.), *Kontinuitäten und Brüche in der Religionsgeschichte: Festschrift für Anders Hultgård zum 65. Geburtstag am 23. Dezember 2001*, Walter de Gruyter, Berlin and New York, pp. 620–650.

Sundqvist, Olof, 2002, *Freyr's offspring. Rulers and religion in ancient Svea society*, Uppsala Universitet, Uppsala.

Sundqvist, Olof, 2009a, 'The question of ancient Scandinavian cultic buildings: with particular reference to Old Norse *hof*', *Temenos*, vol. 45, pp. 65–84.

Sundqvist, Olof, 2009b. 'The hanging, the nine nights and the "precious knowledge" in Hávamál 138–145: the cultic context', in W. Heizmann and H. Beck (eds.), *Analecta Septentrionalia*, Walter de Gruyter, Berlin, pp. 649–668.

Turville-Petre, Gabriel, 1964, *Myth and religion of the north: the religion of ancient Scandinavia*, Greenwood Press, Connecticut.

Uspenskij, Fjodor, 2011, 'The advent of Christianity and dynastic name-giving in Scandinavia and Rus', in I. Garipzanov and O. Tolochko (eds.), *Early Christianity on the way from the Varangians to the Greeks*, Institute of Ukrainian History, Kiev, pp. 108–119.

Vikstrand, Per, 2001, *Gudarnas platser: förkristen sakrala ortnamn i Mälarlandskapen*, Acta Academiae Regiae Gustav Adolphi, Uppsala, pp. LXXVII.

Zachrisson, Torun, 1994, 'The odal and its manifestation in the landscape', *Current Swedish Archaeology*, vol. 2, pp. 219–238.

Zelenin, Dmitrij, 1991 [1927], *Vostochnoslavyanskaya etnografiya*, trans. K. Tsivina, Moscow: Nauka. First published as *Russische (Ostslavische) Volkskunde*. de Gruyter, Berlin and Leipzig.

7 The Ynglingar

This chapter examines the cases of three supposed Ynglingar who are all said to have received public cult in their gravemounds: Freyr, Óláfr Geirstaðaálfr and Hálfdanr svarti. It is argued that all three were associated with a general ancestor cult and that the public and quasipublic aspects of their worship can be explained by recourse to the socio-anthropological theory of superior ancestors (see Chapter 3). It is argued that this theory can be used to account for the evidence examined without recourse to the theory of sacral kingship which has been strongly associated with these cases in the past. Indeed, the Ynglingar have dominated discussion of Old Norse sacral kingship and religious ruler ideology. *Ynglingatal* and other genealogical sources such as *Heimskringla* that trace kings' ancestry from the gods have become central to this discussion, and elements argued to support the framework include the sacred marriage motif and the kings' ability to mediate with the gods due to their own divinity and to thereby secure the *ár ok friðr* ('peace and prosperity'). The focus in connection with the proposed Yngling individuals has been on their divine aspects, overlooking the fact that concepts such as *hieros gamos* are essentially academic constructs which rely heavily on mythological traditions and are patched together from a number of unrelated sources; it is questionable whether such constructs had any real significance in people's beliefs.

7.1 Background on the Ynglingar

7.1.1 Sources

Information about the Ynglingar comes from two main sources: the skaldic poem *Ynglingatal*, believed to be composed by Þjóðólfr from Hvín (c. 885–930), and Snorri Sturluson's *Ynglinga saga*, where *Ynglingatal* is quoted, paraphrased and elaborated on in prose. Preserved mainly in the 13th-century *Heimskringla*, *Ynglingatal* is considered to be one of the oldest recorded skaldic poems. Questions have been raised regarding the pre-Christian date of the poem (see Krag 1991), but most scholars agree that Þjóðólfr composed the poem sometime towards the end of the 9th century (e.g. Lindow 2005; Marold 2012: 3). *Ynglingatal* – alongside a few other poems like *Háleygjatal* – is commonly classified as a genealogical praise poem celebrating an aristocratic lineage. This type of poem focuses on the living ruler and traces the lineage back to his most distant ancestor. *Ynglingatal* – as it is preserved – begins with Fjǫlnir, who according to Snorri was the son of Yngvifreyr (prol p. 4) or Freyr (Yngl ch. 10) and who is associated with Gamla Uppsala, and ends with Rǫgnvaldr heiðumhær of Vestfold. *Ynglingatal* is believed to have been Snorri's main prototype when compiling *Ynglinga saga* – it is unlikely that he followed lost verses of the poem (Faulkes 1978–1979: 5–6; Lindow 2005: 37). In addition to Freyr, he adds Njǫrðr to the lineage prior to Fjǫlnir (chs 4–10). Þjóðólfr does not mention Njǫrðr nor place Freyr at the top of the genealogy, but alludes to some of the Uppsala kings' descent from him.[1] The account is believed to be a combination of at least two different traditions of ancestry: the ancient kings of Sweden and the contemporary Norwegian petty kings who are united by patrilineal kinship and presented as the descendants of Freyr (Faulkes 1978–1979; Lönnroth 1986; Sundqvist 2012a: 237–239). All these rulers have generally become known as the Ynglingar, despite Þjóðólfr himself never using such a title.[2]

However far off *Ynglingatal* (and *Ynglinga saga*) is from historical reality – we are obviously dealing with a pseudo-history for which information was drawn from different sources and places – it exhibits the poet's determination to trace the 10th-century Norwegian district kings' descent from rulers of territory in the Gamla Uppsala region. In the prologue to *Ynglinga saga*, Snorri states that Rǫgnvaldr was the son of Óláfr Guðrǫðarson, a petty king in Vestfold whose brother, Hálfdanr svarti, was according to some sources (e.g. HsHá ch. 1) father to Haraldr hárfagri, in whose court Þjóðólfr was employed. The Norwegian Ynglingar thus seem to represent the Norwegian hárfagri clan, and there is a strong consensus that their artificial attachment to Gamla Uppsala was sparked by the political situation in Norway at the time of composition: the poem is designed to enhance the clan's social dominance and to help reinforce and expand their legal rights to land (e.g. Clunies Ross 2011; Steinsland 2011; Sundqvist 2012a). This motivation offers an explanation as to why Þjóðólfr describes the deaths of the kings and indicates their burial places. That the ability to trace ancestry back at least five generations was a standard process for claiming ancestral land in Scandinavia is well established; incorporating the places where the earlier generations had ruled and died into the poem, which was performed in the relevant circles, cemented the Norwegian rulers' claims to land. Whether the last five generations of Rǫgnvaldr's ancestry are based on authentic traditions is not certain, although other historiographies at least partially support the information provided by Þjóðólfr.

The obstacle in this interpretation, it has been argued, is that Þjóðólfr does not actually specify that the listed individuals are connected in a direct line. Descent is mentioned in connection with Freyr (sts 10, 16), Týr (st. 14), Yngvi (st. 7) and a few others, characters that according to toponymic evidence are to be associated predominantly with southern Sweden and Denmark and who go much further back in time than Rǫgnvaldr's five ancestors. This observation has led to the hypothesis that the entire concept of a dynasty known as Ynglingar, which includes also the later successors of Haraldr hárfagri – Óláfr Tryggvason and Óláfr helgi who notoriously used their ancestry to further their power – is purely the creation of 12th- and 13th-century historiographers (Krag 1991: 88; Bergsveinn Birgisson 2008). Bergsveinn Birgisson (2008: 196–208, 216–224, 413–416) has theorised that *Ynglingatal* was never intended as a 'genealogy', but a satirical *níð*-poem which refers to many different elite families. According to Bergsveinn this was a means of ridiculing the ancient Swedish and Danish kings whose descendants had been the hárfagri clan's greatest rivals in the Mälaren region in Sweden and around Viken in south-east Norway since the beginning of the Viking Age.[3] Several of the non-Norwegians listed in the poem are indeed said to have died in ways which would hardly have glorified the living ruler: one drowns in a mead-vat, another is trapped inside a stone by a dwarf, a third put to death by his own subjects and so on. The preposterous deaths mentioned in the poem – which would be expected to praise the last ruler down the line – have perplexed scholars, and thus Bergsveinn's suggestion has been taken into consideration in recent discussion (e.g. Sundqvist 2009a; Steinsland 2011: 24–25), although not fully accepted.

Sundqvist (2012a: 255–256, note 42), for example, questions the poem's classification as a *níð* and maintains the conventional interpretation that *Ynglingatal* was regarded as a genealogy. Even though the poem contains historically incorrect sequences, it is patched together from real genealogical traditions of different backgrounds. Sundqvist emphasises that both Ari fróði and Eyvindr, the likely authors of *Íslendingabók* and *Háleygjatal*, saw *Ynglingatal* as a genealogical work when they used it as a sample in their own genealogies. Overall, this approach to *Ynglingatal* will be followed here, too. The material for the poem may have been picked erratically, but this is no indication that the final product was not believed to be a genealogy of some sort, including by those who created it. As discussed in Chapter 3, oral genealogies are by their nature adaptable to fit prevailing circumstances and are never static or biologically accurate, in any society or time-period. Considering the hárfagri clan's success in the political arena, the genealogical fabrications were clearly successful from this point of view. That the skald was able to incorporate historically remote 'ancestors' into the dynasty only proves how easily alterable genealogies were at that time in Scandinavia. The strange deaths in the poem are perhaps taken by scholars to be more meaningful than they really are. These tales probably represent remnants of very old traditions about former rulers that had survived in popular memory and resurfaced many times with variations and embellishments. By attaching tales that were generally well known in popular culture – most likely owing to their eccentricity and satirical value – to one's own family must have elevated social visibility and 'particularity'. These attachments demonstrated ancient descent from rulers; the association with entertaining popular tales was a by-product of such a strategy (and a burden every ruler must bear anyway).

7.1.2 The Ynglingar and sacral kingship

Some of the kings in *Ynglingatal* are said to have descended from Freyr, information which Snorri restates in prose when raising Freyr to the very top of the family tree. This has led to the prevailing view that he represents the divine progenitor of the Ynglingar (e.g. Schück 1905–1910; Schröder 1924; Grönbech 1931; von Friesen 1932–1934; Höfler 1952; Ström 1954, 1983; Ström 1959; Turville-Petre 1964: 190–195). Freyr's ability to secure the *ár ok friðr* – which according to Snorri started during his reign in Gamla Uppsala – is shared in other sources by many later 'Yngling' rulers. This ability was seen as compatible with Frazer's sacral kingship paradigm in which a king-priest marries an earth goddess and holds a central position within a fertility cult, which is continued by their offspring. Mythological sources had a central significance in the construction of such identities. Much support was found in *Skírnismál* – an Eddic poem dated to the 13th century – which depicts the meeting of Freyr and Gerðr.[4] In this poem Freyr spots a giantess whilst sitting on Óðinn's high seat which allows him to see into the other worlds. Freyr becomes obsessed with her and sends his alter ego Skírnir to persuade her to sleep with Freyr. After a series of threats Gerðr reluctantly accepts and asks Freyr to meet her in a sacred grove. Even though the arranged meeting, as told in *Skírnimál*, does not end with marriage or offspring, Snorri (Yng ch. 10) adds that they were married and that their son was Fjǫlnir, the first king listed in *Ynglingatal*. Their union was subsequently interpreted by scholars as hierogamous, and as the divine origin of the long lineage of sacral kings listed in *Ynglingatal* (e.g. Olsen 1909; Phillpotts 1920: 144–175; Ström 1983; Steinsland 1991, 1992, 2000, 2011; Svava Jakobsdóttir 2002). Steinsland has studied this aspect most exhaustively and argued that the Ynglingar – beginning with Fjǫlnir, the first earthly ruler – are the outcome of the marriage between a god and a giantess who personifies the land that was to become ruled by the new king. Contrary to earlier theories, she underlines the importance of the female character in the origin myth and that the ideology of rulership was based on the concept of a marriage between two extreme mythical figures: a god and a giantess. The earthly rulers' origin from such a tumultuous mythic union gave them privileges, but also fated them to die ignobly.

Much of the enthusiasm for viewing the Ynglingar as sacral kings has faded away over the last few decades, and scholars increasingly point out the problems with this interpretation. We have discussed the increasingly supported terminological shift from 'sacral kingship' to 'religious ruler ideology' (see Chapter 4), and criticism has also been directed towards methodological issues and the use of sources (e.g. Clunies Ross 2014). The theory about *hieros gamos*, for example, is pieced together from a number of separate and mostly later texts, some of which are copied from each other, so the entire argument is built on circular reasoning. There is no indication of a *hieros gamos* in *Ynglingatal* – this idea derives almost entirely from *Skírnismál*, which Snorri inserted into *Ynglinga saga* (Steinsland 2011: 21–25). The *ár* is mentioned only once in *Ynglingatal*, in connection with Dómaldi (st. 5). The two aspects which were central to the sacral kingship theory are thus linked only to the story by medieval sources, a point made already by Baetke (1964). The allusions to Freyr in *Ynglingatal* are far from suggesting that Þjóðólfr wished to present him as a divinity: both *afspring* ('offspring') and *óttungr* ('descendant') point towards his role as the ancestor of these kings.

106 *Case studies*

Regardless of the extensive criticism recent studies have directed against the earlier application of 'sacral kingship', the century-long debate seems to have generated a lingering reluctance to abandon the divine and mythic aspects of ruler ideology. Despite acknowledging that the conceptual border between pagan gods and human ancestors was probably fuzzy (e.g. 2002: 289–292, 368–369), Sundqvist (2012a: 238–239), for example, seems to take a fairly strict ideological approach when stating that 'it is quite clear that *Ynglingatal* indicates that the father of the royal family was a divinity' and that the 'expressions and denominations of the kings found in *Ynglingatal* [...] clearly indicate that members of the "Ynglingar" were praised for their divine origin'. As noted above, the interpretation is based on phrases found in *Ynglingatal* like *Freys afspring* ('Freyr's offspring'), *Freys óttungr* ('Freyr's descendant'), *Týs óttungr* ('Týr's descendant'), *Yngva þjóðar* ('the people of Yngvi'), *niðkvísl þróttar þrós* ('the descendants of the Þrór; <god> of strength') (tr. Marold 2012: 55), etc., which are assumed to be references to divinities without allowing the ideological contrast between pagan and Christian worldviews to bias the ingrained perspective that Old Norse gods were 'divine'.[5] Þrór, for example, is an unidentified character – Sundqvist himself translates the last phrase as 'the kin-branch of the powerful [potent] man', but assumes that it refers to a divinity. The same line of thought is followed in a typological comparison of pagan Scandinavian rulership with that of pre-Christian Hawaii by Simon Nygaard (2016: 15), who agrees that the above-mentioned phrases 'portray the idea of divine descent quite clearly'. Steinsland's work (e.g. 2011) focuses on mythological subjects, which may not have been central in day-to-day social contexts. The concept of holy marriage between a god and a giantess is fundamentally a mythic construct, and even though it is possible that poems like *Skírnismál* were enacted as ritual drama during real seasonal celebrations (Phillpotts 1920: 13–16; Gunnell 1993), it is questionable how deeply meaningful such performances were in people's beliefs and how the main actors were perceived. Although myths, as embellished folk tales of once-lived and experienced realities, can offer valuable insights into historical events and ideologies, the importance of mythical and divine aspects in the religious cognition of the Norsemen should be deemphasised in discussion of Old Norse rulership and religion.

7.1.3 Ynglingatal: *authorial purpose*

The question that remains is why Þjóðólfr made an effort to create a genealogy which seemingly so ambiguously unites the modern kings of Vestfold and the ancient kings of southern Scandinavia. Considering the power struggles in Haraldr's time, it is tempting to view the poem as stemming from the political rivalry among the Nordic elites. One might therefore wish to consider also the major societal changes thought to have taken place around the period when the ancient Swedish kings – and Freyr in particular – lived and ruled. In this regard, mythology can be used as a map for exploring these broad patterns.

A number of scholars have pointed out that the clash between the *æsir* and *vanir*, which is mentioned by Snorri and in some Eddic poems (e.g. Vsp sts 21–24;

Gylf ch. 22; Skáld ch. 1; Yng ch. 4), reflects changes in religious ideology during the transition from Bronze Age to Iron Age. According to this interpretation, the *vanir* represent an older fertility cult based in south-east Sweden that was gradually overcome by a male-centred warrior cult that started to reach Scandinavia around the middle of the first millennium AD, and which is represented by the *æsir* (Turville-Petre 1964: 159–162; Nordland 1966: 67–68; Motz 1996: 103–124; Gunnell 2007b: 353–361; Hedeager 2011).[6] Freyr is regularly presented as one of the *vanir* in the mythological tradition (e.g. Gylf chs 23–24; Yng ch. 4), and his cult is predominantly associated with Gamla Uppsala where it is believed to have started sometime during the Migration Period, around the 5th or 6th century (we shall return to this in Section 7.2.1). This information is, however, contradicted by some sources such as the early Eddic poem *Grímnismál* (st. 5) – dated to the first half of the 10th century – and *Gylfaginning* (ch. 17), whose content is largely borrowed from the poem, where we find that Freyr had apparently ruled over a place called Álfheimar, which he inherited as his *tannfé* – the present given to a child upon getting its first tooth. This information is curious considering that Freyr's domicile is otherwise strongly established in the Gamla Uppsala area. Freyr's connection to *álfar* – the residents of Álfheimar – is also implied by his association with brightness, which might be an early feature of the *álfar* (Gunnell 2007a; Hall 2007: 24, 38).[7] The *álfar* are sometimes equated with the *vanir* in the literary tradition. For example, while Snorri mentions the *æsir* and *vanir* as the principal races, Eddic poems regularly use the phrase *æsir ok álfar* (e.g. Ls sts 2, 13, 30; Þkv st. 7; Háv sts 143, 159, 160; Skm st. 7; Grm st. 4). Although there is a metrical motivation for the use of *álfar* rather than *vanir* in these cases, it is possible that they represent the same mythological race, the word *álfr* perhaps being used to describe the *vanir* in some circles (Gunnell 2007a: 121–124; Hall 2007: 27, 36–37). However, while the *vanir* are associated with south-east Sweden, the *álfar* seem to be geographically concentrated further to the west.

Since Freyr's ownership of Álfheimar is mentioned only in the mythological tradition, it is commonly assumed that this place does not refer to a real historical land. This assumption has been challenged by Terry Gunnell (2007a: 124), who points out that various, at least semi-historical sources (e.g. Yng ch. 48; Hss ch. 4; HNb ch. 3; Saf ch. 10), refer to Álfheimar as a real place in the Viken area – the region in close proximity to Vestfold, stretching from modern-day Bohuslän between Oslo and Gothenburg and eastwards into Dalsland and Västergötland. This is the area where the *álfar* traditions feature most prominently. For instance, according to an 11th-century skaldic poem, a travelling skald was refused entry to a number of farms in Västergötland on the account of *álfablót* ('sacrifice to the *álfar*') being in progress (Afv st. 5). Also the cup-mark stones which are associated with offerings to the *álfar* – and are known as *älvkvarnar* ('elf-mills') in Swedish – are found copiously in south-west Sweden where they are often carved on gravestones or located near graves and cremation sites (Glob 1969: 119, 128; Bertilsson 1986: 11–17; Kaliff 1997a, 2007), suggesting an association with offerings to ancestors (Widholm 1999; Kaliff 2007: 191–194). The most well-known group of cup-marks is found on the Vitlycke rock-carving in Bohuslän

108 *Case studies*

(Hasselrot & Ohlmarks 1966: 89). The *álfar* tradition there must have been active for an extremely long period – as late as the 18th century, a clergyman in Sweden apparently used to destroy the cup-marks because local people poured milk and placed butter on them (Grundberg 2000). Gunnell (2007a: 124–125) provides a convincing explanation for the geographical discrepancy between the *vanir* and the *álfar* and why Freyr has associations with both: the Álfheimar in present-day south-west Sweden and south-east Norway may once have been under the control of a group led by Freyr's family who at some point during the Migration Period moved to the Gamla Uppsala region in the east. This suggestion is supported by place names that contain Freyr's name and that, although to a much lesser extent than in eastern Sweden, are also present in western Sweden and around modern-day Oslo (Brink 2007: 109–111, 125–127), indicating his presence there (i.e. in Álfheimar).

It seems very unlikely that Freyr was intended to be viewed as the progenitor of many of the ancient kings listed in *Ynglingatal*. He represents one of many in a cluster of historically remote rulers, and his name comes up for the first time almost halfway through the poem. His late appearance is the main reason behind the suggestion that parts of the poem might be missing (e.g. Ström 1954: 34–35); this suggestion itself, however, derives to a great extent from the presumed difference between gods and other characters mentioned in the poem, and probably stems from the presentation of 'gods' in Snorri's mythology. If we follow Snorri's account, the only individuals mentioned in the poem who can be identified as 'gods' are Freyr and Týr. However, simply because he excluded the other names mentioned in *Ynglingatal* from his pantheon (e.g. Fjǫlnir), distributed them to groups other than the *æsir* or *vanir* (e.g. Dúrnir) or chose not to mention them at all (e.g. Þrór), this is not an indication that these individuals should be understood differently from Snorri's 'gods', not least if we accept that the different mythological races are broadly identifiable with different regional groups. The division of kings into 'real', 'legendary' and 'gods' is artificial and fuzzy.

Overall, no systematic genealogical relationship between the named individuals mentioned in *Ynglingatal* seems to be suggested by Þjóðólfr; the references throughout the earlier part of the poem are to different rulers and their followers – whether direct descendants, kinsmen or otherwise – from different parts of southern Scandinavia. The poem does not even seem to favour some rulers over others as we might expect considering power struggles with the Danes. For example, Týr (a god we know practically nothing of) seems to have had a strong presence in Denmark according to placename evidence; the most well-known location associated with him is Tissø in Sjælland (Brink 2007: 119–121), where a large and well-preserved settlement including a chieftain's hall has been excavated on the shore of a lake (Jørgensen 1998). However, he is by no means presented in a way that is derogatory compared to other rulers; the poem simply mentions his offspring. The same applies to Yngvi, who is sometimes conflated with Freyr in the Old Norse tradition (e.g. Yng, prol p. 4; Ls st. 43; Gylf, prol p. 9) and whose documented history is generally complicated. He has been associated with Ing, the ancestor of the Ingaevones who according to Tacitus were a north Germanic tribe living by an ocean (Ger ch. 2, ed. pp. 4–5; tr. p. 102) and who according to *The Old English Rune Poem* (line 67) appeared among the east Danes. The link to Freyr is obscure, and it remains unclear at what point in time the two became connected (Faulkes 1978–1979: 3–4). The geographical origin of Yngvi can be traced roughly to modern-day Denmark according to the written sources, although place names around the Mälaren water system suggest that a certain Yngvi could be linked with this area too (Hellberg 2014). It seems that the names which appear in *Ynglingatal* prior to the last five generations enumerated represent an essentially random selection of rulers across a wide area of southern Scandinavia, although some of them come from the same kin groups, and it is possible that some of these ancient rulers had their roots in the Viken area.

Besides Freyr's potentially south-western Swedish or south-eastern Norwegian origin, the poem mentions, for instance, Álfr who, we might expect, is linked to Álfheimar. Sveigðir, son of Fjǫlnir, who according to *Ynglingatal* (st. 2) was tricked by a dwarf into going inside a rock from which he never returned, made a vow to seek out Goðheimar for the time of his death according to *Ynglinga saga* (ch. 12), which has also an association with the Viken region and its nearby localities. Goðheimar, like Álfheimar, is usually explained in the light of mythological topography as the 'world of gods' because it is used by Snorri as the counterpart of Manheimar, which he interprets as Mannheimar ('world of men') (Yngl chs 8–9).[8] Mythological geography is of course full of anomalies and difficult to interpret.[9] However, the polarised interpretation of Manheimar and Goðheimar as 'humans' versus 'gods' anticipated by the mythical context where they are mentioned is superfluous, and there is once again no reason to think that these places were not historical and linked to specific populations. According to current toponymic evidence, Goðheimar place names occur commonly, but are almost exclusively restricted to Denmark, Bornholm, south-west Sweden and Viken (Brink 2011: 18). This information corresponds more or less with Egill Skallagrímsson's *Sonatorrek* (st. 21), where Goðheimar is mentioned in connection with the Gautar, who most regularly refer to the inhabitants of modern Västergötland. Goðheimar could thus refer to a place where the dead in some parts of Álfheimar were believed to go according to folk tradition and where Sveigðir wished to die – and enter an 'elf-mill' (stone?) – perhaps because this was his or his ancestors' birthplace.

If Álfheimar was the homeland to at least some early 'Ynglingar', the structure of the poem reveals an almost circular migration, beginning and ending in the Viken area. The ancient kings are seen by scholars in two main clusters, those residing by the wide-ranging Mälaren region and those in Gamla Uppsala that lies to the north-east of it (Lönnroth 1986: 87–88; Sundqvist 2012a: 237). As was mentioned before, Freyr's name comes up only around the middle of the poem, at about the same time that Uppsala is mentioned (Yngt sts 10, 16); towards the end of the poem when the focus shifts to the Norwegian kings, we are told that Óláfr trételgja fled from Uppsala towards the west to Värmland (st. 21), which is about halfway between modern-day Uppsala and Oslo; it is then followed by descriptions of his offspring ruling in south-east Norway, first in Oppland and gradually moving towards the south, ending with Óláfr Guðrøðarson in Vestmarir by the south-east coast of Norway.

Presuming that the 9th- and 10th-century petty kings of Vestfold wished to expand their rule over the Viken region, which was the centre of conflict with the Danes at the time, and broadly identifiable as Álfheimar, the attempt to demonstrate their descent from a number of kings who had once inhabited this area makes sense and corresponds broadly to what most scholars believe to be the purpose of the genealogy in *Ynglingatal*. Their interest in the area is demonstrated most obviously in the tale about Óláfr Guðrøðarson, who is Rǫgnvaldr's last ancestor in *Ynglingatal* and who inherits the cognomen Geirstaðaálfr ('*álfr* of Geirstaðir') after he dies. This Óláfr (further discussed in Section 7.4), is in some texts presented as the son of Álfhildr, daughter of Álfr from Álfheimar (e.g. Yng ch. 48; AUk ch. 2). A number of other sources concerned with the Norwegian kings living in this region use *álfr* as a common name-element, for example, Óláfr trételgja's son who died in Oppland and was buried in Skíringssalr, probably located in the region of Vestfold, is called *brynjálfr* ('*álfr* of mail coat') (Yngt st. 22; Yng ch. 44; also HNb ch. 3; Yng ch. 48; Saf chs 8, 10; IsG ch. 5; GD VIII, ed p. 215, tr. p. 239). As Gunnell (2007a: 124–127) explains, it seems that certain kin groups identified themselves as descending from a common ancestor – Álfr – and that the designation *álfr* consequently had a special meaning for people living in the Viken area, probably because this enabled the inheritance of property. The name Geirstaðaálfr is not mentioned in *Ynglingatal*, but the poem states that Óláfr was buried inside a mound at Geirstaðir along the west coast of the Oslo fjord, which corresponds with at least the location (st. 26).

It is possible that Þjóðólfr's purpose when connecting the Swedish and Norwegian kings in *Ynglingatal* was not so much to demonstrate the Norwegians' prestigious descent from a 'royal house' in Gamla Uppsala or from Freyr in particular, but simply to parade knowledge about the past – the poem records the distinguished families who had held important central sites across southern Scandinavia. The passing phrases mentioning Freyr might be less meaningful than is generally supposed. He is not presented as the progenitor of the Ynglingar, but appears alongside a number of other progenitors associated with different distinguished kin groups. Why Snorri chose Freyr as the 'godhead' of the Ynglingar, we do not know; perhaps he knew most about Freyr. The relationships between the individuals mentioned in the first three quarters of the poem are by and large obscure and perhaps were never intended to have anything other than an artistic effect. The latter part of the poem satisfied the five-ancestor requirement; the remainder was an illustration, although a potentially useful one, demonstrating knowledge of and ties of some sort to rulers from the mists of time. Contrary to the traditional view that the Norwegian kings wished to show their descent from the Uppsala kings, it may have been of particular relevance to demonstrate that some of the lineages living in the most important centres had their ancestral origins in the Viken area – the region where the hárfagri family exercised power most actively.

The following sections are concerned with the cults of three 'Yngling' kings – Freyr, Óláfr and Hálfdanr – who are all reported to have received public sacrifices after death. All have been caught up in the sacral kingship framework: Freyr as the divine progenitor, the other two as his descendants. The cults devoted to these kings are conventionally seen as having emerged from their divine associations, probably on account of their public aspects. The present discussion is geared towards an analysis of these characters and cults in order to determine whether the activities dedicated to these men emerged not from associations with divine power, but from the event of death which turned them into ancestors. Naturally, consideration is also given to political underpinnings, instigated by leading families to enable them to manipulate ancestry and to expand their land rights.

7.2 Freyr

Ynglingatal, the earliest written source mentioning Freyr, is silent about his cult, but later texts describe it more or less consistently, placing it in Gamla Uppsala on the northern side of the Mälaren water system, sometimes referring to him as a *blótgoði Svía* ('sacrificial priest of the Svear') (ÓsTF p. 339; prol p. 4; Yng chs 4, 10; GD I, III, VI, ed. pp. 29, 67, 153–154; tr. pp. 30, 73, 172; GH IV, chs 26–27, ed. pp. 174–176; tr. pp. 207–208).

Snorri (Yng ch. 10) explains the origin of Freyr's cult in Gamla Uppsala as follows. In his lifetime Freyr had been an esteemed ruler who received taxes from people. He built a *hof* in Uppsala and made the place his main residence. When Freyr became ill, some *menn* ('people') decided after some consideration to have *fá menn* 'a few people' come to him and build a gravemound with a doorway and three windows. After Freyr died, they secretly carried him into the mound, but told the Svear that he was still alive so that they would continue paying tax to him. They kept him there for three years and stored all the gold, silver and copper that they received from the Svear inside the gravemound; thus their *ár ok friðr* continued.[10] The anonymous *menn* ('people') who took the decision to bury Freyr in secret is probably a reference to his closest alliances or 'kinsmen' who exploited the public in order to protect their own privileges. However, after all the Svear had learned that Freyr was in fact dead, but that the *ár ok friðr* had continued regardless, they came to believe that the situation would hold as long as Freyr's body was in their land. They did not want to cremate him as had been the custom before, and kept on sacrificing to him forever after.

That a large gravemound in Gamla Uppsala was the starting point for Freyr's cult is mentioned also in one version of *Óláfs saga Tryggvasonar* (Flat 1, pp. 400–404), which – like Snorri's *Hákonar saga góða* (Hkr 1, ch. 14) – extends the cult to Norway. More or less consistent with the description in *Ynglinga saga*, it provides Óláfr Tryggvason's explanation of the cult to the farmers of Trondheim before removing and burning the statue of Freyr from a local *hof*. This report, however, adds a further twist to the cult. Since Freyr had been so popular in life, the Svear had thought that it would be appropriate if somebody accompanied him inside the mound. As there were no volunteers, it was decided that two *trémenn* ('treemen') would suffice for this purpose. After many years, it struck some Svear as a good idea to break into the gravemound, since they knew it contained valuable deposits. However, as they were contemplating removing the treasures, they experienced such fear that all they managed to snatch were the treemen: the Svear kept one statue for themselves and sent the other to Trondheim. This passage in *Flateyjarbók* is a component of a longer section about Óláfr's mission through the different parts of Norway to bring Christianity. There is good reason to assume that the person who composed the saga took great pains to promote Óláfr's starring role as a Christian activist in Norway. The influence of learned euhemerism is almost certainly at play; this is not, however, an indication that the perception of Freyr as a once-living ruler is incompatible with a pagan worldview.

Adam of Bremen's *Gesta Hammaburgensis*, the earliest report mentioning Freyr's cult – if we accept the identification of the Fricco who is mentioned in the text with Freyr – also places it in Gamla Uppsala (IV, chs 26–27, ed. pp. 174–176; tr. pp. 207–208).[11] While the above-mentioned sources suggest that the great *haugr* was the primary locus for the cult – although Snorri ascribes the creation of a *hof* to Freyr's own time – by the 11th century it may have moved indoors. Adam describes a cult house (*templum*) decorated entirely with gold where the statue of Fricco, endowed with an extreme phallic extension, was worshipped alongside those of Þórr and Óðinn. Fricco's role was according to the author to confer peace and pleasure and to celebrate marriages, features which are consistent with Freyr's association with fertility known from *Snorra Edda*. Adam does not provide further information about Fricco, but writes that a great sacrifice with human and animal victims hanging from trees in a nearby grove, and in which all the provinces of the Svear participated, was held in Uppsala at nine-year intervals. Scholia to the history (139, 141) add that the temple, encircled with a golden chain, was located on a plain and surrounded by *montes* ('mountains'; i.e. gravemounds) to create a theatrical effect for those who approached it. The great celebrations took place at the time of the spring equinox and lasted for nine days; each day animals and one human were sacrificed. There was also a spring near the temple into which a human victim was plunged to see if people's wishes would be fulfilled; when the body was not found their pleas had been heard.

The great *blót* of Uppsala is also depicted by Snorri (Hsg ch. 14), who writes that Freyr's statue stood alongside those of Óðinn and Njǫrðr in a cult house, and that the current king and all the freeholders were required to attend the event and join the ceremonial beer-drinking in memory of the gods and their own relatives who lay buried in the gravemounds.[12] Saxo adds in his account that a certain Frø who set up his residence not far from Uppsala began the practice of human sacrifice there (GD III, ed. p. 67, tr. p. 73). From these descriptions we gather that Freyr was a former ruler tied to eastern Sweden and to Gamla Uppsala in particular; he was involved in sacrificial ceremonies on a grand scale and he may have been buried in a large gravemound and/or worshipped in a temple-like building in the form of an icon.

7.2.1 Adam's Templum

Much debate has taken place about the existence of the kind of *templum* depicted by Adam in Gamla Uppsala.[13] Traces of settlement in the area go back to the Roman period, but recent archaeological excavations of surrounding settlements reveal that the 5th and particularly the 6th centuries were a period of notable social transformation in the area, when the elite began to assert their status more markedly (Ljungkvist & Frölund 2015). The economic growth of the area, likely fuelled by wider social changes that took place at that time, can be seen in changing burial patterns and in farm units moving close to the 'royal manor complex' – a large settlement area built on artificial plateaus made of soil and clay and elevated so that it would be visible to all around. It is likely that this area was inhabited by the emerging elite and the highest part of the site has revealed also the layout of a very large hall extending 50 metres in length and 4 to 12 metres in width (Ljungkvist & Frölund 2015: 14–20).[14] The hall has been partially excavated and is currently dated to the 6th or 7th century, the same as the two excavated royal mounds (Ljungkvist & Frölund 2015: 6). Although no complete large houses dating from before the 6th century have been found, layers and features underneath later constructions in the manor area have also been dated to the 5th century (Ljungkvist & Frölund 2015: 8). These finds suggest that Gamla Uppsala had already become an important centre with a gradually stratifying society by the Migration Period, and continued to be so until the Middle Ages, as is demonstrated by the medieval church built on the highest ground in the 12th century. Based on archaeological evidence, there is thus good reason to believe that Adam was not far off when he described the magnificent *templum* of Gamla Uppsala, although the construction may have been used for various purposes. Stefan Brink (1996) has suggested that the large halls which Latin writers refer to using the term *templum*, and which have been found by archaeologists at several central sites in Scandinavia – e.g. Lejre in Denmark, where a hall of similar magnitude has been excavated (Christensen 2010) – probably represent banqueting halls where rituals as well as feasts took place. As he points out, in the case of the three icons, Adam actually uses the term *triclinium* ('dining room') and not *templum*.

7.2.2 Adam's account of human sacrifice

The accuracy of the description of the gruesome human sacrifices is difficult to assess, especially considering that it comes not at first hand from Adam, but through the reported observations of other (according to Adam), Christian, witnesses. Ritual killing of humans seems definitely to have occurred during the Viking Age; this is suggested by archaeological analyses of numerous graves from that period where the main burial appears to be accompanied by another, deliberately injured and sometimes tied-up person (e.g. Price 2012b: 266–267; Naumann et al. 2014). It is also part of the surviving 10th-century description of a chieftain's ship burial by the River Volga in *Risala* (pp. 17–18).[15] All these ritual killings, however, are specifically linked to a funeral and thus hardly count as evidence that human sacrifice was a common religious practice during seasonal celebrations like the one Adam describes in the 11th century. Adam's chronicle was of course intended to be read by members of the clergy in Rome and it is possible that he gave some extra colour to the description – for example, as regards the human sacrifices – to emphasise the need for the Catholic Church's involvement.

Communal sacrifices of material objects and animals, too, were commonly conducted even during the Viking Age; however, it is again uncertain if the cultic activities at that time commonly involved human sacrifice.[16] The Lunda grove cult site in Södermanland (south-east Sweden), for example, shows activity from the 2nd century BC until the 10th century AD, but the deposits are mostly burnt bones of livestock, jewellery, weapons, etc. (Andersson 2006, cited in Andrén 2005: 110). The finds from Käringssjön in Halland (south-west Sweden) where sacrificial ceremonies were carried out between AD 200 and 400 are mostly vessels of food, wooden artefacts, stones, etc. and contain no bone material (Carlie 1998). Naturally, human bones have been found in cult sites, for example, at the Röekillorna spring (Stjernquist 1997) or in the sacrificial bog at Skedemosse on Öland which was used until about the 10th century AD (Hagberg 1967). Skedemosse has preserved a unique record of offerings and it is thought that the large deposits were made during collective cultic gatherings that included the entire population of the island (Andrén 2005: 110). Both above-mentioned places are, however, believed to have been used over extremely long periods – Skedemosse for more than a dozen centuries and Röekillorna possibly even longer – so the occurrence of human bones in these sites might be largely fortuitous.

The preserved bodies found in peat bogs in northern Europe – dated from the Mesolithic to the modern era, but with the majority of the most famous finds dating from 500 BC until AD 200 – are often assumed to have been human sacrifices (e.g. Aldhouse-Green 2015) because they often (but not always) show signs of injury and physical force (e.g. hands tied, rope around neck, blindfolded) (see Glob 2004). Although human sacrifice is impossible to rule out, there are other possible explanations for these deaths. Stephen Briggs (1995) has developed a theory according to which all bog bodies should be understood as accidental deaths. Although it is very likely – if not certain – that many of these people must have died by accident, Briggs' argument is not always entirely convincing. Especially dubious is his explanation that the ropes found around the bodies' necks may have resulted from people attempting to pull drowning people out of the bog when the body was slowly sinking and only the head was visible (Briggs 1995: 177); even if we accepted this interpretation and ascribe the irrational rescue method to panic caused by the life-or-death situation, it does not explain the tied hands, physical trauma and the wooden stakes which are sometimes found pinning the bodies down in the bogs.

The most widely favoured theory is that these natural mummies were criminals or social outcasts who were executed by drowning. This argument builds largely on Tacitus who – although not mentioning criminals in this specific context – reports that cowards, men who evaded combat and the *corpore infames* ('infamous of body') were pushed into bogs with wicker hurdles (Ger ch. 12, ed. p. 44, tr. p. 43).[17] Overall, it is probably common sense to recognise that any or all of the above-mentioned reasons, and some others unknown to us, may have been at play at any given time, either separately or in combination. For example, if some of these people were indeed sacrificed, they were probably singled out due to their deviant social position or, as Miranda Aldhouse-Green (2015) emphasises, 'visually special' qualities (also Parker Pearson 2003: 71). War captives and criminals in particular must have presented a serious problem in small-scale agricultural communities – if released they would have been dangerous, if not, food and other amenities had to be provided for them. Execution would have provided a way out of this problem, and we can expect that the grisly nature of the punishments became more palpable in the public eye when adorned with religious regalia. Human life generally must have been too valuable in sparsely populated communities to be thrown away on sacrifice. Although providing fascinating insights, the bog bodies are found piecemeal in isolated contexts and are thus limited in their capacity to help us understand societies as a whole. From the archaeological record it generally seems that human sacrifice was not as common as the provision of other gifts, whoever the intended recipients of the offerings were.

In light of this other evidence, Adam's description of the grand sacrifice of at least ten humans – one for each day of the celebration and at least one plunged into a spring – at the time of writing begins to seem exaggerated, to say the least. It is possible that he used the description of a sacrifice at Lejre by Thietmar (Chr I, ch. 17, ed. p. 11; tr. p. 80) as a model for his work. However, Thietmar's work, too, poses problems. For example, he assigns the last of the great sacrifices at Lejre, with an astonishing 99 humans and numerous animals, to the year 934, which is approximately 80 years before he finished his first book, and thus is by no means contemporary nor based on first-hand observation.[18] The reliability of his insight in this matter is therefore questionable and the information fabricated from speculation. No human bones have been found at the location where the large timber hall – built as an almost identical reconstruction of an earlier 5th- to 6th-century hall nearby, and used until the 10th century – existed in Lejre and where sacrificial ceremonies would have most likely taken place (Christensen 2010: 251–253). Based on archaeological evidence, we are justified in believing that a magnificent hall(s) surrounded by gravemounds and used for public celebrations was indeed present in Gamla Uppsala, most likely from the Migration Period until Adam's own time; the reality of the communal manslaughter he describes is, on the other hand, far more doubtful.

7.2.3 *Icons and processions*

The finds from north European peat bogs bring us to another topic mentioned in connection with Freyr's cult: the wooden statues which supposedly stood in the hall. That wooden icons indeed existed is again confirmed by finds of such objects in peat mosses and bogs dating from as early as the 3rd and 2nd centuries BC (Aldhouse-Green 2004: 59–61; Glob 2004: 180–185); that they were really used in religious contexts is suggested in some early histories as well as in Old Norse sources (e.g. Háv st. 49; ÓsTrF pp. 213–214). Tacitus' oft-quoted

1st-century description of a ritual procession in Jylland, for example, involves a wagon attended by a male priest being driven around containing a wooden icon, entitled Nerthus by the author (Ger ch. 40, tr. p. 58).[19] According to this record, Nerthus was an earth deity and her wagon was kept in a sacred grove on an island, but at certain periods the priest escorted her with the wagon to visit the people, probably to bless the crops. This period was a time of peace, followed by the ritual washing of the goddess and her wagon in a hidden lake; the slaves that performed this act were drowned in the same lake immediately after they had finished, possibly because they had seen and touched her image, which was covered during the journey but exposed to the slaves when they ritually washed her. It is unknown to what extent exactly such consecrated wagons were used; however, here too we find some support from archaeology: the famous Dejbjerg wagons from a west Jutland bog date from about the same period as Tacitus's report (Gunnell 1995: 60) and fragments of similar vehicles are known from elsewhere in Denmark (Klindt-Jensen 1949; Jensen 1980; Hansen 1984), the Netherlands (van der Sanden 2001), etc.[20] A very richly carved ceremonial cart – possibly built before AD 800 – was found also in the Oseberg ship in southern Norway (Brøgger 1928).

Icelanders seem to have accepted the idea that such religious processions involving material representations of venerated persons had really taken place in Scandinavia only a few centuries earlier. A passage preceding Óláfr Tryggvason's demolition of the statue of Freyr in *Flateyjarbók* describes how the Svear appointed a young priestess to transport his statue around settlements in a wagon (Flat 1, pp. 337–339). An Icelandic outlaw suspected of manslaughter became acquainted with the priestess and helped her drive the wagon. Freyr, unappreciative of this act, attacked the man, but having lost the duel, jumped out of the idol and nothing was left but a wooden log. The outlaw dressed himself as Freyr and travelled around Svealand. After some time the priestess became pregnant, but people saw it as a confirmation of Freyr's ability to intervene in the earthly affairs of fertility. The narrative tone here is intentionally satirical; however, the story provides an interesting perspective on what medieval Icelanders thought of the worship of Freyr. Despite a gap of more than a dozen centuries, the accounts of Tacitus and the *þáttr* exhibit a high degree of correlation: both individuals, in the form of icons, are connected to fertility and driven around in a wagon attended by a human guardian of the opposite gender (Gunnell 1995: 53–60); this element has been interpreted as symbolising *hieros gamos* (Gunnell 1995: 59; McKinnell 2005: 55).

It is evident that the *trémenn* served as material representations of individuals from very early on and thus were probably also part of the cult in Gamla Uppsala. Óláfr's satirical tale of the two *trémenn* inserted into Freyr's gravemound as mock human sacrifices seems fanciful. On the other hand, it is very possible that material objects that were used in cultic rituals were 'sanctified' before they were put into use, perhaps by deliberately depositing them into gravemounds or other liminal and intimidating places such as bogs – neither land or sea. Personal items, as well as objects produced especially for burials, were surely given to the dead with the intention of being kept by their owners, simply out of respect, for comfort or to help the departed ward off the unknown. At the same time, archaeologists have long known that pagan graves were reopened regularly and the items inside removed and sometimes replaced. Rather than indicating ransacking, which is mentioned in late sagas (e.g. BsS ch. 20; Grs ch. 18), the predominant reason for this – as was suggested by Anton Brøgger (1945) – was probably of ritual nature, as the buried items would be imbued with the special powers and personal characteristics of their possessors (e.g. Brendalsmo & Røthe 1992; Klevnäs 2007, 2016; Aspöck 2011).[21] It is possible that the *trémenn* which later became cultic representations of Freyr may have been inside his gravemound and were thus believed to have assumed some of Freyr's qualities. Even if we insist that the description in Óláfr's saga is driven by medieval euhemerism, it could represent a real memory of a time-honoured tradition.

That items of value were buried or hidden with the intention to be found again for emotional or practical reasons is also suggested by the fact that objects from wet environments are often discovered near rows of posts and stakes, as well as timber trackways (e.g. van der Sanden 2001; Carlie 1998). The Dejbjerg wagons, for example, were clearly fenced off with stakes, probably to help mark their location. It has been pointed out that it might be thus more appropriate to talk about 'deposits' rather than 'offerings' in these contexts and perhaps even to downplay the religious meaning of such activities (Fabech & Näsman 2013: 68–70). Although graves and bogs were most likely seen as having a special character, owing to associations with their long-term links with past life and societies, deposits in these places may at times have been made simply for safe keeping (Fabech 2006, cited in Fabech & Näsman 2013: 69). Tribute from the Svear, too, was according to Snorri stored in Freyr's gravemound by a selected group of *menn* before public worship and offerings for *ár ok friðr* started; Snorri specifically states that in this way the *ár ok friðr* of these *menn* – not the Svear as a whole – continued. In this specific context, the *ár ok friðr* is thus quite literally the tribute received by a group of manipulators, probably Freyr's kinsmen and allies who thereby continue their own privileged life. The divine connotations which have been read into the phrase *ár ok friðr* owe a great deal to the academic sacral kingship paradigm of which it is a central aspect, and to the expectations embedded in contemporary mindsets, which generally favour the idea of pagan gods as beings that had not previously existed as humans. Freyr was a ruler and his anticipated ability to secure the *ár* would have been a reasonable expectation in a farming society, with no divinity required.

Snorri's comment that the current ruler and all the landholders were required to attend the great *blót* and join in the ceremonial beer-drinking in memory of the gods as well as their own kinsmen that lay buried in the gravemounds implies, too, that the gods were the ideological equals of rulers' ancestors. The absence of these individuals would have meant that access to their ancestors – who had the ability to influence the society as a whole – would have been lost. As legal descendants they had the sole ability to be heard by the 'gods' and other privileged ancestors who had been buried in the large gravemounds surrounding the central manor area. The equal rank of Freyr and ancestors is mentioned also in the 13th-century *Víga-Glúms saga* (chs 25–26) which was written in a very different environment

118 *Case studies*

and probably less concerned with Christian euhemerism than the sagas of kings and Snorri's mythology. This inheritance tale provides a description of a lawsuit over a piece of land which the protagonist Glúmr attempts to retain. He is approached by his *frændur framliðnir* ('departed relatives') in a dream who agree to intercede with Freyr on his behalf and help protect him from being driven away from his land. In this late saga, which takes place in Iceland, we thus witness again the role of ancestors in land laws. Although no longer seen in direct association with specific gravemounds in the memories of the settlers, they provide assistance through a dream and in spirit form. Their interference manifests itself in the earlier passages of the saga by the appearance of the *hamingja* ('spirit') of the protagonist's grandfather who has previously – during a *dísablót* in Norway – provided Glúmr with family heirlooms for protection. The appearance of the spirit – in the form of a supernaturally over-sized woman (a *dís*?) who walks across the land over which Glúmr is fighting – coincides with the grandfather passing away. The dead relatives' interference thus confirms their importance in land laws also in Iceland, which in this tale is featured by the manifestation of ancestral regalia received from the protagonist's grandfather and his appearance in the form of an ancestral being.[22] The fact that the dead kinsmen are proximate to Freyr, or at least have more direct access to him, suggests that the author himself saw them as being of similar rank. Freyr is the most frequently mentioned Scandinavian god in *Landnámabók* and the Icelanders' general familiarity with him is manifested in a number of sagas, which mention activities of ritual nature being dedicated to him (e.g. Vatn chs 10–15; Gís ch. 15; HsF chs 2–6; Fs ch. 26).

The cult of Freyr probably goes back to at least the Migration Period and lasted half a millennium or more. It is predominantly tied to eastern Sweden, as is indicated by the abundance of place names containing his name there, but also to the Viken area (Brink 2007: 109–111, 125–127). It is possible that a group of people with relations to Freyr migrated from the west to the east sometime around the middle of the millennium and settled in Gamla Uppsala where the cult took root after his death. The timeframe corresponds roughly with the changes seen in the archaeological diaspora, which indicates the distancing of the elite and the development of a central state in Gamla Uppsala. Nothing in the descriptions of Freyr screams 'divine'; instead they emphasise his imagined proximity to other ancestors and the existence of his gravemound cult, which must belong to the cult's earliest stage and which may at some point have become represented by a statue inside a large banquet hall. His role as a divine progenitor for the Ynglingar is problematic. It is more likely that in pagan mindsets, he was perceived as a human ruler whose cult was part of more widespread ancestor worship, but had superior qualities attached to him due to his success in the socio-political sphere.

7.3 Hálfdanr svarti

Another Yngling reported to have been worshipped on the public scale at his gravemound(s) is Haraldr hárfagri's father Hálfdanr svarti who ruled in the Oppland area in Norway in the 9th century together with his half-brother Óláfr

Geirstaðaálfr. Hálfdanr is not listed in *Ynglingatal*, which follows his brother's line, but his own lineage and cult are described in *Hálfdanar saga svarta* in *Heimskringla* (ch. 9) and in one version of *Óláfs saga Tryggvasonar* (Flat 1, pp. 566–567), which contains some additional details. Both texts note that the harvests were good during his reign and that much trust was placed in the king even after his death. Following his drowning in a frozen lake, the chieftains from different parts of the land wanted to obtain his body and to bury it in their own district. It is said that the people believed that the dead king's body was *árvænn* ('promising good seasons') and that those who possessed the body could expect to have continuously prosperous seasons. It was decided that the body would be divided between the different districts: each chieftain took home a part of the king's corpse and laid it in a gravemound; this resulted in different cult sites which became known as *Hálfdanarhaugar* ('the mounds of Hálfdanr') where the public could perform ritual practices so that prosperity would continue.[23]

Comparisons to the case of Hálfdanr have been drawn, for example, with modern folk belief in the magic effects of the body (von Sydow 1935: 109) and to the cosmogonic myth of Ymir, whose body is divided to create the universe (Dillmann 1997: 149–158). Others have argued that the cult differs from other examples of gravemound worship found in the Old Norse sources, i.e. Freyr and Óláfr, because Hálfdanr is not presented as belonging to the supernatural world (e.g. the gods or the *álfar*) (Näsström 2001: 90). Instead, his cult resembles the veneration of holy relics found in other cultures; according to the 1st-century historian Ploútarkhos, for example, the senators of Rome killed King Romulus and distributed pieces of his body to each senator to take away (*Romulus* p. 32). The perspective thus dwells on the assumption that deceased kings were seen mostly as non-humans after they died. Lars Lönnroth (1986: 90) has tenuously tied the alleged ritual mutilation of Hálfdanr to the case of another Yngling, Dómaldi, who was murdered by his *árgjǫrn* ('eager for good harvests') subjects (Yngl ch. 15; Yngt st. 5). The verb used for Dómaldi's sacrifice in the poem is *sóa* ('to sow'), meaning that his dismembered body might have been used as seeds to induce the fertility of the land. This suggestion seems far-fetched, building essentially on the aspects associated with sacral kingship at the time of research: the king is ritually sacrificed to the earth goddess to revive the fertility of the land. Even though the physical presence of dead rulers was probably important as it confirmed the legal status of their descendants, Sundqvist (2002: 280) has already commented on the improbability, or at least rarity, of physical mutilation of the sort depicted in Hálfdanr's case.[24] There is no evidence (with the obscure exception of Dómaldi) to suggest that dismembering dead rulers was an active practice in Scandinavia. We should probably favour the versions given in *Fagrskinna* and *Ágrip af Nóregskonungasǫgum*, which is dated to the end of the 12th century, according to which Hálfdanr's body was buried whole in Hringariki. This, however, does not mean that the description of his ritual mutilation in *Heimskringla* and *Flateyjarbók* is worthless or even entirely incorrect. A more pragmatic approach would be to explain this aspect of the cult as a matter of medieval fictitious commodity, coerced by contemporary political expediency, although it is possible that multiple memorial stones or gravemounds (with or without his remains) were indeed dedicated to and named after the king (Ellis 1968: 100). These structures may have served to create a space with a spiritual aura to encourage offerings of tribute by the people living in these areas.

Steinsland (2011: 40–42) has come up with the most convincing ideological rationale behind the narrative. She believes it to be a foundation tale, created to cement the political power of Hálfdanr's descendants – the hárfagri clan – and of Óláfr helgi in particular, who is the central character in the *Heimskringla* collection and notorious for taking advantage of his distinguished ancestry to gain power. The histories preceding Óláfr's own are thus likely to have been composed in a way that would help centralise political control and to justify his rule as a monarch. As Steinsland points out, Hálfdanr is the first Yngling in the chronological sequence of kings' sagas who has a separate account dedicated to him. Following *Ynglinga saga*, the first book of *Heimskringla* that deals with the prehistoric kings of Sweden as a group, and precedes that of Haraldr hárfagri (Óláfr helgi's great-great-grandfather), is the concise saga of Hálfdanr, which features two principal parts. The first involves descriptions of Hálfdanr's conquests over specific places in south-east Norway, and the second is the description of his mutilation and his cult. The conquered areas are also the locations which – albeit with considerable variations between different manuscripts – are listed as the places where the *haugar* are raised. The regions where Hálfdanr had ruled are thus quite literally designated by the author with different parts of the king's body, meaning that Óláfr helgi's claims for each of these geographical territories went back *til haugs ok heiðni*, to his fifth ancestor in the male line (and beyond into prehistory). Tucked between Hálfdanr's conquests and death are descriptions of two dreams. In one, his wife removes a thorn from her clothes which grows into a tree so big that its branches reach all of Norway (Hss ch. 6); in the other, the king's hair has locks of different lengths and colours, but one lock is longer and brighter than others (Hss ch. 7).[25] Steinsland draws the reasonable conclusion that the dreams generated an image of Óláfr as a righteous Christian and the predestined ruler of a unified Norway, while 'burying' his pagan ancestor in the land that would become the first regions of Norway to be united validated his legitimacy in accordance with pagan ideology.

Steinsland's take on the saga is persuasive. Medieval writers were more often than not propagandists with axes to grind and general social, political and religious turmoil was likely to also have been the force behind this product. Regardless of motive, the material provides another reference to a pagan cult that was triggered by a person's death and his anticipated ability to continue to ensure a good life for the wider community. Irrespective of whether the king's corpse was believed to have been buried in different places or buried at all, according to *Óláfs saga Tryggvasonar* (Flat 1, p. 567) people apparently believed in the *haugar* of Hálfdanr and brought him sacrifices until this was finally forbidden by his relatives. 13th- and 14th-century authors and audiences clearly found such activities and the idea of multiple gravemounds dedicated to the same pagan king realistic. The *haugar* were according to this version places of public worship, dedicated to a person we can classify as a 'superior ancestor'. The comment that the king's relatives banned the ongoing ritual activities at the gravemound, again only found in *Flateyjarbók*, may have served the purpose to present the later members of the hárfagri clan as moral Christians. It nonetheless indicates that gravemounds were seen and publicly accepted as the 'property' of the dead person's living relatives. According to the proposed anthropological framework, the family members may have been seen as having the ability to invoke the deceased king for help or to hold back his favours, thus underpinning their social position and limiting succession to their own kin group; this fits well with the general political and economic situation in Norway at the time.

Regardless of the agenda at play, the foundations for the tale of Hálfdanr's cult derive likely from the period when the king died. Large gravemound complexes dating from the 9th century have been found in the Vestfold area and contain incessant offerings, revealing concern for well-being in afterlife (e.g. Christensen et al. 1992; Larsen & Rolfsen 2004; Herschend 2003). A number of these mounds bear Hálfdanr's name even today (Brøgger & Shetelig 1950: 191; Myhre 2006: 301–302), demonstrating a general familiarity with the story of his cult, which must have been so popular that it lived on in re-tellings throughout the centuries. It has been suggested that the part about the dissected body was added by historians in order to find a reasonable explanation for the existence of several gravemounds that already bore the same name in folk tradition (Brøgger 1916: 58–65). This idea cannot be rejected considering that our knowledge of the cult is confined to texts dated to the 13th century and later.

7.4 Óláfr Geirstaðaálfr

A cult to a dead king in a gravemound is found also in the *Flateyjarbók* redaction of *Óláfs saga helga* (2, pp. 6–9) and in a few later *þættir* (see SÓkhh) which also belong to the biography of Óláfr helgi and which contain some additional details.[26] According to these sources, Óláfr Guðrǫðarson who ruled in Vestfold in the 9th century and who is the last ancestor listed in *Ynglingatal* (st. 26; also Yngl ch. 49, prol p. 4) was worshipped by his people after his death. There were no bad years during his reign, but shortly after his death a pestilence broke out and the harvests failed. Despite the king having previously dreamt of the forthcoming events and requested his people not to make sacrifices, people decided to venerate the king with sacrifices to recover the good harvests – they started to call him the *álfr* of Geirstaðir. A detailed study of the later compilations by Anne Heinrichs (1993: 44–50) suggests that regardless of the 12th-century ideology which pervades these *þættir*, they contain components which are of pre-Christian origin. *Ynglingatal* – silent about his cult – notes that the king died of gout; this has led to the character's identification with the man who was found in the Gokstad ship near Gjerstad whose leg revealed signs of injury (Brøgger 1916, 1945: 35–40; see Skre 2007). This remains speculation; tales of a pagan king's burial in Gjerstad, however, must have been widespread as they continued in folk legends until the early 20th century (Bugge 1934: 23–28).

122 Case studies

The *þáttr* that includes the description of the cult is about the birth of Óláfr Haraldsson, posthumously (*inn*) *helgi*. It begins with the reign and death of the pagan king Óláfr Guðrøðarson – Óláfr helgi's ancestor – who lived about a century before the Christian king. He died in Geirstaðir and was buried in a large gravemound with his retinue and many grave goods. The king himself was seated on a chair holding his personal belongings: a sword, a belt, a knife and a bracelet. Since Óláfr had prior to his death dreamed that famine was approaching, he had instructed the people to prepare a large gravemound in which the king and his followers were later to be buried. When preparations were being made for the future burial, the king requested his people to not bring him offerings and sacrifices after he dies because – despite the initial honouring of the dead – their identity becomes forgotten over time and they are 'turned into trolls' (i.e. unidentified ancestors). When the king died, his commands were ignored and people sacrificed to him *til árs sér* ('for fertile seasons'). The famine then subsided.

About 100 years later, the dead Óláfr appears in a dream to a man called Hrani inn víðfǫrli and whom he instructs to break open the large gravemound, to decapitate the occupant with his own sword and to remove the deposited treasures. Hrani should then use the belt to help the present queen to give birth to a son, whom the pagan king appearing in the dream insists must be named Óláfr. His gold ring and sword should later be given to the yet-to-be-born king who is nobody else but Óláfr helgi. When Hrani goes to the queen who is unable to deliver the child and places the belt around her waist – after eliciting a promise from her that the child will be called Óláfr – the baby is born. The description of Óláfr helgi's birth is thus accompanied by a story of the rebirth of his ancestor, which becomes possible only after the removal of the ancestral regalia that has been inside the gravemound for a century and by giving the child the same name as the ancestor who wishes to be reborn; the author specifies that the relatives and in-laws of Óláfr helgi believed that he was the old king reborn and that he thus inherited many great talents from his predecessor (SÓkhh pp. 726, 735). As in other medieval conversion tales, the events are integrated quite illogically, showing how confused they were in the author's mind. However, the misunderstood and artificial settings in a way make the elements contained in the text – the belief in rebirth, the public gravemound cult, the importance of ancestral heirlooms and the motif of having to give a child an ancestral name to make his birth seem preordained – more credible as evidence for a strong ancestor–descendant relationship in 9th-century Norway.

Óláfr's inclusion in *Ynglingatal* and his assumed descent from a god, Freyr, his ability to secure the *ár*, his transformation into an *álfr* and the public worship dedicated to him are all features that have been seen as the necessary pieces to align this king with the sacral kingship model (e.g. Ström 1954: 32–38; Ström 1959; Turville-Petre 1964: 193–195; Ellis Davidson 2001: 100, 136, 142). With the general shift of scholarly focus towards the socio-political situation in Viking Age and early medieval Scandinavia, interpretations of this case have persuasively sought to integrate the folkloristic aspects with the propagandist message behind this literary product. These aspects were considered also by earlier scholars, such as Nora Chadwick (1946); however, the most thorough analysis of the source is by Anne Heinrichs (1993), whose study reasons that the author's determined effort to relate Óláfr helgi to Óláfr Geirstaðaálfr probably served a similar purpose as the story of Hálfdanr: it was necessary to show that Óláfr helgi descended from an ancient distinguished family and was therefore destined to rule the geographical areas where his ancestors had lived. At the threshold of the Christian conversion, pagan legal processes still had to be followed in order to inherit property, so it was necessary to trace ancestry back five generations, approximately 100 years. However, for someone who wished to be shown as an envoy of God, the pagan ethics of legacy must have presented a problem. On the one hand, being obligated to present Óláfr helgi as the foremost promoter of Christianity and a fiercely non-pagan king, and on the other, presenting the five pagan ancestors necessary for legal land claims, whilst eliminating those elements which would have thrown undesirable light on the king, the author of this tale must have found it difficult to find ways of establishing a connection between the two characters.

As Heinrichs argues, the writer solved the issue by presenting the old Óláfr as a dualistic character, combining both pagan and Christian elements. This is visible in the confused passage containing Geirstaðaálfr's speech before his death in which he discourages people from offering him sacrifices after his death, because apparently he fears of becoming a 'troll' as time passes (SÓkhh p. 729) – even in his time, the respectable ancestor of Óláfr helgi had condemned pagan traditions, but had no real power to stop the sacrifices to gravemounds; the gravemound itself, however, had to be present in the story as this became the fundamental element in Óláfr helgi's legal claim to Vestfold. Heinrichs (1993: 47–49) further suggests that the dualism is also apparent in the old king's name – sometimes he is called Geirstaðaálfr, and sometimes *digrbeinn* ('thick-leg'), which is remarkably close to the regnal name *digri* ('stout') used of Óláfr helgi during his lifetime. In her interpretation, the name *digrbeinn* presents a respected king who had secured the welfare of his people, and Geirstaðaálfr a dangerous, supernatural deity who was worshipped at his grave. By using both names, young Óláfr benefited from the old law, but escaped conflict with Christian teachings. This suggestion is less satisfying. As was considered previously, the *álfr* epithet likely held special relevance for the people living in the Viken area where *álfar* traditions seem to go far back in time. As Gunnell (2007a: 124–127) has already explained, if the term *álfar* refers to the groups that had lived in the Viken area, it was useful for later Norwegian rulers to emphasise their relationship with Álfheimar and to present the pagan Óláfr as an inhabitant of this region. It is more likely that the name variations in the surviving texts are due to general confusion in folk memory or among the scribes.[27] Although it is possible that both names were used alongside each other at some point, the *álfr* element was probably more meaningful in legal contexts than *digrbeinn*. Considering that Óláfr Geirstaðaálfr is reported to have died of gout, the pejorative 'thick-leg' is not entirely unexpected. Diana Whaley's (1993: 133) observation that *digri* was used for Óláfr helgi almost exclusively by his enemies in hostile contexts suggests that in his case the name held negative connotations, although it may also refer to his strong physical build (Ósh ch. 3). There seems to be no obvious link between the nicknames of the two kings – *digrbeinn* and *digri* – both seem justified in their own context, although later authors may have made use of the semantic relatedness of the words to reinforce the kings' genealogical relation.

With this reservation, Heinrichs' argument overall is convincing. The potential religious conflict was probably mitigated by the author by linking the two Óláfrs with both pagan and Christian traditions. The old king living in the pagan world is buried in a large gravemound and worshipped with offerings, but this is done against his will. The young king can only be born if the old traditions are followed and the ancestral heirlooms extracted from the gravemound are present, but as a proper Christian he admits no personal role in it. As he passes Geirstaðaálfr's gravemound with a follower who wants to know when he was buried in the grave, the king proclaims that his soul could not possibly exist in two different bodies. The fact that the author made an effort to present the pagan Óláfr as a more righteous pagan than his contemporaries is seen also in several segments of the king's pre-death speech: he first warns people about bringing him sacrifices in the fear of becoming a 'troll', but nonetheless makes the promise that neither he nor his retinue buried in the gravemound will cause people any harm; regrettably for his people, this means that they will have no power to help either. The king relinquishing such powers prior to his death suggests quite clearly that this is how dead people were generally seen and indicates the degree of influence they were believed to wield over the living: potentially harmful and dangerous, yet benevolent and possessing powers that went beyond those of the living. These polarised qualities are characteristic of ancestors across the globe. Pagan Óláfr is presented thus as a transitional character in the story, neither wholly pagan nor wholly Christian. His distancing from the other pagan dead is made most obvious in a passage following his death. It is explained that after the crisis had passed, people apparently went back to keeping the promise they had made to the king and stopped making sacrifices, but this decision angered *hiner illu vætter* ('the other evil beings'), presumably all the other dead that had been turned into 'trolls' and who had been expecting such respect (SÓkhh pp. 729–730).

The pagan Óláfr's involuntary transition into a 'troll' seems to have nonetheless occurred despite his earlier promise: when Hrani enters the great barrow, the residents inside are said to have become raucous, scaring off his followers. Hrani's duty to cut off the king's head in order to get the heirlooms before leaving the mound indicates also a very hostile environment – regardless of the king's efforts to avoid undergoing the precarious transformation from an ancestor to a nameless ghost-figure, he has started to lose control over his actions, presumably until he is allowed to be born again. The rebirth is symbolised through giving a descendant his name and putting his personal belongings into use; the ancestral grave goods seem to have again acquired magical qualities that determine the outcome of an event: the birth of Óláfr helgi. Hrani seems to be singled out for the duty of obtaining the family heirlooms from the ancestral grave because of his kin ties to the family. He is the foster-brother of Óláfr helgi's father Haraldr grenski (who by the time of the described events has himself passed away), and thus the nearest (and possibly oldest) living male relative who must assume the responsibility of interacting with the family's ancestors and who has legal access into the gravemound.

Thus, the aim of this tale as a literary product, which Heinrichs (1993: 45) has so excellently summarised that it would be unreasonable to paraphrase her, was

> to legitimize Óláfr's rule as a *fylkiskonungr* of Vestfold, which would be the legal basis for his claim to sovereignty over all of Norway, like his ancestor Haraldr hárfagri. The story clearly establishes that Óláfr could trace his ancestry back to *haugr* and *heiðni*, that Vestfold was his *óðal* and that he had been expressly chosen by his ancestor to be the owner of the regalia which symbolise his legitimate reign.

These political strategies, however, clearly reveal efforts to fit political manoeuvring into day-to-day social routines and religious conventions, many of which can be recognised as typical constituents of ancestor cults everywhere. Needless to say, practices dedicated to ancestors need not be bound up with the concept of rebirth, but generally speaking, there is a strong association. The possibility of being reborn can be restricted to people with specific positive qualities and status, as well as having a proper burial – something which Óláfr Geirstaðaálfr as a successful ruler buried in a large gravemound seems to fulfil – the idea that a person can experience a series of lifetimes through rebirth, usually into the same family in order to reinforce continuity, is often the driving motivation behind ancestor cults. The elements brought into play in the story of Geirstaðaálfr may have been exaggerated and fantasised by the writers, but they are based on generally familiar concepts that did not conflict with people's understanding of recent paganism. With Óláfr helgi under the spotlight, ancestors are very much the little man behind the scenes in this tale. The *þáttr* depicts, most ornately, the cult of a pagan king who received sacrifices in his gravemound as part of a common ancestor cult.

* * * * *

Freyr is often interpreted as the divine progenitor of rulers in Old Norse scholarship. When we look at the sources, there is no real evidence that he was perceived or presented as a divine being. Instead, the sources quite consistently suggest that he was perceived as a human ruler who had been revered at his gravemound and later inside a cult house. It is rather unfortunate that studies of religion in pagan Scandinavia often judge the sources which depict Freyr as a human ruler to be medieval creations, while texts of a mythological nature which depict him as a god with supernatural features are taken to be authentic. I am not suggesting that mythological motifs were never extracted from their narrative settings to provide real religious insights. However, the divine and mythic aspects are probably overemphasised in discussions of religion, and in Freyr's case, derive to a great extent from the older scholarly theory of sacral kingship, which builds on *Ynglingatal* and *Ynglinga saga*, and insists that Freyr had the role of a divine progenitor. In my view, *Ynglingatal* definitely counts as a genealogy; however, it is also an artistic composition intended to have a dramatic effect, which means that we probably should not try to seek entirely rational consistency in its presentation.

The cases discussed above, especially those of Hálfdanr and Óláfr, were certainly motivated by the desire to augment the prestige and power of the hárfagri dynasty. The strategy behind the narratives, however, does not mean that the reported events were not deep-rooted in social values, nor does their artistic context discredit their core content. Recurring elements such as gravemound worship suggest that people in later times believed the stories to be true or at least found them compelling enough to allow the leading families to exploit these narratives for their own benefit. The very existence of genealogical lore demonstrates how important the representation of the past was to people, especially in relation to political authority. Having buried ancestors was the legal basis for land ownership, inheritance and identity, and they were also a crucial tool for the rising monarchy on the threshold of the country's conversion to Christianity. All the sources are coloured by Christian influences, but they must contain some genuine pagan features and be based on accepted cultural norms.

Since sacrifices to these three men were made by entire communities, they are often excluded from discussion of ancestor worship. Building on the superior ancestor theory, the argument at present is that these public cults were part of a widespread ancestor cult in late Iron Age Scandinavia. It suggests that the artistic genealogies were so easily manipulated because pagan 'gods' were perceived by the populace in essentially the same way as the remote human ancestors of rulers. The possibility of dead rulers being credited with unique abilities that helped protect society as a whole was based on two assumptions: dead rulers were ancestors and thus inherently more powerful than the living, and as rulers they were therefore superior to other social groups, and subsequently earned religious attention on a public scale.

Notes

1 This first appears in the phrase *Freys afspring* ('Freyr's offspring') (Yngt st. 10) and then as *Freys óttungr* ('Freyr's descendant') (Yngt st. 16). Snorri begins the saga with a description of Óðinn, even though he does not link Njǫrðr and Freyr to him by kinship.
2 The title *Ynglingar* is mentioned by Snorri (Yng prol), Ari (Ísb pp. 27–28) and in a few other late texts (e.g. HN ch. 9).
3 A similar idea has been proposed by Lars Lönnroth (1986: 91), who classifies *Ynglingatal* as a satirical *senna*-type poem, a kind of agonistic verbal duel.
4 Gerðr has been identified as Freyja (Bibire 1986). She calls Skírnir her brother's killer, which probably refers to Skírnir taking Freyr's sword as compensation for the journey (Skm st. 9–10) and whose absence brings about Freyr's death at Ragnarǫk (Ls st. 42; Gylf chs 37, 51).
5 The exception here might be *goðkynning* ('descendant of gods') (st. 20); however, it still cannot be considered as a reference to the 'divine' since it is not certain how *goð* was understood by the Norsemen.
6 Schjødt's (2014) latest discussion on this topic includes a more critical analysis to this approach.
7 E.g. the *ljósálfar* 'light *álfar*' who inhabit *Álfheimar* are said to be brighter than the sun (Gylf ch. 17). Freyr's alter ego is Skírnir 'bright, shining', and he is killed by his counterpart Surtr 'swarthy' (Vsp sts 51–52). Freyr is also said to control the shining of

the sun (Gylf ch. 24), and the kenning *álfrǫðull* ('álfr disk', i.e. the sun) in *Skírnismál* (st. 4) probably refers to Freyr (Hall 2007: 30, 38).
8 Snorri's interpretation of Manheimar as 'world of men' is rejected – the meaning is 'worlds of love or desire' (Finlay & Faulkes 2011: 12, n. 31).
9 E.g. Snorri refers to Eyvindr skáldaspillir as his source of knowledge about *Manheimar*, who writes in *Háleygjatal* (st. 2) – a praise poem believed to be modelled after *Ynglingatal* – that Óðinn lived in *Manheimar*. Snorri himself states that Óðinn went to Goðheimar after he died (Yngl chs 9, 12).
10 A similar statement comes from Saxo's report about King Frothi (GD, V, ed. p. 142; tr. p. 157), sometimes identified with Freyr, who is called *inn fróði* in *Skírnismál* (st. 2) and who is associated with *Fróðafriðr* ('Fróði's peace') (Yng p. 24).
11 For discussion of issues with Fricco's identity as Freyr, see Janson (1998).
12 *Skyldi full um eld bera, en sá, er gerði veizluna ok hǫfðingi var, þá skyldi hann signa fullit ok allan blótmatinn, skyldi fyrst Óðins full – skyldi þat drekka til sigrs ok ríkis konungi sínum – en síðan Njarðar full ok Freys full til árs ok friðar. [...] Menn drukku ok full frænda sinna, þeira er heygðir hǫfðu verit.*
13 Useful discussions can be found in Sundqvist and Vikstrand (2013).
14 The origin of the name *Uppsala* is unclear, but according to one interpretation it could mean 'elevated hall' (see Vikstrand 2013).
15 It is generally favoured in Western scholarship that the described group represents North Germanic merchants travelling the Volga trade route (e.g. Duczko 2004; Price 2012a), although their exact identity is indefinite and it is possible that local cultural influence was at play in the described ceremony (see Montgomery 2000; Price 2012a: 267). It is possible that the group, known as Rus, refers to people from the Roslagen province by the south-east coast of Sweden who were accustomed to travelling on the rivers in modern Russia; the name is probably connected to modern Finnish (and Estonian) Ruotsi (Rootsi) for Sweden (Brink 2012: 6–7).
16 For more examples concerning cult sites, see Brink (2001) and Walaker Nordeide and Brink (2013).
17 The greater majority of found bog bodies are of adult males; overall, the proportion of children and women is small. In human societies men exclusively commit the overwhelming majority of crimes and acts of violence according to criminologists (Heidensohn & Silvestri 2012). The *corpore infames* is sometimes understood as a reference to homosexuality, but it more likely refers to people with bodily deformations (Neill 2009: 126–127).
18 It is also noteworthy that Thietmar does not mention the name Lejre in his initial writings about the sacrifice, but only in later additions to the text. He is probably correct though in this aspect, and it is generally accepted that Lejre was an important central location as late as AD 1000 (Christensen 2010: 239).
19 It has been suggested that Nerthus was a male deity, perhaps identifiable with Njǫrðr (North 1997b). Others (e.g. Bibire 1986: 26–27; McKinnell 2005: 55) believe that such fertility figures existed in both male and female forms, i.e. Nerthus and Njǫrðr. This idea is perhaps supported by the bog idols which sometimes come in pairs.
20 For further references, see Egg and Kaul (2001).
21 The importance of dug-up ancestral regalia is evident also in literature (Heinrichs 1993).
22 Very useful discussion about the connection between ancestors and *dísir* is found in Gunnell (2000) and Kaplan (2000).
23 According to Snorri (Hss pp. 92–93) and *Óláfs saga Tryggvasonar* (Flat 1, pp. 566–567), the cadaver was divided among four places: his head was buried at Steinn in Hringariki and the rest was divided among Raumariki, Vestfold and Heiðmörk/Vingulmörk. One version of *Fagrskinna – Nóregs konunga tal* (*viðbætur* p. 366) notes that the body was divided among three places – the entrails were buried in Þengilsstaðr in Haðaland, the body at Steinn in Hringariki and the head in Skírnissalr in Vestfold.

According to another version (*Fagrskinna – Nóregs konunga tal* p. 58) and *Ágrip af Nóregskonungasǫgum* (p. 3) the body was buried undivided at Steinn in Hringariki.

24 The bodies of some Anglo-Saxon kings are known to have been divided in the hope that they would impart luck (Chaney 1970: 95–96).

25 Both *Heimskringla* and *Flateyjarbók* (1, pp. 562–563) note that Hálfdanr was advised to sleep in a *svínabæli* ('pigsty') in order to receive prophetic dreams. Since Freyr has associations with pigs in the mythological tradition and was himself buried inside a mound, it has been speculated that the word in a figurative way refers to a burial mound (Chadwick 1946: 64–65). It is true that contacting the dead through dreams (often by sitting or lying on graves) to learn about the past or to predict the future is a common element in Old Norse literature (see Chadwick 1946: 61–65; Ellis Davidson 2001: 123–125) and is found worldwide (Bulkeley 2008). A list of medieval laws that forbid the *útiseta* ('sitting-out') custom performed at gravemounds can be found in Tolley (2009: 133–134). Concerning memories about *útiseta* in later times, see Jón Árnason's folktale collection *Íslenzkar þjóðsögur og æfintýri* (1862: 436–440). As far as I am aware, only one other character is mentioned in connection with the word *svínabæli* and that is Jarl Hákon, who hides in it from Óláfr Tryggvason (ÓsT chs 48–49). It is said that his slave dug a large *grǫf* ('pit') under the *svínabæli*, which was then covered with timber and earth. This description does not clearly state that the hiding place is a grave, however, one of the many meanings of *grǫf* is also 'grave' (de Vries 2000: 193) and Hákon dies in it. The description finishes with the odd statement that the *svínabæli* was under a great stone; unless the indication is that the sty was under a shadow of the stone, it seems more likely that the underlying meaning is that the *grǫf* symbolises Hákon's grave that is under a memorial stone. What the exact relationship between the *svínabæli* and Hálfdanr's dream might be is unclear.

26 The *þáttr* has survived in six late medieval manuscripts. The oldest text, contained in the *Legendary saga* of Óláfr helgi, dates from approximately 1200 (Johnsen 1922: 1–4); four variants of the same manuscript are from the 14th- and 15th-century *Independent* or *Separate saga* of Saint Óláfr by Snorri (Johnsen & Jón Helgason 1941, II: 715–735) and one separate *þáttr* known as *Þáttr Óláfs digrbeins* is dated to the 15th century (Heinrichs 1993).

27 The texts are inconsistent regarding the kings' identities and names. For example, according to one text, the son of Haraldr hárfagri (i.e. Óláfr helgi) was the one called Geirstaðaálfr and had a dream about the approaching famine (SÓkhh pp. 725–726). The episode is followed by Hrani's dream and the description of young Óláfr being born and named after Óláfr digrbeinn. It seems that the writer exchanged the two names and by accident attached a story elsewhere linked to Óláfr digrbeinn (or Geirstaðaálfr) to Óláfr helgi.

Secondary sources

Aldhouse-Green, Miranda (ed.) 2004, *An archaeology of images: iconology and cosmology in Iron Age and Roman Europe*, Routledge, London.

Aldhouse-Green, Miranda, 2015, *Bog bodies uncovered: solving Europe's ancient mystery*, Thames & Hudson, London.

Andrén, Anders, 2005, 'Behind "Heathendom": archaeological studies of Old Norse religion', *Scottish Archaeological Journal*, vol. 27, no. 2, pp. 105–138.

Aspöck, Edeltraud, 2011, 'Past "Disturbance" of graves as a source: tophonomy and interpretation of reopened early medieval inhumation graves at Brunn Am Gebirge (Austria) and Winnall II (England)', *Oxford Journal of Archaeology*, vol. 30, no. 3, pp. 299–324.

Baetke, Walter, 1964, *Yngvi und die Ynglinger. Eine quellenkritische Untersuchung über das nordische 'Sakral-köningtum'*, Sächsische Akademie der Wissenschaften zu Leipzig. Philologisch-historische Klasse: Sitzungsberichte, 109, 3, Akademie-Verlag, Berlin.

Bergsveinn Birgisson 2008, *Inn i skaldens sinn. Kognitive, estetiske og historiske skatter i den norrøne skaldediktningen*. Doctoral dissertation. University of Bergen. Available from: https://bora.uib.no/handle/1956/2732?show=full (accessed 16 August 2018).

Bertilsson, Ulf, 1986, 'Rock carvings and graves: spatial relationships', in G. Steinsland (ed.), *Words and objects: towards a dialogue between archaeology and history of religion*, Norwegian University Press, Oslo, pp. 9–20.

Bibire, Paul, 1986, 'Freyr and Gerðr: the story and its myths', in R. Simek et al. (eds.), *Sagnaskemmtun: studies in honour of Hermann Pálsson on his 65th birthday, 26th May, 1986*, Hermann Böhlaus Nachf, Wien, Köln and Graz, pp. 19–40.

Brendalsmo, Jan, and Gunnhild Røthe, 1992, 'Haugbrott eller de levendes forhold til de døde – en komarativ analyse', *Meta*, vol. 1–2, pp. 84–119.

Briggs, Stephen, 1995, 'Did they fall or were they pushed? Some unresolved questions about bog bodies', in R. Turner and R. Scaife (eds.), *Bog bodies: new discoveries and perspectives*, British Museum Press, London, pp. 168–182.

Brink, Stefan, 1996, 'Political and social structures in early Scandinavia. A settlement-historical pre-study of the central place', *Tor*, vol. 28, pp. 235–281.

Brink, Stefan, 2001, 'Mythologizing landscape. Place and space of cult and myth', in M. Stausberg (ed.), *Kontinuitäten und Brüche in der Religionsgeschichtem*, de Gruyter, Berlin and New York, pp. 76–112.

Brink, Stefan, 2007, 'How uniform was the Old Norse religion?' in J. Quinn et al. (eds.), *Learning and understanding in the Old Norse world: essays in honour of Margaret Clunies Ross*. Medieval Texts and Cultures in Northern Europe, 18, Brepols, Turnhout, pp. 105–135.

Brink, Stefan, 2011, 'Gudhem – the toponymic evidence (or rather challenge)', in O. Grimm and A. Pesch (eds.), *Gudme/Gudhem phenomenon. Papers presented at a workshop organized by the Centre for Baltic and Scandinavian Archaeology*, Schleswig, April 26th and 27th, 2010, Karl Wachholtz Verlag, pp. 15–23.

Brink, Stefan, 2012 [2008]. 'Christianisation and the emergence of the early Church in Scandinavia', in S. Brink and N. Price (eds.), *The Viking world*, Routledge, London and New York, pp. 621–628.

Brøgger, Anton, 1916, 'Borrefundet og Vestfoldkongernes graver', *Videnskapsselskapets Hist. Filos. Klasse*, vol. 1, pp. 1–67, Videnskapsselskapet, Kristiania.

Brøgger, Anton, 1928, *Osebergfundet*, 2, Universitetets Oldsaksamling, Oslo.

Brøgger, Anton, 1945, 'Oseberggraven–Haugbrottet', *Viking: Tidsskrift for norrøn arkeologi*, vol. 9, pp. 1–44.

Brøgger, Anton, and Haakon Shetelig, 1950, *Vikingeskipene*, Dreyer, Oslo.

Bugge, Kristian, 1934, *Folkeminne-optegnelser. Et Utvalg*, Norsk Folkeminnelag, Oslo.

Bulkeley, Kelly, 2008, *Dreaming in the world's religions: a comparative history*, New York University Press, New York and London.

Carlie, Anne, 1998, 'Käringsjön: a fertility sacrificial site from the late Roman Iron Age in South West Sweden', *Current Swedish Archaeology*, vol. 6, pp. 17–37.

Chadwick, Nora, 1946, 'Norse ghosts: a study in the *Draugr* and the *Haugbúi*, 1–2', *Folklore*, vol. 57, no. 2 and 3, pp. 50–65, pp. 106–127.

Chaney, William, 1970, *The cult of kingship in Anglo-Saxon England: the transition from Paganism to Christianity*, University of California Press, Berkeley and Los Angeles.

130   Case studies

Christensen, Arne et al., (eds.) 1992, *Osebergdronningens grav: vår arkeologiske nasjonalskatt i nytt lys*, Schibsted, Oslo.

Christensen, Tom, 2010, 'Lejre beyond the legend – the archaeological evidence', *Settlement and Coastal Research in the Southern North Sea Region*, vol. 33, pp. 237–254.

Clunies Ross, Margaret, 2011 [2005]. *A history of Old Norse poetry and poetics*, DS Brewer, Cambridge.

Clunies Ross, Margaret, 2014, 'Royal ideology in early Scandinavia: a theory versus the texts', *The Journal of English and Germanic Philology*, vol. 113, no. 1, pp. 18–33.

Dillmann, François-Xavier, 1997, 'Pour l'Etude des Traditions relatives á l'Enterrement du Roi Halfdan le Noir', *Sagas and the Norwegian Experience: 10th International Saga Conference, Trondheim, 3–9 August 1997*. Senter for middelalderstudier, NTNU, pp. 149–158.

Duczko, Wladyslaw, 2004, *Viking Rus: studies on the presence of Scandinavians in Eastern Europe*, Brill, Leiden.

Egg, Markus, and F. Kaul, 2001, 'Kultwagen', in H. Beck et al. (eds.), *Reallexikon der germanischen Altertumskunde*, 17: Kleinere Götter – Landschafts-archaäologie, De Gruyter, Berlin, pp. 463–478.

Ellis, Hilda, 1968, *The road to Hel: a study of the conception of the dead in Old Norse literature*, Greenwood Press, New York.

Ellis Davidson, Hilda, 2001 [1993]. *The lost beliefs of Northern Europe*, Routledge, London and New York.

Fabech, Charlotte, and Ulf Näsman, 2013, 'Ritual landscapes and sacral places in the first millennium AD in South Scandinavia', in S. Walaker Nordeide and S. Brink (eds.), *Sacred sites and holy places: exploring the sacralization of landscape through time and space*, Brepols, Turnhout, pp. 53–109.

Faulkes, Anthony, 1978–1979, 'Descent from the Gods', *Medieval Scandinavia*, vol. 11, pp. 92–125.

Finlay, Alison, and Anthony Faulkes (trans.), 2011, *Snorri Sturluson. Heimskringla, 1. The beginnings to Óláfr Tryggvason*. Viking Society for Northern Research, University College of London, London.

Glob, Peter, 1969, *Helleristninger i Danmark*. Jysk Arkæologisk Selskabs Skrifter, 7, i kommission hos Gyldendalske Boghandel, Copenhagen.

Glob, Peter, 2004 [1969], *The bog people: Iron Age man preserved*. New York Review Books, New York.

Grönbech, Wilhelm, 1931 [1909–1912]. *The culture of the Teutons*, 1, trans. W. Worster, Oxford University Press and Jespersen og pios forlag, London and Copenhagen.

Grundberg, Leif, 2000, 'Älvkvarnskult och offerkällor', in L. Ersgård (ed.), *Människors platser – tretton arkeologiske studier från UV*. Riksantikvarieämbetet arkeologiska undersökningar skrifter, 31, Riksantikvarieämbetets förlag, Stockholm, pp. 89–106.

Gunnell, Terry, 1993, 'Skírnisleikur og Freysmál: Endurmat eldri hugmynda um "forna norræna helgileika"', trans. Jón Karl Helgason. *Skírnir*, vol. 167, pp. 421–459.

Gunnell, Terry, 1995, *The origins of drama in Scandinavia*, D. S. Brewer, Cambridge.

Gunnell, Terry, 2000, 'The season of the *Dísir*: the winter nights and the *Dísablót* in early Scandinavian belief', *Cosmos*, vol. 16, pp. 117–149.

Gunnell, Terry, 2007a, 'How Elvish were the Álfar?' in A. Wawn et al. (eds.), *Constructing nations, reconstructing myth: essays in honour of T. A. Shippey*, Brepols, Turnhout, pp. 111–130.

Gunnell, Terry, 2007b, 'Viking religion: Old Norse mythology', in R. North and J. Allard (eds.), *Beowulf & other stories: a new introduction to Old-English, Old Icelandic & Anglo-Norman literatures*, Pearson, New York, pp. 351–375.

Hagberg, Ulf, 1967, *The archaeology of Skedemosse*, 1–2, Almqvist & Wiksell, Stockholm.

Hall, Alaric, 2007, *Elves in Anglo-Saxon England. Matters of belief, health, gender and identity*, The Boydell Press, Woodbridge.

Hansen, Henrik, 1984, *Fragmenter af en bronzebeslået pragtvogn fra Dankirke. Aarbøger for Nordisk Oldkyndighed og Historie*. Copenhagen, pp. 217–243.

Hasselrot, Pehr, and Åke Ohlmarks, 1966, *Hällristningar*, Nordisk Rotogravyrs Förlag and Norstedt & Söner, Stockholm.

Hedeager, Lotte, 2011, *Iron Age myth and materiality: an archaeology of Scandinavia AD 400–1000*, Routledge, London and New York.

Heidensohn, Frances, and Marisa Silvestri, 2012, 'Gender and crime', in M. Maguire et al. (eds.), *The Oxford handbook of criminology*, Oxford University Press, Oxford, pp. 336–369.

Heinrichs, Anne, 1993, 'The search for identity: a problem after the conversion', *Alvíssmál*, vol. 3, pp. 43–62.

Hellberg, Lars, 2014, 'Ortnamnen och den forntida sveastaten. Presentation av ett forsknings- projekt. Med en efterskrift av Thorsten Andersson', *Namn och Bygd*, vol. 101, pp. 9–31.

Herschend, Frands, 2003, 'Material metaphors: some late Iron and Viking Age examples', in M. Clunies Ross (ed.), *Old Norse myth, literature and society*, University Press of Southern Denmark, Odense, pp. 40–65.

Höfler, Otto, 1952, *Germanisches Sakralkönigtum*, 1. *Der Runenstein von Rök und die Germanische Individualweihe*, Niemeyer, Tübingen, München and Köln.

Janson, Henrik, 1998, *Templum nobilissimum: Adam av Bremen, Uppsalatemplet och konfliktlinjerna i Europa år 1085*, Göteborg Universitet, Göteborg.

Jensen, Stig, 1980, 'Fredbjergfundei. En bronzebesldet pragtvogn pa en veslhimmerlatidsk jernatder boptads', *Kuml*, pp. 169–216.

Johnsen, Oscar (ed.) 1922, *Olafs saga hins helga: efter pergamenthaandskrift i Uppsala Universitetsbibliothek*. Delagardieske samling nr. 8, Jacob Dybwad, Oslo.

Johnsen, Oscar, and Jón Helgason (eds.) 1941, *Saga Óláfs konungs hins helga. Den store saga om Olav den hellige. Efter pergamenthandskrift i Kungliga Biblioteket i Stockholm nr. 2 4to med varianter fra andre handskrifter*, vol. 2, Norsk Historisk Kjeldeskrifts-Institutt, Oslo.

Jørgensen, Lars, 1998, 'En storgård fra vikingetid ved Tissø, Sjælland', in L. Larsson and B. Hårdh (eds.), *Centrala platser, centrala frågor: samhällsstrukturen under Järnåldern: en vänbok till Berta Stjernquist*. Acta Archeologica Lundensia, 28, Almqvist and Wiksell, Lund.

Kaliff, Anders, 1997, *Grav och kultplats. Eskatologiska föreställningar under yngre bronsålder och äldre järnålder i Östergötland*. Aun 24, Uppsala University, Uppsala.

Kaliff, Anders, 2007, *Fire, water, heaven and earth: ritual practice and cosmology in ancient Scandinavia: an Indo-European perspective*, Riksantikvarieämbetets forlag, Stockholm.

Kaplan, Merrill, 2000, 'Prefiguration and the writing of history in "Þáttr Þiðranda ok Þórhalls"', *The Journal of English and Germanic Philology*, vol. 99, no. 3, pp. 379–394.

Klevnäs, Alison, 2007, 'Robbing the dead at Gamla Uppsala, Sweden', *Archaeological Review from Cambridge*, vol. 22, no. 1, pp. 24–42.

Klevnäs, Alison, 2016, 'Imbued with the essence of the owner: personhood and possessions in the reopening and reworking of Viking-Age burials', *European Journal of Archaeology*, vol. 19, no. 3, pp. 456–476.

Klindt-Jensen, Ole, 1949, 'Foreign influences in Denmark's early Iron Age', *Acta Archaeologica*, vol. 20, pp. 1–230.

132 Case studies

Krag, Claus, 1991, *Ynglingatal og Ynglingesaga: en Studie i historiske kilder.* Studia humaniora, 2, Rådet for humanistisk forskning, Oslo.

Larsen, Jan, and Perry Rolfsen (eds.) 2004, *Halvdanshaugen – Arkeologi, historie og naturvitenskap*, University of Oslo, Oslo.

Lindow, John, 2005 [1985]. 'Mythology and mythography', in C. Clover and J. Lindow (eds.), *Old Norse-Icelandic literature: a critical guide*, University of Toronto Press, Toronto, pp. 21–67.

Ljungkvist, John, and Per Frölund 2015, 'Gamla Uppsala – the emergence of a centre and a magnate complex', in F. Herschend, P. Sinclair and N. Price (eds.), *Journal of Archaeology and Ancient History*, 16, Uppsala University, Uppsala.

Lönnroth, Lars, 1986, 'Dómaldi's death and the myth of sacral kingship', in Lindow et al. (eds.), *Structure and meaning in Old Norse literature: new approaches to textual analysis and literary criticism*, Odense University Press, Odense.

Marold, Edith, 2012, 'Þjóðólfr ór Hvini, *Ynglingatal*, 26', in D. Whaley (ed.), *Poetry from the Kings' Sagas 1: from mythical times to c. 1035. Skaldic poetry of the Scandinavian Middle Ages*, *1*, Brepols, Turnhout.

McKinnell, John, 2005, *Meeting the other in Norse myth and legend*, D. S. Brewer, Cambridge.

Motz, Lotte, 1996, *The king, the champion and the sorcerer. A study in Germanic myth*, Fassbaender, Vienna.

Myhre, Bjørn, 2006 [1992]. 'The royal cemetery at Borre, Vesfold: a Norwegian Centre in a European periphery', in M. Carver (ed.), *The age of Sutton Hoo: the seventh century in North-Western Europe*, Boydell Press, Woodbridge.

Naumann, Elise et al., 2014, 'Slaves as burial gifts in Viking Age Norway? Evidence from stable isotope and ancient DNA analyses', *Journal of Archaeological Science*, vol. 41, pp. 533–540.

Näsström, Britt-Mari, 2001, *Blot: Tro og offer i det førkristne Norden*, Paf Forlag A/S, Oslo.

Neill, James, 2009, *The origins and role of same-sex relations in human societies*, McFarland and Co., Jefferson, North Carolina and London.

Nordland, Odd, 1966, 'Valhall and Helgafell: syncretistic traits of the Old Norse religion', in S. Hartman (ed.), *Syncretism: based on papers read at the Symposium on Cultural Contact, Meeting of Religions, Syncretism held at Åbo on the 8th–10th of September, 1966*, Almqvist & Wiksell, Stockholm, pp. 66–99.

North, Richard, 1997, *Heathen gods in Old English literature*. Cambridge Studies in Anglo-Saxon England, 22, Cambridge University Press, Cambridge.

Nygaard, Simon, 2016, 'Sacral rulers in pre-Christian Scandinavia: the possibilities of typological comparisons within the paradigm of cultural evolution', *Temenos*, vol. 52, pp. 9–35.

Olsen, Magnus, 1909, 'Fra gammelnorsk myte og kultus', *Maal og Minne*, pp. 17–36.

Parker Pearson, Michael, 2003 [1999], *The archaeology of death and burial*, Sutton Publishing, Stroud.

Phillpotts, Bertha, 1920, *The elder Edda and ancient Scandinavian drama*, The University Press, Cambridge.

Price, Neil, 2012, 'Dying and the dead: Viking Age mortuary behaviour', in S. Brink and N. Price (eds.), *The Viking world*, Routledge, London and New York, pp. 257–273.

Schjødt, Jens Peter, 2014, 'New perspectives on the Vanir God in pre-Christian mythology and religion', in T. Tangherlini (ed.), *Nordic mythologies: interpretations, intersections, and institutions*, North Pinehurst Press, Berkeley and Los Angeles, pp. 19–34.

Schröder, Franz, 1924, *Germanentum und Hellenismus. Untersuchungen zur germanischen Religionsgeschichte*, C. Winter, Heidelberg.

Schück, Henrik, 1905–1910, *Studier i Ynglingatal*, Akademiska boktryckeriet, Uppsala.

Skre, Dagfinn (ed.) 2007, *Kaupang in Skiringssal*. Norske oldfunn, 22. Kaupang Excavation Project, 1, Aarhus University Press, Aarhus.

Steinsland, Gro, 1991, *Det hellige bryllup og norrøn kongeideologi: En analyse av hierogami-myten i Skírnismál, Ynglingatal, Háleygjatal og Hyndluljóð*, Solum, Oslo.

Steinsland, Gro, 1992, 'Myte og ideologi – bryllupsmyten i eddadiktning og hos Snorri – om det mytologiske grunnlaget for norrøn kongeideologi', in Úlfar Bragason (ed.), *Snorrastefna, 25.–27. júli 1990*, pp. 226–240.

Steinsland, Gro, 2000, *Den hellige kongen. Om religion og herskemakt fra vikingtid til middelalder*, Pax Forlag, Oslo.

Steinsland, Gro, 2011, 'Origin myths and rulership. From the Viking Age ruler to the ruler of medieval historiography: continuity, transformations and innovations', in G. Steinsland et al. (eds.), *Ideology and power in the Viking and Middle Ages. Scandinavia, Iceland, Ireland, Orkney and the Faeroes*, Brill, Leiden and Boston, pp. 15–67.

Stjernquist, Berta, 1997, *The Röekillorna spring: spring-cults in Scandinavian prehistory*, Almqvist & Wiksell, Stockholm.

Ström, Åke, 1959, 'The king god and his connection with sacrifice in Old Norse religion', in *The sacral kingship. Contributions to the Central Theme of the VIIIth International Congress for the History of Religions*. Studies in the History of Religions, 4, Brill, Leiden, pp. 702–715.

Ström, Folke, 1954, *Diser, norner, valkyrjor. Fruktberhetskult och sakralt kungadöme i norden*, Almqvist & Wiksell, Stockholm.

Ström, Folke, 1983, '*Hieros gamos*-motivet i Hallfreðr Óttarssons Hákonardrápa och den nordnorska jarlavärdigheten', *Arkiv för nordisk filologi*, 98, 67–79.

Sundqvist, Olof, 2002, *Freyr's offspring. Rulers and religion in ancient Svea society*, Uppsala Universitet, Uppsala.

Sundqvist, Olof, 2009, 'The question of ancient Scandinavian cultic buildings: with particular reference to Old Norse *hof*', *Temenos*, vol. 45, pp. 65–84.

Sundqvist, Olof, 2012, '"Religious ruler ideology" in pre-Christian Scandinavia. A contextual approach', in C. Raudvere and J. P. Schjødt (eds.), *More than mythology: narratives, ritual practices and regional distribution in pre-Christian Scandinavian religions*, Nordic Academic Press, Lund, pp. 225–261.

Svava Jakobsdóttir, 2002, 'Gunnlöð and the precious mead', in P. Acker and C. Larrington (eds.), trans. K. Attwood, *The Poetic Edda: essays on Old Norse mythology*, Routledge, New York and London, pp. 27–58.

Tolley, Clive, 2009, *Shamanism in Norse myth and magic*, Academia Scientiarum Fennica, Helsinki.

Turville-Petre, Gabriel, 1964, *Myth and religion of the North: the religion of ancient Scandinavia*, Greenwood Press, Connecticut.

van der Sanden, Wijnand, 2001, 'From stone pavement to temple – ritual structures from wet contexts in the Province of Drenthe, the Netherlands', in B. Purdy (ed.), *Enduring records. The environmental and cultural heritage of wetlands*, Oxbow, Oxford, pp. 132–147.

Vikstrand, Per, 2013, 'Namnet *Uppsala*', in O. Sundqvist and P. Vikstrand (eds.), *Gamla Uppsala i ny belysning*, Swedish Science Press, Uppsala, pp. 135–160.

von Friesen, Otto, 1932–1934, 'Har det nordiska kungadömet sakralt ursprung?' *Saga och Sed*, pp. 15–34.

von Sydow, Carl, 1935, 'Övernaturliga väsen', in N. Lid (ed.), *Folketro*. Nordisk kultur, 19. Stockholm, Oslo and Copenhagen: Albert Bonniers Förlag, H. Aschehoug & Co.s Forlag and J. H. Schultz Forlag, pp. 95–159.

Walaker Nordeide, Sæbjørg, and Stefan Brink (eds.) 2013, *Sacred sites and holy places: exploring the sacralization of landscape through time and space*, Brepols, Turnhout.

Whaley, Diana, 1993, 'Nicknames and narratives in the Sagas', in *Arkiv för nordisk filologi*, vol. 108, pp. 122–146.

Widholm, Dag, 1999, 'Rock art as a part of Bronze Age funerary rites – the case of the Hjortekrog Cairn', in J. Goldhahn (ed.), *Rock art as social representation. Papers from a session held at the European Association of Archaeologists Fourth Annual Meeting in Göteborg, 1998*, Archaeopress, Oxford, pp. 65–75.

8 The Háleygjar

This chapter reviews evidence to support the idea that members of the Háleygjar dynasty, and in particular Þorgerðr holgabrúðr, were the objects of ancestor – and superior ancestor – worship. The extant material concerning Þorgerðr has often been strongly folklorised and is clearly driven by Christian religious and political motivations, but it exhibits characteristics which might be traced to the early stages of her cult. The sources suggest that Þorgerðr was a protecting – albeit capricious – patron of Jarl Hákon and his family, and was worshipped by them in the northern parts of Norway. It is possible that her cult grew out of practices performed at her gravemound, but expanded at later stages and moved inside cult houses. Increasingly supernatural characteristics were probably attached to her person over time, leading to her full demonisation by Christian authors. However, this chapter argues that the sources contain a number of elements which allow her to be identified as a prototypical ancestor figure. Her position as a superior ancestor is less clear than in the case of the previously discussed male characters, as less is known about the extent and magnitude of her cult. However, identifying her at least as a venerated ancestor offers a more adequate explanation of her varied role in the sources than, for example, linking her with sacral kingship or religious ruler ideology; such links are here therefore rejected.

8.1 The Háleygjar and sacral kingship

Another genealogical praise poem similar to *Ynglingatal* is *Háleygjatal* ('enumeration of the Háleygjar') by the 10th-century Norwegian skald Eyvindr Finsson *skáldaspillir* (perhaps 'plagiarist'). It was written in honour of Jarl Hákon Sigurðarson (c. 937–995) of Hlaðir (east Trondheim), who ruled over a part of Norway in the second half of the 10th century and who has entered history as the last pagan king of Norway, despite him never claiming such a title (Krag 2012: 647).[1] The poem begins by emphasising the distinguished descent of the family, tracing it back 'to the gods' (*til goða*); this time, however, the union of Óðinn and a woman called Skaði is claimed to form the genealogical basis of the lineage.[2] Sæmingr – the first jarl of Hlaðir, whose offspring ruled over Trøndelag and Hálogaland between the 9th and 11th centuries – is said to descend from this couple. The poem contains similar elements to those in *Ynglingatal* and it is generally accepted that Eyvindr, for reasons of political rivalry between Trondheim and Vestfold (the geographical battleground where the formation of a united Norway started), used it as a model for his *Háleygjatal* (North 1997b: 39; Steinsland 2011: 26–35).

Eyvindr came from a noble family in Hálogaland and probably descended from Haraldr hárfagri on his mother's side and also from the Hlaðir group through his father (Marold 1993: 175–176). He served as a court poet to Hákon góði Haraldsson – a son of Haraldr hárfagri – who was on friendly terms with the jarls of Hlaðir because they supported him against the sons of Eiríkr blóðøx – another son of Haraldr hárfagri – who were allied with the Danes. After Hákon góði's death in a battle against Eiríkr's sons, which Eyvindr depicts in his *Hákonarmál*, the crown passed to Haraldr gráfeldr, one of Eiríkr's sons. The relationship between the new king and Eyvindr did not remain peaceful, so he renounced his interest in the power struggles between the Haraldssons and Eiríkssons of the hárfagri dynasty and instead joined the court of Jarl Hákon. After Jarl Hákon's victory over a group of mercenaries from the southern shores of the Baltic Sea – the Jómsvíkingar – Eyvindr composed *Háleygjatal*, in all probability intended as a propagandistic response to the political enmity between the hárfagri family and the jarls of Hlaðir (Steinsland 2011: 33). An account tracing Jarl Hákon's ancestry back to Óðinn, and thereby creating an analogy to Þjóðólfr's *Ynglingatal* with Freyr at the top, proved that he and his kindred were the social equals of the hárfagri clan. Like Þjóðólfr, Eyvindr alludes to former rulers' deaths and burial places, most likely to validate and to lend weight to the Hlaðir family's long-term presence in the Trøndelag area since time immemorial and thus their rightful claim to it. The two poems are very similar in gist.

The alliance between Óðinn and Skaði at the top of the Hlaðir family tree – and which results in the birth of Sæmingr (the equivalent to Fjǫlnir in *Ynglingatal*) – has again been discussed in connection with sacral kingship (e.g. von Friesen 1932–1934; Höfler 1952; Turville-Petre 1964: 190–195; Ström 1983). For earlier scholars who followed the Frazerian paradigm, the sacral king represented a cultic priest and a divinity who took part in the *hieros gamos* with a fertility goddess. Óðinn, who is conventionally understood as a god, thus became seen as the divine progenitor of the jarls of Hlaðir, and marries Skaði, a female character linked to Jǫtunheimar and to the northern regions in general in the mythological tradition.[3] Even though Skaði has little to do with fertility and is not always listed as a goddess – she appears as a giantess to be associated, like Óðinn, with warfare and fighting – scholars supporting the sacral kingship theory were not disheartened by this and instead focused on the male members of the lineage.

This framework did not change until Gro Steinsland (1991), who, as was discussed previously (see Chapter 7), took *Ynglingatal* and the union between Freyr and Gerðr in *Skírnismál* as her starting point and proposed that Skaði, the foremother of the Háleygjar according to the poem, played a crucial role in the motif. Steinsland has discussed this relationship in a series of studies (e.g. 2000, 2011) in the context of the *hieros gamos* as the basis of an origin myth. She believes that the mythic motif of an alliance between two socially opposite groups – the gods of Ásgarðr and the giantesses of Útgarðr – was used in later times by the leading families to legitimise their power (Steinsland 2011: 27–28). The outcome of their *hieros gamos* – the ruler – embodied the cosmic conflict which provided the following generations with special powers, but also predestined them to die early (Steinsland 2011: 28). Steinsland also emphasises Skaði's link to the earth – *Háleygjatal* refers to land as *brúðr Val-Týs* ('bride of slaughter-Týr'), i.e. Óðinn, which on account of the alliance in this poem could refer to Skaði (Chadwick 1950) – and reckons that the origin myth formed the basis for the entire ideology of rulership. This ideology was founded on an erotic bond between the jarls and the geographical territory over which they ruled, symbolically represented by Skaði (Steinsland 2011: 30–31). Steinsland's hypothesis has been generally well received, although less favourably in recent years. Margaret Clunies Ross (2014), for example, criticises Steinsland's work on methodological grounds. The poems – composed long before their recording by medieval Icelandic authors to suit their own purposes, usually in prose contexts – are essentially the authors' constructs; the surviving stanzas of *Háleygjatal* in particular are spread across various prose compositions. Although the poems have certainly preserved authentic material from the time of their original composition, interpretation must be cautious as the scattered nature of the poems in their preserved form does not allow us to fit their content into a uniform mythical structure, something which forms the basis for Steinsland's theory, Clunies Ross argues. The present study, too, questions the relevance and existence of such rounded mythical constructs in human religious consciousness, although Steinsland makes convincing points regarding the political background and purpose of the poem; her emphasis on the importance of the female aspect of genealogical lore in general is thought-provoking. The element of Steinsland's study which is relevant to the present study, however, concerns not Skaði, but the enigmatic Þorgerðr hǫlgabrúðr – a potential antecedent to the Óðinn–Skaði genealogy according to Steinsland (2011: 33–34).

According to a different tradition, the Háleygjar did not descend from Óðinn and Skaði, but from King Hǫlgi of Hálogaland, whose daughter was Þorgerðr hǫlgabrúðr (Skáld ch. 55). This name runs like a unifying thread through many sources concerned with Jarl Hákon, known for his close relationship with her. Skaldic poetry does not mention Þorgerðr; however, emerging from the hotchpotch of different Þorgerðr personages in the sources, earlier scholars (e.g. Chadwick 1950: 400–402, 414–415; Ellis Davidson 1998: 177–178) detected her character in the 10th-century *Hákonardrápa* by Tindr Hallkelsson (Skald 1, st. 1), which depicts Jarl Hákon's conquest of the land and contains the kenning *gims gerði* ('Gerðr' of a jewel). This find subsequently led to the proposal that Þorgerðr's original name had been *Gerðr*, which was in turn linked to Saxo's work where a woman called Lathgerda from Gaulardalr at Hlaðir is mentioned (GD IX, ed. pp. 251–255, tr. pp. 280–283); since Gaulardalr is the area where the cult of Þorgerðr was most prominent according to the extant sources, Lathgerda was identified as cognate with *Hlað(a)-Gerðr* ('Gerðr of Hlaðir') (Chadwick 1950: 414–415; Ellis Davidson 1998: 151–152, note 9).

138 Case studies

The purported connections do not, however, stop there, but in turn lead to others being proposed; since Freyr's partner in *Skírnismál* is Gerðr, sometimes recognised as Freyja (Ström 1954: 53–69; Bibire 1986: 26–27), the identification of Þorgerðr and Gerðr was taken as an indication that Þorgerðr, too, might be identical with Freyja (Lid 1942: 136–137; Chadwick 1950; Ellis Davidson 1998: 177–178). Evidence for this was seen in the fact that Þorgerðr's statue is sometimes mentioned together with that of Freyr (e.g. Flat I, pp. 407–409) and that Freyja, like Þorgerðr, is called *brúðr* (e.g. Skáld ch. 44). Since Freyja is in the mythological tradition presented as a sexually triumphant goddess of the *vanir* stock – a group inherently associated with the fertility cult by scholars – this link elicited discussion about the *hieros gamos* in connection with Þorgerðr and with Hákon's role as a sacral king (e.g. Chadwick 1950: 417; Ström 1983: 68–79; North 1997b; Ellis Davidson 1998: 177–178).[4] Steinsland (1991: 220–225, 2011: 33–34), for example, emphasises that Þorgerðr, like Skaði, is a giantess and an 'Útgarðr-woman'. She suggests that the relationship between Þorgerðr and Hǫlgi, representing a marriage rather than a father-daughter bond, resulted in the birth of a prototypic ruler and formed the basis for the later *hieros gamos* between Þorgerðr and Hákon, Hǫlgi's descendant; she was a patron goddess – the land personified – and *brúðr* of many successive rulers.[5] The idea that Þorgerðr is an embodiment of the land and thereby linked to many rulers has also been put forward by other scholars (e.g. Ström 1983: 75; North 1997b; McKinnell 2005: 84). Abram (2011: 127–142), for instance, has discussed the possibility that Hákon's relationship with the land might be symbolised in literature by his notorious sexual misdeeds towards the female community, although the author concludes that there is nothing godly about such abuse and that overall Hákon's role as a sacral king is unlikely.

The relation between these different versions of Þorgerðr and related characters had obviously become confused in the minds of medieval historians, and even if some authentic connections exist, it would be impossible to reconstruct a genuine successional history for any of them, because such clear-cut personalities probably never existed. Everything has a beginning, but these beginnings cannot be understood as isolated phenomena because beliefs, worldviews and values are in constant flux and religious–cultural concepts are adapted to changing and often idiosyncratic realities. Mythological topography in particular is exceedingly multifaceted and different races and beings blend and interact with each other, which means that concocting systematic yet intricate connections (such as those between the above-mentioned characters and sources) in order to fill the missing gaps in an academic theory is a slippery path. Much uncertainty remains about the degree to which these forms are identifiable with the Þorgerðr, who is said to have been worshipped in cult houses by Hákon and other members of his family. In recent years, scholars such as Terry Gunnell (2014) have encouraged and facilitated looking beyond the boundaries of conventional approaches to Old Norse religion and mythology in order to recognise that the present literary corpus is itself, too, folklore – a literary report of folk life, belief and memory at a specific point in time. When applying a more flexible, folklore-friendly approach to the material, we must presuppose that if an 'original' Þorgerðr ever did exist, the way in which she was perceived would likely have varied between different localities and even households from very early on. However, the confused and manifold traditions need not be seen necessarily in a pessimistic way. The more scattered and tangled up they are, the more they enable appropriate focus on those characteristics that occur regularly and that must have been the most well-known 'facts' about Þorgerðr's character.

It has become clear that Old Norse society was a typical lineage society where kinship ideology ran deep and legitimised inheritance rights; in such societies, the creation of the genealogies must be sourced in historical, matter-of-fact traditions and processes that allowed the establishment of the elite in the first place. It therefore seems fair to ask if studies which anticipate a genuine belief in the divine – albeit abandoning the outdated 'sacral kingship' term and acknowledging the underlying political aims – might not go a step too far given the religious and social realities of pre-literate Nordic societies. As was discussed in Chapter 3, the very foundation of religious practice in most ethnic societies is ancestors, and even if it is accompanied by beliefs in supernatural entities like creators or transcendental gods, these beliefs are hazy, ancillary and often sceptical. If we trust this socio-anthropological perspective, we are justified in reasoning that the Norsemen, too, are more likely to have believed in the humanity of gods than the divinity of rulers. Literary metaphors and names are also too often interpreted at face value instead of as poetic allegories or umbrella terms for broader concepts. For example, taking *brúðr* – a variant of Þorgerðr's ever-changing epithet – as a reference to her role as a 'bride' or 'wife' of Hǫlgi or Hákon and therefore as a link to 'sacral kingship' or 'ruler ideology' is misleading considering that it occurs so frequently and in different contexts, essentially meaning 'woman', which could refer to any female. The same meaning and frequency of use apply to *Gerðr*, disallowing identification with a single character – Freyja – simply because it sometimes concurs with her name. Rulers' relationship with the land as an epitomised fertility goddess, too, is a pervasive figure of speech in poetry and as Roberta Frank (2007) underlines, symptomatic of power, not belief in a sexual relationship with a mythical entity. Hákon's genealogical connection to the gods, his supposed participation in *hieros gamos* and his role as a sacral king is an overemphasised concept in Old Norse studies of religion and ruler ideology.

However, the question of Hákon's status as a sacral king is not relevant to this study. What is important is that the sources reckoned to contain elements suggestive of Hákon's *hieros gamos* do not seem to concern Þorgerðr; the theory of her participation in a sacred marriage is dependent on and derived solely from the mythic Freyr–Gerðr and Óðinn–Skaði model. Evidence nonetheless points towards a devoted relationship of some kind between her and Hákon's family, which sometimes takes on quite fanatical dimensions. This relationship will be examined in the next chapter which evaluates the content of the texts concerned with Þorgerðr; the point in focus is Þorgerðr's role as a foremother of the Háleygjar family, an idea previously examined by scholars like Else Mundal (1974) and Gunnhild Røthe (2007), who have classified her character as a *fylgja*.

8.2 Þorgerðr hǫlgabrúðr

Belief in Þorgerðr's existence is attested in various sources, ranging from sagas and historical writings to a grammar book, mythological accounts and, later, folk songs. The most frequently occurring designations for her – *hǫlgabrúðr*, *hǫrðabrúðr*, *hǫldabrúðr*, *hǫrgabrúðr* and *hǫrgatrǫll* (see Storm 1885; Røthe 2007) – all make sense in their own way.[6] *Hǫrðabrúðr* ('bride of Hǫrða(land)') and *hǫldabrúðr* ('bride of Holde') might relate to farmers in specific regions in Norway and imply associations with fertility and the land (Storm 1885: 124–125), an aspect that was earlier seen as forming a bridge to sacral kingship. *Hǫlgabrúðr* ('bride of Hǫlgi') indicates her relation to the Háleygjar or to Hǫlgi, as is suggested by Snorri and Saxo; the 'bride' element is taken to have a sexual undertone, again seen in connection with the 'sacred marriage'. *Hǫrgabrúðr* ('bride of *hǫrgar*') and *hǫrgatrǫll* ('troll of *hǫrgar*') might suggest an association with gravemounds (Røthe 2007: 53). Whether a single original name for her ever existed is uncertain, although it is by and large accepted that the *trǫll* component, which usually occurs in later (c. 14th-century) texts, evolved as a Christian reaction to reverence for her and that the name-forms containing *brúðr* are older (Storm 1885: 126; McKinnell 2005: 84). It has also been proposed that to her family, Þorgerðr was a *brúðr* and to rivals, a *flagð* ('troll woman') (McKinnell 2005: 85).

The often overlooked detail that the *trǫll* element was already in use at the beginning of the 12th century – the First Grammarian used it as a linguistic example in the *Fyrsta Málfræðiritgerðin* (c. 1130) – probably does not undermine the argument above, considering that also by that time Iceland had been Christian for more than a century and that this period would have been long enough to turn her character into a demonic being. Albeit intended as a treatise on orthography and therefore not shedding any ground-breaking information on the nature or role of Þorgerðr, this work is relevant as it is the earliest surviving record of Þorgerðr's existence (and one of the earliest surviving texts written in Icelandic).[7] The treatise also highlights two factors that account for the public image of her character in early 12th-century Iceland: she is tall, corresponding with later sources that similarly emphasise her height (e.g. BrN ch. 88), and she is placed on an equal footing with Þórr.[8] The grammarian's familiarity with Þorgerðr implies that she was easily recognisable to the Icelandic audience despite her cult being associated mainly with northern Norway; this shows that the traditions about her were widely known and entrenched in people's memory. Her equal footing with Þórr suggests, too, that she may have been seen as equally well known and important by the grammarian, despite Snorri leaving her out from the *ásynja* group in his *Edda*.

For a number of scholars, Snorri's failure to include Þorgerðr has meant that she was not considered to be a 'goddess', and various alternative suggestions have been made concerning her identity, e.g. giantess (Motz 1987: 221; Steinsland 1991), *valkyrja* (Lid 1942: 136), *dís* (Ström 1983: 75; Tolley 2009: 153), *fylgja* (Chadwick 1950; Mundal 1974; Røthe 2007) or a *vanir* woman (McKinnell 2005: 81–85). The boundaries among all these supernatural beings in the mythological tradition are – to put it mildly – hazy, so the idea that Þorgerðr was not listed as an *ásynja* by reason of her different 'identity' can hardly explain her marginal role in the *Edda*. Røthe (2007: 35, 51) has come up with the more convincing explanation that Snorri's perception of Þorgerðr was that of a real historical person. Geographical and temporal remoteness from the historians' own time and place may certainly have impelled them to assign, perhaps intuitively, some characters to a more eminent or supernatural status than others; then again, how could we ascertain the historians' perception and grasp of the mythological landscape? We need not necessarily assume that pagan gods and historical people were clearly differentiated in the minds of medieval authors. A simple lack of information about Þorgerðr does not explain her modest appearance in the *Edda* either, because most of the *ásynjur* (and essentially all women with the exception of Freyja) are also elusive in Snorri's mythology, but he nonetheless deemed them worthy of mentioning. On the other hand, it cannot be ruled out that Snorri's knowledge of Þorgerðr may have been far more abundant than indicated by the sources. If we are correct in assuming that she was known in the middle to northern coastal areas of Norway and that she was related to one of the foremost families there, then Snorri's familiarity with Þorgerðr-lore might have been on a more advanced level compared to the mythological goddesses who probably represented local deities from many different parts of Scandinavia (Mundal 1990; Gunnell 2007b). The lack of background facts concerning these other female deities from remote areas may have given Snorri more freedom to clump them all into a pantheon-like configuration, whereas Þorgerðr may have been distinctly linked to a specific kin group in his mind and therefore less malleable.

Whatever the reasons, the *Edda* was obviously crafted with different intentions than historiography, and Snorri accordingly ties her character to an enigmatic king called Hǫlgi in the *Edda* (Skáld ch. 55) and to the historical ruler Hákon in *Heimskringla* (ÓsTr chs 41–42, 48). While her role in the last source is limited to marriage to Hákon, *Skáldskaparmál* states that a spectacular gravemound was raised for both her and Hǫlgi – consisting of layers of earth and stones and of gold and silver offerings to them – where they were *blótuð* ('worshipped with sacrifices'). John McKinnell (2005: 84) has proposed that the Hǫlgi character is a late development, created with the purpose of explaining the origin of the name Hálogaland. Although there is no evidence for Hǫlgi's historical existence, skaldic verse reveals familiarity with this name already in the late 9th or early 10th century – Þórbjǫrn hornklofi mentions *Hǫlga ætt* ('Hǫlgi's kin') in *Hrafnsmál* (SKALD 1, st. 14), composed around the year 900, and the early 11th-century *Poem about Svǫldr* (SKALD 3, st. 4) by Skúli Þorsteinsson contains the kenning *Hǫlga haugþak* ('the thatch of Hǫlgi's gravemound', i.e. gold). McKinnell (2005: 84) rejects the relevance of the above-mentioned skaldic verses for the evaluation of the Háleyjar cult due to their enigmatic nature. Indeed, skaldic poetry as a genre was deliberately created in an enigmatic manner by the poets according to Snorri (e.g. Skáld ch. 8), and it is possible that aesthetic form was prioritised over content (Würth 2007). According to the rapidly expanding field of cognitive poetics, poetry has the capacity to exploit and to stimulate the spectators' cognitive processes for artistic purposes, often through metaphorical expression. This can be learned by the audiences through repetition, somewhat like with cross-word puzzles. This means that the human brain can, through recurring patterns, become familiar with and even begin to perceive fictitious stories and characters as if they were real.[9] However, it is hard to believe that the practice of verse-making would have continued through the centuries had its content been entirely beyond peoples' understanding. We do not know how skilled exactly the Norsemen were at recognising the kennings, and it is possible that an eponymous ancestor for the people of Hálogaland was invented (perhaps by these skalds). However, I think we are justified in assuming that Hǫlgi's *haugþak* as a kenning for 'gold' created a clever association for readers in the 10th century – ancient rulers were worshipped in gravemounds which were ornamented with precious offerings. We also know that the name and association with a gravemound cult goes back about 85 years before the composition of *Háleygjatal* and more than 300 years before *Snorra Edda*. Regardless of Hǫlgi's dubious existence, these skaldic pieces vouch for the description of the cult in the *Edda* and for the commonsense hypothesis that Þorgerðr's cult started at her gravemound.

Røthe (2007: 49–51) is probably correct when she explains the *hǫrgr* element in Þorgerðr's name in connection with her gravemound cult; even though *hǫrgr* has multiple meanings (Heide 2014) and the variant is almost certainly not an original one (it occurs in manuscripts from the 14th century onwards), it again signposts a ready association with gravemounds, even if only for Christian audiences.[10] Since there is little phonetic difference between *hǫlga* and *hǫrga*, it was not a far step for the later audiences to make this modification, probably in jest. One late *þáttr* which addresses Þorgerðr as *hǫrgabrúðr* extends this alteration to Hǫlgi, who is here called Hǫrgi – both are presented as sinister beings and Hákon as their idolator (Þþj pp. 213–214). This source clearly views pagan religion with a strong sense of amusement; however, the satirical epithet still suggests that pagan cults were remembered predominantly as gravemound cults.

Þorgerðr makes her foremost appearance in a sequence of *þættir* in the *Flateyjarbók* version of *Ólafs saga Tryggvasonar*. The biography of Óláfr Tryggvason is believed to have been written in Latin in the early 12th century by the Icelandic priests Oddr Snorrason and Gunnlaugr Sveinsson (Ashman Rowe 2005).[11] Intended to contain the biographies of Óláfr Tryggvason and Óláfr helgi and probably dedicated to Óláfr Hákonarson, the last living descendant at the time of composition, the scribe undoubtedly hoped to manipulate people's awareness of the political–religious turmoil at the time by praising the Christian kings and reprimanding their opponents (Ashman Rowe 2005: 22–23, 43, 54–61). The tales about Þorgerðr which consistently present her as the demonic companion of Jarl Hákon were quite obviously designed by the author as attacks on Hákon, the archenemy of Óláfr Tryggvason. The descriptions which derive mainly from independent manuscripts compiled in the 13th and 14th centuries as well as skaldic poems (Würth 1991) nonetheless represent the memories and public understanding of pagan cult at the time.

Þorgerðr is mentioned in four thematically ordered *þættir*. Beginning with *Færeyinga þáttr* (Flat 1, pp. 144–145), Hákon visits an enclosed cult house of Þorgerðr to receive her support for maintaining an alliance with Sigmundr Brestisson, who wishes to re-establish his rule over the Faroe Islands and so avenge his father who had been defeated by a man named Þrándr. It describes Hákon's attempt to attain a ring from Þorgerðr as a symbol of her willingness to help. Þorgerðr exchanges the ring for a substantial offering of silver, and Sigmundr defeats the rival. The storyline is simple and straightforward: Hákon attempts to establish an alliance with Sigmundr to expand his own power and in order to do so, turns to a patron for aid. However, the tale also unveils the hazards of pagan practices: when Sigmundr joins Óláfr Tryggvason and goes to the Faeroes to introduce Christianity there, he is killed by a farmer who desires the precious ring. As Røthe reasons, the pagan artefact obtained from the cult house, which had prior to the betrayal symbolised the friendship between Hákon and Sigmundr, now leads to death. The moral of the story is what every commoner should hear: favours sought and items obtained from the pagan world, albeit tempting and desirable, should be avoided at best because they can easily backfire. As variants of the interpolated *þættir* had probably circulated in oral tradition long before they reached the surviving manuscripts, these tales may have served the practical purpose of discouraging people from taking valuables from ancient graves and cult houses, probably for the profit of their rulers and affiliates. The Christian kings themselves have a reputation of having been active in the looting of pagan cultic places; e.g. Óláfr helgi was noted as having removed valuables from a pagan gravemound (ÓshF ch. 36).

The sequence continues with a tale about the *Jómsvíkingar* (Flat 1, pp. 191–193) which depicts Hákon's victory over a Danish force in a naval battle at a place called Hjǫrungavágr (see below), followed by *Þorleifs þáttr jarlsskálds* (Flat 1, pp. 213–214), where Hákon makes offerings to Þorgerðr in gratitude for her implementing vengeance on an Icelandic skald who composed *níð* against his father. Guided by her advice, Hákon crafts a *trémaðr* ('tree man'), kills a man and places his heart inside the idol, clothes the figure and names it Þorgarðr. Then he evokes the tree man with the 'devil's might' and instructs him to kill the skald. The narrative is, as expected, not confined to ridiculing Hákon, but it also conveys a further message, which praises Óláfr Tryggvason as the promoter of the Christian mission in the last tale concerned with Þorgerðr, *Rauðs þáttr ramma* (Flat 1, pp. 407–409). The Þorgerðr cult is brought to a miserable end by the king who removes her statue from the *hof* and burns it to stop her bringing about evil; he then strips the remains of the statue, binds it to his horse's tail and rides away. He places her on a high *stallr* ('altar'), adorns her with treasures and makes the people swear in the presence of Þorgerðr that they will now regard her with contempt.

The most exciting and perhaps valuable description of Þorgerðr in *Flateyjarbók* comes from the above-mentioned *Jómsvíkingar þáttr* (Flat 1, pp. 191–193), which describes how Hákon lands on an island and after reaching a clearing in a forest says prayers to his *fulltrúi* ('trusted friend') Þorgerðr and her sister Irpa, asking them for victory in battle. He prays to the north, but receives no answer. He offers sacrifices, but she again refuses. She finally accepts a human sacrifice and

144 Case studies

so Hákon decides that his son should be given to her in exchange for her help in battle. After the sacrifice is completed and Hákon invokes her, a magical storm ensues from the north, the sky turns black and thunder and hail arrive. Þorgerðr and Irpa are seen standing side by side with Hákon on his ship and it is said that it looked as if arrows were shooting from all of their fingers.

The *þættir* are indubitably driven by a particular purpose and influenced by their Christian ideological context. We find support for the idea that her cult was associated with the northern areas with respect to the location of Hjǫrungavágr: probably on the middle coastal area of Norway (Megaard 1999), which at the time was an interlace of Norse and Sámi communities. Considering the rationale and time of composition of *Flateyjarbók*, Þorgerðr's connection to the north might be coloured by medieval Christian theological associations of the north with the Devil and his servants. The negative connotations with the north have various roots and go back a long way; however, for medieval Scandinavian authors, these associations must have been at least partially buttressed by the fact that the Sámi peoples who held their ancestors in high regard remained pagan until the 18th century.[12] If Þorgerðr's original domicile was in the north, which is likely considering that nowhere in the reasonably copious sources is she linked to individuals other than the Háleygjar, it might be expected that the traditions about her reveal aspects attributed to the Sámi. The fact that Hákon prayed to the north and that the enchanted storm arrived from the north indicates Þorgerðr's residence there; however, this detail alone could be easily attributed to Christian influence. The associated weather magic, on the other hand, is regularly tied to the northern regions and the Sámi in particular in both vernacular and Latin literature (Perkins 2001), building a somewhat stronger ground for her 'northernness'.

Sources that associate the ability to cause storms at will with the *Finnar*, i.e. the different north Scandinavian groups, range from histories (e.g. *De Proprietatibus Rerum* p. 100, *Historia de Gentibus Septentrionalibus* pp. 172–173, *Norges historie* p. 236) and missionary reports (e.g. Thurenius 1910: 395; Solander 1910: 22–23; Forbus 1910: 32–33) to sagas (e.g. Ósh p. 11) and modern folklore (Kvideland & Sehmsdorf 1999: 151–152).[13] Some of these combine this ability with extraordinary skills in archery, offering a direct parallel to Þorgerðr and Irpa shooting arrows like no one else after having raised the storm (Chadwick 1950: 401–402). A remarkably similar description is found also in *Gesta Danorum* (I, pp. ed. 30–31, tr. p. 31), where an old man who fought against the Bjarmians – a group living around the White Sea (Simek 1986) – 'drew out […] a cross-bow, […] projected in an extensive arc, he fitted ten shafts to its cord and, briskly shooting them all at once'. Like Þorgerðr, the Bjarmians awoke a storm, but the old man fought back by raising clouds of his own. Weather witching is a form of incantation found all over the world and one that has lasted the test of time – during the major witch-hunt in the 16th century in Central Europe, for example, weather-magic was still one of the most frequent accusations (Behringer 2002). All aspects of (farm)life are connected to the weather and the practice cannot of course be confined to only a set of people known as Sámi in northern Europe. From the point of view of the Germanic Scandinavian cultural sphere, however, it seems that weather-magic was associated predominantly with the Sámi, and not necessarily regarded with contempt, but with curiosity and as a chance to learn (see Perkins 2001: 1–26). The recurring associations between weather-magic and the Sámi in different sources suggest they were widely known. Some of these associations are also found with Þorgerðr and were in circulation long before the composition of *Flateyjarbók*. A certain holgabrúðr causing grim weather and storms from the north is also mentioned in *Jómsvíkingadrápa* by Bjarni Kolbeinsson from 1222 (SKALD 1, st. 32), and *Búadrápa* (SKALD 1, sts 9–10) by Þórkell Gíslason – composed in the first half of the 12th century – notes that a 'very ugly troll-woman' shot arrows from her fingers and that after the battle Hákon's men weighed the massive hailstones that fell during the battle.[14] Regardless of Jón Þórðarson's effort to present Hákon as a raucously pagan king and idolator, it is likely that Þorgerðr's northern domain was an original feature, even if reinforced by the author due to the lucky coincidence that Hákon happened to come from this area.

A potential link to the Sámi might also be found via Þorgerðr's proposed sister, Irpa, who appears in later prose texts (BrN ch. 88; Þþj pp. 213–214). McKinnell (2005: 84–85) explains Irpa, whose name has cognates in ON (*jarpr*), OE (*eorp*) and OHG (*erpf*), designating 'brown, dark, swarthy' as a reflection of Þorgerðr's double character: her dark and dangerous characteristics, the same way Skírnir ('shining') is the light alter ego of Freyr in *Skírnismál*. Symbolism of this kind cannot be ruled out; for example, according to one late and heavily folkloric source, Þorgerðr also had a brother Sóti ('soot coloured') (Cleasby and Vigfússon 1874: 580), who was a demonic character. However, according to a recent study *jarpr* is not a general term for colour, but refers exclusively to human hair (Crawford 2014: 105–106, 127).[15] If the connection to the name Irpa is trustworthy, it would simply mean that Irpa was imagined as a dark-haired (Sámi?) woman.[16] Support for this idea might be found in the personal name Erpr, which in poetry (e.g. *Akv* st. 38) is given to the sons of foreign fathers (see McKinnell 2005: 84, note 16). Again, considering the Norsemen's dense interactions with the Sámi, who are typically viewed with a hopeful eye in regard to marriage, and with curiosity in regard to magic practices, the 'foreign' born sons could refer to the half-Sámi.

We know almost nothing else about Irpa, except that she may have been worshipped in a cult house together with her sister. According to *Færeyinga þáttr* (Flat 1, pp. 144–145), they stood alongside Horgi and many other gods whose identity is left to the imagination, while *Brennu-Njáls saga* (88: 214–215) aligns the two sisters with Þórr who, as was discussed previously, is mentioned in conjunction with Þorgerðr also in the *Fyrsta Málfræðiritgerðin*, albeit in a very different context. In *Rauðs þáttr ramma* (Flat 1, pp. 400–405, 408–409), the last tale in the Þorgerðr sequence, we find a portrayal of Freyr that mirrors the defacing of Þorgerðr's statue. There is no documentation of Þorgerðr sharing a place of worship with Freyr; however, his statue – which instead of a cult house had apparently been held inside his *haugr* – is also confiscated by Óláfr and burned together with Þorgerðr. Røthe (2007: 39) reasons that the relationship to Freyr and Þórr probably belongs to a later stage of Þorgerðr's cult; this might be, but the assumption is weakened by the lack of toponymic evidence for the existence of these male gods in the mid-coastal regions of Norway (Brink 2007: 109–111, 113–115). It is more likely that these relationships gave the authors a chance to broach Þorgerðr in a way that would speak to people. Creating a public image of Hákon's antagonistic patron that was equal to Freyr and Þórr – characters that people in southern Norway, where the plan for a unified Christian nation was launched, were more familiar with – helped to permanently smear her character. If we eliminate the idea of her co-existence with Þórr and Freyr by reason of authorial tactic, then we are left with Hǫrgi, Irpa and a number of anonymous 'gods' in her cult house; it starts to become more likely that the *hof* depicted in the sources may have been a sanctuary restricted to the members of the Háleygjar family.

That other Háleygjar besides Hákon were involved in visiting the *hof* is documented in *Harðar saga ok hólmverja* (chs 15, 19), where the cult of Þorgerðr expands to Iceland. A man named Grímkell – a close relative of Hákon – goes to the *hof* to ask Þorgerðr's blessing for a successful marriage for his daughter; she, however, refuses by reason of Grímkell's son having carried out *haugbrot* ('grave-breaking') of her brother Sóti's gravemound, stealing a gold ring; she prepares to abandon the cult house and says that Grímkell does not have long to live. Annoyed with her, Grímkell puts fire on the *hof*, but later that evening suddenly falls dead. This late source, preserved in two 15th-century manuscripts, is characterised by Christian and folkloristic motifs. For example, Þorgerðr does not refuse to bestow good luck on Grímkell's daughter, but fears that they will be forced to separate because great light shines over the daughter's head; the indication is obviously that conversion is imminent and she is getting ready to take her leave. However, she will not go without first taking vengeance for disloyalty; perhaps offended by the *haugbrot*, she goes after Grímkell.

McKinnell (2002: 269–270) has explained the death of Grímkell as Þorgerðr's demand for a human sacrifice. The idea that she received human offerings is indeed present, as was noted earlier, in *Jómsvíkinga þáttr*, *Jómsvíkingadrápa* (SKALD 1, st 30) and also in later prose texts, where some variations state that Hákon sacrificed his child; a similar motif is found in the whimsical tale of Hákon murdering a man in order to conjure up the tree man (Þþj pp. 213–214).[17] The rate of recurrence in which human sacrifice is associated with Hákon in the different sources suggests that the *idea* of pagans sacrificing humans was generally associated with the recent past. It is unlikely though that ritual murder was a common phenomenon in the 10th century – medieval authors would have probably deemed it less worthy of mention if it had been (Ellis Davidson 1992). It is more likely that it served a literary purpose, illustrating the pagan patron's final act of vengeance before releasing her followers, who would then switch faiths, as Kaplan (2000) has convincingly argued with regard to the *dísir* in *Þiðranda þáttr ok Þorhalls* (Flat 1 ch. 335). The conversion to Christianity must have been a critical time as it posed a direct threat to kinship alliances and family unity which were vital for success and even survival. The story of Þiðrandi is similar to the description in *Harðar saga*; the underlying theme there is the conversion to Christianity, which following the internal strife between the ancient dark and new light *dísir* – a set of

The Háleygjar   147

beings explained as foremother spirits of the family – culminates with the murder of a chieftain's son and the ancient spirits vacating the landscape (Mundal 1974; Kaplan 2000). The dark *dísir* being overthrown by their light counterparts clearly symbolise the acceptance of Christianity; however, Kaplan argues that the two opposing types of *dísir* also served another purpose: the replacement of the former dark *dísir* with the comparable light *dísir* allowed the continuity of earlier kinship ties and allegiance to ancestors. The *þáttr* consequently permitted 'historical continuity between the Christian and pre-Christian periods in Iceland conceived of in terms of kinship' (Kaplan 2000: 379). The narrative about Þorgerðr is not as vivid as that in *Þiðranda þáttr*, but it contains similar elements – a protective female linked to a specific family is preparing to abandon them in the face of approaching conversion, but dealt a final strike before surrendering. Familial allegiance is probably important also to this narrative. The kin relationship is extended even to Sóti, who also appears in other texts as a vicious mound-dweller (e.g. BsS ch. 20). Þorgerðr's relationship with Sóti conveys strong folkloristic colour and is almost certainly not an original feature. It is possible, however, that this association was implemented in order to emphasise Þorgerðr's initial place of worship – the gravemound – which by then had become associated with a cult house in Iceland (Røthe 2007: 52–53).

Unlike Snorri, *Flateyjarbók* and *Íslendingasǫgur* make no mention of a gravemound and instead refer to an isolated cult house – sometimes surrounded by a fence – as a place where Þorgerðr's icon rested. In different sources, the building is referred to as *hof* (e.g. Flat 1, p. 214; Hs ch. 19), *hús* (e.g. Flat 1, pp. 144–145, 408) and *goðahús* (e.g. BrN ch. 88), and is always said to be very beautiful and the statue to be very tall and adorned with fine-looking clothes and jewellery made of gold and silver. These details have been considered to be imaginary in scholarship ever since the mid-1960s, when Olsen's study of the *hof* claimed that separate cult buildings never existed. However, as was noted previously, archaeologists have now been able to recover new evidence supporting the presence of such buildings. Simply because the sources are conflicting in this regard does not mean that one is correct and the other not; in my opinion Røthe (2007: 50–51, 53) makes a valid and justified point when she assumes that Þorgerðr's gravemound was probably the natural starting place for her cult, which expanded over time and moved inside cult houses; somewhere along the line there may have been the *hǫrgr* – an altar-like semi-house built on her grave and at other locations where she was held in respect.

It was discussed in the context of superior ancestors that the ability to call upon ancestors is as a rule confined to their kin. This secures the leader's privilege to command; however, the rule itself applies to ancestor worship among all kin groups. 'Familial' boundaries with regard to burials, activities on gravemounds and the ability to invoke ancestors are suggested, as was reviewed previously (see Chapter 3, Sections 3.3 and 3.4); they are also in some Scandinavian laws and in connection with individuals such as Geirstaðaálfr and Hálfdanr, and similar elements are also found in sources concerned with Þorgerðr. Her releasing of the ring, for example, as well as the 'theft' of the ring from her brother, both part of the debate about

148 *Case studies*

the sacred marriage motif (e.g. McKinnell 2005: 84; Steinsland 2005b: 83), imply that these were in effect ancestral artefacts. For example, it is Hákon – Þorgerðr's descendant – who succeeds in persuading her to pledge the ring, not the friend who acquires help from her. The ring taken from Sóti is presented as an act of robbery by the author; however, the fact that it is carried out by a family member seems odd and without a motive. It is possible that this instance, too, alludes to a former religious act which in the eyes and memories of medieval historians had started to look like grave robbery, or which they simply attempted to stop for the advancement of their patrons, albeit under the veneer of Christian morality. Archaeologists have been able to recover supporting evidence for the deliberate and continuous insertion and removal of objects from gravemounds, likely driven by the purpose of sustaining a relationship with the buried person who transfers personal qualities into the grave goods, and the idea is also present in literature. In Óláfr's case, let us remember that the ancestral items removed from his mound were used to ease the birth of the new king, and in Freyr's, the items included wooden icons that were later used as representations of Freyr himself and were, according to *Flateyjarbók*, burned along with Þorgerðr. Written as a satire, the author of *Þorleifs þáttr*, too, seems to have had this motif in mind when he introduces the assassinating *trémaðr* into the narrative and gives him a weapon retrieved from Hǫrgi in the *hof* which he shares with Þorgerðr and Irpa, allegedly his daughters. If we accept the existence of a predecessor called Hǫlgi, along with his identification with Hǫrgi, the weapon represents another powerful ancestral object used to avenge the family's honour. We could hypothesise that the story of the ring, 'stolen' by a family member from a notorious and sinister mound-dweller (artificially assigned the role of the brother) falls into a similar category. Or perhaps the introduction of a 'tainted' ring was meant to discourage removing grave goods in earlier times. In any case, such beliefs and practices were accepted by the authors and their audiences as having been followed only a few centuries previously.

* * * * *

The information about Þorgerðr has been weaved into academic theories about sacral kingship and ruler ideology, and her character has been fitted into mythical frameworks. She is identified with a number of beings known from Old Norse literature, e.g. *jǫtnar*, *valkyrjur*, *dísir*, *fylgjur*, etc. It cannot be denied that Þorgerðr has aspects characteristic of each and every one of these – sometimes purely mythological – beings, considering that their generally confounded identities and conceptions overlap with each other. Sources which provide the main portion of information about her are written not only from a Christian perspective, but are also biased by political objectives and are made up of numerous diffuse traditions, which are then selected, edited and penned on behalf of the 13th- and 14th-century elite. Mentions of her in literature are consequently diffuse and often of a negative nature. Some aspects of the imagined early medieval versions of Þorgerðr are nonetheless comparatively consistent and permit some rationalisation of her character in the pagan context.

Þorgerðr was considered to be a splendidly proportioned woman in magnificent clothes, transformed into a wooden icon, which was worshipped by a (prominent kin) group of people in a cult-house-type structure. This structure, or structures, may have evolved from a cult of her gravemound which went through different stages of development and various designs. Aspects of her character, such as her extraordinary skills in archery and weather-magic, point in the direction of the Sámi; considering their geographical vicinity and dense interaction with north Norwegians, this supports Þorgerðr's origin in the northern regions. She is protective yet vengeful, and the cult appears to have been limited to the 'family' affined with Hákon. No matter how artificial some (or all) of these relationships may be – there is no historically valid data which would help us determine the existence of Hǫlgi or Irpa or even to prove whether Hákon ever really worshipped Þorgerðr – medieval scribes clearly saw kinship as a prerequisite in their descriptions of pagan cults. Whether a woman named Þorgerðr was held in particular honour in the northern regions or whether she was singled out by the skalds because she was an easy object for ridicule – perhaps the worship of a female character was seen as more unfitting for a ruler in their eyes and thus served their purpose more effectively – is impossible to know. Seeking for an original name of the character of Þorgerðr's from the copious epithets would, too, most likely be in vain – the chances are that they all belong to the Christian era. Whether *hǫrga* or *hǫlga*, *brúðr* or *trǫll*, all these epithets sound external in the sense that they were probably used by people outside the group actually involved in her cult; for insiders – a group of north Norwegians living in the Hálogaland region – it would have been unnecessary to refer to their patron as the 'bride of Háleygjar'. The constructed surviving corpus of Þorgerðr-lore was intended primarily as a parody of a pagan cult; however, the underlying pattern which emerges from it points towards a typical ancestor cult where the helpful and capricious foremother was involved in the lives of her family, potentially alongside other dead relatives, and where kinship was important social glue. The medieval sources' perceptions of Þorgerðr, which were exaggerated and constructed with antagonistic intent towards Hákon, are nonetheless real and meaningful.

Forcing Þorgerðr into mythic ideology and the sacral kingship paradigm masks her true character because both insist on the presence of specific characteristics lacking in the sources. While the Óðinn–Skaði duo was attached to Hákon by Eyvindr in order to generate a genealogy broadly corresponding with that of the hárfagri clan for aesthetic effect and for political reasons (although its importance in the religious context is questionable), according to the sources Þorgerðr appears to have no association with this paradigm; evidence used in arguments is obscure and the groundwork for this theory is built on sources unrelated to Þorgerðr. The sources about her hint at her popularity in the northern Norwegian region possibly being equal to that of gods in other areas who have become more well known in scholarship due to their eminent appearance in *Snorra Edda* and elsewhere, but this must remain conjecture. Despite her affiliation with a petty kingdom in Hálogaland, her role as a superior ancestor remains unclear because we do not have sufficient information on the magnitude of her cult. However, she

150 *Case studies*

nonetheless seems to represent a dead foremother worshipped by a distinguished family in northern Norway.

Notes

1 Only a limited number of stanzas of the poem have survived, but based on parallel genealogies from other sources, scholars have reconstructed a lineage that is as long as that in *Ynglingatal*, arguably going back to Óðinn and Skaði (see Steinsland 2011: 26, n. 26).
2 It has been argued that Óðinn's position at the top of the Háleygjar genealogy is due to Anglo-Saxon influence (Faulkes 1978–1979: 3–4; Dumville 1979; cf. Sundqvist 2012a: 240).
3 Some scholars argue that the *jǫtnar* (conventionally translated as 'giants'), who were the primeval inhabitants of the world, offer a parallel to the Sámi as the 'original' people of Scandinavia (Lindow 1995; Mundal 2000). A link to Sámi has also been seen in connection with the name Sæmingr (Steinsland 2011: 29). A kenning for Skaði – *ǫndurdís* 'ski-*dís*' – too, suggests a connection to the Sámi who are called *skritfinni* 'sliding Finns' by historians as early as the 1st century AD and after (e.g. Germ I, chs 1, 46, ed. pp. 3, 47–48; Get ch. 3, ed. p. 59; tr. p. 56; GH IV, chs 24–25, ed. pp. 172–173; tr. pp. 205–206; GD V, IX, ed. pp. 133, 138, 258; tr. pp. 148, 153, 28).
4 Freyja's erotic exploits are depicted in e.g. Sþ ch. 1; Ls sts 30, 32.
5 The man-wife model is suggested by Saxo (GD III, ed. p. 65; tr. p. 71) according to whom Helgi of Hálogaland tried to win the love of Þóra, the daughter of a chieftain of the Finns and Biarmians, while Snorri (ÓsT ch. 48) comments that a woman named Þóra owned land near Hlaðir and was married to Jarl Hákon.
6 The article by Gustav Storm from 1885 is still useful in providing a detailed survey of Þorgerðr's name variants in the different sources. The name variants appear also in medieval Norwegian legends and ballads available at:
  http://www.dokpro.uio.no/ballader/lister/alfa_titler/tittel_326.html (accessed: 16 July, 2018).
7 The grammarian used this name in an example of the difference between *d* and double *d*: *HÓ dó, þá er Hǫlgatroll dó, en heyrði til hǫDo, þá er Þórr bar hverinn* (a tall [woman] died when Hǫlgatrǫll died, but one could hear the handle [rattle] when Þórr carried the cauldron (*Fyrsta Málfræðiritgerðin* ed. pp. 30, 77; tr. p. 245).
8 Icelandic records from the 18th century mention a Háa-Þóra 'tall Þóra' who is believed to have a pre-Christian origin in Scandinavia and have reached Iceland in the medieval period (Gunnell 1995: 150–155).
9 For further reading and discussion of cognitive poetics generally, see Tsur (2002); Csabi (2018). Concerning Old Norse poetry and cognition, see Würth (2007) and Bergsveinn Birgisson (2008).
10 For example, a manuscript of *Brennu-Njáls saga* (ch. 88, note 2) from c. 1300, and *Harðar saga* and *Ketils saga hængs*, both from the 15th century.
11 The Latin manuscripts are almost entirely lost, but three Old Norse translations have survived: one in *Heimskringla* (c. 1230), one in *Óláfs saga Tryggvasonar en mesta* (14th century) and one in *Flateyjarbók* (14th century). The last two manuscripts were likely copied from the text of Snorri, who primarily followed Oddr's text, but expanded it with information from Oddr and Gunnlaugr's manuscripts and other related texts, as well as oral tradition (Óláfr Halldórsson 2001: v–lvi; Ashman Rowe 2005: 35–38).
12 For discussion of ancestor worship among the Sámi, see Bäckman (1975, 1983); Bäckman and Hultkrantz (1978).
13 Bartholomaeus Anglicus' *De Proprietatibus Rerum* (ed. p. 100) from the 13th century and Olaus Magnus' *Historia de Gentibus Septentrionalibus* (I, ed. pp. 172–173) from the 16th century note that Finnish wizards can regulate the order of nature by putting

spells on natural elements and that they sell wind to traders by giving them 'knots tied in a strap'; untying the knots could then help the traders regulate the winds.
14 The weighing of the hailstones in connection with this battle is also mentioned by Snorri (ÓsT ch. 41) and Saxo (GD X, ch. 4, ed. pp. 8–9), although nothing is said about Þorgerðr.
15 For discussion of colour terms in Old Norse literature, see Wolf (2006); Crawford (2014).
16 The different *Finnar* are often described in the sagas as dark-looking and sinister (e.g. Hs ch. 17; QOs ch. 19; Krm ch. 3; Þþb chs 7, 8, 11). The tendency to consider the dark appearance of the *Finnar* as ugly and demonic must derive to a great extent from associations with the medieval geography of the Devil whose realm often exist in the north (see Russell 1984: 69–71). However, even if the texts were influenced by Christian theological views, we must consider that these views could have, in turn, been influenced by local religions and environments. The fact that the northern regions of Scandinavia became known as the entrance to hell in the middle ages and the Sámi people as the Devil's most potent tools derives to a great extent from these people's association with magic performances and superstitions, and from the fact that the Sámi stayed officially pagan for more than half a millennium longer than the Germanic Scandinavians, which probably generated a degree of anxiety among their southern neighbours (Willumsen 2013: 358–360). The genetic origin of the Sámi and the Finns is still debated and they represent a very heterogeneous group in terms of physical features. However, one of the dominant physical characteristics of the Sámi – dark hair and skin – resembles that of some Asian populations further east (Beckmen et al. 2001). The dark-looking *Finnar* were probably easy targets for such demonisation in the sagas.
17 Snorri notes that according to 'the people's tales', Hákon sacrificed his son for his benefit in battle (ÓsTr ch. 42), while Saxo states that two sons were killed in order to win the battle (GD X, ch. 4); neither source mentions Þorgerðr.

Secondary sources

Abram, Chris, 2011, *Myths of the pagan north: the gods of the Norsemen*, Continuum International Publishing Group, London and New York.
Ashman Rowe, Elizabeth, 2005, *The development of Flateyjarbók. Iceland and the Norwegian dynastic crisis of 1389*, University Press of Southern Denmark, Odense.
Bäckman, Louise, 1975, *Sájva: Föreställningar om hjälp-och skyddsväsen i heliga fjäll bland samerna*, Almqvist & Wiksell International, Stockholm.
Bäckman, Louise, 1983, 'Förfäderskult? En studie i samernas förhållande till sina avlidna', *SáDS áigecála*, vol. 1, pp. 11–48.
Bäckman, Louise, and Åke Hultkrantz, 1978, *Studies in Lapp shamanism*, Acta Universitatis Stockholmiensis, Stockholm.
Beckman, L. et al., 2001, 'Haemochromatosis gene mutations in Finns, Swedes and Swedish Saamis', *Human Heredity*, vol. 52, no. 2, pp. 110–112.
Behringer, Wolfgang, 2002, 'Weather, hunger and fear. Origins of the European witch-hunts in climate, society and mentality', in D. Oldridge (ed.), *The witchcraft reader*, Routledge, London, pp. 69–86.
Bergsveinn Birgisson, 2008, 'What have we lost by writing? Cognitive archaisms in skaldic poetry', in E. Mundal and J. Wellendorf (eds.), *Oral art forms and their passage into writing*, Museum Tusculanum Press, Copenhagen, pp. 163–184.
Bibire, Paul, 1986, 'Freyr and Gerðr: the story and its myths', in R. Simek et al. (eds.), *Sagnaskemmtun: studies in honour of Hermann Pálsson on his 65th birthday, 26th May, 1986*, Hermann Böhlaus Nachf, Vienna, Cologne and Graz, pp. 19–40.

152 Case studies

Brink, Stefan, 2007, 'How uniform was the Old Norse religion?' in J. Quinn et al. (eds.), *Learning and understanding in the Old Norse world: essays in honour of Margaret Clunies Ross*. Medieval Texts and Cultures in Northern Europe 18. Brepols, Turnhout, pp. 105–135.

Chadwick, Nora, 1950, 'Þorgerðr Hölgabrúðr and the *Trolla Þing*: a note on sources', in C. Fox and B. Dickins (eds.), *The early cultures of north-west Europe (H.M. Chadwick Memorial Studies)*. Cambridge University Press, Cambridge, pp. 395–417.

Cleasby, Richard, and Guðbrandur Vigfússon (eds.) 1874. *Icelandic-English dictionary*, Clarendon Press, Oxford.

Clunies Ross, Margaret, 2014, 'Royal ideology in early Scandinavia: a theory versus the texts', *The Journal of English and Germanic Philology*, vol. 113, no. 1, pp. 18–33.

Crawford, Jackson, 2014, *The historical development of basic color terms in Old Norse-Icelandic*. Germanic and Slavic Languages and Literatures Faculty Contributions. 1, University of Colorado, Boulder, Doctoral Dissertation.

Csabi, Szilvia (ed.) 2018, *Expressive minds and artistic creations: studies in cognitive poetics*, Oxford University Press, Oxford.

Dumville, David, 1979, 'Kingship, genealogies and Regnal lists', in P. Sawyer and I. Woods (eds.), *Early medieval kingship*, University of Leeds, Leeds, pp. 72–104.

Ellis Davidson, Hilda, 1992, 'Human sacrifice in the late pagan period in North-Western Europe', in M. Carver (ed.), *The age of Sutton Hoo: the seventh century in North-Western Europe*, Boydell, Woodbridge, pp. 331–340.

Ellis Davidson, Hilda, 1998, *Roles of the northern goddess*, Routledge, London.

Faulkes, Anthony, 1978–1979, 'Descent from the gods', *Medieval Scandinavia*, vol. 11, pp. 92–125.

Forbus, Henric, 1910 [1727], 'En korrt beskrifning om Kongl. Missions Collegio i Dannemark, om Missionen, LapScholarne, och Lapparnes fasliga afguderi, författad in Martio 1727', in E. Reuterskiöld (ed.), *Källskrifter till lapparnas mytologi: Bidrag till vår odlings häfder*, Nordiska Museet, Stockholm, pp. 28–41.

Frank, Roberta. 2007, 'The lay of the land in skaldic praise poetry', in S. Glosecki (ed.), *Myth in early Northwest Europe*, ASMAR and Brepols, Turnhout, pp. 175–196.

Gunnell, Terry, 1995, *The origins of drama in Scandinavia*, D. S. Brewer, Cambridge.

Gunnell, Terry, 2007b. 'Viking religion: Old Norse mythology', in R. North and J. Allard (eds.), *Beowulf & other stories: a new introduction to Old-English, Old Icelandic & Anglo-Norman literatures*, Pearson, New York, pp. 351–375.

Gunnell, Terry, 2014, 'Nordic folk legends, folk traditions and gravemounds: the potential value of Folkloristics for the study of Old Norse religions', in E. Heide and K. Bek-Pedersen (eds.), *New focus on retrospective methods*. Folklore Fellows' Communications 307. Academia Scientarum Fennica, Helsinki, pp. 17–41.

Heide, Eldar, 2014, '*Hǫrgr* in Norwegian names for mountains and other natural features', *Namn og Nemne*, vol. 31, pp. 7–51.

Höfler, Otto, 1952, *Germanisches Sakralkönigtum*, 1. *Der Runenstein von Rök und die Germanische Individualweihe*, Niemeyer, Tübingen, München and Köln.

Kaplan, Merrill, 2000, 'Prefiguration and the writing of history in "Þáttr Þiðranda ok Þórhalls"', *The Journal of English and Germanic Philology*, vol. 99, no. 3, pp. 379–394.

Krag, Klaus 2012 [2008], 'The creation of Norway', in S. Brink and N. Price (eds.), *The Viking world*, Routledge, London and New York, pp. 645–651.

Kvideland, Reimund, and Henning Sehmsdorf, 1999 [1988], *Scandinavian folk belief and legend*, University of Minnesota Press, Minneapolis.

Lid, Nils, 1942, 'Gudar og Gudedyrkning', in N. Lid (ed.), *Religionshistorie*. Nordisk Kultur, 26. Albert Bonniers Förlag, H. Aschehoug & Co.s Forlag and J. H. Schultz Forlag. Stockholm, Oslo and Copenhagen, pp. 80–153.

Lindow, John, 1995, 'Supernatural others and ethnic others: a millennium of world view', *Scandinavian Studies*, vol. 67, no. 1, pp. 8–31.

Marold, Edith, 1993, 'Eyvindr Finsson skáldaspillir', in P. Pulsiano et al. (eds.), *Medieval Scandinavia: an encyclopedia*, Garland, New York, pp. 175–176.

McKinnell, John, 2002, 'Þorgerðr Hölgabrúðr and Hyndluljóð', in R. Simek and W. Heizmann (eds.), *Mythological women: studies in memory of Lotte Motz*, Studia Medievalia Septentrionalia, Vienna, pp. 265–290.

McKinnell, John, 2005, *Meeting the other in Norse myth and legend*, D. S. Brewer, Cambridge.

Megaard, John, 1999, 'Hvor sto "Slaget i Hjorungavágr"? Jomsvikingeberetningens stedsnavn og Sæmundr fróði', *Alvíssmál*, vol. 9, pp. 29–54.

Motz, Lotte, 1987, 'The family of Giants', *Arkiv för nordisk filologi*, vol. 102, pp. 216–236.

Mundal, Else, 1974, *Fylgjemotiva i norrøn litteratur*. Skrifter fra Instituttene for nordisk språk og litteratur ved Universitetene i Bergen, Trondheim og Tromsø. Universitetsforlaget, Oslo.

Mundal, Else, 1990, 'The position of the individual gods and goddesses in various types of sources – with special emphasis to the female divinities', in T. Ahlbäck (ed.), *Old Norse and Finnish religions and cultic place-names*, Donner Institute for Research in Religious and Cultural History, Åbo, pp. 294–315.

Mundal, Else, 2000, 'Coexistence of Saami and Norse culture: reflected in and interpreted by Old Norse myths', in G. Barnes and M. Clunies Ross (eds.), *Old Norse myths, literature and society: proceedings of the 11th International Saga Conference 2–7 July 2000*. University of Sydney, Sydney, pp. 346–355.

North, Richard, 1997b, *Heathen gods in old English literature*. Cambridge Studies in Anglo-Saxon England, 22. University Press, Cambridge.

Ólafur Halldórsson, 2001, *Text by Snorri Sturluson in Óláfs saga Tryggvasonar en mesta*, University College London, London.

Perkins, Richard, 2001, *Thor the Wind-Raiser and the Eyrarland image*. Viking Society for Northern Research, 15. University College London, London.

Røthe, Gunnhild, 2007, 'Þorgerðr Hölgabrúðr. The *fylgja* of the Háleygjar family', *Scripta Islandica*, vol. 58, pp. 33–55.

Russell, Jeffrey, 1984, *Lucifer: the devil in the Middle Ages*, Cornell University Press, Ithaca and London.

Solander, Carl, 1910 [1726], 'Kort relation, om den Danska Missions tillstånd uti Norrige […] som skiedde 1726', in E. Reuterskiöld (ed.), *Källskrifter till lapparnas mytologi: Bidrag till vår odlings häfder*, 10. Nordiska Museet, Stockholm, pp. 17–27.

Simek, Rudolf, 1986, 'Elusive Elysia or which way to Glæsisvellir?' in R. Simek et al. (eds.), *Sagnaskemmtun: Studies in honour of Hermann Pálsson on his 65th birthday, 26th May, 1986*, Hermann Böhlaus Nachf, Wien, Köln and Graz. pp. 247–275.

Steinsland, Gro, 1991, *Det hellige bryllup og norrøn kongeideologi: En analyse av hierogami-myten i Skírnismál, Ynglingatal, Háleygjatal og Hyndluljóð*, Solum, Oslo.

Steinsland, Gro, 2000, *Den hellige kongen. Om religion og herskemakt fra vikingtid til middelalder*, Pax Forlag, Oslo.

Steinsland, Gro, 2005b, 'The mythology of rulership and the saga of the Faroe Islanders', in A. Mortensen and S. Arge (eds.), *Viking and Norse in the North Atlantic. Selected*

154 Case studies

papers from the proceedings of the fourteenth Viking congress, Tórshavn, 19–30 July 2001. The Faroese Academy of Sciences in collaboration with Historical Museum of the Faroe Islands, Tórshavn, pp. 76–86.

Steinsland, Gro, 2011, 'Origin myths and rulership. From the Viking Age ruler to the ruler of medieval historiography: continuity, transformations and innovations', in G. Steinsland et al. (eds.), *Ideology and power in the Viking and Middle Ages. Scandinavia, Iceland, Ireland, Orkney and the Faeroes*, Brill, Leiden and Boston, pp. 15–67.

Storm, Gustav, 1885, 'Om Thorgerd Hölgebrud', *Arkiv för nordisk filologi*, vol. 2, pp. 124–135.

Ström, Folke, 1954, *Diser, norner, valkyrjor. Fruktberhetskult och sakralt kungadöme i norden*, Almqvist & Wiksell, Stockholm.

Ström, Folke, 1983, '*Hieros gamos*-motivet i Hallfreðr Óttarssons Hákonardrápa och den nordnorska jarlavärdigheten', *Arkiv för nordisk filologi*, vol. 98, pp. 67–79.

Sundqvist, Olof, 2012a, 'Religious ruler ideology in pre-Christian Scandinavia. A contextual approach', in C. Raudvere and J. P. Schjødt (eds.), *More than mythology: narratives, ritual practices and regional distribution in pre-Christian Scandinavian religions*, Nordic Academic Press, Lund, pp. 225–261.

Thurenius, Petrus, 1910 [1724], 'Om vidskepelser i Åsele Lappmark, En Kort Berättelse Om the Widskeppelser, som uthi Åhrsilla Lapmark ännu äro i bruk', in I. Fellman (ed.), *Handlingar och uppsatser angående finska Lappmarken och lapparne, samlade och utgifna af Isak Fellman*, 1. Finska Litteratursällskapets tryckeri, Helsingfors, pp. 389–399.

Tolley, Clive, 2009, *Shamanism in Norse myth and magic*, Academia Scientiarum Fennica, Helsinki.

Tsur, Reuven, 2002, 'Aspects of cognitive poetics', in E. Semino and J. Culpeper (eds.), *Cognitive stylistics: language and cognition in text analysis*, John Benjamins Publishing Company, Amsterdam and Philadelphia, pp. 279–318.

Turville-Petre, Gabriel, 1964, *Myth and religion of the north: the religion of ancient Scandinavia*, Greenwood Press, Connecticut.

von Friesen, Otto, 1932–1934, 'Har det nordiska kungadömet sakralt ursprung? En ordhistorisk utredning', *Saga och Sed*, vol. 1, pp. 15–34.

Willumsen, Liv, 2013, *Witches of the North: Scotland and Finnmark*, Brill, Leiden.

Wolf, Kirsten, 2006, 'Some comments on Old Norse-Icelandic color terms', *Arkiv för nordisk filologi*, vol. 121, pp. 173–192.

Würth, Stefanie, 1991, *Elemente des Erzählens: Die þættir der Flateyjarbók*. Beiträge zur nordischen Philologie 20. Helbing & Lichtenhahn, Basel.

Würth, Stefanie, 2007, 'Skaldic poetry and performance', in J. Quinn, K. Heslop and T. Wills (eds.), *Learning and understanding in the Old Norse world: essays in honour of Margaret Clunies-Ross*, Brepols, Turnhout, pp. 266–274.

9 The Settlers of Breiðafjǫrðr

Haraldr hárfagri made a series of conquests over the independent petty kingdoms in Norway around 870 and shortly after, sometime between the years 870–900, defeated a united group of local chieftains at the naval battle of Hafrsfjǫrðr, near modern-day Stavanger, thus establishing his position as the king of Norway (Bagge & Walaker Nordeide 2007: 128). After this battle many leading chieftains are known to have fled to Iceland, the Faroes, the Orkneys, the Hebrides and Shetland. The westward emigration had nevertheless started already some time before these events and the opponents of Haraldr from the Norse settlements in the western islands are said to have conducted raids on his kingdom. According to *Eyrbyggja saga* (chs 1–3) – an Icelandic family saga written in the 13th century – Haraldr commanded Ketill flatnefr, the son of an early 9th-century Norwegian *hersir* called Bjǫrn Buna, to undertake an expedition to the isles in the west with an army and stop the raids. Having at first refused this command, Ketill finally travelled to the west with an army and his family, fought many battles and became a great chieftain there. During Ketill's absence, Haraldr took hold of his lands in Norway. Ketill's son Bjǫrn, who lived in Jämtland at that time, returned to Norway and took back his father's lands, but was declared an outlaw by Haraldr. When fleeing towards the south, Bjǫrn met a man named Hrólfr (or Þórólfr mostrarskegg), who agreed to help him, but who himself fell out with Haraldr as a result of this act and immigrated to Iceland. Hrólfr married the daughter of Auðr djúpúðga, the daughter of Ketill flatnefr.

According to the written sources, Þórólfr and Auðr were among the first settlers in Iceland, where they both had roles as cult leaders – Þórólfr was an adherent of Þórr and Auðr held prayers to the Christian God – and where they may themselves have acquired a cultic status after they died. The descriptions come chiefly from *Eyrbyggja saga* and *Landnámabók*. Even though *Landnámabók* contains fictional scenes, its purpose is generally believed to be historical and therefore realistic in terms of major historical events, such as how, when and by whom the land was settled. *Eyrbyggja saga* is full of paranormal occurrences and encounters with the supernatural. However, since the saga and particularly its beginning, which is of most concern to the present discussion, are believed to be based on *Landnámabók*, we can assume that the descriptions contain elements of genuine pagan traditions. The main subject and structure of the saga, too, is similar to *Landnámabók*: it

156 *Case studies*

is a generational history that traces the members of specific families in specific regions through the period from settlement in the late 9th century to conversion in the early 11th century.

This chapter discusses the descriptions of Þórólfr mostrarskegg and Auðr djúpúðga, among the first settlers and cult leaders in Iceland according to the written sources. Since these characters are not kings and did not claim divine descent from the gods of mythological tradition, they have been excluded from previous discussions of sacral kingship. Recent scholarship – increasingly critical of the earlier use of the restricted term 'sacral kingship' to describe the relationship between aristocracy and religion, and instead using the broader expression 'religious ruler ideology' – emphasises that the traditions of Icelandic chieftains, too, display a ruler ideology. As in previous chapters, it is argued that this ideology was built on the veneration of ancestors, which had to be adapted to suit the local environment and which consequently became associated with natural forms in the landscape as abodes for the dead, carrying the symbolic function of gravemounds. The assumption tested at present is whether these descriptions display characteristics suggestive of an ancestor cult and if they allow us to identify these characters as the 'superior ancestors' of their kin in Iceland.

9.1 Þórólfr Mostrarskegg

According to *Eyrbyggja saga* (chs 2–4) and *Landnámabók* (pp. 124–126) a man named Hrólfr was a great Norwegian chieftain and a believer of Þórr. It is said that he watched over a *hof* ('cult house') dedicated to the god on the island of Mostr in south-western Norway and therefore earned himself the name Þórólfr mostrarskegg. After quarrelling with Haraldr hárfagri for defending the outlawed son of Ketill flatnefr, Þórólfr held a sacrificial feast for Þórr, who advised him to leave Norway and go to Iceland. It is said that Þórólfr had the image of Þórr carved on his high-seat pillars, which stood in the *hof*, and that he took these with him to guide him to his new home in Iceland. Þórólfr landed at the place where the high-seat pillars were washed ashore, south of Breiðafjǫrðr on Snæfellsnes, and established a farm where he built another great *hof* dedicated to Þórr. This is said to have taken place about a decade after the settlement of Ingólfr Árnarson, who, according to *Íslendingabók* (ch. 1), threw his high-seat pillars overboard and settled near modern-day Reykjavík shortly after the year 870.

Olof Sundqvist (2012: 241–244) has argued that the story of Þórólfr displays a type of religious ruler ideology where Þórólfr and his offspring had the role of cultic priests devoted to Þórr. He emphasises that Þórólfr was involved in the naming of places after Þórr in the area where he settled (e.g. Þórsnes 'Þórr's ness') and which he consecrated with a fire ritual.[1] It is said that Þórólfr was a good friend of Þórr's (Eyr chs 3, 4). His offspring, like him, were named after Þórr and dedicated to the god: his son Steinn was called Þorsteinn and his grandson Grímr Þorgrímr; his family became known as the Þórsnesingar. Þórólfr himself was regarded as a *hofgoði*, leading a cult devoted to Þórr; this position was later inherited by his descendants. His son and grandson became *goðar* (Eyr chs 11–12, 48), as well as his great grandson Snorri goði Þorgrímsson (Eyr ch. 15). Sundqvist (2012: 244) concludes that the Þórsnesingar's association with Þórr legitimised their dominant position in a public cult in the same way that kings used their divine descent in Scandinavia. However, the ideology was different because their relation to Þórr was reinforced through a close friendship with him, not their own divine nature or descent from the god.

I think there is no need to question Sundqvist's hypothesis concerning the Icelandic chieftains' policy of taking advantage of their special relationship with the known gods to legitimise their authority. However, the other central subject in the same description, namely Þórr's ideological proximity to ancestors which is of interest at present, deserves no less attention in this context. Both *Eyrbyggja saga* (ch. 4) and *Landnámabók* (p. 125) state that alongside placing much trust in Þórr, Þórólfr also believed that he and all his kinsmen living in the area would after their death 'go into' Helgafell ('Holy Mountain') which stood between the farm and the fjord where the high-seat pillars had come to land. The mountain was sacred and everyone had to take care to not taint the area. A further description of the mountain, which is omitted from *Landnámabók*, follows after Þórólfr's death, when his son Þorsteinn goes missing on a fishing trip and is seen being welcomed by his father inside a great hall in the mountain Helgafell (Eyr ch. 11). A large fire burned in the courtyard-like interior, and laughter, the sound of drinking-horns and voices inviting Þorsteinn to take a place at the high seat across from Þórólfr were heard. The next morning the news arrived that Þorsteinn had died in the night. The author of the saga clearly made an effort to give the dead members of the family an equal social standing with Þórr, who was given the privilege of a private cult house in the close vicinity of Helgafell.

The description of Þórólfr and Þorsteinn entering a mountain is not unique in the Icelandic context. In fact, although the majority of references to the dead passing into the mountains in Iceland derive from one source, *Landnámabók*, it is mentioned so regularly that we must regard the belief as having some historical validity.[2] As expected, the descriptions are sparse and offer no specific details or explanations as to the ideological background on the emergence of such a belief in Iceland, although it has left traces in later Norwegian folklore, where it again involves the dead emerging from the mountains in order to visit farms (see Nordland 1966).[3] Attempts have therefore been made to connect the Icelandic material with aspects of Sámi religion, in which the belief in the *sájva* or *passe vare* world located in mountains and occupied by ancestors is particularly prominent (Nordland 1966; Bäckman 1975; 1983; Bäckman & Hultkrantz 1978: 80–81, 103; DuBois 1999: 75–77). Due to the Sámi remaining pagan significantly longer than their southern neighbours, the descriptions of their religious mediators' visits into these mountains to convene with the ancestors are much better documented and overall correspond with that in *Eyrbyggja saga* in that these visits also involve drinking, dancing and singing and are considered generally delightful (Bäckman & Hultkrantz 1978: 80). While the earlier assumption was that these Sámi beliefs were probably influenced by Old Norse practices (Arbman 1960: 127), later studies have argued that the prominence of these beliefs among the

158 *Case studies*

Sámi, as well as in other circumpolar areas, suggests that the tradition is probably of genuine Sámi origin (Bäckman 1975; Pettersson 1987: 72–74). Even though cultural borrowing – most likely bidirectional – certainly took place between the distinct but closely situated ethnic groups of Scandinavia, the practice of honouring mountains as abodes for the dead occurs globally in so many places where suitable geographical features are available (Rivers 1906: 446; Eliade 1961: 49–50; Hori 1966; Reinhard 1985) that we probably cannot attach much significance to any possible borrowing in this particular context. However, regardless of its origin, the tradition was in any case present in Iceland, where according to the author of *Eyrbyggja saga* it co-existed with the cult of Þórr; since it is associated with people of Norwegian ancestry, many of whom probably came from the middle coastal regions coinhabited by the Sámi (Zachrisson 2005; Price 2000), the belief is unlikely to have emerged entirely independently in Iceland.

That said, mountains as abodes for the dead may have acquired a particularly sacred character for Icelanders, perhaps much more so than it had in Norway. Although it is unclear to exactly what extent burial grounds in Scandinavia were used for cultic purposes during the first millennium, literary sources and archaeological evidence (Baudou 1989; Zachrisson 1994; Artelius 2004) indicate that they had an important role in religious activities, and we can assume that the earliest and most basic place for communicating with the dead was the gravemound, which over time merged with other practices. For Icelanders the situation was different. The ancestral graves which had symbolised family cohesion for centuries and which had been the physical markers of territory and claims of inheritance had been left behind along with their inhabitants, leaving them no obvious way to signpost their claims to the new land. Visualising the desolate, volcanic, Icelandic terrain, it is not surprising that the outstanding natural formations in the landscape would have taken over this function. That the flat-topped shape of Helgafell actually resembles that of a gravemound has been highlighted previously (Lid 1942: 142–144; Ellis Davidson 1988: 13–14). Considering the number of references to this belief in Iceland (e.g. BrN ch. 14; Lnd pp. 98–99, 139–140, 233), it would not be too much to suggest that perhaps most major farms – at least in the western parts of the land, and especially in Breiðafjǫrðr which seems to be the epicentre of the belief – had their own 'ancestral' mountain or hill that was regarded as a symbol of family property where distant and recent ancestors could be symbolically joined and contacted for counsel, similarly to the deep-rooted gravemound cult in Scandinavia. In one case in *Landnámabók*, the name, Þórir, of an original settler and founder of a farm and the first ancestor in Iceland is devoted to the mountain which his relatives later 'die into'.[4]

The use of the expression *að deyja í* ('to die into') to describe the ancestral mountain practice is confined to the author of *Landnámabók* and is absent elsewhere in Old Norse literature. His systematic use of this unusual phrase, however, is consistent with his firm favouring of the settlers in the Breiðafjǫrðr region as the people who most frequently enter mountains after death. Þórólfr and his relatives living in Breiðafjǫrðr believed they would *dæi allir í fjallit* 'all die into the mountain' (Lnd p. 125), the kinsmen of the daughter of Ketill flatnefr, Auðr djúpúðga, who lived in Hvammur not far from Breiðafjǫrðr believed that they would 'die into hillocks' (dæi í hólana) (Lnd pp. 139–140) and Sel-Þórir Grímsson's relatives who 'died into' (dó í) Þórisbjǫrg (Lnd pp. 97–98) lived at Ytri-Rauðamelur near Breiðafjǫrðr; Kráku-Hreiðarr Ófeigsson 'chose to die into' (kaus að deyja í) a mountain in the south of Iceland (Lnd p. 233), though he was also connected to those in Breiðafjǫrðr by kinship (Ellis 1968: 89). Saga traditions, as we have already seen in connection with Þórólfr, simply mention 'going into' mountains after death: according to Eyrbyggja saga (ch. 4) Þórólfr and his relatives 'would go there [i.e. to Helgafell] when they died' (mundi þangað fara) and Brennu-Njáls saga (ch. 14) remarks that a man called Svanr – another one of Ketill flatnefr's direct descendants – was seen 'going inside a mountain' (ganga inn í fjallit) in north-western Iceland. Thus, not only do most of the documented instances of people passing into specific mountains link these cases to Breiðafjǫrðr, they exclusively connect the belief to individuals who had close kinship ties to the inhabitants of Breiðafjǫrðr.[5] The regional origins of the colonists are considered somewhat unclear (see Vésteinsson 1998: 4–5); however, the social groups that dominated Iceland in the 11th and 12th centuries are believed to have traced their lineages back to three main kinship groups among the first settlers. A major part of Breiðafjǫrðr's population comprised of people with relations to the western Norwegian chieftain Bjǫrn Buna, father of Ketill flatnefr (Gísli Sigurðsson 2004: 88–89), who were predominantly behind the establishment of the Alþingi and who, as was mentioned earlier, frequently held the important political office of goði (Nordal 1942: 111–119). It thus seems that the author of Landnámabók made a conscious and deliberate effort to affiliate a specific kin group of settlers – the members of the Buna clan – with a tradition that helped legally mark their territory by dotting the landscape with the spirits of their first ancestors in Iceland. We may also assume a common transmission for the relevant passages in later sagas.

It seems, however, that the author of Landnámabók did not stop there. Although the description of Þórr's cult in Breiðafjǫrðr comes only from Eyrbyggja saga, Þórr is regularly associated with the Buna family in Landnámabók, too. Despite Þórr's more frequent appearance in the later Íslendingasǫgur, in Landnámabók he is mentioned in connection with half a dozen individuals: Þórólfr mostrarskegg (Lnd pp. 124–125), his son Hallsteinn (Lnd pp. 163–164) and Kráku-Hreiðarr, who all, as discussed, 'died into' mountains; Ketill's son-in-law Helgi magri (Lnd pp. 250–253) and Ketill's nephew Kollr (Lnd p. 53–55), who both called upon Þórr at sea on their way to Iceland; and Ásbjǫrn Reyrketilsson (Lnd pp. 344, 346), who dedicated his settlement to Þórr, calling it Þórsmǫrk. The pattern that consistently emerges is Þórr associated with the land-taking of one specific kin group. Theoretically, it would not be unlikely that specific 'gods' were to be associated with specific groups of people who moved to Iceland in clusters from the same regions in Scandinavia, except that according to the current state of toponymic evidence, known Þórr place names in Norway come almost exclusively from the south-east and that only limited, problematic toponyms are found in its western parts (Brink 2007: 114–115).[6] This places a big question mark over Bjǫrn Buna's descendants' actual familiarity with Þórr at the time of their settlement in Iceland

160 *Case studies*

and suggests that Þórr must have been linked to them artificially by the authors of *Eyrbyggja saga* and *Landnámabók*, I imagine, with the purpose of enhancing the following generations' reputation and political influence, precisely as Sundqvist (2012) suggests.

However, while Sundqvist emphasises the role of friendship between Þórólfr and Þórr, which he sees as being different from the way rulers enforced their pretensions to supremacy in Scandinavia, Þórr's intended role as the ancestor of the family might be veiled in the author's attempt to present him as the provider of the *ǫndvegissúlur* ('high-seat pillars') that the settlers used to help them decide where to establish their farms, as *Landnámabók* and other sources (e.g. Eyr ch. 4; Laxd ch. 5) suggest.[7] Þórólfr had the image of Þórr carved on one of the high-seat pillars which led him to Iceland (Lnd p. 124), and his son Hallsteinn is reported to have called upon Þórr in order to receive *ǫndvegissúlur* from him after which a large piece of wood drifted to land and was used to make high-seat pillars for every household in the area (Lnd p. 163–164), while Kráku-Hreiðarr apparently did not throw his high-seat pillars overboard because he deemed it wiser to ask Þórr directly (Lnd p. 233). The primary sources fail to explain what prompted this practice and since the prevailing association in these descriptions is with Þórr, who is presented as a god in the mythological pantheon and subsequently seen as having divine character, the high-seat pillars, too, are often discussed in mythological terms as divinely charged devices, the *axis mundi* connecting the earthly realm to the divine (e.g. Böldl 2005: 163–176).[8] Support for this is found in the accompanying phenomenon called *reginnaglar*, which are said to have been inside Þórólfr's high-seat pillars and which are commonly translated as 'god's nails' or 'sacred nails', supposedly derived from *regin* ('powers', 'rulers', 'gods') (Clunies Ross 2012: 11). The problem with this interpretation is that the *reginnaglar* are mentioned in only one other source besides *Eyrbyggja saga – Glælognskviða* (Skald 1, st. 9) – an 11th-century skaldic poem that describes how Óláfr helgi began to mediate between people and God after his death; according to Margaret Clunies Ross (2012) the *reginnaglar* there is a kenning for priests, for Óláfr or for the decorations on the cover of a liturgical book.[9] Recorded literature suggests that the high-seat pillars, although probably regarded as important religious symbols, were a reasonably commonplace item that belonged to many farms that all had 'gods' of their own, and the only god of the mythological tradition directly associated with *ǫndvegissúlur* (and by only two authors, one of whom is probably borrowing from the other) is Þórr.[10] The connection between *ǫndvegissúlur*, *reginnaglar* and the divine seems vague, at best.

Emil Birkeli's (1932, 1943: 177–186, 1944: 19–37, 68–73) study of the use of the high-seat pillars as depicted in Old Norse literature and in later Norwegian folk traditions emphasises that they served primarily a domestic purpose in ancestor cults. The *ǫndvegi* or high seat that held the pillars was the seat of the chieftain, but it carried special significance because it was also previously the seat for the initial house-father: the first ancestor. Birkeli supports the argument by stressing that the literal meaning of the word *ǫndvegi* is 'spirit-path', suggesting that the seat symbolised an access point to ancestors. Its central significance as a passage between the living and the dead members of the household was obstinately retained also for centuries to come: in much later Norwegian folklore the *ǫndvegi* still marks the resting place for the visiting dead during Yule (Birkeli 1944: 26–29). It is of course difficult to determine with any degree of certainty the origin or precise sentiments attached to the tradition of casting the *ǫndvegissúlur* overboard. As the study by Jonas Wellendorf (2010) shows, the custom was not restricted to the use of high-seat pillars – bench boards, doors, plain pieces of timber and even coffins were used for the purpose of determining the location of settlements – and it finds parallels also in hagiographic texts, suggesting that it probably represents a more basic tradition that had various expressions, for both pagans and Christians. However, it does seem that the early Icelanders in any case readily adopted the tradition of using *ǫndvegissúlur* as guides, and it is not unlikely that the powers believed to direct the timber were the ancestors whose presence materialised through the pillars on the way to a new land. This finds support in *Egils saga* (chs 27–28), where Kveld-Úlfr foresees his imminent death before reaching Iceland and instructs his men to throw his body overboard inside a coffin that will lead to the location of his son's future settlement. As Wellendorf (2010: 10–11) has pointed out, this instance makes it explicitly clear that Kveld-Úlfr (who attains the status of an ancestor during the journey and is buried inside a mound on the headland once the travellers have landed) becomes the legal marker of his descendant's land-claim, essentially substituting for guidance from the *ǫndvegissúlur*. Sundqvist (2015: 230) has pointed out that in various instances chieftains are also said to have gone on their high seats to die (e.g. Vatn chs 22–23; Eyr ch. 33), which also suggests that the high seat itself was seen as a kind of a symbolic crossing point to another dimension, the passport to which was death.[11]

These things considered, the high-seat pillars may well have been understood as ancestral artefacts in their own right and their association with Þórr must thus be interpreted along similar lines. In my view, there is no more reason to attribute any kind of cosmic or mythological powers to the high-seat pillars merely due to their association with Þórr than to believe that the perception of Þórr (in the early medieval period and previously) was that of a remote ancestor and for this reason linked to a domestic, albeit important and meaningful, item by the authors of *Landnámabók* and *Eyrbyggja saga*. The Breiðfirðingar's relationship to Þórr persistently expressed by the authors through a fundamentally ancestral object and the interlacing of his cult with that of Helgafell (where the members of the family passed once they attained their own status as ancestors) suggests that for the medieval writers, the pagan gods and ancestors represented conceptually very close categories.

The representation of *Eyrbyggja saga* as a whole certainly gives the reader a feeling that the religious history of Helgafell (which by the 13th century when the saga was written had become a prosperous monastery and educational centre) was of particular concern to the author, who seems to regard Snorri goði, who had the first Christian church built there, particularly highly. By inserting Þórólfr and Þorsteinn – Snorri goði's first ancestors in Iceland – into Helgafell,

162 *Case studies*

the later Christian members' original connection to the area and thus hereditary rights were established. The introduction of Þórr was probably intended to simply add some weight and colour to the narrative, although his presentation as a *vinr* ('friend') perhaps also added enough ambiguity to protect the Christian reputation of later generations. Another theory is that it served the tacit purpose of emphasising Þórr's human-like persona, which by the time the saga was written had probably started to attain somewhat devilish proportions. While the author of *Landnámabók*, who is generally considered, although not proven, to have been Ari fróði, a man who himself was born at Helgafell and who traced his ancestry to the male line to Ketill flatnefr's son-in-law Óleifr hvíti (Ísb p. 28), was somewhat more modest in his description of Þórólfr, he clearly used similar components in his literary project as the saga author. The consistency with which the members of the Buna lineage are guided to their settlements by Þórr and 'die into' strategically visible spots across western Iceland, and Breiðafjǫrðr in particular, helped the Buna clan to progressively establish its political influence. The authorial intent of the text does not, however, reduce or discount the significance of its underlying context: the belief that ancestors continue life inside mountains.

9.2 Auðr djúp(a)úðga

Auðr djúp(a)úðga Ketilsdóttir, the daughter of Ketill flatnefr and herself another important settler in western Iceland, is mentioned in a range of Old Norse sources.[12] According to these, she married a Norse king in Dublin with whom she had a son named Þorsteinn rauðr, who became a great chieftain over the northern regions of Scotland. After her husband's death, Auðr travelled to the Hebrides and from there to Orkney, the Faroe Islands and finally to Iceland. It is said that Auðr, like Þórólfr, took land in the Breiðafjǫrðr area, and that from her the greatest families of the above-mentioned lands are descended. She negotiated important marriages for her kindred, thus establishing a strong network of connections across the eastern Atlantic (Jesch 1991: 80–83, 193–202). Auðr has come to be known as one of the foremost settlers of Iceland and one of the most remarkable women mentioned in Old Norse literature.[13]

The most exciting part of the descriptions of Auðr's life concerns her death, after which she may have become something of a local cult figure. It is said in *Landnámabók* (pp. 146–147) that before her death Auðr invited her family to a great banquet that went on for three days. Afterwards, she instructed them to continue the gathering for another three days so that it could be her funeral feast. She gave gifts and counsel to her kindred and asked them to bury her in the space upon the seashore between the high and low watermarks because she was a Christian and did not wish to lie in unholy land. This is followed by a passage – absent in other sources – stating that after she died the faith of her kinsfolk grew corrupt. They ignored her wish, turned back to old traditions and brought sacrifices to a *hǫrgr*, which they raised in the place where Auðr had held prayers – known as Krosshólar 'Cross-hillocks' – and believed that they would 'die into the hillocks' (*at þeir dæi í hólana*) (Lnd pp. 139–140). This might have occurred because the family, having lost their Christian leader, lapsed back into paganism (see Jón Hnefill Aðalsteinsson 1997: 39–40). However, it is possible that Auðr's death triggered the ritual activities in a more meaningful sense, emerging from her new role as the progenitor for her kin in Iceland. She was an outstanding settler of prestigious Norwegian descent and a foremother to many important families. That a small-scale cult could have been dedicated to a deceased ancestress who had brought people to their new settlement is certainly a possibility.[14]

The 'hillocks' that Auðr's relatives believed they would 'die into' obviously share an ideological similarity with the mountains mentioned in the previous section. The meaning of the word *hólar* (sgl. *hóll*) itself is somewhat ambiguous in literature and seems to designate a knoll in the land, often occupied by different inhabitants of supernatural nature like *álfar* (e.g. Krm ch. 22), *dísir* (e.g. Þþ) and various kinds of *vættir* ('spirits') (e.g. ÓsT ch. 33).[15] Our knowledge about these beings is hazy, and we do not know to what extent their portrayal in the sources is fictional, but at least the *dísir* and *álfar* appear to have a long history in Scandinavia, strongly associated with ancestor cults (e.g. Kaplan 2000; Gunnell 2000, 2007a).[16] Since the *hólar* in *Landnámabók* are referred to as Krosshólar, where Auðr practised Christianity, the pagan use of the locality seemingly occurred only after her death. Whether she was actually buried at Krosshólar is unclear. Her relatives' subsequent actions suggest that they may have ignored her dying wish to be buried on the seashore, and we know that according to another tradition Auðr received a pagan ceremony: she was placed inside a boat and put in a gravemound, the precise location of which is unknown (Laxd ch. 7). Boat burials, albeit mentioned in some sagas (e.g. Gís ch. 17; Vatn ch. 23), were not particularly common in Iceland (Eldjárn 2000: 115–119, 564, 592–594, 605), which perhaps weakens the authenticity of this passage. On the other hand, the sacrifices to the *hǫrgr* might strengthen its likelihood of having taken place. The exact purpose of the *hǫrgr*, as was discussed previously (see Chapter 6), is unclear. However, medieval laws (e.g. GÞL p. 18; NC p. 308; GL p. 9; SC p. 430), later folklore (Nordland 1966: 84–85; Heide 2014) and archaeological evidence (Kaliff 2011: 56–57) point towards an association of some sort with gravemounds. It is possible that the special aura attributed to the *hólar* by Auðr's pagan relatives derived from an understanding of it as a space for the spirits of the dead, just as Helgafell in *Eyrbyggja saga*.[17]

The fact that Krosshólar had religious importance for the family for many generations and that it was perceived as a point where power had accumulated is demonstrated by the remark about Þórðr gellir – Auðr's great-grandson – who became a great chieftain and one of the main individuals that later generations of law speakers traced their ancestry from (Gísli Sigurðsson 2004: 88–89). It is said that Þórðr was taken to Krosshólar before he assumed the status of manhood (Lnd p. 140). What was expected from such an act is not specified, but the implication is that the place was associated with a kind of authoritative endorsement. Whether it was consent, blessing, advice or something else that was expected, or whether it was an act committed simply under the impulse of convention, some kind of ritual requisition of power from the focal point of worship of the first foremother

164 *Case studies*

in Iceland seems to have been represented by the act of paying the place a visit to celebrate an important stage of Þórðr's life. This is not a far step from the way new rulers in Scandinavia exercised their judicial and legislative power at *Þing* sites that were surrounded by ancient family graves (Brink 2004a, 2004b).

It has been suggested that the presentation of the boat burial in *Laxdæla saga* might derive from the author's wish to present Auðr as pagan and subsequently reserve the fame of introducing Christianity to a later male character (DuBois 1999: 86). To me it seems that there is no less reason to assume that the author of *Landnámabók* might have had an ulterior motive in presenting Auðr as a Christian. Considering her abundant travels in the British Isles she may have been a practising Christian. However, only one other source, *Eiríks saga rauða* (ch. 1), which was based on *Landnámabók*, mentions that Auðr was a Christian. We know that the transition from paganism to Christianity was a long-term process both in terms of broader societal changes and personal beliefs. The majority of people probably did not have rigid convictions about religious matters nor did these change abruptly. The author's claim that the kinsmen suddenly reverted to paganism, suggesting that in Auðr's lifetime they had followed the Christian faith, does not sound entirely convincing. Considering that Ari fróði, who claimed descent from her (Ísb p. 28), was probably at least partly behind the creation of *Landnámabók* at the time when no more than six or seven generations had lived in Iceland, we are justified in believing that the presentation of Auðr as a devout Christian may have served a particular purpose for Ari. The presentation of Auðr as a noble and knowledgeable matriarch who herself had followed the right faith already a few centuries earlier, on some level exalted later generations' righteousness. The less distinguished relations, however, became conveniently associated with an eye-catching feature in the landscape, helping mark the family's heritable land that all its members, like in the case of Helgafell, quite literally 'died into' according to the pagan tradition.

Jesse Byock (1990: 56–58), among others, has previously suggested that the description of the cult was probably motivated by Auðr's family's need to control other landowners. *Landnámabók* emphasises that besides claiming a large piece of land for herself, Auðr gave land to many people who went with her to Iceland. As Byock (1990: 56–57) points out, even though it is likely that her own family continued to have an influential role in major decision-making processes in the area, the initial settlers' deaths must have caused some changes in terms of social relations between the different farm owners on their land. As there was no common law in the early Icelandic community concerning land inheritance, the unwritten rules of the initial land division, which must have been based on the settlers' personal knowledge and memories of laws from different areas in Scandinavia, were probably forgotten within a few decades after the first settlers' deaths. Byock (1990: 56–57) reasonably adds that this probably meant that parts of the land that had been initially distributed by Auðr were gradually coming to be seen as the rightful possession of each family who held it, which started causing problems for her own descendants whose social authority and right to the land was thereby compromised. Realising what little authority and means of control they had – and this authority being acknowledged only by immediate associates, not the entire population – the following generations started to recognise the need for administrative law (Byock 1990: 57). According to *Íslendingabók* (p. 9) all usable land in Iceland had been taken about 60 years after its settlement. This timeframe matches with the foundation of the *Alþingi* in 930 which was initiated chiefly by the group that traced their descent from Bjǫrn Buna, Auðr's grandfather (Nordal 1942: 111–119). After the establishment of the *Alþingi*, the land was divided into four *goðorð*, each controlled by nine *goðar* chosen in accordance with their respectable descent and kinship ties: many of these positions, as was mentioned previously, were held by the members of the line traced from Bjǫrn Buna (Byock 1990: 57–58).

*****

However distant specific details in these descriptions are from historical reality, they capture the cultural norms and beliefs that existed in early medieval Iceland, which clearly rested to a great extent on ancestry and kinship. Þórólfr and Auðr were among the initial settlers of prominent descent from western Norway who settled in western Iceland, and they were tied to one another by kinship. Their deaths triggered beliefs and ritual activities among their living descendants, possibly turning them into local cult objects. Þórólfr was 'inserted' into Helgafell where he dwelt alongside other ancestors and was joined by new ones, and Auðr's relatives' ceremonial visits to the *hólar* suggest a similar purpose. Later family members 'dying into' these natural features probably served a political purpose, designed by the authors to secure the power of a group of people descending from Bjǫrn Buna and to maintain control over other landowners. However, the descriptions also show that such concepts and practices were real and alive in the settlers' minds at the time of the composition of the sources. Belief in ancestral mountains probably already existed in western Norway, but this phenomenon must have carried particular meaning for the first generations of Icelanders whose ancestors had been left behind on the move to a previously uninhabited land. However, we must give credit to their imagination with regard to the lands' invisible residents, whose depictions blended with older concepts. Assigning a ritual purpose to outstanding forms in the landscape that resembled gravemounds – thus giving a physical form to the symbolic presence of ancestors – would have been a natural way of continuing and preserving the old traditions in the new environment.

While *Landnámabók*, regardless of its fantastical elements, is a genealogical record of the settlers, the author of *Eyrbyggja saga* had the opportunity to add a more dynamic touch to the 'genealogy' by describing a pagan chief who had worshipped and sacrificed to Þórr. This association might be a literary invention considering the lack of toponymic evidence for Þórr's popularity in western Norway, and it probably served to reinforce the Buna clan's authority at Helgafell. It is, however, remarkable that Þórr – residing alongside the ancestors in mountains which were the visible markers of heredity – also counsels the kin through an inherently

166 *Case studies*

ancestral object. The author's consistent presentation of the high-seat pillars exclusively in connection with Þórr and one specific kin group cannot be unintentional. Auðr's relationship to God could not be used for the validation of land ownership, so this was manifested via the *hólar*; the presentation of her Christian character, however, may have distinguished her later Christian descendants in much the same way, allowing them to take pride in their foremother. As colonists, founders and leaders, both Þórólfr and Auðr were likely recipients of ritual attention from their descendants and kinsmen. The two descriptions probably served a similar purpose: both sought to instil feelings of respect and authority towards their descendants. However, in these descriptions, we can also see the ancestor cult's most concrete literary embodiment in Iceland. These characters' 'superior' ancestral role is perhaps more doubtful than in Scandinavia considering that we are dealing with a very different society in terms of its size, age, structure, organisation, social roles, politics and general way of life. However, these cases unequivocally show that simple human ancestors, although perhaps not elevated to the status of gods, did acquire the role of cult figures, underpinning the wider argument that the large-scale cults of the king-gods in Scandinavia, too, were extended ancestor cults.

Notes

1 It is unclear how much religious significance the fire-carrying ritual mentioned in *Eyrbyggja saga* has. According to *Landnámabók* (pp. 337, 339), the initial settlers were troubled by how much land the later arrivals took and Haraldr hárfagri established a rule according to which the new arrivals could only take possession of areas no larger than they could carry fire over in one day.

2 Lnd pp. 97–98, 125, 139–140, 233; Eyr ch. 4; BrN ch. 14. The 14th-century *Bárðar saga Snæfellsáss* also contains the motif of an ancestor in a mountain. It describes the transition of an initial settler called Bárðr into a godlike being after his disappearance into the Snæfellsnes mountain, again in western Iceland (chs 1–6). It is said that people living on the peninsula worshipped him after he died and had him as their god. The saga and especially its beginning which is concerned with Bárðr is heavily folklorised – he is all at once depicted as *mennsk* ('human'), a *risi* ('giant'), a *trǫll* ('troll'), a *bergbúi* ('mountain dweller'), a *bjargvættr* ('mountain spirit'), a *heitguð* ('votive god') and an *áss*. However, since many of the saga's characters also appear in *Landnámabók*, it probably has some historical basis in terms of later characters. It is a story about the transition to Christianity of Bárðr's son Gestr, who, after being spiritually led by Óláfr helgi to victory against a *haugbúi* ('mound dweller') and his 500 companions in a buried ship, decides to convert, but suffers an irrevocable punishment inflicted by his pagan ancestor for renouncing the faith of his forefathers. The intention of the author was clearly to present Bárðr as one of the founding fathers of Snæfellsnes and a dead pagan ancestor residing in a mountain. The story seems to have been well-known and was alive in folk memories even into the 18th century (Olafsen 1772). For an analysis of *Bárðar saga*, see Ármann Jakobsson (1998–2001, 2005); and discussions in Sävborg & Bek-Pedersen (2014).

3 The dead *oskoreia* riders who usually emerge from gravemounds sometimes appear from mountains in Norway (Birkeli 1944: 174).

4 For further discussion about naming landscape features in Iceland, see Clunies Ross (1998); Barraclough (2012).

5 For example, Auðr was the granddaughter of Bjǫrn Buna and daughter of Ketill flatnefr, Þórólfr was married to Auðr's daughter, Unnr, and Svanr was Auðr's great-grandson's

brother-in-law. A genealogical diagram linking the other individuals associated with this belief is found in Ellis (1968: 89).
6 Considering the settlers' travels in the British Isles where Þórr may have become known through other channels, the tradition may have reached Iceland from there, although Þórr place names in Britain are few and their links are considered to be questionable (Jesch 2015: 136–137).
7 For the latest discussions of the high-seat pillars, see Böldl (2005); Wellendorf (2010); Sundqvist (2015: 199–263); Hoefig (2017: 79–82).
8 See also Gunnell (2005); Sundqvist (2015: 199–263).
9 See also Sundqvist (2015: 236–237).
10 The only other reference to a god in connection with the high-seat pillars is in *Vatnsdœla saga* (ch. 15), where a lost amulet with Freyr's image is found inside the ground where the high-seat pillars are to be set up (also Lnd p. 218).
11 As Verena Hoefig (2017: 79) has pointed out, the word *áss* for the class of gods to which Þórr belongs according to Snorri has the literal meaning of 'beam' or 'post', suggesting a connection to the high-seat pillars. This can be again interpreted in two ways. The traditional approach would be to choose to see this as an attribute that supports the high-seat pillars' numinousity. However, there is nothing to oppose the emergence of the concept of *æsir* from ideas about ancestors.
12 For example, see Lnd (pp. 50–51, 136–145, 209, 397); Ísb (pp. 6, 26); Laxd (chs 1–7); Eyr (chs 1, 6); Grs (ch. 26); BrN (ch. 1); HsHá (ch. 22); Gís (ch. 1).
13 For a recent discussion about Auðr, see Vanherpen (2013, 2017).
14 The initial settler of the Faroe Islands, Grímr kamban, is also said to have received sacrifices for his popularity after death (Lnd p. 59; Fær p. 122).
15 See Byock et al. (2005: 196); Jón Hnefill Aðalsteinsson (1998: 136–138).
16 The *landvættir* inhabiting *hólar* and mountains in Iceland are quite vague and probably represent a product that incorporates a vast spectrum of beliefs and traditions which blended over time. Both *dísir* and *álfar* seem to merge with the land spirits in Iceland (Turville-Petre 1963; Gunnell 2007a: 118–121).
17 See Nordland (1966); Ellis (1968: 90).

Secondary sources

Arbman, Ernst, 1960, 'Underjord och heliga fjäll i de skandinaviska lapparnas tro', *Arv*, vol. 16, pp. 115–136.
Artelius, Tore, 2004, 'Minnesmakarnas verkstad. Om vikingatida bruk av äldre gravar och begravningsplatser', in Å. Berggren et al. (eds.), *Minne och myt. Konsten att skapa det förflutna*.Vägar till Midgård 5. Nordic Academic Press, Lund, pp. 99–120.
Bagge, Sverre, and Sæbjørg Walaker Nordeide, 2007, 'The kingdom of Norway', in N. Berend (ed.), *Christianization and the rise of Christian monarchy: Scandinavia, Central Europe and Rus' c. 900–1200*, Cambridge University Press, Cambridge, pp. 121–166.
Barraclough, Eleanor, 2012, 'Naming the landscape in the *Landnám* narratives of the *Íslendingasǫgur* and *Landnámabók*', *Saga-Book*, vol. 36, pp. 79–101.
Baudou, Evert, 1989, 'Hög – gård – helgedom i Mellannorrland under den äldre järnåldern', *Arkeologi i norr*, vol. 2, pp. 9–43.
Birkeli, Emil, 1932, *Høgsetet: Det gamle ondvege i religionshistorisk belysning*, Dreyers Grafiske Anstalt, Stavanger.
Birkeli, Emil, 1943, *Fedrekult fra norsk folkeliv i hedensk og kristen tid*, Dreyer, Oslo.
Birkeli, Emil, 1944, *Huskult og hinsidighetstro. Nye studier over fedrekult i Norge*. Skrifter utgitt av Det Norske Videnskaps-Akademi i Oslo II. Hist.-Filos. Klasse, no. 1. i kommisjon hos Jacob Dybwad, Oslo.

168 Case studies

Brink, Stefan, 2004a, 'Mytologiska rum och eskatologiska föreställningar i det vikingatida Norden', in A. Andrén et al. (eds.), *Ordning mot kaos. Studier av nordisk förkristen kosmologi.* Vägar till Midgård 4: 291–316. Nordic Academic Press, Lund.

Brink, Stefan, 2007, 'How uniform was the Old Norse religion?' in J. Quinn et al. (eds.), *Learning and understanding in the Old Norse world: essays in Honour of Margaret Clunies Ross.* Medieval Texts and Cultures in Northern Europe 18. Brepols, Turnhout, pp. 105–135.

Bäckman, Louise, 1975, *Sájva: Föreställningar om hjälp- och skyddsväsen i heliga fjäll bland samerna*, Almqvist & Wiksell International, Stockholm.

Bäckman, Louise, 1983, 'Förfäderskult? En studie i samernas förhållande till sina avlidna', *SáDS áigecála*, vol. 1, pp. 11–48.

Bäckman, Louise, and Åke Hultkrantz, 1978, *Studies in Lapp Shamanism*, Acta Universitatis Stockholmiensis, Stockholm.

Böldl, Klaus, 2005, *Eigi Einhamr: Beiträge zum Weltbild der Eyrbyggja und anderer Isländersagas.* Ergänzungsbände zum Reallexikon der Germanischen Altertumskunde, 48. Walter de Gruyter, Berlin and New York.

Byock, Jesse, 1990 [1988], *Medieval Iceland: society, sagas, and power*, University of California Press, Berkeley and Los Angeles.

Byock, Jesse et al., 2005, 'A Viking Age valley in Iceland: the Mosfell archaeological project', *Medieval Archaeology. Journal of the Society for Medieval Archaeology*, vol. 49, no. 1, pp. 195–218.

Clunies Ross, Margaret. 1998, 'Land-taking and text-making in medieval Iceland', in S. Tomasch and S. Gilles (eds.), *Text and territory: geographical imagination in the European Middle Ages*, University of Pennsylvania Press, Philadelphia, pp. 159–184.

Clunies Ross, Margaret, 2012, 'Reginnaglar', in M. Kaplan and T. Tangherlini (eds.), *News from other worlds: studies in Nordic folklore, mythology and culture. In honor of John F. Lindow*, North Pinehurst Press, Berkeley, pp. 3–21.

DuBois, Thomas, 1999, *Nordic religions in the Viking Age*, University of Pennsylvania Press, Philadelphia.

Eldján, Kristján, 2000, *Kuml og haugfé úr heiðnum sið á Íslandi*, Mál og Menning, Reykjavík.

Eliade, Mircea, 1961. *Images and symbols: studies in religious symbolism*, Princeton University Press, Princeton.

Ellis, Hilda, 1968, *The road to hel: a study of the conception of the dead in Old Norse literature*, Greenwood Press, New York.

Ellis Davidson, Hilda, 1988, *Myths and symbols in pagan Europe. Early Scandinavian and Celtic religions*, Syracuse University Press, New York.

Gísli Sigurðsson, 2004, *The medieval Icelandic saga and oral tradition: a discourse on method*, Harvard University Press, Cambridge.

Gunnell, Terry, 2000, 'The season of the *Dísir*: the winter nights and the *Dísablót* in early Scandinavian belief', *Cosmos*, vol. 16, pp. 117–149.

Gunnell, Terry, 2005, 'Hof, Halls, Goðar and Dwarves: an examination of the ritual space in the pagan Icelandic hall', *Cosmos*, vol. 17, pp. 14–17.

Gunnell, Terry, 2007a, 'How Elvish were the Álfar?' in A. Wawn et al. (eds.), *Constructing nations, reconstructing myth: essays in honour of T. A. Shippey*, Brepols, Turnhout, pp. 111–130.

Heide, Eldar, 2014, '*Hǫrgr* in Norwegian names for mountains and other natural features', *Namn og Nemne*, vol. 31, pp. 7–51.

Hoefig, Verena, 2017, 'Foundational myth in Sturlubók: an analysis of the tale of Ingólfr and Hjörleifr', in Jón Víðar Sigurðsson and Sverrir Jakobsson (eds.), *Sturla Þórðarson: Skald, Chieftain and Lawman*, Koninklijike Brill NV, Leiden, pp. 70–82.

Hori, Ichiro, 1966, 'Mountains and their importance for the idea of the other world in Japanese Folk religion', *History of Religions*, vol. 6, no. 1, pp. 1–23.

Jakobsson, Ármann, 1998–2001, 'History of the trolls? *Bárðar saga* as an historical narrative', *Saga-Book*, vol. 25, pp. 53–72.

Jakobsson, Ármann, 2005, 'The good, the bad, and the ugly: *Bárðar saga* and its giants', *Mediaeval Scandinavia*, vol. 15, pp. 1–15.

Jesch, Judith, 1991, *Women in the Viking Age*, Boydell, Woodbridge.

Jesch, Judith, 2015, *The Viking diaspora*, Routledge, London and New York.

Jón Hnefill Aðalsteinsson, 1997, *Blót í norrænum sið*, University of Iceland Press, Reykjavík.

Jón Hnefill Aðalsteinsson, 1998, *A piece of horse liver: myth, ritual and folklore in old Icelandic sources*, trans. T. Gunnell and J. Turville-Petre, Háskólaútgáfan, Félagsvísindastofnun, Reykjavík.

Kaliff, Anders, 2011, 'Fire', in T. Insoll (ed.), *The Oxford handbook of the archaeology of ritual and religion*, University Press, Oxford, pp. 51–62.

Kaplan, Merrill, 2000, 'Prefiguration and the writing of history in "Þáttr Þiðranda ok Þórhalls"', *The Journal of English and Germanic Philology*, vol. 99, no. 3, pp. 379–394.

Lid, Nils, 1942, 'Gudar og Gudedyrkning', in N. Lid (ed.), *Religionshistorie*. Nordisk Kultur, 26, Albert Bonniers Förlag, H. Aschehoug & Co.s Förlag and J. H. Schultz Förlag, Stockholm, Oslo and Copenhagen, pp. 80–153.

Nordal, Sigurður, 1942, *Íslenzk Menning*, 1, Mál og Menning, Reykjavík.

Nordland, Odd, 1966, 'Valhall and Helgafell: syncretistic traits of the Old Norse religion', in S. Hartman (ed.), *Syncretism: based on papers read at the Symposium on Cultural Contact, Meeting of Religions, Syncretism held at Åbo on the 8th–10th of September, 1966*, Almqvist & Wiksell, Stockholm, pp. 66–99.

Olafsen, Eggert, 1772, *Vice-Lavmand Eggert Olafsens og Land-Physici Biarne Povelsens Reise igjennem Island, foranstaltet af Videnskabers Sælskab i Kiøbenhavn*, Jonas Lindgrens Enke, Sorøe.

Pettersson, Olof, 1987, 'Saami ideas about the realm of the dead', in T. Ahlbäck (ed.), *Saami religion: based on papers read at the Symposium on Saami Religion held at Åbo, Finland, on the 16th–18th of August 1984*, Donner Institute, Åbo, pp. 69–80.

Price, Neil, 2000, 'Drum-time and Viking Age: Sámi-Norse identities in early medieval Scandinavia. Identities and cultural contacts in the Arctic', in M. Appelt et al. (eds.), *Proceedings from a conference at the Danish National Museum*, The Danish National Museum & Danish Polar Center, Copenhagen, pp. 12–27.

Reinhard, Johan, 1985, 'Sacred mountains: an ethno-archaeological study of high Andean Ruins', *Mountain Research and Development*, vol. 5, no. 4, pp. 299–317.

Rivers, William, 1906, *The Todas*, Macmillan, London.

Sävborg, Daniel, and Karen, Bek-Pedersen (eds.) 2014, *Folklore in Old Norse. Old Norse in Folklore*, Nordistica Tartuensia 20, Tartu, University of Tartu Press.

Sundqvist, Olof, 2012, '"Religious ruler ideology" in pre-Christian Scandinavia. A contextual approach', in C. Raudvere and J. P. Schjødt (eds.), *More than mythology: narratives, ritual practices and regional distribution in pre-Christian Scandinavian religions*, Nordic Academic Press, Lund, pp. 225–261.

Sundqvist, Olof, 2015, *An arena for higher powers. Ceremonial buildings and religious strategies for rulership in late Iron Age Scandinavia*, Brill, Leiden.

Turville-Petre, Gabriel, 1963, 'A note on the Landdisir', in A. Brown and P. Foote (eds.), *Early English and Old Norse studies: presented to Hugh Smith in honour of his sixtieth birthday*, Methuen, London.

Vanherpen, Sofie, 2013, 'Remembering Auðr/Unnr djúp(a)uðga Ketilsdóttir. Construction of cultural memory and female religious identity', *Mirator*, vol. 14, no. 2, pp. 61–78.

Vanherpen, Sofie, 2017, 'In search of a founding mother: the case of Auðr *djúpauðga* in *Sturlubók*', *Amsterdamer Beiträge zur älteren Germanistik*, vol. 77, pp. 559–583.

Vésteinsson, Orri, 1998, 'Patterns of settlement in Iceland: a study in pre-history', *Saga-Book*, vol. 25, pp. 1–29.

Wellendorf, Jonas, 2010, 'The interplay of Pagan and Christian traditions in Icelandic settlement myths', *The Journal of English and Germanic Philology*, vol. 109, no. 1, pp. 1–21.

Zachrisson, Inger, 2005, 'Ethnicity – conflicts on land use. Sámi and Norse in Central Scandinavia in the Iron Age and the Middle Ages', in I. Holm et al. (eds.), *'Utmark': the outfield as industry and ideology in the Iron Age and the Middle Ages*, Universitetet i Bergen, Bergen, pp. 193–201.

Zachrisson, Torun, 1994, 'The odal and its manifestation in the landscape', *Current Swedish Archaeology*, vol. 2, pp. 219–238.

10   General conclusion

The case studies that have been presented are all – to varying degrees and in varying ways – concerned with the cult of the gravemound. Erik of Birka is said to have a cult house dedicated to him, but the way in which he is permitted to join the 'owners of the land' indicates ancestor ideology behind the cult. Freyr's cult is in several medieval sources said to have started at his gravemound, and this also applies to Hálfdanr svarti and Óláfr Geirstaðaálfr, who received offerings and sacrifices at their respective gravemounds. Þorgerðr holgabrúðr's story, too, points in this direction – she is, at least according to one tradition, said to have been buried in a great mound where she received offerings. The deaths of some settlers in Iceland are associated with gravemound-shaped natural features in the landscape, which were seen as the abodes of deceased family members. The gravemound cult itself is a key indicator of a worldview where ancestors were crucial religious and political actors. The political and legal motivations behind these medieval descriptions do not undermine their potential to provide a realistic image of a pagan worldview, and indeed demonstrate the continued significance of ancestors and gravemound worship even into the early medieval period.

Some of the individuals discussed here received ritual attention from large communities and this has led to an understanding among contemporary scholars that they were 'gods' or supernatural figures, a concept which is inevitably tinged by notions of the 'divine' in the minds of modern Western audiences. This has barred these figures from scholarly discussion of ancestors, which is more accustomed to looking at ancestors and ancestor worship from a domestic or folkloristic perspective. When looking at the sources, however, there is little evidence found for the idea that these individuals were seen as 'gods' in the sense of 'divine beings'. Instead they are quite regularly described as having associations with concepts that are inherently related to beliefs about ancestors. There are different, often scattered and indirect pieces of information about these characters which suggest that they were perceived as once-living human beings. These pieces of texts were likely influenced by classical writings, which often refer to the ruler as a human being who had been turned into a god. Such euhemerisations in Old Norse literature have accordingly been interpreted as medieval scribes' fabrications, created with the purpose of promoting Christianity and disparaging the pagan gods who were reduced to mere human status. This study has argued that regardless of the high probability that medieval authors did consciously follow a learned euhemeristic strategy, this method could be applied and accepted by the populace so readily because it was already a part of the Norsemen's social and religious reality.

This book has argued that the public or semi-public aspect of the cults of those scrutinised here is consistent with the possibility that their worship was an integral part of the general worship of ancestors. The public aspects of these cases can be explained by recourse to the anthropological theory of superior ancestors. According to this theory, ancestor cults are not only a personal and domestic convention; they can also attain the status of a politico-religious institution with the distancing of the elite in societies with established social hierarchies. In such cases the leading groups present their own ancestors as having more influential qualities than those of common ancestors, which helps them strengthen their political position. It is important, however, that the basis for this kind of manipulation is kinship rather than a link to the divine and that each family's ancestors are equally important, albeit on a lesser scale. Given the framework of superior ancestors, there is no need to imbue these king-gods with divine and mythic elements, which are often present in discussion of sacral kingship or religious ruler ideology. The claim is not made, however, that there was no ruler ideology in pagan Scandinavia. The ruling groups certainly used their distinguished ancestry as a tool to reinforce and secure power and authority. However, this was done so easily because the important predecessors were seen by the people, and perhaps by the rulers themselves, as real once-living ancestors rather than divinities.

Any examination that is concerned with religion is bound to be subjective and limited in its capacity to fit the events, of which we have partial knowledge, into a neat historical narrative. Since in addition to its inherent complexity, religion is not only a sociological or historical phenomenon that affiliates a person with a particular group, but also has a profound psychological significance for each individual, the varieties it can encompass are almost infinite. It would therefore be impossible and misleading to make any conclusive observations about religion generally, let alone about religion in one specific corner of Europe more than a millennium ago. The aim here has not been to oversimplify the complexity of spirituality and religiousness or even to claim that all pagan 'gods' were seen as mere extensions of mortal men whose followers had managed to trick their way to wealth and status. The concept of omnipotent creators (and destroyers) was certainly also present in pagan Scandinavians' religious sentiments and over time merged and blended with conceptions about ancestors and other forces that were believed to influence human life more directly. Religious conceptions are not temporally static and it is also likely that many regionalised 'superior ancestors' whose gravesites were turned into communal cultic places, but whose precise identities were eventually forgotten, lost some of their realism and over time acquired qualities which made them somewhat less human-like. In Freyr's case, at least, there is sufficient evidence to suggest that the perception of him, even more than a few centuries after his cult potentially commenced, was that of a human: he was remembered as an ancestor in a gravemound. Placing trust in anthropological analogues from other analysed historical and contemporary cultures, we may assume that ancestors were more directly addressed by their kin in ritual invocation in pagan Scandinavia as well, and that the 'god' concept was by and large inherently closer in status to ancestors and less compatible with the demanding theological conception of a Christian God.

The research question at the beginning of this book asked whether the phenomena observed in the corpus of examined material – traditionally accounted for by a number of disparate underlying processes (sacral kingship, worship of dead chieftains, learned euhemerisation) – can be reasonably accounted for in a unified and principled way through a single underlying belief in 'superior ancestors'. The evidence adduced in the course of this study allows us to give a tentative but positive answer to the question.

Primary sources

Aeneid, 2000, *Virgil, Aeneid 7. A commentary*, N. Horsfall (ed.), Brill, Leiden, Boston and Cologne.
Ágrip af Nóregskonungasǫgum, 1985, Bjarni Einarsson (ed.), Hið íslenzka fornritafélag, Reykjavík.
Chambers Dictionary of Etymology, 1988, R. Barnhart (ed.), Chambers Harrap Publishers Ltd., Edinburgh and New York.
Chronicon, 1889, *Thietmari Merseburgensis Episcopi Chronicon*, J. Lappenberg (ed.), Impensis Bibliopolii Hahniani, Hannoverae.
Chronicon, 2001, *Ottonian Germany: the chronicon of Thietmar of Merseburg*, trans. D. Warner, Manchester University Press, Manchester.
Corpus iuris Sueo-Gotorum antiqui: Samling af Sweriges gamla lagar, vol. 1, Codex Iuris Vestrogotici. Westgötalagen, 1827, H. Collin and C. Schlyter (eds.), Z. Haeggström, Stockholm.
Corpus iuris Sueo-Gotorum antiqui: Samling af Sweriges gamla lagar, vol. 6, Helsingelagen, Kristnu-balken af Smålands lagen, Bjärköarätten, 1844, H. Collin and C. Schlyter (eds.), Berlingska Bogtryckeriet, Lund.
De Proprietatibus Rerum, 1905, *Mediæval Lore from Bartholomew Anglicus*, R. Steele (ed.), The De La More Press, London.
Diarium Vazstenense ab ipsis initiis monasterii ad ejusdem destructionem, 1721, E. Benzelius (ed.), Russworm, Upsaliæ.
Diplomatarium Norvegicum. Oldbreve til kindskab om norges indre og ydre forhold, sprog, slægter, sæder, lovgivning og rettergang i middelalderen, 1855, C. Lange and C. Unger (eds.), vol. 3, P. T. Mallings Forlagshandel, Christiania.
Eddukvæði, 1998, Gísli Sigurðsson (ed.), Mál og Menning, Reykjavík.
Fagrskinna – Nóregs konunga tal, 1985, Bjarni Einarsson (ed.), Hið íslenzka fornritafélag, Reykjavík.
Flateyjarbok. En samling av norske konge-sagaer, 1860–1868, Guðbrandur Vigfússon and C. R. Unger (eds.), 3 vols, P. T. Mallings Forlagsboghandel, Christiania.
Fornaldarsǫgur norðurlanda, 1954, Guðni Jónsson (ed.), vols 1–4, Íslendingasagnaútgáfan, Reykjavík.
Fornmanna sögur eptir gömlum handritum. Saga Ólafs konúngs hins helga, 1829, Sveinbjörn Egilsson et al. (eds.), vol. 4, H. Popp, Kaupmannahøfn.
Fyrsta Málfræðiritgerðin, 1972, *First grammatical treatise: the earliest Germanic phonology. An edition, translation and commentary*, E. Haugen (ed.), Longman, London.

Primary sources

Fyrsta Málfræðiritgerðin, 1972, *The first grammatical treatise: introduction, text, notes, translation, vocabulary, facsimiles*, trans. Hreinn Benediktsson, University of Iceland Publications in Linguistics, 1, Institute of Nordic Linguistics, Reykjavík.
Geographia, 1843, C. Nobbe (ed.), Umptibus et Typis Caroli, Lipsiae.
Germania, 1885, *Cornelii Taciti de Origine, Situ, Moribus ac Populis Germanorun*, G. Egelhaaf (ed.), F. A. Perthes, Gotea.
Germania, 1999, *Tacitus. Agricola and Germany*, trans. A. Birley, University Press, Oxford.
Geographia, 1991, *The geography*, trans. E. Stevenson, Dover Publications, New York.
Gesta Danorum. Danorum Regum Heromque Historie, 1980, books 9–16, trans. E. Christiansen (ed.), vol. 1, BAR International Series, Oxford.
Gesta Danorum. The history of the Danes, 1998, books 1–9, trans. P. Fisher, H. Ellis Davidson (ed.), D. S. Brewer, Cambridge.
Gesta Danorum. Saxonis Gesta Danorum, 1931, books 1–9, J. Olrik and H. Ræder (eds.), Det Danske Sprog- og Litteraturselskab, Copenhagen.
Gesta Hammaburgensis, 1876, *Adami Gesta Hammaburgensis Ecclesiae Pontificum*, J. Lappenberg (ed.), Scriptores Rerum Germanicarum. Impensis Bibliopolii Hahniani, Hahniani.
Gesta Hammaburgensis, 2002, *History of the archbishops of Hamburg-Bremen*, trans. F. Tschan, Columbia University Press, New York.
Getica, 1882, *Monvmenta Germaniae Historica: Iordanis Romana ed Getica*, part 1, T. Mommsen (ed.), vol. 5, APVD Weidemannos, Berolini.
Getica, 1915, *The Gothic history of Jordanes*, trans. C. Mierow, University Press, Princeton.
Guta lag. The law of the Gotlanders, 2009, trans. C. Peel (ed.), Viking Society for Northern Research, 19, University College London, London.
Guta saga. The history of the Gotlanders, 2010, trans. C. Peel (ed.), Viking Society for Northern Research, 12, University College London, London.
Hauksbók, 1892–1896, *Hauksbók udgiven efter de Arnamagnæanske Håndskrifter No. 371, 544 og 675, 4o samt Forskellige Papirshåndskrifter*, Eiríkur Jónsson and Finnur Jónsson (eds.), 2 vols, Thieles Bogtrykkeri, Copenhagen.
Historia de Gentibus Septentrionalibus, 1996–1998, *A description of the northern peoples Rome 1555*, P. Foote et al. (ed.), The Hakluyt Society, London.
Historia Ecclesiastica Gentis Anglorum, 1907, *Bede's ecclesiastical history of England. A Revised Edition*, A. Sellar (ed.), George, Bell & Sons, London.
Historia Langobardorum, 1878, L. Bethmann and G. Waitz (eds.), Impensis Bibliopolii Hahniani, Hannoverae.
Historia Langobardorum, 1974, *History of the Lombards*, trans. W. Foulke, University of Pennsylvania Press, Philadelphia.
Historia Rerum Norvegicarum, 2008, *Norges historie*, I. Titlestad (ed.), trans. Å. Ommundsen and V. Roggen, Eide Forlag, Bergen.
Íslenzk fornrit, 1933, Multiple editors, 35 vols,Hið Íslenzka fornritafélag, Reykjavík.
Íslenzkar þjóðsögur og æfintýri, 1862, Jón Árnason (ed.), J. C. Hinrichs, Leipzig.
Norges gamle love indtil 1387, 1846–1849, R. Keyser and P. Munch (eds.), 3 vols, Trykt hos Chr. Gröndahl, Christiania.
Norges historie, 2008, I. Titlestad (ed.), trans. Å. Ommundsen and V. Roggen, Eide Forlag, Bergen.
Ohthere's Voyages. A late 9th-century account of voyages along the coasts of Norway and Denmark and its cultural context, 2007, J. Bately and A. Englert (eds.), Maritime Culture of the North, 1, The Viking Ship Museum, Roskilde.

Ravennatis anonymi Cosmographia et Gvidonsis Geographica, 1860, M. Pinder and G. Parthey (eds.), Aedibvs Friderici Nicolai, Berolini.

Risala, 2000, trans. J. Montgomery (ed.), 'Ibn Fadlan and the Rusiyyah*.' *Journal of Arabic and Islamic Studies*, vol. 3, pp. 1–25.

Romulus, 1889, *Plutarch's lives of Romulus, Lycurgus, Solon, Pericles, Cato, Pompey, Alexander the Great, Julius Cæsar, Demosthenes, Cicero, Mark Antony, Brutus, and others, and his comparisons*, W. Langhorne and J. Langhorne (eds.), John W. Lovell Company, New York.

Saga Óláfs konungs hins helga. Den store saga om Olav den hellige. Efter pergamenthandskrift i Kungliga Biblioteket i Stockholm nr. 2 4to med varianter fra andre handskrifter, 1941, O. Johnsen and Jón Helgason (eds.), vol. 2, Norsk Historisk Kjeldeskrifts-Institutt, Oslo.

Skaldic Poetry of the Scandinavian Middle Ages, 1. Poetry from the Kings' Sagas 1: From Mythical Times to c. 1035, 2012, D. Whaley (ed.), Brepols, Turnhout.

Skaldic Poetry of the Scandinavian Middle Ages, 3. Poetry from Treatises on Poetics, 2017, K. E. Gade and E. Marold (eds.), Brepols, Turnhout.

Skånske lov og Eskils skånske Kirkelov, tilligemed Andreæ Suonis lex Scaniæ prouincialis, Skånske Arvebog og det tilbageværende af Knud den 6.' Og Valdemar den 2.' Lovgivning vedkommende Skånske Lov, 1853, P. Thorsen (ed.), Nordiske Litteratursamfund, Copenhagen.

Snorra Edda, 2003, Heimir Pálsson (ed.), Mál og Menning, Reykjavík.

The Old English rune poem, 1981, *The old english rune poem: a critical edition*, M. Halsall (ed.), University of Toronto Press, Toronto.

Vita Ansgarii, 1884, *Scriptores rerum Germanicarum in usum scholarum ex Monumentis Germaniae historicis recusi, vol. 55. Vitae Anskarii et Rimberti*, G. Waitz (ed.), impensis bibliopolii Hahniani, Hannoverae.

Vita Ansgarii, 1921, *Anskar, the Apostle of the north. 801–865*, trans. C. Robinson, The Society for the Propagation of the Gospel in Foreign Parts, London.

Index

Note: The 'Þ' character is alphabetized as 'th'.

Adam of Bremen: *Gesta Hammaburgensis* 19, 76–77, 91, 93, 97n3, 112–115
að deyja í ('to die into') 158–159
æsir and *vanir* 12, 75, 98n15, 106–108; see also *álfar*
Africa, rituals in 49; see also specific peoples
afterlife 11–13
Ágrip af Nóregskonungasǫgum 119
ahnenkult ('ancestor cult') 72
Aldhouse-Green, Miranda 115
álfar 12, 39, 41, 107–108, 123, 163, 167n16; see also *vanir*
Álfheimar 107, 109, 110, 126n7
álfskot ('elf-shot') 39
Alþingi 165
ancestors and ancestor worship: academic research on 31–37; and burial grounds, significance of 14–15; defining 48–50; and *dei* 96; diverse beliefs and practices surrounding 47, 62; and fear 35–36, 63–64n2; and folk religion 50–53; and Freyr 118; and king-god cults 166; and public offerings to prominent persons 87; of ruling groups 54; socio-anthropological treatment of 1–3; Swanson's categories of 55–56; Tylor on 33–34; see also superior ancestors and superior ancestor worship
'ancestral soul' concept 42n5
animism 33–34
anthropology: evolutionary 31–33; and functionalist perspectives on ancestor worship 36–37; social 1–3, 31, 39, 41
'anti-pantheon' work 11
archaeology 39
Arctic culture 91

Ari fróði Þorgilsson 19–21, 77, 104, 162, 164
ár ok friðr ('good harvests and peace') 40, 117
Aryans 32
Ashanti people 57
áss 166n2, 167n11
Auðr djúpúðga 155–156, 158–159, 162–167n5

Baetke, Walter 90–91, 105; *Yngvi und die Ynglinger* 71–73
Bantu-speaking people 57
Bárðar saga Snæfellsáss 166n2
Bartholomaeus Anglicus: *De Proprietatibus Rerum* 150–151n13
Ba-Thonga people 57–58
Bede 77; *Historia Ecclesiastica Gentis Anglorum* 18
bergrisi 14, 24n8
Biezais, Haralds 91, 92
Birgisson, Bergsveinn 104
Birkeli, Emil 39, 40, 160–161
Bjarni Kolbeinsson: Jómsvíkingadrápa 145
Bjǫrn Buna 155, 165, 166n5
blood sacrifices 76
blótgoði 76, 77, 111
blót practice 76, 117
boat burials 163
bog bodies (Northern Europe) 114–115, 127n17
Breiðafjǫrðr region (Iceland) 158–159, 162
Brennu-Njáls saga 145, 159
Briggs, Stephen 114
Brink, Stefan 11, 93, 113
British Isles 167
Brøgger, Anton 117

brúðr 138–140
Buna family 159–160, 162; *see also* Bjǫrn Buna
Byock, Jesse 164

Catholic Church 114
Chadwick, Nora 40, 122–123
chieftains' dwellings 98n13
China, religion in 16
Christianity: and biography of Óláfr Tryggvason 142; and euhemerism 74–75; and humanisation of pagan gods as men 74–76; and kinship alliances 146–147; and paganism 17–18; variety within 8
Christiansen, Reidar 40
Christmas celebrations 39
classical writings 3, 10, 75, 77, 171
Clunies Ross, Margaret 137, 160
'collective unconscious' 42n5
corpore infames 114, 127n17
Crovan, Guðrøðr 97n10
cult houses *see hof*
'cult of the dead' 41, 63n2
Cunnison, Ian 55
cup-mark stones 107–108
Czaplicka, Maria 51

Dahomean people 58
Darwin, Charles: *On the Origin of Species by Means of Natural Selection, or the Preservation of Favoured Races in the Struggle for Life* 33
death-beliefs, customs and rituals 12, 39–40; *see also* afterlife; graves and gravemounds; *specific rituals*
dei 89, 91, 93, 96–97n2
Dejbjerg wagons (Jutland) 116, 117
Denmark: and Goðheimar place names 109; political organisation in 86; Snoldelev memorial runestone 94; vehicle fragments in 116
deus term 76
the Devil 144
de Waal Malefijt, Annemarie 63n2
Diana (goddess) 70–71
digri and digrbeinn 123–124
dísir 18, 40, 41, 146–148, 163, 167n16
dismembering of dead rulers 119, 127–128n23
'divine' concept 72–73, 89, 106, 126n5, 139, 171
Dómaldi 119

draugr ('ghost') or *haugbúi* ('mound-dweller') cults 40
Dumézil, George 10
Durkheim, Émile 34–35

Egils saga 161
Eiríkr blóðǫx 136
Ellekilde, Hans 38
elves 24n9
ǫndvegissúlur ('high-seat pillars') 160–161, 167n7, 167n11
Enlightenment period 31
Erik of Birka 86, 89–97n2, 171
eriksgata (ceremony) 89, 92, 96, 97nn7–8, 97n10
ethnology 39
etymological studies 39
euhemerism: of Bede 78; defined 74; emergence of 63, 74–75; and Freyr cult 112; of Icelandic historians 78–79; Lang on 35; in Latin histories 75; medieval 1–3; and Rimbert 91; and ruler ideology 78; and sacral kingship hypotheses 90; of Saxo 19; of Scandinavian rulers 76; of Snorri 78; of Spencer 34, 74
European imperialism 33
Eyrbyggja saga 98n15, 155–163, 165, 166n1
Eyvindr Finsson *skáldaspillir*: *Hákonarmál* 136; *Háleygjatal* 87, 104, 127n9, 135–136, 142, 150n1; and hárfagri clan genealogy 149

Færeyinga þáttr 145
Fagrskinna 119, 127–128n23
families *see* kinship and family systems
farm guardians 13, 36, 38–39, 40
farmhouses 98n13
Faroe Islands 167n14
fedrekult ('forefather cult') 39
Feilberg, Henning 38, 40
fertility rituals: and dísir cult 40; and Dómaldi's sacrifice 119; and Erik of Birka 89; and Frazerian sacral kingship 136; and Freyr 116; and rulers' relationship with the land 139; and sacral kingship 70–71; and *vanir* 107
Finnar groups 144, 151n16
Finno-Ugric cultures 9, 91, 95
First Grammarian 140, 150
five-generation principle 13, 55, 61, 103, 110, 123
Flateyjarbók 112, 116, 119, 121, 128n25, 142, 147–148, 150n11

folklore: and approach to Old Norse religion and mythology 138; and evolutionary anthropology 32; and *Finnar* 144; and folklore studies 36, 39; about graves 15; theories of 31
folk religion 15–17, 23, 50–53
förfäderskult 40
forn siðr ('old customs') 7–8
Fortes, Meyer 49, 52, 54
Frank, Roberta 139
Frazer, James 87, 105, 136; *The Golden Bough: A Study of Comparative Religion* 70–71
Freedman, Maurice 57
Freeprose and Bookprose theories 20
Freud, Sigmund 36
Freyja 11–12, 87, 126n4, 138, 139
Freyr: and ancestor worship 41; blood sacrifices to 76; death of 126n4; as divine progenitor 111, 125; and fertility 10, 11, 116; and Gamla Uppsala 95, 103, 107, 108, 111–112, 118; gravemound of 12, 148, 171; icons and processions relating to 115–118; offerings to 95; and pig associations 128n25; and rulers' ancestors 117–118; and *Skírnir* 126–127n7; Snorri on 71; and Þorgerðr 145–146; and *vanir* 107; in *Vatnsdæla saga* 167n10; and Ynglingar 104–105; in *Ynglinga saga* 103; Yngvi 75
functionalism 7, 35, 37
fylgja 139, 148
Fyrsta Málfræðiritgerðin 140, 145

Gamla Uppsala pagan cult house: Catholic Church descriptions of 19; and Freyr 95, 103, 107, 108, 111–112, 118; significance of 73; *templum* at 93, 113
Gapt (king) 75
Gaulardalr area 137
Geirstaðaálfr 147
genealogical knowledge 55, 78; *see also* five-generation principle
'genealogical schizophrenia' 61
Gerðr (goddess) 71, 105, 126n4, 137, 138
'Germania' 18–19
Germanic culture 9, 31, 36
Gesta Danorum 24n8, 144
Gesta Hammaburgensis 91
giants *see jǫtnar*
Gísla saga 91
Glælognskviða (poem) 160

goðar (gods) 76, 77, 126n5
'god' concept and worship 15, 23, 35, 36, 75, 171
Goðheimar 109
Good, Anthony 57
Goths 75, 76
graves and gravemounds: and ancestors in Old Norse religion 13–15; in election ceremonies 93; and *fedrekult* 39; in folktales and legends 38; and Hálfdanr 119–121; and *hǫrgr* 163; in Iceland 12; and Óláfr helgi 123, 124; and prohibition of gravemound offerings 41, 94; and public cults dedicated to kings 72; tampering with 116–117, 127n21, 143, 148; and Þorgerðr 142, 147
Grímkell 146
Grimm brothers 31–33
Grímnismál 98n15, 107
Grímr kamban 167n14
Grjótgarðsson, Hákon 86
Grottasǫngr (poem) 24n8
guardian-like figures 40; *see also* farm guardians
Gunnell, Terry: on Álfheimar 107, 108; on *álfr* 110, 123; 'anti-pantheon' work by 11; approach of 138; on chieftains' dwellings 98n13; on Yule time 38, 39
Gunnlaugr Sveinsson 142, 150n11
Guta saga 76–77
Gylfaginning 98n15, 107

Hagberg, Louise 40
hailstones 145, 151n14
Hákonarson, Jón: *Flateyjarbók* 21
Hákon góði Haraldsson 136
Hákonsson, Magnús 13
Háleygjar 75, 139, 150n2
Hálfdanr 147
Hálfdanr svarti 103, 118–121, 126, 127–128n23, 128n25, 171
Hálogaland region (Norway) 149
Hamburg–Bremen diocese 91
Haraldr gráfeldr 136
Haraldr grenski 124–125
Haraldr hárfagri 20, 21, 85–87, 103–104, 136, 155, 156, 166n1
Haraldsson, Óláfr 86
Harðar saga 146–147
hárfagri family 21, 63, 87, 136
haugar 120–121, 125
haugbrot ('grave-breaking') 146
Hawaii, nobility in 58, 106

heiðinn siðr ('heathen customs') 8
Heinrichs, Anne 121, 123, 125
hekura (spirits) 52–53
Hel (goddess) 11
Helgafell ('Holy Mountain') 157–159, 161–164, 165
Helgi magri 18
Hǫlgi of Hálogaland (King) 137, 141–142, 145–146, 148
Helms, Mary 60
hǫrgar 13, 94–95, 98n15
Hǫrgi *see* Hǫlgi of Hálogaland
hǫrgr 142, 147, 162, 163
hieros gamos motif 70, 71, 102, 105, 116, 136–139
'high mythology' and 'lower mythology' 36
high-seat pillars *see ǫndvegissúlur*
Hlaðir group 136
Hoefig, Verena 167n11
hof ('cult house' or 'cult building') 93–95, 98n13, 98n15, 112, 143, 146–147; *see also* Gamla Uppsala; *templum*
hólar (knoll) 163, 166
holy scriptures 8, 16
'homeostatic process of forgetting' 61
Hrólfr 156
Hsu, Francis 56
human sacrifice 77, 112–115, 143–144, 146, 151n17
Hyndluljóð 94

Ibn Fadlan 77
Iceland: Alþingi in 86; boat burials in 163; Breiðafjǫrðr region 158–159, 162; chieftaincies in 85, 86, 156; Christianity in 147; *ǫndvegissúlur* custom in 161; Freyr in sagas of 118; guardian-like figures in 40; *hof* in 94; land inheritance in 164–165; *landvættir* in 167n16; Medieval Christians in 8; mountain motif in 157–158; patrilineal kinship systems in 56; Snæfellsnes mountain 166n2
indigenous cultures 32, 33, 49; *see also specific cultures*
Ing and Ingaevones 108–109
Ingólfr Árnarson 156
intergenerational bonds 41; *see also* kinship and family systems
Ireland, settlers from 86
Irpa 143–146, 148, 149
Íslendingabók 19–20, 23, 104, 156, 165
Íslendingasǫgur 147, 159

Japan, imperial ancestors in 58
Jarl Hákon Sigurðarson 86, 128n25, 135–136, 138–139, 142, 145–146, 148–149, 150n5, 151n17
jarls of Hlaðir 87
Jennbert, Kristina 8
jǫtnar 12, 148, 150n3
Jómsvíkinga þáttr 143–144, 146
Jordanes 75, 76
Jung, Carl 42n5

Kaplan, Merrill 146–147
Käringssjön site (Sweden) 114
Ketill flatnefr 155, 156, 166n5
kings and kingship 39; *see also* sacral kingship
kings' sagas 20–22
kinship and family systems: and ancestor worship 34, 37; and cohesion in folk religion 16–17; defining 57; and kinship-based societies 1–2, 37; Malinowski on 36; manipulation of 61; and superior ancestors 53–57; and 'superior ancestor worship' 57–63; *see also* ancestors and ancestor worship
kristinn siðr ('Christian customs') 8–9
Krosshólar 'Cross-hillocks' 162, 163
Kuhn, Adalbert 32
!Kung people 51
Kveld-Úlfr 161

landdísir 40
land inheritance 13–14, 86–87, 103, 117–118, 126, 139
Landnámabók 11, 19–20, 23, 118, 155–165, 166nn1–2
landvættir 167n16
Lang, Andrew 35
Lares Praestites ('city ancestors of Rome') 58
Lathgerda 137
laws pertaining to graves 13
Laxdœla saga 164
Lejre sacrifices 115, 127n18
Lid, Nils 39, 41
lineages and clans 55, 56, 62, 64n4
literacy 18, 61, 63
Littledale, Richard 32
Lönnroth, Lars 119, 126n3
'lower mythology' and 'high mythology' 36
Lugbara people 51
Lunda grove cult site (Sweden) 114

182 Index

Madagascar 39
Mälaren region (Sweden) 86, 89, 104, 109
Malinowski, Bronislaw 31, 37, 55
Manheimar 109, 127nn8–9
Mannhardt, Wilhelm 15, 36, 38, 70
man-wife model 150n5; *see also* sacred marriage motif
Manx folklore 97n10
Mardu people 52
Mayan society 58
Mbiti, John 49
McKinnell, John 141
McTurk, Rory 72
memory 64n2
methodology 23
missionaries and merchants 33, 144
monotheistic God 8
Mora stone (Sweden) 92
Morgan, Lewis Henry 60
mountain motif 157–158, 163, 166n2
Müller, Max 32
Mundal, Else 139
mythological geography 109

naming customs 91–92, 97nn5–6
nationalism and folklore 32
nature-myth school 32
Nerthus (deity) 116, 127n19
Njáls saga 91–92, 97n6
Njǫrðr 76, 103, 126n1, 127n19
Nordberg, Andreas 8–9
Nordic pantheon 73
Norway: Freyr cult in 111; genealogies in 93; *hof* in dialects of 94; landowners in 85; mountain motif in folklore of 157–158; northern areas of 144, 149; petty kings of 103; *Þórr* place names in 159; Yule traditions in 161
Norwegian kings, burial places of 71
numina 76
Nygaard, Simon 106
nýi siðr ('new customs') 8–9

Oddr Snorrason 142, 150n11
Óðinn (god) 10–12, 75–76, 126n1, 127n9, 135–136, 149, 150nn1–2
Óláfr Geirstaðaálfr tale 41, 110, 121–125, 128n27, 171
Óláfr Guðrøðarson 103, 110, 121
Óláfr Hákonarson 142
Óláfr helgi 21, 103–104, 120–123, 126, 128nn26–27, 142, 166n2
Óláfr trételgja 109, 110

Óláfs saga helga 121
Óláfs saga Tryggvasonar 21, 86, 103–104, 111–112, 116, 120, 127n23, 128n25, 142–143, 148, 150n11, 151n14, 151n17
Olaus Magnus: *Historia de Gentibus Septentrionalibus* 150–151n13
The Old English Rune Poem 109
Old Norse literature and mythology 23, 31–32, 37–41, 62, 98n13
Old Norse religion 1, 9–11
Óleifr hvíti 162
Olrik, Axel 38–39
Olsen, Magnus 71
Olsen, Olaf 94, 95, 147
oral traditions 20, 31, 60–61, 62–63, 78, 104
Oree (or Orry) 97n10
origin myths 136–137
Oseberg ship (Norway) 116
oskoreia riders 166n3
oskoreia tradition 39, 92
otherworld concepts and perceptions 11–13; *see also* Valhǫll

pantheon of Old Norse gods 10–11, 71, 73, 108, 160; *see also* individual gods by name
patrilineal systems 56
political strategies 125, 172
Price, Neil 12
primary sources 18–23
Primiano, Leonard 15
public and domestic cults 37, 57, 63, 172

Radcliffe-Brown, Alfred 31, 37
Radin, Paul 79
Rauðs þáttr ramma 143, 145
rebirth 91, 124, 125
reginnaglar ('god's nails' or 'sacred nails') 160
Rǫgnvaldr 103, 110
Reichborn-Kjennerud, Ingjald 38–39
religion, defining 7–9
religious ruler ideology 2–3, 73–74, 78, 105, 156; *see also* sacral kingship
Rígr (or Heimdallr) 97n10
Rimbert: Birka rulers mentioned by 97n4; *dei* of 93; *Vita Ansgarii* 19, 73, 76–77, 89–91, 95–96, 97n3
risahaug 13–14
rituals and religion 8–9
Rivers, William 51–53, 60
rock carvings and picture stones 14

Röekillorna spring site 114
Roman emperor cult 58
Romantic School 31
Røthe, Gunnhild 139, 141–143, 145–147
Royal Road (Isle of Man) 98n10
Russia, gravesite constructions in 95

sacral kingship: *vs.* ancestor worship 39–41; elements of of 70–71; and Erik of Birka 90; and euhemerism 78; and general ancestor cults 87; and the Háleygjar 135–139; and land, associations with 140; and public cult for dead rulers 63; and terminology issues 2; and Ynglingar 104–106; *see also* religious ruler ideology; Ynglingar
sacred marriage motif 140, 148
Sæmingr (first jarl of Hlaðir) 135, 136, 150n3
Saint Ansgarius 19, 89, 90, 96
Saint Óláfr 128n26
Sakalava monarchy (Madagascar) 58
salhauku(m) ('on the hall of mounds') 94
Sámi (or *Fenni*) people and language: and death-beliefs 12; influence of 9–10; and *jǫtnar* 12, 24n5; naming conventions of 92; negative associations with 151n16; as 'original' people of Scandinavia 150n3; and paganism 157–158; and Þorgerðr 149; and Þorgerðr cult 144; and weather magic 144–145
Samoyed people 51–52
Saxo Grammaticus: *Gesta Danorum* 19, 112, 127n10, 137, 151n14, 151n17; on *Hǫlgabrúðr* 140; and man-wife model 150n5
Scandinavia: deaths of rulers in 59, 104; and 'deifications' of individuals 60; *hof* in 94; landowners in 85; northern regions of 151n16; paganism in 7
Schetelig, Haakon 38
Schjødt, Jens Peter 60, 73, 74, 76, 79
Schleicher, August 10
Schwartz, Wilhelm 15, 36
Scotland: *broonie* 39; settlers from 86
sequential development 95
Setberg 24n8
Shang dynasty (China) 58
Sheils, Dean 57, 58, 60
siðaskipti ('change of customs') 9
Sigmundr Brestisson 143
Sigurðsson, Gísli 20
Skaði 135–137, 149, 150n1

skaldic verses 21–23, 141–142
Skallagrímsson, Egill: *Sonatorrek* 109
Skedemosse site 114
Skírnir 126n4, 126n7, 145
Skírnismál 105, 136, 145
skritfinni ('sliding Finns') 150n3; *see also* Sámi (or *Fenni*) people and language
Skúli Þorsteinsson: *Poem about Svǫldr* 141
Snæfellsnes mountain (Iceland) 166n2
Snorri goði 161–162
Snorri Sturluson: *Edda* 21–23, 75, 140, 142, 149; euhemerism of 78; Freyr's cult 117–118; on Freyr's cult 112; *Hákonar saga góða* 111; *Heimskringla* 21, 75, 77, 102, 112, 119, 128n25, 141, 150n11; on *Hǫlgabrúðr* 140; pantheon of 10–11; significance of work by 14; and Valhǫll concept 11, 12; *Ynglinga saga* 71, 75, 87, 102–103, 105, 108–110, 120, 126n1, 150n1
'solar mythology' 32
Sóti 147, 148
the soul 49
Sparlösa runestone 97n4
Spencer, Herbert 32–35, 38, 74
Stammbaumtheorie ('language-tree theory') 10
Steadman, Lyle 52
Steinsland, Gro 105, 106, 120, 136–137
Storm, Gustav 150n6
Ström, Åke 71, 91, 92
Ström, Folke 40, 41
'structural amnesia' 61
structural–functionalist methods 1
substantive ideologies 7
Sundqvist, Olof 2–3, 72–74, 79, 91–92, 97n4, 104, 119, 156, 160–161
superior ancestors and superior ancestor worship 2, 53–57, 59–60, 62, 72–74, 78, 87, 89, 96, 120–121, 147, 172–173
'supernatural' concept 72, 78
Svealand 73
Swanson, Guy 55
Swaziland, protective nature of ancestors in 57
Sweden: and Goðheimar place names 109; kings of 71, 103; Mälaren region 86, 89, 104, 109; Roslagen province 127n15
systematic introspection 37

Tacitus: *Germania* 18–19, 75, 76, 108–109, 115–116
Tallensi people 54

Tanimbar islanders 58
tannfé 107
Tatje, Terrence 56
templum ('temple') 93–94, 96, 112, 113; see also *hof*
Þáttr Óláfs digrbeins 128
Thietmar of Merseburg 76, 127n18; *Chronicon* 19, 115
þing sites 92–93, 97n9, 97–98n10, 164
Þiðranda þáttr 18, 146–147
Þjóðólfr úr Hvíni: *Ynglingatal* 21, 87, 102–104, 108–110, 125–126, 126n3, 135–136
Þóra 150n5, 150n8
Þórbjǫrn hornklofi: *Hrafnsmál* 141
Þorgerðr 135, 137–139; description of 149–150; in *Flateyjarbók* version of *Ólafs saga Tryggvasonar* 142–144; gravemound cult of 146–149, 171; identity of 140–141; ring story 147–148
Þorgilsson, Ari 75
Þórhallson, Magnús: *Flateyjarbók* 21
Þórkell Gíslason: *Búadrápa* 145
Þorleifs þáttr 143, 148
Thornton, David 61
Þórðr 163–164
Þórólfr mostrarskegg 155–156, 158–159, 165, 166n5
Þórr 10–11, 145–146, 156–162, 165–166, 167n6
Þórsnesingar family 156–157
til haugs ok heiðni ('to gravemounds and heathen time') 13, 93, 120
Tindr Hallkelsson: *Hákonardrápa* 137
Tiv people 60–61
Toda people 51–53
Torfason, Þormóður: *Historia Rerum Norvegicarum* 24n5
totemism 34–35
tradition *vs.* belief 49
translation of indigenous terms 52
trǫll 140, 166n2
trémaðr and *trémenn* ('tree man/men') 116–117, 143
tripartite paradigm of social structures 10
Trøndelag area 135–136
Tuan, Yi-Fu 16

Tungus people 51–52
Turville-Petre, Gabriel 41
Tylor, Edward 32–35
Tynwald Hill (Isle of Man) 97n10
Týr (god) 11, 108

Ugarthilocus (mythical figure) 24n8
Ullr (god) 11
unilineal kinship systems 56, 64n3
'unique abilities' of elite 62
Uppsala 127n14; see also Gamla Uppsala
Útgarða-Loki 24n8

vættir ('spirits') 163, 167n16
Valhǫll (otherworld) 11, 12; see also otherworld concepts and perceptions
valkyrjur 148
vanir stock 138
Vatnsdœla saga 98n15, 167n10
vegetation cults and magic 40, 70, 71; see also fertility rituals
Vǫluspá 98n15
Vestfold area, gravemounds in 110, 121
Víga-Glúms saga 117–118
Viken region 109
Viking Rus 77
Virgil (poet) 70
Volga trade route 127n15

wagons 116
weather magic 144–145
Wellendorf, Jonas 161
Westermarck, Edward 34
west Nordic language 9
Whaley, Diana 21, 123
winter traditions 39; see also Yule traditions
wizards 150–151n13
world *vs.* folk religion 16–17

Yanomamö people 52
Ymir 119
Ynglingar 21, 63, 71, 73, 75, 103–106; see also hárfagri family
Yngvi (king) 75, 108–109
Yule traditions 38, 39, 161

Zachrisson, Torun 38

Printed in Great Britain
by Amazon

Printed in Great Britain
by Amazon

Thank you...

We hope this journey into the world of plant-based living has inspired and empowered you to embrace a healthier, more sustainable way of eating. But our story together doesn't end here. For a treasure trove of the latest plant-based recipes, essential store cupboard items, recommended buys and other publications to assist you on your ongoing plant-based journey, we invite you to explore our website at www.myplantbasedlife.co.uk and subscribe to our mailing list.

Stay connected with us on social media, too! Follow us at @myplantbasedlife and share your culinary masterpieces with the world. We can't wait to see your creativity shine and share in your delicious plant-based adventures.

Thank you for choosing plant-based living, not only for your well-being but also for the health of our planet. Together, we can make a difference—one delectable dish at a time. Here's to your vibrant, plant-powered life!

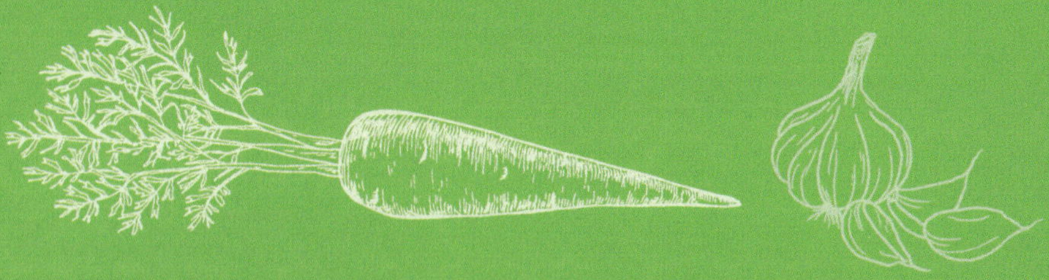

Special thanks go out to all our friends and family who have been invaluable in testing and refining these recipes and generously sharing their experiences with us along this incredible journey. And rest assured, there's much more in store to come!

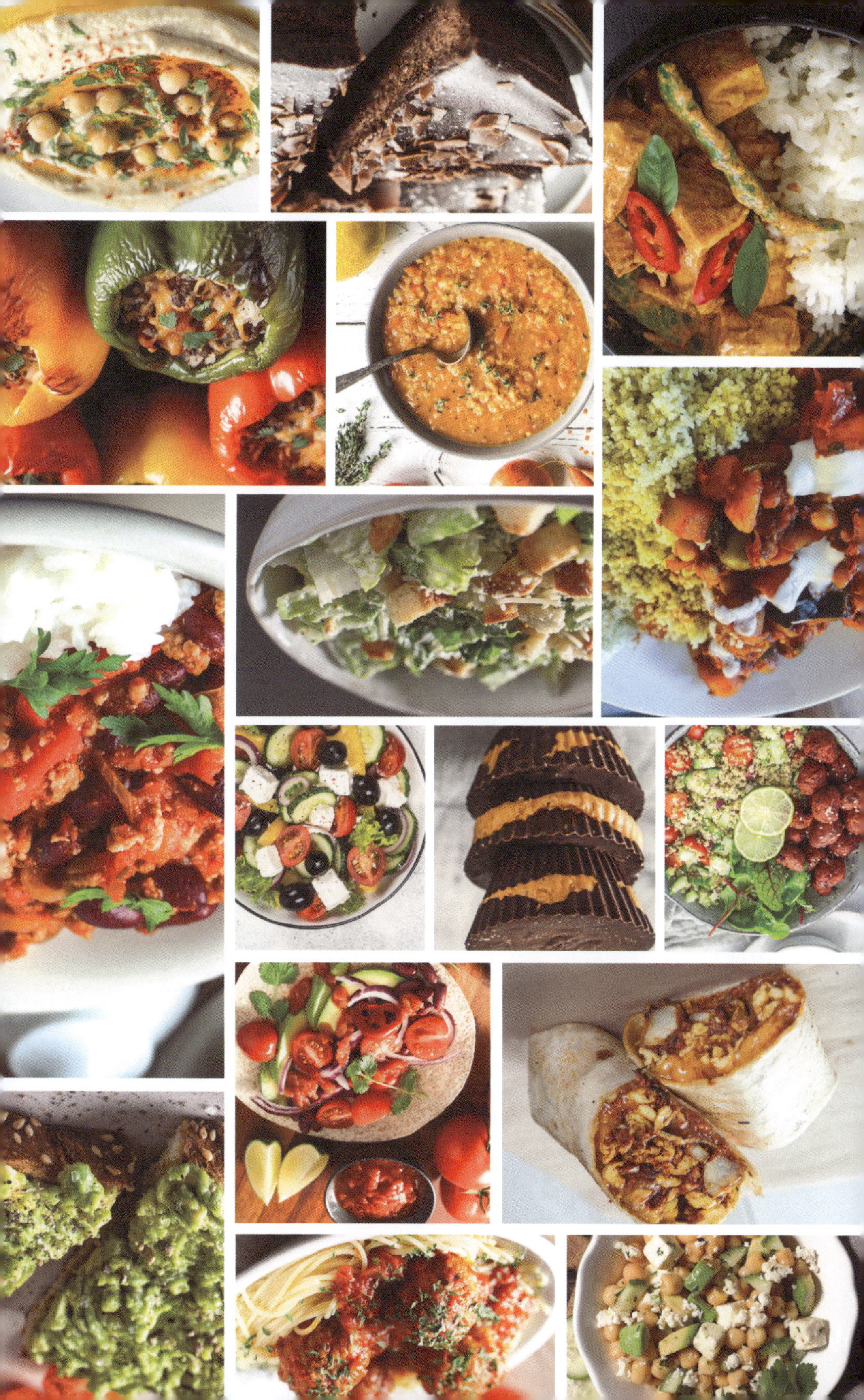

BONUS

PEANUT BUTTER OAT CUPS

SERVES 6

PREP TIME: 10 MINS. 2 HOURS CHILL TIME
COOKING TIME: 20 MINS

INGREDIENTS

- 70g rolled oats used gluten-free if necessary
- 2 tbsp smooth peanut butter or nut butter of choice
- 2 tbsp maple syrup
- Pinch of salt
- 100g smooth peanut butter
- 1 tbsp maple syrup
- 140 g dark chocolate melted
- Optional drizzle of melted Biscoff spread

PER SERVING

Calories: Approx 210 kcal
Protein: Approx 5g
Carbohydrates: Approx 26g
Dietary Fiber: Approx 3g
Sugars: Approx 12g
Fat: Approx 10g

DIRECTIONS

- Prepare the Base: Drizzle a small amount of dark chocolate into the base of each cup in a 6-cup silicone muffin tray. Freeze for 5 minutes to set the chocolate.
- Prepare the Oat Mixture: In a mixing bowl, combine the remaining rolled oats, smooth peanut butter, maple syrup, and a pinch of salt. Mix all the base ingredients in this bowl, ensuring they are well combined.
- Remove the muffin tray from the freezer. Press the oat mixture firmly on top of the chocolate layer in each cup, creating a solid base. Freeze for an additional 15 minutes.
- Prepare the Peanut Butter Layer: In a small bowl, mix the peanut butter and maple syrup together until well combined. This will be the middle layer of your cups.
- Spread the peanut butter and maple syrup mixture evenly over the oat bases in the muffin tray, creating the middle layer.
- Top with Melted Chocolate: Melt the remaining chocolate and spoon it over the peanut butter layer, ensuring each cup is generously covered. Use the back of a spoon to smooth out the top.
- Refrigerate Until Set: Place the muffin tray in the refrigerator and let the cups refrigerate until the chocolate hardens and the layers are set, usually for a few hours or overnight.
- Once the cups are completely set, remove them from the muffin tray.

Feel free to adjust the chilling times based on your preference for the texture of the cups. Enjoy your homemade treats!

PEANUT BUTTER OAT CUPS

CHOCOLATE TOFU CHEESECAKE

BONUS

SERVES 12

PREP TIME: 2 HOURS 45 MINS. 2 HOURS CHILL TIME
COOKING TIME: 30 MINS

INGREDIENTS

- 250 g Biscoff Biscuits, crumbled
- 2 tbsp vegan butter, or coconut oil
- 6 tbsp Biscoff Spread
- 1 tbsp maple syrup
- 500 g silken tofu
- 200 g Biscoff Spread
- 300 g melted vegan chocolate
- 1 tsp vanilla bean paste or extract
- melted vegan chocolate
- chopped chocolate
- Biscoff Biscuits, broken
- salted popcorn
- sea salt flakes

PER SERVING

Calories: Approx 703 kcal
Protein: Approx 12g
Carbohydrates: Approx 63g
Dietary Fiber: Approx 5g
Sugars: Approx 40g
Fat: Approx 44g

DIRECTIONS

- Preheat your oven to 180°C (Gas Mark 4, 350 °F).
- Begin by crushing the biscuits in a food processor until they turn into fine crumbs. In a small pan, melt the remaining crust ingredients together. Add the crumbs to the melted mixture, stirring thoroughly until well combined.
- Transfer the mixture to a baking tin and firmly press it down, ensuring it covers the bottom and sides evenly, creating a compacted base. Bake the crust in the oven for 10-15 minutes, then remove it and let it cool.
- For the filling, place all the required ingredients in a clean food processor or blender. Blend until the mixture becomes smooth and well combined.
- Once the base has cooled, pour the filling into the tin and refrigerate for at least 2 hours, preferably overnight, to allow it to set.
- After the cheesecake has set, carefully remove it from the tin and place it on a cake stand or serving plate. Decorate the top with your preferred toppings. Chill the cheesecake again until you're ready to serve. Enjoy!

After the cheesecake has set and cooled, cover it tightly with plastic wrap or aluminum foil. This helps prevent it from drying out or absorbing odors from other items in the fridge.

CHOCOLATE TOFU CHEESCAKE

CHOCOLATE NUTTY FUDGE

BONUS

SERVES 20

PREP TIME: 10 MIN

INGREDIENTS

- 200 g vegan baking chocolate
- 140 g almond or another nut butter
- 80 g mixed nuts, chopped small
- Sea salt, optional

PER SERVING

Calories: Approx 180 kcal

Protein: Approx 5g

Carbohydrates: Approx 10g

Dietary Fiber: Approx 3g

Sugars: Approx 4g

Fat: Approx 14g

DIRECTIONS

- Break up the chocolate and set in bowl over a pan of simmering water and add the nut butter. Melt together until silky smooth.
- Pour into moulds or lined container and sprinkle over the chopped nuts and a tiny pinch of salt, if you like. Allow to set in the fridge for 2 hours.
- Slice into bites or remove from the mini moulds. Store in the fridge.

Enjoy your delicious and nutritious homemade no-bake protein balls!

CHOCOLATE NUTTY FUDGE

BONUS

NO BAKE PROTEIN BALLS CINNAMON AND RAISIN

SERVES 24

PREP TIME: 10 MIN

INGREDIENTS

- 150g old fashioned rolled oats
- 250g cashew butter
- 60ml honey or maple syrup
- 2 scoops (about 50-60 grams) vanilla protein powder
- 30g raisins
- 1/4 teaspoon cinnamon

PER SERVING

Calories: Approx 210 kcal
Protein: Approx 9g
Carbohydrates: Approx 20g
Dietary Fiber: Approx 2g
Sugars: Approx 9g
Fat: Approx 11g

DIRECTIONS

- Mix Dry Ingredients: In a large bowl, combine the rolled oats, vanilla protein powder, raisins, and cinnamon. Mix well to ensure even distribution of ingredients.
- Add Cashew Butter and Sweetener: Add the cashew butter and honey (or maple syrup) to the dry ingredients. Mix until the mixture comes together and forms a dough-like consistency. If the mixture is too dry, you can add a bit more honey or maple syrup.
- Form Balls: Take small portions of the mixture and roll them between your palms to form balls. The size can vary based on your preference, but a typical size is about 1 inch (2.5 cm) in diameter.
- Chill: Place the protein balls on a tray or plate lined with parchment paper. Chill them in the refrigerator for at least 30 minutes to firm up.
- Serve: Once the protein balls have hardened, they are ready to be enjoyed. Store any leftovers in an airtight container in the refrigerator for freshness.

Enjoy your delicious and nutritious homemade no-bake protein balls!

NO BAKE PROTEIN BALLS

TAHINI DRESSING

BONUS

PREP TIME: 20 MIN

INGREDIENTS

- 1/4 cup tahini (sesame paste)
- 2 tablespoons fresh lemon juice
- 2 tablespoons water
- 1 clove garlic, minced
- 1 tablespoon maple syrup or agave syrup
- 1/2 teaspoon ground cumin
- Salt and black pepper, to taste
- Optional: 1-2 tablespoons chopped fresh parsley or cilantro for garnish

PER SERVING

Calories: Approx 120 kcal

Protein: Approx 3g

Carbohydrates: Approx 6g

Dietary Fiber: Approx 1g

Sugars: Approx 3g

Fat: Approx 10g

DIRECTIONS

- Prepare the Tahini: If your tahini has separated in the jar, stir it well until it's smooth and creamy.
- Mix Ingredients: In a bowl, whisk together the tahini, fresh lemon juice, water, minced garlic, maple syrup, and ground cumin. Whisk until the mixture is well combined and smooth.
- Adjust Consistency: Depending on your preference, you can adjust the thickness of the dressing by adding more water, a tablespoon at a time, until you reach your desired consistency. Remember that the dressing will thicken slightly when refrigerated.
- Season and Taste: Season the dressing with salt and black pepper to taste. Remember that a little salt goes a long way, so start with a small pinch and adjust as needed. Taste the dressing and adjust the lemon juice or sweetness if necessary.
- Garnish (Optional): If desired, garnish the dressing with chopped fresh parsley or cilantro. This adds a burst of fresh flavour and a pop of colour to your salad.
- Store or Serve: Use the dressing immediately over your favourite salad or store it in an airtight container in the refrigerator. Before using leftovers, give the dressing a good stir, as it might thicken in the fridge. If it's too thick, you can thin it out with a little water before serving.
- Enjoy: Drizzle the vegan tahini salad dressing over your salad just before serving. It's also great as a dipping sauce for vegetables or a marinade for grilled tofu and vegetables.

Enjoy your vegan tahini salad dressing! Feel free to customise the recipe by adding herbs like parsley, dill, or chives for extra flavour variations.

TAHINI DRESSING

BONUS

DAISY'S FAVOURITE HUMMUS

PREP TIME: 20 MIN

INGREDIENTS

- 1 can (400g) of chickpeas, drained and rinsed
- 3 tablespoons tahini (sesame paste)
- 2 cloves garlic, minced
- 1 large fresh lemon juice
- 2 tablespoons extra virgin olive oil
- 1/2 teaspoon ground cumin
- Salt, to taste
- 2 to 3 tablespoons water
- Optional toppings: a drizzle of olive oil, a sprinkle of paprika, chopped fresh parsley, or pine nuts

PER SERVING

Calories: Approx 140 kcal

Protein: Approx 4g

Carbohydrates: Approx 11g

Dietary Fiber: Approx 3g

Sugars: Approx 1g

Fat: Approx 9g

DIRECTIONS

- Prepare Chickpeas: Drain and rinse the chickpeas thoroughly under cold running water. If you have time, you can remove the skins for an even smoother hummus. (this is a step I wouldn't skip as it makes such a difference to the texture)
- Blend Ingredients:
- In a food processor, combine the chickpeas, tahini, minced garlic, lemon juice, olive oil, ground cumin, and a pinch of salt.
- Blend the ingredients until they form a thick paste. Scrape down the sides of the food processor with a spatula as needed.
- Adjust Consistency: With the food processor running, slowly add 2 to 3 tablespoons of water, one at a time, until the hummus reaches your desired creamy consistency. Add more water if you prefer a smoother hummus.
- Taste and Adjust Seasoning: Taste the hummus and adjust the seasoning. You might want to add more salt, lemon juice, or cumin according to your preference. Blend again to incorporate the additional seasonings.
- Transfer the hummus to a bowl. Create a shallow well in the center of the hummus with a spoon and drizzle a bit of olive oil into the well. Sprinkle with paprika and chopped parsley for a burst of colour and flavour. You can also add a few pine nuts for extra crunch.
- Enjoy: Serve the hummus with warm pita bread, vegetable sticks, or your favourite crackers. It's also great as a spread in sandwiches or wraps.

Hummus can be stored in an airtight container in the refrigerator for up to one week. If it thickens in the fridge, simply stir in a little water or lemon juice to reach the desired consistency again before serving.

DAISY'S FAVOURITE HUMMUS

BONUS

Bonus recipes

THINGS TO KNOW

- **Vegan cheese isn't always replacement:** in fact the taste is somewhat acquired. in fact i would go as far as to say vegan cheese is the devil! but if you do need to add cheese to a dish there are some ways of doing it without that weird after taste. here are some tips from our guys ... (then i will add in tips)

There is always an option to make your own, not only is this an interesting project, you can make sure the ingredients are to you liking and no hidden nasties. Check out this one we found on amazon https://amzn.to/3PByhon

I'm a big fan of the vegan Parmesan and Greek cheeses, these are so versatile and can be used as an actual replacement for their diary counterparts. most supermarkets stock these too.

if you do want some grated cheese or one you want to use on top of pizzas or melted then we've reviewed some of the larger brands....

"Vegan Cheese is the devil!" - Michelle

- **Store Cupboard Essentials:** Starting on this plan might appear to require a substantial selection of herbs and spices, but always keep in mind that these aromatic treasures can serve you for weeks, if not months, and will soon become pantry essentials. For excellent value, consider a visit to Aldi or Lidl, where you can find a wide range of affordable dry herbs and spices
- **Don't be hard on yourself:** The most important thing to remember is, to not be so hard on yourself and be realistic. Transitioning to a new way of eating takes time and is a process. Every little helps and eating more plant based meals is a win.

- **Eating out isn't as hard as you think:** Eating out at your favorite restaurants while maintaining a plant-based diet isn't as challenging as it may seem. In fact, it's now easier than ever as many eateries are offering vegan options to cater to their diverse customer base. However, where I found it most challenging was during holidays in Spain and Italy, where vegan options weren't always readily available. During such trips, I sometimes had to temporarily shift to a vegetarian diet until I could return to being 100% plant-based. On occasion, I even asked restaurants to create a custom dish from the items on their menu, which didn't always receive the warmest reception, especially in Italy. However, it's essential not to be too hard on yourself and to savor the dining experiences with friends and family while on holiday. Fortunately, these situations have been the exception rather than the rule, and most of my dining-out experiences have been absolutely delightful

- **Planning is Key:** Planning may appear straightforward, but it can prove challenging for those who weren't natural planners before. Personally, I used to relish the spontaneity of choosing meals on the day rather than pre-planning them. However, with the responsibilities of parenthood and the increasing cost of living, I've found it necessary to embrace this structured approach to weekly meal planning. Having a set meal plan not only helps you stay on budget but also promotes healthier eating habits. I encourage you to give our 14-day meal plan a try and see how it works for you.

- **Egg Substitutes**: Vegan egg substitutes have revolutionised plant-based cooking. One popular substitute is **aquafaba**, the thick liquid found in canned chickpeas, which mimics egg whites and can be whipped. **Tofu**, especially silken or soft varieties, can be blended to a smooth consistency, resembling the texture of scrambled eggs, or used in baking as an egg replacer. **Bananas and applesauce** serve as excellent binding agents in baking. **Flaxseed meal and chia seeds**, when mixed with water, form a gel-like substance that emulates the binding properties of eggs. Additionally, commercial vegan egg replacers, often made from starches and leavening agents, offer a convenient and reliable option for both baking and cooking needs.

THINGS TO KNOW

So when I decided to join the world of plant based eating, it wasn't always smooth sailing, we came across some stumbling blocks and i wanted to arm you with the knowledge we have gathered the past few years:

- **Mindset is everything:** Mindset is everything when it comes to embracing a plant-based lifestyle. We've all grown up in a world where meat and two veg are the norm, so shifting our mindset towards a plant-based diet can be a real challenge. For me, it took several months to overcome that feeling of missing something on my plate, especially during dinner. Initially, I relied on meat-free alternatives to ease the transition, but that soon became monotonous. It was when I started exploring the vibrant world of vegetables that I truly found my stride, and I've never looked back. Don't get me wrong; I still enjoy a Beyond Meat burger or some vegan chicken nuggets for a quick meal fix, but the realm of plant-based cuisine goes far beyond these options. With our collective experiences and a well-structured meal plan, we hope to make your journey into this lifestyle even smoother

- **Preparing Tofu (firm tofu):** To prepare firm tofu and unleash its full potential, it's essential to begin by efficiently draining the liquid from the packet. Once you've removed the tofu block, carefully wrap it in kitchen towels to absorb any excess moisture. This step is crucial as it not only improves the tofu's texture but also makes it easier to handle and crisp up if desired. After draining, consider marinating the tofu in your favorite sauce or seasoning to infuse it with flavor. You can then proceed to pan-fry, bake, or grill the tofu to achieve a delicious crispy exterior while maintaining a tender inside. Remember that firm tofu works exceptionally well in stir-fries, salads, and sandwiches, absorbing the flavors of the accompanying ingredients. Mastering the art of draining and marinating firm tofu ensures a satisfying culinary experience, allowing you to explore a wide range of tasty and nutritious dishes.

CHAPTER
06

THINGS WE WISH WE'D KNOWN BEFORE

- **Vegan Protein Powder:** If you're looking to boost your protein intake in a convenient shake form, consider exploring the world of vegan proteins. There's a wide variety available on the market, but here are a few of our favorite options:

- **Earth Champ in delicious vanilla flavor (available at https://amzn.to/48blFvn),**
- **Bodyme protein (find it at https://amzn.to/3ZiUxrx),**
- **Free Soul (available at https://amzn.to/3PA6LbW).**

These vegan protein choices not only offer a sustainable and cruelty-free protein source but also deliver a tasty and satisfying experience for your taste buds. So, whether you're a dedicated vegan or simply looking to try something new, these options can help you meet your protein goals while tantalising your palate

- **Vegan Omega 3:** Omega-3s are vital for heart and brain health, among other things. By choosing a vegan option, you not only avoid the potential environmental and ethical concerns associated with fish oil but also ensure that your dietary choices align with your values. We'll share our favorite vegan Omega-3 supplements that provide all the goodness without any compromise.

- **Nothing but... (find it at https://amzn.to/3PfwEML)**
- **Freshfield (find it at https://amzn.to/45GRqff)**
- **Supplemented (find it at https://amzn.to/464Nlf8)**

- **Additives and Fillers:** Read the ingredient list to check for any unnecessary additives, fillers, or artificial colors or flavors. Opt for supplements with minimal additional ingredients.

- **Monitor Your Health:** Regularly assess your nutrient levels through blood tests to ensure that your chosen supplements are effectively addressing any deficiencies or imbalances.

Remember that supplements should complement a well-balanced diet rich in a variety of whole, plant-based foods. They are not a substitute for a healthy diet but can be essential for filling nutrient gaps and supporting overall health when chosen wisely and used in conjunction with a nutritious vegan lifestyle.

We've researched a small selection of supplements available on the market for you. Our aim is to assist you in making informed choices that align with your nutritional needs, dietary preferences.

We hope to simplify the process of selecting vegan supplements, empowering you to support your health and well-being with confidence.

However, it's essential to remember that individual nutrient requirements can vary, so consulting with a healthcare provider or registered dietitian remains an essential step in tailoring your supplement regimen to your specific needs.

When choosing vegan supplements, there are several important factors to consider to ensure you are meeting your nutritional needs effectively and safely:

- **Individual Nutrient Needs:** Your specific nutrient requirements may vary based on factors such as age, gender, activity level, and overall health. Consult with a healthcare provider or registered dietitian to determine which supplements are necessary for you.

- **Quality and Purity:** Look for supplements from reputable brands that undergo third-party testing for quality and purity.

- **Bioavailability:** Some nutrients are more easily absorbed in specific forms or combinations. For example, vitamin D3 is typically more effective than D2 for raising blood levels of the vitamin. Consider the bioavailability of the supplement

- **Whole Food vs. Isolated Nutrients:** Whenever possible, choose whole food-based supplements or those derived from natural sources. Whole food supplements often provide a broader range of nutrients and phytonutrients that work together synergistically.

- **Dosage and Frequency:** Follow the recommended dosage and frequency provided on the supplement label or as advised by a healthcare professional. Avoid mega-dosing

- **Interactions:** Be aware of potential interactions between supplements and medications you may be taking. Consult your healthcare provider to ensure there are no adverse effects or interactions.

- **Form and Delivery:** Consider the form of the supplement, such as capsules, tablets, liquids, or powders, based on your preferences and ease of consumption. Also, think about the delivery method; some nutrients are more effectively absorbed when taken with food or at specific times of the day.

SUPPLEMENTS

Vegan supplements play a crucial role in helping individuals maintain a balanced and nutritionally complete plant-based diet.

- **Vitamin D:** supports bone health, immune function, and overall well-being. Many vegans opt for vitamin D supplements, especially if they have limited sun exposure, as our bodies can produce this vitamin when exposed to sunlight.

- **Omega-3 Fatty Acids:** specifically EPA and DHA, are essential for cardiovascular health and brain function. Vegan sources include algae-based supplements, providing a sustainable alternative to fish oil.

- **Iron:** Plant-based iron is less easily absorbed than heme iron from animal products. Vegans may take iron supplements, particularly if they are at risk of iron deficiency, to maintain healthy blood and energy levels.

- **Calcium:** is crucial for strong bones and teeth. While plant sources like fortified foods, leafy greens, and almonds provide calcium, some vegans choose calcium supplements to meet their daily needs.

- **Iodine:** is essential for thyroid function and overall health. Vegans who avoid iodised salt may consider iodine supplements or consume iodine-rich foods like seaweed.

- **Zinc:** supports immune function, wound healing, and metabolism. While plant foods contain zinc, vegan diets may benefit from zinc supplements, especially if consuming foods that contain phytates that can inhibit zinc absorption.

- **Vitamin K2:** is important for bone and cardiovascular health. Vegans can consider vitamin K2 supplements or opt for fermented foods like natto and sauerkraut as dietary sources.

CHAPTER
05

SUPPLEMENTS

CHICKPEA AND SWEETCORN BURGER

DINNER

SERVES: 2

PREP TIME: 15 MIN

COOKING TIME: 10 MIN

INGREDIENTS

1 x 400g tin of chickpeas, drained and rinsed

1 x 340g tin of sweetcorn

1/2 a bunch of fresh coriander (about 15g)

1/2 teaspoon paprika

1/2 teaspoon ground coriander

1/2 teaspoon ground cumin

1 lemon

3 heaped tablespoons plain flour, plus extra for dusting

Rapeseed oil (or any cooking oil of your choice)

1 small round lettuce

2 large ripe tomatoes

Tomato ketchup

4 wholemeal burger buns

PER SERVING

Calories: Approx 280-320 kcal

Protein: Approx 10-12g

Carbohydrates: Approx 50-55g

Dietary Fiber: Approx 8-10g

Sugars: Approx 6-8g

Fat: Approx 4-5g

DIRECTIONS

- In a food processor, combine the drained chickpeas, sweetcorn, fresh coriander (including stems), paprika, ground coriander, and ground cumin.
- Blend the mixture until it's fairly smooth but still has some texture. You don't want it completely pureed; a little texture is good.
- Zest the lemon and add the zest to the chickpea and sweetcorn mixture.
- Add the plain flour to the mixture. Mix everything together until well combined. The mixture should be firm enough to shape into burgers. If it's too wet, you can add a bit more flour.
- Divide the mixture into four equal portions and shape them into burger patties. You can use your hands for this. Dust each patty with a little extra flour.
- Cook the Burgers: Heat a bit of rapeseed oil in a large frying pan over medium-high heat. Once the oil is hot, add the burger patties. Cook for about 3-4 minutes on each side, or until they are golden brown
- Prepare the Burger Fixings: While the burgers are cooking, wash and dry the lettuce leaves and slice the tomatoes.
- Spread a little tomato ketchup on the bottom half of each wholemeal burger bun. Place a lettuce leaf and tomato slices on top of the ketchup.
- Add a cooked chickpea and sweetcorn burger patty on top.

These nutritional values are approximate and can vary based on the specific brands and quantities of ingredients you use. You can use a choice of condiments and potato wedges as a side dish

CHICKPEA AND SWEETCORN BURGER

MOROCCAN TAGINE WITH CHICKPEAS

DINNER

SERVES: 2

PREP TIME: 15 MIN

COOKING TIME: 40 MIN

INGREDIENTS

1 red onion, chopped

2 cloves garlic, chopped

a spray olive oil

½ tsp ground cumin

½ tsp ground coriander

½ tsp ground cinnamon

1 red pepper, seeded and chopped

1 courgette, chopped

1 aubergine, chopped

4 vine tomatoes, chopped

400g tin chickpeas, drained

250ml vegetable stock

2 tbsp harissa or siriacha if you haven't got harissa

4 prunes, pitted and sliced

flat-leaf parsley, to serve

steamed couscous or Bulgar, to serve

PER SERVING

Calories: 187kcal

Protein: 8.2g

Carbohydrates: 24.6g

Dietary Fiber: 11.7g

Sugars: 14.1g

Fat: 3.6g

DIRECTIONS

- Sauté Onions and Garlic: Heat a large, deep skillet or tagine over medium heat and spray with olive oil.
- Add the chopped red onion and garlic. Sauté for about 2-3 minutes until they start to soften.
- Add Spices: Sprinkle in the ground cumin, ground coriander, and ground cinnamon. Stir well to coat the onions and garlic with the spices. Sauté for another 1-2 minutes to release the fragrance of the spices.
- Add Vegetables: Add the chopped red pepper, courgette, and aubergine to the skillet or tagine. Sauté for about 5-7 minutes, stirring occasionally, until the vegetables start to soften.
- Incorporate Tomatoes and Chickpeas:
- Stir in the chopped vine tomatoes and drained chickpeas.
- Add Vegetable Stock and Harissa: Pour in the vegetable stock and add the harissa (or sriracha). Stir well to combine.
- Reduce the heat to low, cover, and let the tagine simmer for about 15-20 minutes or until the vegetables are tender and the flavors meld together. If the mixture becomes too dry, you can add a bit more vegetable stock.
- Add Prunes: Add the sliced prunes to the tagine and stir to combine. The prunes will add a sweet and tangy element to the dish.
- Serve and Garnish: Serve the Moroccan tagine hot, garnished with fresh flat-leaf parsley.
- Accompany it with steamed couscous, rice, or Bulgar

These nutritional values are approximate and can vary based on the specific brands and quantities of ingredients you use. You can also add in sriracha sauce instead of Harissa

MOROCCAN CHICKPEA TAGINE

VEGAN TACOS WITH KIDNEY BEANS

DINNER

SERVES: 2

PREP TIME: 15 MIN

COOKING TIME: 15 MIN

INGREDIENTS

1 can kidney beans, drained and rinsed

1/2 tps Cumin

1 avocado, peeled, pitted, and sliced

1 cup salsa (store-bought or homemade)

2 cups shredded lettuce

1 teaspoon olive oil

For the Taco Shells or Tortillas:

8 taco shells or small tortillas

PER SERVING

Calories: 180-220 kcal (per taco)

Protein: 6-8g

Carbohydrates: 25-30g

Dietary Fiber: 6-8g

Sugars: 3-4g

Fat: 7-9g

DIRECTIONS

- Prepare the Kidney Beans Drain and set aside.
- Warm the Taco Shells or Tortillas: Preheat your oven to 350°F (175°C). Place the taco shells or tortillas on a baking sheet and warm them in the oven for 5-10 minutes, or until heated through.
- Prepare the Kidney Bean Filling: In a skillet, heat the optional teaspoon of olive oil over medium heat
- Add the drained kidney beans to the skillet. Cook for about 5 minutes, mashing some of the beans with a fork or potato masher to create a slightly chunky consistency sprinkle the cumin and mix well.
- Assemble the Tacos: Fill each warmed taco shell or tortilla with a generous scoop of the kidney bean filling.
- Top the filling with sliced avocado, salsa, and shredded lettuce.
- Serve and Enjoy

These nutritional values are approximate and can vary based on the specific brands and quantities of ingredients you use. You can also add in sriracha sauce or more seasoning to the mix.

TACOS WITH KIDNEY BEANS

SPAGHETTI AND VEGAN MEATBALLS WITH MARINARA SAUCE

DINNER

SERVES: 2

PREP TIME: 40 MIN

COOKING TIME: 30 MIN

INGREDIENTS

1 package frozen Quorn meatballs
1 tablespoon olive oil
For the Marinara Sauce:
1 can of chopped tomatoes
2 cloves garlic, minced
1 teaspoon dried oregano
1 teaspoon dried basil
Salt and pepper to taste
Red pepper flakes
For the Spaghetti:
225g of spaghetti
Salt (for cooking pasta)
For the Side Salad:
Mixed greens
Cherry tomatoes, halved
Cucumber slices
Red onion slices (optional)
Balsamic vinaigrette dressing
Vegan parmesan cheese

PER SERVING

Calories: 500-600 kcal
Protein: 20-25g
Carbohydrates: 65-70g
Dietary Fiber: 7-10g
Sugars: 8-10g
Fat: 18-20g

DIRECTIONS

- Follow the package instructions for cooking the frozen Quorn meatballs. Typically, they can be baked in the oven or pan-fried in a bit of olive oil. Cook until they are heated through and golden brown.
- Marinara Sauce: In a saucepan, heat a tablespoon of olive oil over medium heat.
- Add the minced garlic and sauté for about 1 minute until fragrant but not browned.
- Stir in the crushed tomatoes, dried oregano, dried basil, salt, pepper, and red pepper flakes (if using).
- Simmer the sauce for 15-20 minutes, stirring occasionally, until it thickens and the flavours meld together. Adjust seasonings to taste.
- Cook the spaghetti according to package instructions in a pot of salted boiling water until al dente. Drain and set aside.
- Side Salad: In a salad bowl, combine the mixed greens, cherry tomatoes, cucumber slices, and red onion slices.
- Drizzle with balsamic vinaigrette dressing or your preferred vegan dressing.
- Toss the salad to coat the vegetables evenly.
- Assemble the Meal: Serve the cooked Quorn meatballs over a portion of cooked spaghetti.
- Spoon the marinara sauce over the meatballs and spaghetti.
- Serve with the side salad on the side and sprinkle with vegan parmesan cheese if desired.

These nutritional values are approximate and can vary based on the specific brands and quantities of ingredients you use.

SPAGHETTI AND VEGAN MEATBALLS

RED THAI CURRY WITH TOFU AND MIXED VEGETABLES

DINNER

SERVES: 2

PREP TIME: 15-20 MIN

COOKING TIME: 30 - 40 MIN

INGREDIENTS

1 block of firm tofu

2 tablespoons vegetable oil

1 onion, thinly sliced

2 cloves garlic, minced

1 red bell pepper, sliced

150g Mangetout

1 carrot, sliced into rounds

1 courgette, into rounds

2 tablespoons vegan red Thai curry paste

1 can coconut milk

1 cup vegetable stock

1 tablespoon soy sauce

1 tablespoon brown sugar or agave nectar

Salt and pepper to taste

Fresh basil leaves

Cooked jasmine rice

PER SERVING

Calories: 350-400 kcal

Protein: 12-15g

Carbohydrates: 20-25g

Dietary Fiber: 5-7g

Sugars: 8-10g

Fat: 25-30g

DIRECTIONS

- Prepare the Tofu: Press the tofu to remove excess water, then cut it into cubes. You can also lightly pan-fry or bake the tofu until it's golden brown for added texture.
- Heat the Oil and Saute Vegetables: In a large pan or wok, heat the vegetable oil over medium-high heat. Add the minced garlic and sliced onion. Stir-fry for 2-3 minutes until fragrant and the onion starts to soften.
- Add Curry Paste: Add the vegan red Thai curry paste to the pan. Stir-fry for another 1-2 minutes to release its aroma and flavor.
- Add Vegetables: Add the sliced red and yellow bell peppers, Mangetout, carrot rounds, and courgette rounds to the pan. Stir-fry for about 5-7 minutes or until the vegetables start to soften.
- Pour in Coconut Milk and Vegetable stock: Pour in the can of coconut milk and vegetable stock. Stir well to combine and let it come to a gentle simmer.
- Add Tofu and Seasonings: Add the cubed tofu to the pan. If desired, season with soy sauce or tamari for umami flavor and brown sugar. Season with salt and pepper to taste.
- Simmer and Serve: Allow the curry to simmer gently for 10-15 minutes, or until the vegetables are tender and the flavors have melded together.
- Serve hot over cooked jasmine rice or rice noodles, garnished with fresh basil leaves.

These nutritional values are approximate and can vary based on the specific brands and quantities of ingredients you use.

■ RED THAI CURRY WITH TOFU

STUFFED BELL PEPPERS WITH CHILLI

DINNER

SERVES: 2

PREP TIME: 10 MIN

COOKING TIME: 20 MIN

INGREDIENTS

Leftover Chili with Crumbled Tofu (from the previous recipe)
2 large bell peppers (any color)
200g cooked rice (white or brown, your choice)
100g vegan shredded cheese
Fresh parsley, for garnish

PER SERVING

Calories: 300-350 kcal (per stuffed bell pepper)
Protein: 12-15g
Carbohydrates: 40-45g
Dietary Fiber: 7-9g
Sugars: 7-10g
Fat: 10-12g

DIRECTIONS

- Preheat your oven to 350°F (175°C).
- Prepare the Bell Peppers: Cut the tops off the bell peppers and remove the seeds and membranes from the inside. Rinse them thoroughly.
- Stuff the Bell Peppers: Spoon the leftover Chili with Crumbled Tofu into each bell pepper, filling them to the top.
- Add Rice and Cheese (Optional):
  - If desired, mix the cooked rice into the remaining chili to add some extra texture.
  - Sprinkle vegan shredded cheese on top of each stuffed bell pepper for a cheesy finish.
- Bake the Stuffed Bell Peppers: Place the stuffed bell peppers in a baking dish. Cover the dish with aluminum foil and bake in the preheated oven for 30-40 minutes or until the bell peppers are tender.
- Garnish and Serve: Remove the stuffed bell peppers from the oven and let them cool slightly. Garnish with fresh parsley if desired. Serve hot.

These nutritional values are approximate and can vary based on the specific brands and quantities of ingredients you use.

STUFFED PEPPERS WITH CHILLI

DINNER

CHILLI WITH CRUMBLED TOFU

SERVES: 6

PREPPING TIME: 15 MIN

COOKING TIME: 45 MIN

INGREDIENTS

2 tablespoons olive

1 large onion, diced

1 red bell pepper, diced

4 garlic cloves, minced

1 package extra firm tofu

2 tablespoons chili powder

2 teaspoons ground cumin

1 teaspoon paprika

2 cans chopped tomatoes

2 tablespoons tomato paste

1 can black beans

1 can kidney beans

Salt and pepper to taste

PER SERVING

- Calories: 320 kcal
- Protein: 15g
- Carbohydrates: 40g
- Dietary Fiber: 11g
- Sugars: 7g
- Fat: 11g

DIRECTIONS

- Prepare the Tofu: Crumble the extra firm tofu into small pieces using your hands and set it aside.
- Saute the Aromatics: Heat the olive oil in a large pot over medium heat.
- Add the diced onion and red bell pepper. Cook for 5-7 mins, or until the vegetables become soft and translucent.
- Stir in the minced garlic and cook for 1-2 mins.
- Add the crumbled tofu to the pot and stir well to combine it with the vegetables.
- Sprinkle in the chili powder, ground cumin, paprika, chili powder, and cayenne pepper. Stir to evenly coat the tofu and vegetables with the spices.
- Pour in the chopped tomatoes and tomato paste. Stir
- Add the drained and rinsed black beans and kidney beans, stirring to incorporate them into the mixture.
- Reduce the heat to low and let the chili simmer for about 20-30 mins, stirring occasionally.
- Season with salt and pepper to taste. Adjust the spices as needed to suit your preference.
- Serve and Enjoy: Ladle the chili into bowls and serve hot. You can garnish with toppings like vegan cheese, chopped green onions, or fresh cilantro, if desired.

Keep leftover Chilli and for the stuffed peppers recipe to follow, this will last for 3 days in the fridge

CHILLI WITH CRUMBLED TOFU

DINNER
The main event

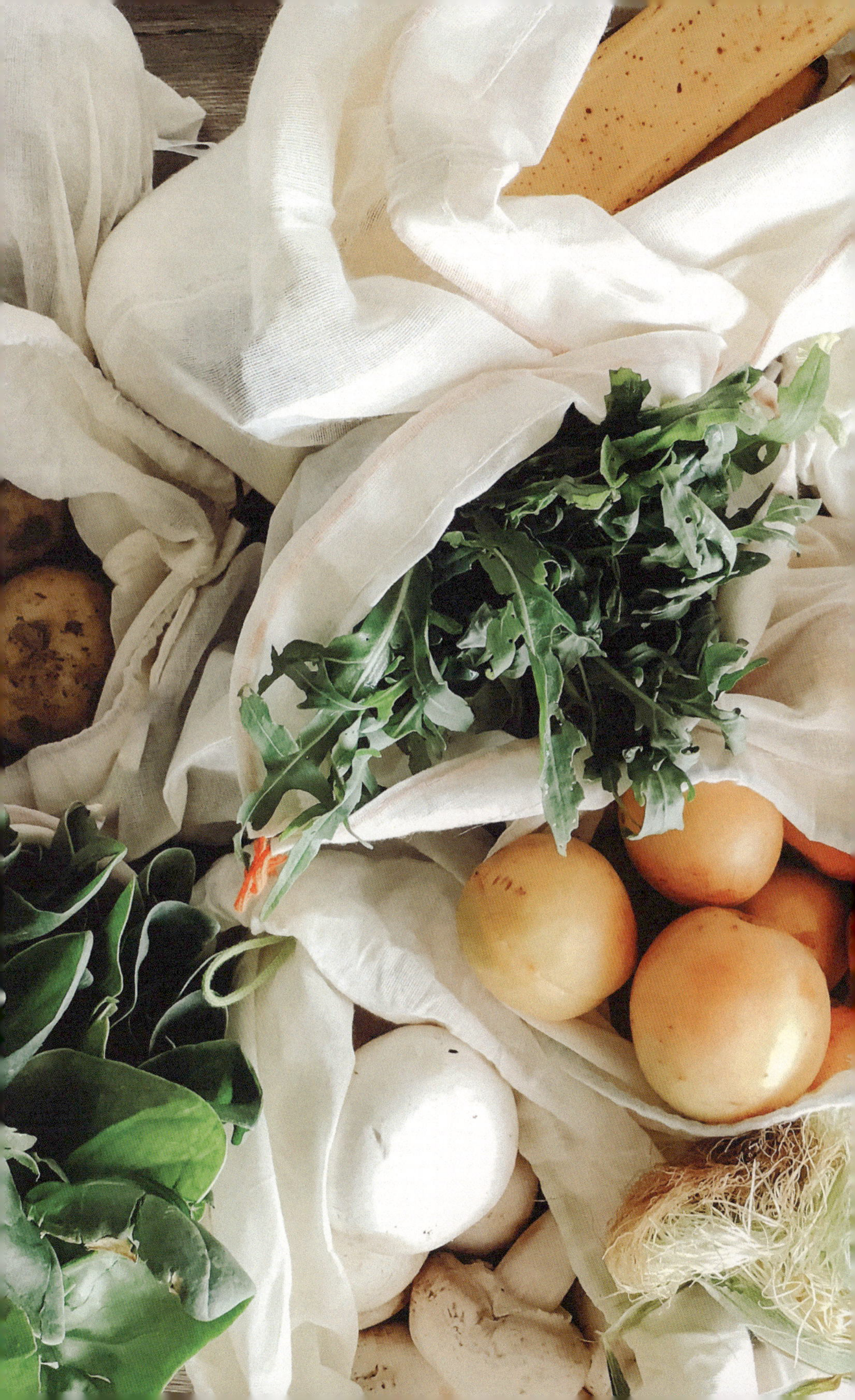

LUNCH

CAESAR SALAD WITH CHICKPEA CROUTONS

SERVES: 2

PREP TIME: 25 MIN

INGREDIENTS

100g of Romaine lettuce

100g of Vegan Caesar
dressing

100g of chickpeas (canned or
cooked)

50g of bread (for croutons)

PER SERVING

Calories: 350 kcal

Protein: 11g

Carbohydrates: 37g

Dietary Fiber: 8g

Sugars: 4g

Fat: 18g

DIRECTIONS

- Prepare the Chickpea Croutons: Preheat your oven to 375°F (190°C).
- Cut the bread into small cubes to make croutons.
- Place the bread cubes on a baking sheet and lightly drizzle with olive oil. Toss them to coat evenly.
- Bake in the preheated oven for 10-12 minutes or until the croutons are golden and crispy. Remove from the oven and let them cool.
- Prepare the Chickpeas: If using canned chickpeas, drain and rinse them under cold water. If using cooked chickpeas, make sure they are cooked and ready to use.
- Assemble the Salad: Wash and chop the Romaine lettuce into bite-sized pieces.
- In a large salad bowl, combine the Romaine lettuce, chickpeas, and chickpea croutons.
- Dress the Salad: Pour 100g of Vegan Caesar dressing over the salad.
- Toss Gently: Carefully toss all the ingredients together until the salad is well coated with the dressing and the croutons are evenly distributed.

You can make your own casear dressing and store it in the fridge for up to 3 days - recipe on our website visit www.myplantbasedlife.co.uk

■ CAESAR SALAD WITH CROUTONS

GREEK SALAD WITH FETA, OLIVES AND FALAFEL

LUNCH

SERVES: 2

PREP TIME: 20 MIN

INGREDIENTS

75g of Feta-style vegan cheese

50g of Kalamata olives

100g of falafel

100g of tomatoes

100g of cucumbers

For the Dressing:

2 tablespoons of olive oil

1 tablespoon of lemon juice

Salt and pepper to taste

PER SERVING

Calories: 450 kcal

Protein: 13g

Carbohydrates: 20g

Dietary Fiber: 6g

Sugars: 4g

Fat: 36g

DIRECTIONS

- Prepare the Ingredients: If you have frozen or dried falafel, cook them according to the package instructions until they are crispy and hot.
- Wash and dice the tomatoes.
- Wash and dice the cucumbers.
- Cut the Feta-style vegan cheese into small cubes.
- Pit and slice the Kalamata olives.
- Make the Dressing: In a small bowl, whisk together 2 tablespoons of olive oil and 1 tablespoon of lemon juice until well combined. Season with salt and pepper to taste. Set the dressing aside.
- Assemble the Salad: In a large salad bowl, combine the diced tomatoes, diced cucumbers, cubed vegan Feta cheese, and sliced Kalamata olives.
- Add the Falafel:
- Once the falafel is cooked and crispy, break it into pieces or leave it whole, depending on your preference.
- Drizzle with Dressing: Pour the prepared lemon juice and olive oil dressing over the salad ingredients.
- Toss Gently: Carefully toss all the ingredients together until the salad is well coated with the dressing.

> *These nutritional values are approximate and can vary based on the specific brands and quantities of ingredients you use.*

■ GREEK SALAD WITH VEGAN FETA

LUNCH

VEGAN WRAP WITH HUMMUS

SERVINGS: 2

PREP TIME: 10 MIN

COOKING TIME: 15 MIN

INGREDIENTS

2 whole-grain wraps or tortillas
75g of hummus
100g of roasted red peppers
50g of fresh spinach
100g of chickpeas (canned or cooked)

PER SERVING

Calories: 355 kcal
Protein: 11g
Carbohydrates: 57g
Dietary Fiber: 13g
Sugars: 4g
Fat: 10g

DIRECTIONS

- Prepare Your Ingredients: drain chickpeas and rinse them under cold water.
- Cut the red peppers into slices and drizzle with olive oil and roast for 15 mins then leave them aside
- Wash and dry the fresh spinach.
- If you have whole-grain wraps or tortillas that need heating, warm them up according to the package instructions.
- Spread Hummus: Lay out one whole-grain wrap or tortilla on a clean, flat surface. Using a butter knife or the back of a spoon, spread half of the hummus (approximately 37.5g) evenly over the wrap, leaving a border around the edges.
- Add Roasted Red Peppers: Place 50g of roasted red peppers evenly over the hummus.
- Layer with Spinach: Add 25g of fresh spinach leaves on top of the roasted red peppers.
- Add Chickpeas: Spread 50g of chickpeas evenly over the spinach.
- Wrap it Up: Carefully fold in the sides of the wrap and then roll it up tightly from the bottom, ensuring all the fillings are enclosed.
- Repeat for the Second Wrap:

> *These nutritional values are approximate and can vary based on the specific brands and quantities of ingredients you use.*

VEGAN WRAP WITH HUMMUS

LENTIL SOUP

LUNCH

SERVES: 4

PREP TIME: 25 MIN

COOKING TIME: 40 MIN

INGREDIENTS

200g dried red lentils

1 litre vegetable stock

1 onion, chopped

2 carrots, chopped

2 celery stalks, chopped

2 cloves garlic, minced

1 bay leaf

1 teaspoon dried thyme (or other preferred herbs)

Salt and pepper to taste

Olive oil for sautéing

PER SERVING

Calories: 250-300 calories

Protein: 15-20 grams

Carbohydrates: 45-50 grams

Dietary Fiber: 15-20 grams

Sugars: 6-8 grams

Fat: 1-2 grams

DIRECTIONS

- Rinse Lentils: Start by rinsing the lentils under cold water and removing any debris.
- Sauté Vegetables: In a large soup pot, heat a drizzle of olive oil over medium heat. Add the chopped onion, carrots, and celery. Sauté for about 5 minutes, or until the vegetables start to soften.
- Add Garlic and Herbs: Add the minced garlic, dried thyme (or other preferred herbs), bay leaf, salt, and pepper to the pot. Sauté for another minute until fragrant.
- Add Lentils and Broth: Stir in the rinsed lentils and pour in the vegetable or chicken broth (or water). Bring the mixture to a boil.
- Simmer: Reduce the heat to low, cover the pot, and let the soup simmer for about 25-30 minutes or until the lentils and vegetables are tender. Stir occasionally.
- Adjust Seasoning: Taste the soup and adjust the salt and pepper as needed.
- Serve: Remove the bay leaf, and ladle the soup into bowls. You can garnish with fresh herbs or a drizzle of olive oil if desired.

> *These nutritional values are approximate and can vary based on the specific brands and quantities of ingredients you use.*

LENTIL SOUP

MEDITERRANEAN BOWL WITH FALAFEL

LUNCH

SERVES: 2

PREP TIME: 15 MIN

COOKING TIME: 15 MIN

INGREDIENTS

200g falafel mix (store-bought)
For the homemade tabbouleh:
25g cup fresh parsley, finely
chopped
75g cup tomatoes, diced
200g cup cooked bulgur wheat
(cooled)
Juice of 1 lemon
2 tablespoons olive oil
Salt and pepper to taste
150g hummus (store-bought
or homemade)

PER SERVING

Calories: 400-500 calories
Protein: 10-15 grams
Carbohydrates: 35-45 grams
Dietary Fiber: 7-10 grams
Sugars: 3-5 grams
Fat: 25-30 grams

DIRECTIONS

- Prepare Homemade Tabbouleh: In a mixing bowl, combine the finely chopped fresh parsley, diced tomatoes, and cooked and cooled bulgur wheat.
- In a separate small bowl, whisk together the lemon juice and olive oil. Season with salt and pepper to taste.
- Pour the lemon juice and olive oil mixture over the parsley, tomatoes, and bulgur. Toss everything together until well combined. Taste and adjust the seasoning if needed. Set the tabbouleh aside.
- Prepare Falafel: Follow the instructions on the store-bought falafel mix packaging. Typically, you'll need to combine the falafel mix with water and let it sit for a few minutes to hydrate. Form the hydrated falafel mixture into small patties or balls, following the instructions on the package.
- Cook the falafel according to the package instructions. This usually involves baking them in the oven or pan-frying them until they are golden brown and cooked through.
- Assemble the Meal: On each plate, place a portion of the homemade tabbouleh.
- Arrange the cooked falafel on top of the tabbouleh.
- Serve with a side of hummus.

You can serve it as a plated dish or as a DIY falafel wrap by using the tabbouleh and hummus as toppings or fillings for warm pita bread.

MEDITERRANEAN BOWL WITH FALAFEL

LUNCH

CHICKPEA SALAD

SERVES: 2

PREPPING TIME: 15 MIN

INGREDIENTS

400g chickpeas (canned or cooked)

200g mixed greens

200g cucumbers

200g tomatoes

200g tahini dressing

Vegan Feta Cheese (Optional)

PER SERVING

Calories: 350-400 calories

Protein: 10-15 grams

Carbohydrates: 30-35 grams

Dietary Fiber: 7-10 grams

Sugars: 5-7 grams

Fat: 20-25 grams

DIRECTIONS

- Prepare the Chickpeas: If using canned chickpeas, drain and rinse them under cold water. If using cooked chickpeas, make sure they are cooled. Set them aside.
- Chop Vegetables: Wash and chop the cucumbers and tomatoes into bite-sized pieces. You can also slice the cherry tomatoes in half for a burst of color and flavor.
- Assemble the Salad: In a large mixing bowl, combine the mixed greens, chopped cucumbers, tomatoes, and chickpeas.
- Add Tahini Dressing: Pour the tahini dressing over the salad ingredients. You can adjust the amount of dressing to your taste. Start with a portion and add more as needed.
- Toss and Serve: Gently toss the salad until all the ingredients are well coated with the tahini dressing.
- Serve: Divide the salad into two serving bowls or plates. Optionally, you can garnish with additional tahini dressing or a sprinkle on sesame seeds and crumbled Vegan Feta Cheese (See image).

make double the amount to have it prepared for another day, it will keep for 3 days in the fridge (leave the tahini dressing to the side and drizzle when eating to avoid it going soggy)

CHICKPEA SALAD

LUNCH

Light & healthy bites

BREAKFAST

BREAKFAST BURRITO

SERVES: 4   **PREP TIME: 20 MIN**   **COOKING TIME: 15 MIN**

INGREDIENTS

4 tortillas

400g tofu (for scrambling)

300g mixed vegetables (e.g.,
bell peppers, onions,
mushrooms)

100g vegan cheese (optional)

200g vegan salsa

1/2 teaspoon chili powder

1/2 teaspoon garlic powder

1/2 teaspoon turmeric

PER SERVING

Calories: 350-400 calories

Protein: 15-20 grams

Carbohydrates: 30-35 grams

Dietary Fiber: 5-8 grams

Sugars: 3-5 grams

Fat: 20-25 grams

DIRECTIONS

- Prepare Tofu: Press the tofu to remove excess water. Crumble it into a bowl, and then add the chili powder, garlic powder, and turmeric. Mix well to coat the tofu evenly with the spices.
- Sauté Vegetables: Heat a non-stick skillet over medium heat. Add a bit of oil or use cooking spray. Add the mixed vegetables (bell peppers, onions, mushrooms) to the skillet and sauté until they become tender and slightly Remove the vegetables from the skillet and set them aside.
- Cook Tofu: In the same skillet, add a little more oil if needed. Add the seasoned tofu and cook for about 5-7 minutes, stirring occasionally until it's heated through and slightly crispy.
- Warm Tortillas: While the tofu is cooking, warm the tortillas. You can do this in the oven, on a dry skillet, or in the microwave for about 15 seconds.
- Assemble Tacos: Lay out the warm tortillas, and divide the cooked tofu scramble, sautéed vegetables, vegan cheese (if using), and vegan salsa evenly between the two tortillas.
- Fold and Serve: Carefully fold the tortillas over the fillings to form tacos. Serve immediately, and enjoy your Tofu Scramble Breakfast Tacos!

Refrigerate leftover burritos wrapped in foil for about 2 to 3 days. You can also heat them up a bit in the microwave before serving.

BREAKFAST

WHOLEGRAIN TOAST WITH AVOCADO AND CHERRY TOMATOES

SERVINGS: 2

PREP TIME: 15 MIN

INGREDIENTS

2 slices of whole-grain bread

1 medium avocados

100g cherry tomatoes

1/2 lime

1/2 teaspoon Sriracha sauce
(adjust to taste)

PER SERVING

Calories: 250-300 calories

Protein: 5-7 grams

Carbohydrates: 25-30 grams

Dietary Fiber: 8-10 grams

Sugars: 2-4 grams

Fat: 15-20 grams

DIRECTIONS

- Toast the Bread: Start by toasting the whole-grain bread slices until they are crispy and golden brown.
- Prepare the Avocado: While the bread is toasting, cut the avocado in half, remove the pit, and scoop the flesh into a bowl. Mash the avocado with a fork until you achieve your desired level of creaminess. squeeze lime juice to the mashed avocado for extra flavor.
- Prepare the Cherry Tomatoes: Wash the cherry tomatoes and slice them in half or quarters, lightly season them with a pinch of salt and pepper.
- Assemble the Avocado Toast: Once the bread is toasted to your liking, spread the mashed avocado evenly over the two slices of bread.
- Add Cherry Tomatoes: Arrange the sliced cherry tomatoes on top of the mashed avocado, distributing them evenly.
- Drizzle with Sriracha Sauce: Drizzle Sriracha sauce over the avocado and tomatoes to add a spicy kick. Adjust the amount to your taste preferences.

Adapt this recipe to suit your tastes. You can leave the hot sauce out for a milder flavour or add vegan feta cheese crumbled on top

BREAKFAST

SMOOTHIE WITH SPINACH, BANANA

SERVES: 4   **PREP TIME: 10 MIN**

INGREDIENTS

Spinach: 100g

Banana: 200g

Almond milk: 400ml

Peanut butter: 40g

PER SERVING

Calories: 150-200 calories

Protein: 5-7 grams

Carbohydrates: 20-25 grams

Dietary Fiber: 3-5 grams

Sugars: 8-12 grams (naturally occurring from the banana)

Fat: 7-10 grams

DIRECTIONS

- Add Almond Milk: Pour the almond milk into a blender. You can adjust the quantity of almond milk based on your preferred smoothie thickness. If you like a thicker smoothie, start with less milk and add more if needed.
- Add Spinach: Add the spinach leaves to the blender. If you're using frozen spinach, there's no need to thaw it in advance.
- Add Banana: Peel and chop the banana into smaller pieces. Add the banana chunks to the blender. If you prefer a colder smoothie, you can use frozen banana slices.
- Add Peanut Butter: Measure out the peanut butter and add it to the blender. Make sure it's unsweetened peanut butter to keep the smoothie on the healthier side.
- Blend Until Smooth: Secure the blender lid and blend all the ingredients until the mixture is smooth and creamy. This may take a minute or two, depending on your blender's power.
- Check Consistency: After blending, check the consistency of your smoothie. If it's too thick, you can add a bit more almond milk and blend again until it reaches your desired thickness.

Adapt this recipe to suit your tastes. You can add other fruits, seeds and even protein powder for the perfect healthy breakfast

BREAKFAST

OVERNIGHT OATS

SERVES: 4   **PREP TIME: 10 MIN**   **CHILLING TIME: 4 HOURS**

INGREDIENTS

Rolled oats: 200g

Almond milk: 400ml

Chia seeds: 40g

Mixed berries: 200g

Cinnamon 2 tps

PER SERVING

Calories: 250 kcal

Protein: 8g

Carbohydrates: 37g

Dietary Fiber: 12g

Sugars: 5g

Fat: 7g

Calcium: 300mg

Iron: 3mg

DIRECTIONS

- Prepare Your Container: Choose a clean, airtight container or a jar with a lid. This will be used to store your overnight oats.
- Combine Oats and Chia Seeds: In your container, add the rolled oats and chia seeds.
- Add Cinnamon: Sprinkle the cinnamon over the oats and chia seeds. Cinnamon adds a warm, comforting flavor to your overnight oats.
- Pour in Almond Milk: Carefully pour the almond milk (or your preferred milk) over the oats, chia seeds, and cinnamon. Make sure the liquid covers all the dry ingredients in the container.
- Mix Well: Use a spoon or a long-handled utensil to stir everything together thoroughly.
- Add Berries: Gently fold in the mixed berries into the oat mixture. You can use a variety of berries like strawberries, blueberries, raspberries, or blackberries. If you're using frozen berries, they will thaw and release juices as they sit overnight, adding extra flavor.
- Seal and Refrigerate: Close the container with an airtight lid. Place it in the refrigerator and let it sit for at least 4 hours, but preferably overnight.

Adapt this recipe for overnight oats to suit your tastes. You can add dried fruit, seeds and nuts, grated apple or pear or chopped tropical fruits for the perfect healthy breakfast

BREAKFAST

Best meal of the day

SHOPPING LIST

Proteins:
Tofu (firm): 800g 2 large
Kidney beans: 800g (canned or cooked)
Black beans: 400g (canned or cooked)
Quorn Meatballs
Split Red Lentils 400g

Fruits and Vegetables:
Spinach: 200g
Banana: 200g 2 medium
Avocado: 2 (medium)
Cherry tomatoes: 400g
Mixed salad greens: 400g
Cucumbers: 2
Tomatoes: 800g
Bell Peppers x 4
Courgette x 2
Carrots x 2
Mangetout 150g
Onions x 3
Red Onions x 2
Mushrooms 250g
Lemon juice
Lime 1
Garlic bulbs x 3
Basil
Parsley

Dairy Alternatives:
Almond milk: 800ml
Coconut milk: 400ml
Feta style cheese 150g
Cheddar style 200g

Nuts and Seeds:
Chia seeds
Peanut butter
Walnuts

Spices and Condiments:
Salsa: 200g
Thai red curry paste: 100g
Tahini dressing: 200g
Cinnamon
Sriracha
Chilli powder
Garlic powder
Turmeric
Cayenne pepper
Smoked Paprika
Vegetable stock 2 ltr
Dried Oregano
Coriander
Bay Leaf
Thyme
Balsamic Dressing
Soy Sauce
Cumin
Vegan Caesar dressing: 200g
Hummus: 450g
Olive oil

Canned and Dry Goods:
Rolled oats: 200g
White or brown rice 200g
Chickpeas: 4x 400g tins
Falafel: 300g
Bulgur (for tabbouleh): As needed
Whole-grain bread: 8 slices
Tortillas pack x 2
Kalamata olives: 100g
Bread (for croutons): 100g
Spaghetti: 600g
Chopped Tomotoes x 3
Dried Prunes
Wholemeal burger buns x 4
Sweetcorn
Plain Flour

MEAL PLAN

Day 1:
- **Breakfast:** Overnight oats with almond milk, chia seeds, and berries.
- **Lunch:** Chickpea salad with mixed greens, cucumbers, tomatoes, and a tahini dressing.
- **Dinner:** Chilli with Crumbled Tofu, Kidney Beans, Black Beans, and Vegetables

Day 2:
- **Breakfast:** Smoothie with spinach, banana, almond milk, and peanut butter.
- **Lunch:** Vegan Mediterranean Bowl with Falafel, Tabbouleh, and Hummus
- **Dinner:** Stuffed Bell Peppers with Leftover Chilli and Corn

Day 3:
- **Breakfast:** Whole-grain toast with avocado and cherry tomatoes.
- **Lunch:** Lentil soup with a side of whole-grain bread.
- **Dinner:** Vegan Tacos with Kidney Beans, Avocado, Salsa, and Shredded Lettuce

Day 4:
- **Breakfast:** Breakfast Burrito
- **Lunch:** Vegan wrap with hummus, roasted red peppers, spinach, and chickpeas.
- **Dinner:** Vegan Thai red Curry with Tofu and Mixed Vegetables

Day 5:
- **Breakfast:** Overnight Oats with Almond Milk, Chia Seeds, and Berries
- **Lunch:** Greek Salad with Feta, Olives, and Falafel
- **Dinner:** Moroccan Chickpea Tagine

Day 6:
- **Breakfast:** Breakfast Burrito
- **Lunch:** Vegan Caesar Salad with Chickpea Croutons
- **Dinner:** Vegan Chickpea and Sweetcorn burger

Day 7:
- **Breakfast:** Smoothie with Spinach, Banana, Almond Milk, and Peanut Butter
- **Lunch:** Lentil Soup with a Side of Whole-Grain Bread
- **Dinner:** Vegan Spaghetti and meatballs with Marinara sauce

CHAPTER
04

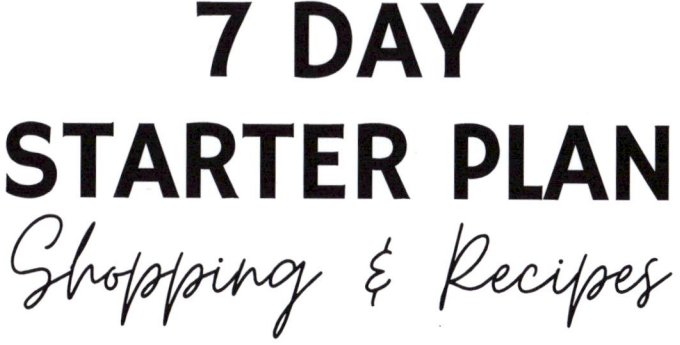

7 DAY
STARTER PLAN
Shopping & Recipes

PROTEINS

- **Textured Vegetable Protein (TVP): Usage:** TVP is a versatile and sustainable alternative to traditional meat consumption and can be used in the same way as animal proteins. **Protein Content**: (TVP) typically contains a massive 48 grams of protein per 1 cup (dry) serving.

- **Soy Milk and Yogurt: Usage:** These dairy alternatives can be used in place of cow's milk and yogurt in recipes, cereals, and smoothies. **Protein Content**: They contain approximately 6-9 grams of protein per cup.

- **Plant-Based Protein Powders: Usage:** These can be added to smoothies or used in baking to boost protein content. **Protein Content:** The protein content varies by brand and type but typically ranges from 15 to 20 grams per serving.

Incorporating a variety of these vegan protein sources into your diet can help you meet your protein needs while enjoying a diverse range of delicious and nutritious meals. Remember to balance your protein intake with other essential nutrients for a well-rounded plant-based diet.

A general guideline for adults is to aim for approximately 0.8 grams of protein per kilogram of body weight per day.' - World Health Organisation

PROTEINS

- **Seitan (Wheat Gluten)**: **Usage:** Seitan has a meaty texture and is often used as a meat substitute. It's great for making vegan "steaks," sausages, and stir-fries. **Protein Content**: It's exceptionally high in protein, containing about 25 grams of protein per 3.5 ounces (100 grams).

- **Nuts and Nut Butters**: **Usage:** Nuts and nut butters can be eaten as snacks or added to oatmeal, yogurt, and smoothies. They also work well in baked goods and as toppings for salads. **Protein Content**: The protein content varies, but generally, nuts contain around 5-7 grams of protein per ounce.

- **Seeds (Chia, Flax, Hemp, Sunflower, Pumpkin)**: **Usage:** Seeds can be sprinkled on top of yogurt, added to smoothies, or used as a base for homemade energy bars. Chia seeds can be turned into puddings. **Protein Content**: Depending on the type, seeds contain roughly 2-9 grams of protein per ounce.

- **Quinoa**: **Usage:** Quinoa is a versatile grain that can be used as a base for salads, bowls, and side dishes. It can also be incorporated into soups and stews. **Protein Content:** Quinoa is a complete protein source, offering about 8 grams of protein per cooked cup.

PROTEINS

Here's a guide to some common vegan protein sources and how they can be used in your diet:

- **Legumes (Beans, Lentils, Chickpeas): Usage**: Legumes are incredibly versatile and can be used in numerous dishes, including soups, stews, salads, and curries. **Protein Content:** They are rich in protein, with around 15-18 grams of protein per cup of cooked legumes.

- **Tofu: Usage**: Tofu is known for its ability to absorb flavors, making it a great addition to stir-fries, sandwiches, salads, and smoothies. It can be pan-fried, grilled, or used as a creamy base for sauces and desserts. **Protein Content:** Firm tofu contains about 10-15 grams of protein per 3.5 ounces (100 grams).

- **Tempeh: Usage**: Tempeh has a nutty flavor and firm texture, making it ideal for grilling, sautéing, or crumbling into salads and sandwiches. It absorbs marinades well. **Protein Content**: It's a protein powerhouse, with roughly 21 grams of protein per 3.5 ounces (100 grams).

CHAPTER

03

PROTEINS

OUR STORIES - Wayne

I grew up in the 70's with my Mum being vegetarian, so eating veggies and meat substitutes became second nature to me and my sister. My mum was a really experimental cook and was always trying out new recipes on us from veggie curries and stews to her amazing Marmite Nutloaf.

In my 20's I shared a flat with a friend who had very strict dietary need, this led to me researching and trying out vegan alternatives and healthier food choices. I've always had a love for Asian cooking, and eating purely plant-based came easy to me. I love sharing ideas and recipes with my kids (now grown), and helping them become passionate about cooking. My love for nutrition and food has developed along with Michelle, into plant-based cooking. Introducing more plants into your diet has been consistently shown to positively improve physical health.

"Introducing more plants into your diet has been consistently shown to positively improve physical health" - Wayne

OUR STORIES – John

My dad had been advised by the doctors that he would need to increase his medication for blood pressure, diabetes, and cholesterol. After some persistent nudging from me and my suggested Netflix shows to watch, he finally decided to give a plant-based diet a try for 4 weeks to see if it would make a big difference to his health. He wholeheartedly committed to the diet and followed it strictly for a solid month. When he returned to the doctors and received his test results, the difference was nothing short of incredible. Every aspect had improved, and, in fact, his cholesterol levels hadn't been that low since he was a boy, if ever.

It's fair to say he's been converted to a fully plant-based lifestyle for life. The doctors even mentioned that if his next test results are as low as this, he may no longer be classified as having type 2 diabetes and could potentially come off the medication. To say I was pleased would be an understatement.

"The difference was nothing short of incredible" – John

OUR STORIES - Michelle

As I ventured further into my vegetarian journey, I couldn't help but feel the positive effects on my health and well-being. I had more energy, clearer skin, and a sense of vitality that I hadn't experienced in years. But there were moments when I wished I had known a few key things from the start to make my transition even smoother.

One of the first things I wish I had known was the importance of diversifying my diet. Initially, I stuck to the basics, relying heavily on salads, pasta, and simple vegetable stir-fries. It wasn't until later that I discovered the wide variety of plant-based foods available. I wished I had explored new recipes and ingredients earlier, as it would have made my meals more exciting and nutritious.

Another valuable lesson was learning about proper nutrition. It's easy to assume that being vegetarian automatically means you're eating healthy, but that's not always the case. I wish I had educated myself about essential nutrients like B12, iron, and protein to ensure I was getting everything my body needed. Supplements and fortified foods became my allies in maintaining a balanced diet.

As time passed, I naturally transitioned into being vegan. It was a smooth shift, thanks to the foundation I had built during my vegetarian phase. I realised that making this change wasn't just about my health but also about contributing to a more compassionate and sustainable world.

In honor of my husband's memory and my daughter's future, I decided to compile my experiences and insights into a book, sharing what I've learned along the way. It's my hope that this book will help others make their journey toward a plant-based lifestyle easier, more fulfilling, and ultimately, a force for positive change in their lives and the world.

OUR STORIES - Michelle

My journey into vegetarianism and eventually a fully plant-based lifestyle began after a life-altering event. It all started when my husband and I watched "Seaspiracy" on Netflix one night, sparking our curiosity about a vegan diet. We decided to give it a try for a week, thinking we had nothing to lose. Little did we know that during that week, my husband had been suffering from heart attacks, and one fateful night, he experienced heart failure and passed away instantly, shocking our family and leaving us heartbroken, especially given that he was only 36 years old at the time. This devastating loss compelled me to make a profound change in my life. I realised that prioritsing a healthy lifestyle was crucial, not just for my own well-being but also for the sake of our 5-year-old daughter. So, I made the transition to vegetarianism, which surprisingly wasn't as challenging as I had anticipated. Initially, my family struggled with the change and would offer meat alternatives at dinner when i visited them, but over time, they became incredibly supportive and joined me in learning more about and embracing this plant-based journey together.

There are so many things I wish I had known when I started this journey, so we've compiled some of those questions and tips for you in this book in the hopes that it makes that transition as smooth and easy as possible.

"Veganism is not just a diet its a prescription for a healthier you! - Michelle

MAKING THE TRANSITION

Transitioning to a plant-based diet can be a fulfilling and sustainable choice for both your health and the environment. Here are some tips and easy-to-follow ideas to help you make the transition smoothly:

Take it slow:

Transitioning doesn't have to be abrupt. Start by designating a few meatless days per week and gradually increase them as you become more comfortable.

Educate Yourself:

Learn about plant-based nutrition to ensure you're meeting your dietary needs. Understanding the importance of various nutrients will help you make informed food choices. This is where My Plant Based Life can help you.

Explore Plant-Based Proteins:

Incorporate plant-based protein sources such as tofu, tempeh, legumes (beans, lentils, chickpeas), nuts, and seeds into your meals. These are rich in protein and can be used in various dishes.

Plan Your Meals:

Plan your meals in advance to ensure you're getting a balanced diet. Check out our 30 day meal plan and shopping list to give you some ideas and pointers

CHAPTER
02

MAKING THE
TRANSITION
Easy does it

WHAT IS PLANT BASED?

Being plant-based means adopting a diet primarily composed of foods derived from plants, such as vegetables, fruits, grains, legumes, nuts, and seeds, while excluding the consumption of animal products like meat, dairy, and eggs.

Pros

The pros of eating a plant-based diet are numerous. It's associated with lower risks of chronic diseases, including heart disease and diabetes, as well as potential weight management benefits.

Why

People choose this lifestyle for various reasons, including health, environmental concerns, and ethical considerations, such as animal welfare. Having knowledge about plant-based living is crucial to ensure a balanced diet and reap the full spectrum of health benefits.

Help

Our Plant-Based Life is here to provide you with valuable insights, tips, and all the information we wish we knew when starting our own plant-based journey.

CHAPTER 01

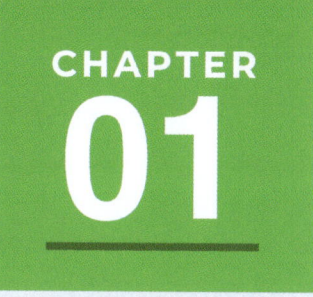

WHAT IS PLANT BASED?

More than just a diet

CONTENTS

CHAPTER 01

WHAT IS PLANT BASED?
PAGE 2 - WHAT IS PLANT BASED

CHAPTER 02

MAKING THE TRANSITION
OUR STORIES
PAGE 5 - MAKING TRANSITION
PAGE 6 - 9 - OUR STORIES

CHAPTER 03

PROTEINS
PAGE 10 - 13 - PROTEINS

CHAPTER 04

7 DAY MEAL PLAN, SHOPPING LIST
AND RECIPES
PAGE 15 - PLAN
PAGE 16 - SHOPPING LIST
PAGE 17 - BREAKFASTS
PAGE 22 - LUNCHES
PAGE 35 - DINNERS

CHAPTER 05

SUPPLEMENTS
PAGE 50 - 54 - SUPPLEMENTS

CHAPTER 06

THINGS WE WISHED WE'D KNOWN
PAGE 55 - 58 - THINGS WE WISHED
PAGE 60 - 73 - BONUS RECIPES
PAGE 74 - THANK YOU